THE
BIG BOOK
OF
ILLINOIS
GHOST STORIES

THE

BIG BOOK

OF

ILLINOIS

GHOST STORIES

TROY TAYLOR

Globe
Pequot

Guilford, Connecticut

Globe
Pequot

An imprint of The Rowman & Littlefield Publishing Group, Inc.
4501 Forbes Blvd., Ste. 200
Lanham, MD 20706
www.rowman.com

Distributed by NATIONAL BOOK NETWORK

British Library Cataloguing in Publication Information available

Library of Congress Cataloging-in-Publication Data available

ISBN 978-1-4930-4380-4 (paperback)
ISBN 978-1-4930-4381-1 (e-book)

♾™ The paper used in this publication meets the minimum requirements of American National Standard for Information Sciences—Permanence of Paper for Printed Library Materials, ANSI/NISO Z39.48-1992

Printed in the United States of America

Contents

Central Illinois

Northern Illinois

Chicago

Introduction

*I*llinois is a very haunted place. Now that we have that out of the way, we have to address the questions that always follow such a pointed and matter-of-fact statement about the ghostly denizens of the Prairie State—questions like, why is it so seemingly haunted? If forced to choose a single reason, it would likely be the violent, bloody, and often tragic history of the state. Ghosts and hauntings are born from violence, murder, and bloodshed. The tragedies of yesterday often beget the ghost stories of today.

Illinois was, in many ways, born in blood. From the Indian massacres of the War of 1812 to the feuds and vendettas in the late 1800s, there was a long history of violence and death written in blood during the early days of the state. During the early 1800s, when it was sparsely populated, Illinois was often the scene of open crime. Outlaws, fleeing in desperation from the restraints of civilization where the law was strictly enforced, found the wilderness a region where they could carry on their lawless ways. The settlements in those days were small and widely scattered, with broad spaces of unknown forest and prairie lying in between. The beleaguered upholders of the law were unable to be everywhere at once, if they existed at all. It was easy in those days to operate in secrecy, and the very life of the frontier bred a class of rough and desperate men, capable of committing almost any crime.

In 1819, a western traveler wrote, "Illinois is the hiding place for villains from every part of the United States and, indeed, from every quarter of the globe. A majority of the settlers have been discharged from penitentiaries and jails or have been the victims of misfortune or imprudence. Many of those will reform, but many, very many, are made fit for robbery and murder."

This may have been a bit of an overstatement, but it's not hard to understand how the often gruesome and macabre tales of thieves and bandits, death and destruction, created ghostly stories that are still being told today. Illinois has often been a violent place, from the days of the French settlers and soldiers who walked the land, to the Native Americans who fought for their territory with bloody massacres, to the outlaws who left death in their wake, and to the gangsters of modern times who inflicted violence throughout the state.

Illinois is a strange and haunted place, and the history of the state reveals a chilling past that has left more than bloodstains in its wake—it has also left behind more than its share of ghosts.

Southwestern Illinois

The Curse of Kaskaskia

When the first French settlers began to move southward and westward into the Illinois Territory, they began colonizing the fertile plain along the Mississippi River. A new settlement, called Kaskaskia, was started near the western edge of the region in 1703. For more than a century, it was the commercial and cultural capital of Illinois. Although it was once a prosperous and thriving settlement, little of the city remains today. Strangely, many believe that the city was destroyed because of an old curse, leaving behind nothing but a scattering of houses and ghosts.

Many years ago, Kaskaskia was a part of Illinois' mainland, a small peninsula that jutted out just north of present-day Chester. There still remains a portion of what was once Kaskaskia that is accessible from Illinois today, but the peninsula is now an island, cut off from the state by a channel change in the Mississippi River that took place decades ago. Much of the area was flooded at that time and is now largely a ghost town, consisting of a few scattered homes and a handful of residents. The remains of the town, while still considered part of Illinois, can now only be reached from Missouri. There is an ancient bridge between St. Genevieve and St. Mary's that crosses the Mississippi to the island. It is the only physical link this desolate spot has to either state. Only a few scattered buildings remain to indicate that the city ever existed at all.

The French settlers founded the vanished town, once considered the "metropolis" of the Mississippi Valley and the main rendezvous point for the whole territory. It also served as a springboard for explorations to the West and, in time, became the state and territorial capital of Illinois. The area grew, and Kaskaskia became a land-office town in 1804 and the territorial capital in 1809. The town was made up of stone mansions and homes of typical French architecture that—according to contemporary sources—were inclined to be "shabby."

Half of the inhabitants were of French or French-American Indian background; they raised cattle, horses, and hogs, and worked small farms. The city also boasted a post office and a number of general stores, a hat shop, and three tailor shops. There was only one tavern in town, which was constantly overcrowded by state officials, soldiers, adventurers, and land speculators.

In 1818, the state capital was moved to the new city of Vandalia in the central part of the state. Illinois had just gained its statehood, and legislators began searching for a place that was more centrally located than Kaskaskia. The move was made with some regret, but of course no one knew that the river city would be destroyed in just a few more years.

About twenty-five years later, the waters of the Mississippi began to shift in their channel, and flooding assailed the edges of Kaskaskia, destroying homes and farms. By 1881, the peninsula was completely cut off by the river and the city nearly ceased to exist.

But what happened to change the fates of this once marvelous city? Was it simply nature taking its course—or were more dire circumstances the cause of Kaskaskia's demise?

According to some, there was a terrible curse placed on the town many years before that predicted the city and the land around it would be destroyed and that the dead would rise from the graveyard in eternal torment. Believe it or not, these events actually came to pass.

The legend of the curse dates back to 1735, when Kaskaskia was a thriving community of French settlers. A wealthy fur trader lived there who is remembered only by the name of Bernard. He lived in a luxurious stone home in the company of his daughter, Maria, a beautiful young girl who was the pride of his life. Bernard owned a trading post on the edge of the city, and he frequently hired local men, both French and Indian, to work for him. Most of the Indians were hired to do the menial work, as Bernard cared little for them and considered them a "necessary evil" at best. At some point, he hired a young Indian to work for him who had been educated by French missionaries. As the two spent time together, Bernard actually began to become fond of the young man, at least until he realized that his daughter had also become fond of him. In fact, Maria and the Indian had fallen in love.

When Bernard learned this, he became enraged. He immediately fired the young man and spoke to friends and other merchants, who then refused to put him to work. Eventually, the young man left town. Before he left, he promised Maria that he would return for her.

Maria was heartbroken by her father's actions. She pretended that nothing was wrong so as to not arouse her father's curiosity, but deep down she secretly hoped, waited, and watched for the return of her lover. Several local men attempted to court her, but while she feigned interest in their attentions, she secretly pined away for the young Indian.

A year passed and one day, a group of unknown Indians visited Kaskaskia from the west. Among them was Maria's lover, wearing a disguise so that Bernard would not recognize him. Maria and her lover arranged to meet in secret and then quickly fled Kaskaskia to the north.

When Bernard learned what had happened, he vowed to seek vengeance on the Indian. He gathered several of his friends and began hunting his daughter and the young man. They captured them near Cahokia. Maria begged her father to understand, but he refused to hear her cries. He decided to kill the young man by drowning him. The Indian was silent as the rough trappers tied him to a log and then set him adrift on the Mississippi. Just as they placed him in the water, he swore a terrible curse. He swore that Bernard would be dead within the year, and soon he and Maria would be reunited forever. Kaskaskia was damned and would be destroyed, along with all of the land around it. The altars of the churches would be destroyed and the homes along with them. Even the dead of Kaskaskia would be disturbed from their graves!

The river then swallowed the Indian beneath the muddy water. He was silenced, but the curse eventually came to pass. Within the year, the prophecy began to come true. Maria became distraught over her lover's fate and refused to leave the house or eat. She soon died and rejoined her lover on the other side. Bernard became involved in a bad business deal and challenged the man that he believed to have cheated him to a duel. He was killed by the other man.

The river also began to seek the Indian's revenge on Kaskaskia. The river channels shifted and flooded the peninsula over and over again until, by 1881, Kaskaskia was completely cut off from the mainland. The homes and farms were abandoned, and people began to slowly leave the island. The church was moved over and over again, but it did no good. The altar was eventually destroyed in the 1973 flood. In that year, Kaskaskia became a desolate ghost town; eerily, the local cemetery washed away and the bodies of those buried there erupted to the surface and vanished beneath the river. The dead of Kaskaskia, as predicted by the curse, had risen from their graves.

The Phantom Funeral of Fort de Chartres

Down an old road near the small town of Prairie du Rocher, one of America's most famous phantom funeral processions is said to walk on a summer night when Independence Day falls on a Friday. The legend of the phantom funeral began in July 1889 when two women witnessed a mourning entourage of more than forty wagons, thirteen groups of soldiers, and a casket rolling along the road outside the village. Eerily, it made no sound. The procession began at the ruins of old Fort de Chartres and disappeared in the direction of the small cemetery located outside of town. Although they did not yet realize it, the women (and one other witness) had glimpsed what has become known as one of the most famous and enduring mysteries of the Mississippi River region.

Fort de Chartres has a rich, violent, and bloody history in Illinois. The first French settlers in the region established trading posts in places such as Kaskaskia and Cahokia, near the Mississippi River, and not far from the present-day town of Prairie du Rocher, which was the site of Illinois' earliest military post, Fort de Chartres.

Several different forts stood at this site, the first having been built around 1720. The area was beginning to be settled by this time, and the fort became an outfitting location for colonization. In 1751, an Irish soldier of fortune named Richard MacCarty became commander of the French fort. The original fort had fallen into ruin by this time, and it was his responsibility to construct a new one using slave labor and local limestone. The new fort housed more than four hundred soldiers, and it enclosed an area larger than four acres. It boasted a powder magazine, a storehouse, a prison with four dungeons, barracks, and quarters for officers.

After France's defeat in the French and Indian War, the Illinois Territory was ceded to Britain in 1763. The Indians, led by Chief Pontiac, were hostile to the new British rulers, however, and two years would pass before the English could take possession of Fort de Chartres. Under British command, the fort declined and fell into ruin and was nearly destroyed by river flooding. The British military garrison was transferred to Kaskaskia, and Fort de Chartres was never occupied again.

As time wore on, the ruins fell apart and the site was largely forgotten until the middle 1900s, when historic restoration efforts began. Today, the original foundations have been exposed, and a few of the old buildings have been restored, serving as an isolated time capsule of early Illinois history.

Time has never completely forgotten about Fort de Chartres. The events of the past never died completely, and it is said that at least one of them replays itself over and over again in the form of a phantom funeral procession that has become one of the most famous haunts in Illinois. According to the legend, three people along the road leading from Fort de Chartres to a small cemetery in Prairie du Rocher will be able to witness the funeral procession between the hours of eleven and midnight, but only when July 4 falls on a Friday.

The modern version of this intriguing story began in July 1889. A woman named Mrs. Chris and her neighbor were sitting on the front porch of the Chris house near Prairie du Rocher one night. It was near midnight, and the two women had escaped the heat of the house by going out into the cooler air of the porch. They talked quietly for a short time, and then one of the women noticed a large group of people coming toward them on the road. She caught the attention of her friend and they both puzzled over why such a procession of people and wagons would be on the road from the old fort at such an hour. As they spoke, the wagons rolled into view, looking strange and eerie in the pale light of the moon. Behind the wagons came carriages and men and women walking along the dusty road. There was no clue as to their purpose on this night until a low wagon holding a casket came into view.

The two women continued to watch and they counted nearly forty wagons, followed by horsemen and mourners on foot. Then, they noticed something very peculiar about the grim parade. Even though the wagon wheels seemed to pound the earth and the feet of the men and women stirred up clouds of dust, none of them made any sound at all. The entire procession was impossibly silent. The only sounds came from the rustling of the trees in the breeze and the incessant barking of the Chris's family dog, which also sensed that something was not quite right with the spectral and silent procession. The barking of the dog awakened the neighbor woman's husband, who also looked out and witnessed the strange entourage on the road. He verified the women's account early the next morning, but other than those three people, no one else saw the phantom funeral march.

Eventually, the procession passed by and faded away into the darkness. The two women waited the entire night for the funeral to return, but it never did. What was it that they had seen, and whose funeral was being conducted? The answers would come some years later when they would learn that the procession had apparently been seen in the past. In fact, it was a replaying of an actual event that occurred many years before.

During the French occupation of Fort de Chartres, a prominent local man had gotten into a violent disagreement with one of the officers of the garrison. The two men exchanged heated words and the local merchant was killed. Unsure of how to handle the affair, the fort's commander sent a delegation to the government offices in Kaskaskia. According to legend, they advised keeping the incident quiet and ordered the local man be buried at midnight in the small cemetery that is now outside of Prairie du Rocher. It was believed that Mrs. Chris and her neighbors were witness to an eerie reenactment of that funeral more than a century after it occurred. Since 1889, accounts have been sketchy, but there are those who claim that the phantom funeral continues to be seen.

Intrigued by the tale? You might have the chance to search for the phantom funeral on your own in the future. July 4 will again fall on a Friday in the years 2014 and 2025. If you are feeling brave, take along two friends and stake out the old road that leads to Fort de Chartres. You might just be in the right place at the right time when the dead decide to walk once more.

Ghosts of the Devil's Bake Oven

Legends of death haunt the rivers of Illinois, telling tales of bloodshed, piracy, and murder. Violence often occurred along the Mississippi, and during the first half of the 1800s, pirates and Native Americans attacked boats and travelers that passed along the river.

Perhaps the most dangerous place along the Mississippi was the area near present-day Grand Tower, where a menacing collection of outcroppings marked a place of death for river travelers. The Native Americans were convinced that evil spirits lurked there, waiting to claim the lives of unwitting victims. The white men who settled the area would later acknowledge these beliefs by giving the towering rocks suitable names. There is one landmark called the Devil's Backbone, which is a rocky ridge about one-half mile long. A steep gap at the north edge of the Backbone separates it from the Devil's Bake Oven, a larger rock that stands on the edge of the river and rises to heights of nearly one hundred feet.

The river ran red with blood in 1786 when a band of immigrants ascending the Mississippi River from the Ohio was attacked by Indians at the south edge of the Devil's Backbone. The settlers were scalped, mutilated, and killed—all except one. The lone survivor was a young man named John Casper Moredock; he was able to hide in the rocks until the killers had departed. He buried his family and then made his way upstream to Kaskaskia. He related his horrifying story there and managed to assemble a group of men who helped him wreak vengeance on the Indians who took his family's lives.

Moredock's party traveled south to the ambush site but was unsuccessful in finding the guilty parties. However, Moredock was unwilling to give up. Two years after the massacre, he attacked and killed a group of Indians near the massacre site. Whether or not these particular Indians were involved in the bloody ambush is unknown, but by this time, Moredock didn't care. As far as he was concerned, all Indians were guilty, and he began a relentless campaign to kill as many as he could. He stalked and killed dozens of Indians, many of them unarmed, and later, as head of a volunteer militia, he reportedly shot and killed Native Americans who had surrendered to his troops. Word spread of his obsession, and he became known as the "Indian Slayer."

In the years that followed the Moredock Massacre, river navigation came to the Mississippi, and keelboats and flatboats passed the area in great numbers. During this time, the Devil's Bake Oven served as a landmark for river pilots. It also afforded an excellent lookout point from which boats could be seen coming from miles away. The two outcroppings of rocks also made excellent hiding places for river pirates to lie in wait for their victims to come along. In fact, river-pirate raids became so bad that in 1803, a detachment of federal cavalrymen were dispatched to drive the outlaws from the area. They set up camp at the Devil's Bake Oven from May to September of that year. While the soldiers waited, the river pirates simply moved their camp to a rock overhang on the Big Muddy River. The place is still known today as Sinner's Harbor. Once the military left, the outlaws returned to attacking boats on the river. Later, as settlers and a semblance of civilization arrived, the pirates moved on, and the rapids beneath the Devil's Bake Oven became a much safer place. They also, however, became home to one of the region's most haunting legends.

After the departure of the pirates, years passed and Grand Tower began to grow. It became a busy river port where goods were shipped and received daily. On the west side of the Devil's Backbone, between the rock formation and the river, is the site of two vanished iron furnaces that operated there until around 1870. Iron ore was brought to these furnaces from Missouri, and they were fired with coal from Murphysboro. It is said that Andrew Carnegie once considered making Grand Tower the "Pittsburgh of the West."

The population soon expanded and a lime kiln was started in Grand Tower, along with a box factory and a shipyard. A number of river barges and steamers were constructed here. New businesses came to the area, and even an amusement park was opened on Walker's Hill, just east of town. Time marched on, and the city seemed poised to become a major population center until a cholera epidemic swept through the area and wiped out most of the residents. Within a short time, the coming of the railroads and the decline in river traffic drove away most of the remaining residents. Grand Tower was once a town of more than four thousand souls, but only a fraction of them still remain.

It was the expansion of the iron industry in Grand Tower that brought about the great legend that still haunts the town today. The Devil's Bake Oven became the site of Grand Tower's first ironworks. When the new industry came, several attractive homes were built for the officials of the company, including one for the superintendent. This house was constructed on top of the Devil's Bake Oven. The foundation of the old house can still be seen on the eastern side of the hill today, which is where a lonely ghost reportedly walks. It has been said that her voice is sometimes heard among the ruins of the old house, a once happy place that became one of tragedy and despair.

According to the old story, the ghost is that of the superintendent's young daughter. The girl was said to be very beautiful but also sheltered and naïve about life. Her doting father kept her away from the rough men of the foundry, and although she had a number of suitors seeking her hand in marriage, her father accepted none of them. Finally, one day, the girl fell in love with one of the young men who came to court her. Her father did not approve and therefore forbid his daughter to see the young man. After she slipped away to meet the young man a few times in the night, he confined her to the house. The young man eventually left Grand Tower. After he departed, the young girl wept over him for days and weeks. At last, either because of grief or because of some illness brought on by her despair, the young woman died. But she did not leave the Devil's Bake Oven.

The spirit of the young girl is said to have lingered at the site of the house. For many years after her death, visitors to the area reported seeing a strange, mistlike shape that resembled the dead girl, walking along the pathway and vanishing among the rocks near the old house. Her disappearance was often followed by the sounds of moans and wails. It was also believed that when thunderstorms swept across the region, those moans and wails would become blood-curdling screams.

How long the girl haunted the place, and whether she still does or not, is unknown. Some believe that her spirit, seeking vengeance for her lost life and love, was the cause for the ruin of Grand Tower. It was after her death that the foundries and businesses failed, the epidemic swept through the region, and the residents of the once thriving town vanished. Legend has it that not long after the girl's death, her guilt-ridden father—unable to cope with what he had done—committed suicide. When the foundry closed down soon after, his once fine home was razed and its timbers were used to build a railway station. Only its stone foundations remain today.

But does the ghost still haunt the Devil's Bake Oven? If she does, she probably finds the area unfamiliar to her now. The town of Grand Tower has faded into a scattering of houses, and there is little to remind us of the history that once enriched this small area. And little to remind us of the young girl who once died here of a broken heart and whose spirit refuses to rest in peace.

The Lingering Spirit of Elijah Lovejoy

I don't believe there is any other Illinois town along the Mississippi River that is as haunted as Alton. Mark Twain once called the place a "dismal little river town," but it has since earned a more distinguished reputation as "one of the most haunted small towns in America." The history of the place is filled with all of the makings of ghost stories—death, murder, disease, tragedy, the Civil War, the Underground Railroad, and much more.

One of the most tragic events in the history of Alton occurred on November 7, 1837, with the brutal murder of abolitionist and newspaper publisher Elijah P. Lovejoy. Although largely forgotten today, the events surrounding his death galvanized the abolitionist cause and helped start America on the path toward civil war. They also created a ghost story that haunted Alton for generations.

Elijah Lovejoy, the man who came to be known as the first martyr to freedom, came to the West from Maine and settled with his family in St. Louis. When he arrived in 1827 to teach school, he was warmly received by the citizens, but his views about the abolitionist movement in America would soon wear out his welcome in the pro-slavery state of Missouri. For a short time, he taught school and began to make a name for himself as a writer. He eventually gave up his teaching career, however, to become a Presbyterian minister. After completing his studies at the seminary, he returned to St. Louis and started a religious newspaper called the *St. Louis Observer*. Articles with an anti-slavery bent began appearing in the newspaper in 1834 and, despite warnings from a number of prominent citizens, continued to appear into 1835. Threats began to come from angry slave owners who feared that a slave rebellion could start in the city, and in 1836, vandals broke into the offices of the newspaper several times and severely damaged his printing press.

Lovejoy realized he was finished in St. Louis. The city would no longer tolerate him, and he feared for his family's safety. He sent his wife and son to her mother's home in St. Charles and made plans to move his newspaper to Alton, Illinois.

He arrived in Alton in late July 1836. He sent for his family with the hopes that the free state of Illinois would provide a better environment for his abolitionist work, but that was not to be. On July 23, a steamboat delivered Lovejoy's new printing press to the Alton docks, and shortly before dawn, a group of vandals wrecked the press and dumped it into the river. A short time later, another press was also destroyed, but it is the story surrounding the arrival of the fourth printing press that inspired the ghostly legend of Elijah Lovejoy.

On November 7, 1837, Lovejoy's final printing press was delivered to the Alton docks and was taken to a warehouse along the river that belonged to the Godfrey, Gilman & Company. Lovejoy and a number of his friends gathered at the warehouse with guns to defend the press, but the day passed without incident. Later that night, however, a mob gathered outside the warehouse. Most of them were intoxicated, and they called loudly for the press to be surrendered to them. Once that demand was refused, they tried a different approach and used rocks to shatter the windows of the warehouse. Several members of the mob waved guns, and Lovejoy—or someone else inside the building—fired a shot through a broken window. One of the men outside crumpled to the ground and the mob was enraged. They stormed the warehouse, intent on revenge.

Someone placed a ladder against the building and climbed to the roof, a burning torch in his hand. Lovejoy ran outside with a pistol and ordered the man to come down. Before he could fire his own weapon, several men in the crowd opened fire on the editor and he was hit five times. After he fell to the ground and died, the defenders inside the warehouse surrendered. The mob pushed its way inside and broke the printing press into pieces, and then flung the remnants into the Mississippi River.

Lovejoy's body was left in the warehouse overnight. The next day, a grave was hastily dug in a local cemetery and the body, without a proper ceremony, was thrown in and haphazardly covered up. Some years later, Lovejoy's body was exhumed and moved to another location. Today, a fine monument stands in tribute to the fallen abolitionist, and while he is highly regarded in these less troubled times, his death was never avenged.

The tragedy of the Lovejoy murder spawned what seemed like a curse to many of Alton's citizens. Property values in the city shrank, and when the tales of the riots spread across America, the press attacked from all directions. The abolitionist newspapers loudly condemned the city, as did the free press, which feared the rights of the First Amendment were in jeopardy.

The court proceedings surrounding the affair made the city look even more corrupt. At a January 1838 session of the Alton munici-

pal court, the grand jury brought indictments against both Lovejoy's defenders and some of the rioters. The cases later came to trial
and Lovejoy's friends were acquitted of all charges, but so were the
members of the mob. Alton was branded a lawless place, and
thanks to this, new settlers avoided the area and many current residents packed up and moved out, believing that Alton had little
future. It would be years before the city struggled back to life.

Legend states that the Godfrey, Gilman & Company warehouse
was never used again after the terrible events of 1837. The place was
avoided for the simple reason that it was believed to be haunted.
Local dock workers and freight wagon drivers, who had occasion to
pass by the place at night, spread tales of mysterious lights that were
seen shining in the windows and of loud cries, shouts, and gunshots
that would echo in the darkness. Others claimed that the terror
experienced there left an impression on the area that reverberated
for years. Many who visited the location claimed to feel the madness of the crowd, the desperation of Lovejoy and his friends, and
the energy pulsing through the entire incident. Most eerie were the
tales of a spectral figure that would exit the side door of the building and begin to run along the street. The figure would then stumble, clutch his hands to his chest, and fall to the ground. It was
believed that this figure was the ghost of Elijah Lovejoy, reliving his
final moments over and over again.

The spirit is said to have roamed the riverfront in despair for
many years, but the ghostly tale came to an end with the destruction of the warehouse—and with the proper burial of Lovejoy's
missing body. Fearing reprisal and desecration of his corpse, Lovejoy's friends had secretly buried his body in what was then a small
cemetery in town. A wooden marker with Lovejoy's initials on it
was first used to mark the grave, but this was quickly removed. After
that, only two distinctive trees remained as a rough guide to the
grave's location. After the cemetery came into general use, the trees
were cut down, and the grave would have been lost if not for the
superintendent, William Burdon. He marked the site with two
pieces of limestone and told no one what they were for, or even
that anyone was buried at the site. And then he died, leaving no
clue as to Lovejoy's whereabouts.

In 1865, Thomas Dimmock, a former resident of Alton, decided to try and track down the abolitionist's remains. He sought out the last survivor of those who buried Lovejoy, William "Scotch" Johnson, and learned the location of the remains. Lovejoy's grave was properly recognized at last and his restless ghost was finally laid to rest.

Ghosts of the Alton Penitentiary

One of the darkest periods in the history of Alton occurred during the years of the Civil War, when the town became a military post thanks to its location on the Missouri border and its access to the river. It was during this period that Alton's penitentiary, the first in the state of Illinois, was turned into a prison for Confederate soldiers, leading to death, a terrible epidemic, and a relentless haunting.

Construction had been completed on the penitentiary in Alton in 1833. Conditions were grim from the beginning, and the prison became known as a horrific place plagued by rats, vermin, and disease. There was always a lack of clean clothing, fresh water, edible food, and medical care, and according to records, many of the men who served time here died within a few months of their release. Their health had simply been broken by the conditions of the prison.

By the 1850s, things were so bad that Dorothea Dix, a social reformer and leader in the movement to improve conditions for prisoners, the insane, and the mentally ill, led a crusade to stop the Alton prison from being used. Her reports about the place led to a heated controversy that eventually ended in a legislative investigation and the construction of a new prison near Joliet. It was completed in 1859 and prisoners from Alton were soon transferred there. By 1860, the Alton penitentiary was abandoned.

By 1862, it had become apparent that the war was not going to come to a swift end and more space was needed for the growing numbers of Confederate prisoners of war. Permission was granted to Union commanders to take over the empty Alton Penitentiary for use as a military prison. Within three days of the arrival of the first prisoners, the penitentiary was already overcrowded. The maximum capacity of the institution was estimated at eight hundred but throughout most of the war, it held between one thousand and fifteen hundred prisoners, and often more—sometimes as many as five thousand.

Most of the prisoners remained in their cells or had limited access to the yard where the drinking water and the latrines could be found. The prison had no water supply. A well was located on the grounds, but soon after the prisoners of war were transferred there, the water was found to be contaminated. The situation was remedied by hauling huge water kegs from the river using a six-mule-team wagon. The drinking water was stored in a trench just a short distance away from a similar container that was used as the latrine. Wood-burning stoves that had been set up in the corridors supplied heat to the prison.

As the war continued, new prisoners arrived in Alton on a regular basis. Living conditions in the prison were unbearable: most of the men were badly clothed, food was often withheld as a punishment or was not edible when it was given, bathing facilities were not available, and gnats, lice, rats, and other vermin were common. The prevailing diseases at the Alton prison included malaria, pneumonia, dysentery, scurvy, and anemia; these diseases felled more men than gunshots ever could. Then, in 1863, several isolated cases of smallpox broke out among the prisoners. The disease began to spread and quickly turned into an epidemic.

At the time of the outbreak, the prison population numbered almost two thousand in quarters that were designed for many less. The men slept three in a bed, ate standing up, and used a common latrine. Nothing was clean in the prison, and the men were often unshaved and filthy. Their sleeping mattresses were never changed or washed, and the prison yard was filled with pools of stagnant water and urine.

Smallpox swept through the penitentiary and soon both prisoners and guards began to die. Before it was over, the disease also spread into the city of Alton itself, killing many residents. In the early days of the epidemic, as the prison death toll first began to climb, Alton's mayor, Edward T. Drummond, refused to have any of the prisoners treated away from the prison. There were no hospitals in the city of Alton in those days. The patients were quartered in hallways, storage rooms, and stables as the prison hospital was woefully inadequate with only five beds. Before the outbreak, there had been about a half dozen deaths per week in the prison, but soon they were counting more than five a day. Once the disease started to spread, there was no way to stop it. The men were weakened by poor diets and filthy living conditions and were helpless against the disease.

The sick and dying men were overflowing from the converted hospitals and sick rooms and there became a dire situation over what to do with the bodies of the dead. The prison "dead house" was simply a shed in the yard where bodies were kept until they could be buried, but this was soon overflowing with corpses. The people of Alton began to panic and demanded that the sick and the dead be taken somewhere outside of the city limits. The sick were subsequently taken to a small island in the Mississippi called Sunflower Island. Located on one end of the island was a dilapidated summer cottage, which was commandeered and turned into a hospital pesthouse. Prisoners, guards, and doctors feared going to the island, afraid they would never return. Prisoners and guards also transported wrapped bodies to the island, where they were placed in trenches.

The smallpox epidemic continued to rage at the prison throughout the winter of 1863 and into the following spring. In the summer of 1864, a group of St. Louis nuns from the Daughters of Charity arrived at the prison. They demanded better medical supplies, an actual hospital building, and permission to conduct burial services for the men. The new hospital was authorized for the grounds and construction was completed by that autumn. By the end of the summer, new cases of smallpox were no longer reported and the pesthouse on Sunflower Island was closed down. Those who were buried there remain unknown today and their graves have vanished due to flooding along the Mississippi River. Some believed that Alton residents shunned the island because of the chance that traces of smallpox might linger there. Others believed that it was avoided for another reason altogether—because the ghosts of the men buried there in unmarked graves still roamed the island.

The Alton Penitentiary was abandoned after the war. The walls around the prison yard were torn down between 1870 and 1875, and most of the stone was hauled off for road construction projects. The area where the prison yard was located was turned into a public park. Some of the walls of the old prison remained standing for years, but by the 1940s, only scattered ruins remained. The last section was finally moved in 1973 and reconstructed nearby as a monument to the past. The area where the prison was located is now a public parking lot. Today, only this small portion of the wall remains on the site of the penitentiary, where visitors can find historical information and displays about the prison and the Civil War.

As the years have passed, the old Alton Penitentiary has become the source of a number of ghostly legends around the area. For years, the historic site and the surrounding area has been the scene of ghostly reports. Many of the tales date back even further than recent times.

In the days after the war, the old prison building remained on the back of the lot, slowly crumbling into ruin. The temptation of the old prison proved too much for most visitors to resist, and many of them explored the empty corridors, abandoned cells, and deserted staircases. These visitors soon learned, however, that the former prison was not as "empty" as they first believed. Tales began to filter out of the prison about ghostly voices, strange sounds, screams, cries, eerie weeping, and moaning that came from places where no living person could be found. The disturbing tales continued for decades, even up until the time that the remainder of the prison was finally demolished.

In addition to the sounds, people also spoke of seeing the spectral images of former prisoners still wandering about on the property. These figures had the chilling habit of vanishing without a trace when approached or confronted. They would be there one moment and gone the next; turning the old prison yard into a parking lot seemed to have little effect on them.

Even in recent years, passersby have claimed to see the apparitions of men and soldiers still lingering on these grounds. They are usually described as being very ragged, and they will appear and vanish without warning. Are these strange visions truly the lost souls of soldiers who suffered and died here in the past? Or are they merely a small piece of time that has been left behind on the atmosphere of this place? We may never know, but the ghosts serve as a record of the horror and tragedy that occurred here during some of America's darkest days.

The Mansion House

One of the most legendary haunted sites in the city of Alton is the Mansion House. It was built on State Street in 1834 by a Captain Botkin, who operated the place for many years as a hotel. He offered lodging to travelers and to those who were living in the area on a temporary basis. For a short period in 1836, it was the only hotel in Alton.

Nuns of the Ursuline Order and the Daughters of Charity later used the building as a Catholic boarding school. In 1864, during the height of the smallpox epidemic at the Alton Penitentiary, the house was turned into a hospital, and in fact was the very first hospital in the city. Three Daughters of Charity nuns from St. Louis responded to a plea from President Abraham Lincoln to come to Alton and try to get the smallpox epidemic under control. They began treating the sick townspeople at the hospital and at the isolation camp on Smallpox Island. Gradually, under their watchful care, the epidemic began to subside. Legend states that many people who came down with the dreaded disease died in the Mansion House. Supposedly, their ghosts still walk there, restless and frightened of the illness that suddenly ended their lives. And if these ghosts walk here, they may not walk alone.

According to stories, anecdotes, and even historical records, this house was haunted long before the Civil War. In fact, the Mansion House has the rather dubious honor of being one of the first documented haunted houses in the city of Alton.

The most famous otherworldly resident of the place is the ghost of a man named Tom Boothby. He was a grizzled old Indian fighter who came to live in the hotel in 1836. Boothby had seen more than his share of adventure during the Indian battles of the War of 1812. As a result, he had retired to Alton with only one arm and one eye, an arrow having put out the other one. Boothby took a downstairs room in the back left corner of the house and quickly became known as an eccentric recluse. It is believed that he did not leave his room until his death in 1838, and supposedly he had a boy deliver his meals to him each morning. The following day, Boothby would leave a payment and the empty tray for the young man to exchange for a full one.

Boothby soon became well-known at the Mansion House. He was obsessed with the idea that the ghosts of the Indians he had killed in the past were coming to murder him, and he would often wake up screaming in the middle of the night. This would also rouse the other tenants in the house, and soon someone would be pounding on Boothby's door to settle him down. Although he never opened the door, he would normally murmur a few words of apology to the guests in the hallway outside his room and the rest of the night would pass in peace.

How often this late-night screaming occurred is unknown, but apparently it happened often enough that Boothby gained a reputation among the guests. Only the most recent tenants ever bothered to venture out into the dark corridors when Boothby began crying out in the night. They, too, soon learned to ignore the chilling sounds. And so it went for the next two years. Whispers spread throughout the city that Boothby had been moving from town to town along the Mississippi, always hoping to stay one step ahead of the ghostly attackers who pursued him. He was dismissed as a lunatic, but perhaps Tom Boothby was not as crazy as everyone believed he was.

One night, Boothby's screams were different than in the past. This time, instead of crying that the Indians were coming to kill him, he screamed that they had finally found him. Boothby yelled that the savages were strangling him. If his screams roused anyone that night, they did not come to his aid. The other guests had been awakened so many times before that they had trained themselves to simply ignore the ruckus. Perhaps they flinched in their sleep at the urgency of Boothby's call, but if they did, they did not come to help him.

The next day passed like all the others. The young man who came to deliver Boothby's meals picked up the empty tray and left a full one, just as he always did. It would not be until the following morning that he realized something was wrong. The tray from the day before had been untouched, something which had never happened in the previous two years. Concerned, (probably more for his future salary than for Boothby's welfare) the young man fetched the owner of the hotel, who opened the door to Boothby's room. They found the old man inside, sprawled sideways across the bed. His night shirt was ripped and torn, as if he had been involved in a struggle, and his one good eye stared wide with fright.

The Indians were strangling him, Boothby had screamed—but it was the man's own remaining hand that was so tightly holding his throat!

As the years have passed, it has been said that Tom Boothby has never rested. His cries and frantic footsteps have often been heard in the house and still continue to echo there today. During the period when the Mansion House was still used as a hotel, only guests who were unaware of the story of Tom Boothby were given his old room. That way, when they were awakened by the sounds of his spirit screaming in the darkness, they would think that it was coming from some other room.

The house today is leased as private apartments and is not open to the public; however, this does not stop new stories about Tom Boothby from being told. On certain nights, tenants in the house are still awakened by the sound of a man screaming, echoing in the darkness from another place and time.

One of the Most Haunted Houses in Illinois

If you ask anyone who lives in southwestern Illinois to think of a haunted house, one of the first places they'd mention would be the infamous McPike Mansion located on Alby Street in Alton. And these days, even those who live far beyond the borders of the region also think of the McPike Mansion. They have read about it in books, discovered it on Web sites, and seen it on television programs. But could all of those stories be true? Could this old house really be as haunted as the owners and various ghost hunters have claimed? I can answer those questions quite simply with just one word—yes.

The McPike Mansion was built in 1869 for a man named Henry Guest McPike, a prominent Alton citizen. McPike's family can be traced back to Scotland. His ancestry includes a number of patriots who fought during the Revolutionary War, including Captain Mose Guest McPike of New Jersey, as well as Captain James McPike; both were at Valley Forge with George Washington. James McPike came west to Kentucky in 1795, bringing with him his sons, John and Richard. Henry McPike was a son of John McPike and came to Alton as a very young man in 1847. McPike soon became active in the business and political community of Alton, and over a period of years, was involved in a number of different companies, working as a real estate agent, box manufacturer, and insurance executive, amongst other things. He also became the president of the oldest horticultural society in Illinois.

McPike's political aspirations did not get off to a quick start, however, although he did have an interest in the abolitionist movement. His father had been the editor of a Whig newspaper (the Whig party later became the Republicans in the time of Abraham Lincoln) and was an early advocate of the abolition of slavery. He was also one of the organizers of the Lincoln–Douglas debate in Alton and had a place on the platform during the event. Despite this, McPike never sought political office, although it was offered to him many times. During the Civil War, he was called upon to act as deputy provost marshal of the district, which placed him in a management position in the War Department. After this, he was said to have begun acting as a representative in many conventions and with the city council. This would eventually lead to a stint as the mayor of Alton in 1887–91.

The McPike Mansion was constructed in an Italianate-Victorian style and stands as one of the more elaborate homes in Alton. It contains sixteen rooms and a vaulted wine cellar and was originally built on a country estate of fifteen acres that McPike called "Mount Lookout." Thanks to McPike's interest in all things horticultural, the estate was planted with rare trees and shrubs, orchards, flowers, and extensive vineyards. The owner became the propagator of the McPike grape, which became known across the country. The grape was known for its great winemaking properties and it won gold medals in almost every competition in which it was entered. There is no question that the mansion was one of the most beautiful homes in the area.

The McPike family lived at the estate for some time after the death of Henry McPike, but records are unclear about some of the dates. It has been stated that they stayed in the house until around 1936, while others records say that the home was owned by Paul A. Laichinger, who purchased the house in 1925 and lived there until his death around 1945. Laichinger either lived in the house or rented it out to tenants, but it's likely that it became a rooming house after his death. There have been a number of people who have come forward and spoken to the current owners about living in an apartment in the house in years past. One woman even mentioned the strange experiences she and her family had with ghosts in the house—long before the place earned the reputation that it has today for being haunted.

For years, the house remained silent and empty, but then it was sold to an individual who planned to develop the remaining four acres of property by demolishing the house and turning the site into a shopping center. When the new owner encountered problems with the city in regards to the zoning of the property, the plans for the stores were scrapped and the house was abandoned once again. It was not long after this that the condition of the McPike Mansion started to go rapidly downhill.

Word got out that anyone who was looking for anything from the house could easily come in and take it, and soon thieves and vandals descended on the place. They stole everything from the house that was not nailed down and many things that were, from the marble fireplace mantels to even the toilets. The staircase banisters soon disappeared, as well as the massive interior doors that had been custom-made for the home's twelve-foot ceilings. Chandeliers and light fixtures were torn out, radiators were removed, and even plumbing fixtures and copper pipes were taken. Perhaps even worse than the scavengers were the vandals that followed in their wake. Soon, spray-painted graffiti was covering the walls, windows were broken, and plaster walls were broken apart. It was destruction for the sheer thrill of it, which is the worst kind of crime to commit on an old house.

Time had not been kind to the old house either. In the 1980s, the box gutters failed and water began to seep into the house. The roof started to deteriorate and leak, causing the floors to fall into such ruin that many of them are no longer safe to walk on. With all of the window glass broken out of the house, the damaged interior was left to the elements, and the days of Mount Lookout seemed to be numbered.

In 1990, a contractor from St. Louis purchased the house. He had come to Alton in search of a modest Victorian home but became entranced with the McPike Mansion instead. Even after viewing all of the destruction that the elements and the vandals had wreaked on the house, he still had hope for the place and almost immediately began renovating it. As a stickler for detail, his plans for the house were extensive, and he estimated that it would take him at least two years to restore the mansion to its former glory. He began remaking the eaves brackets of the house with old lumber (since modern lumber was not the same) and planned to floor the solarium with white marble, along with many other improvements and enhancements. When he finished the work on the interior, he planned to also build a new carriage house for the property and a Victorian gazebo for the lawn.

Unfortunately, the house was never finished, and in 1994, it was put up for auction and purchased by the current owners, George and Sharyn Luedke. Sharyn, a teacher in the Edwardsville School District, stopped by the house on the day that it was to be auctioned off. She and her husband, an associate professor at Southern Illinois University–Edwardsville, had always dreamed of buying an old house and fixing it up. Almost on a lark, Sharyn put in a bid on the house. She was more than a little surprised to later learn that she had won it. A few months later, when the brick ranch house next door to the mansion came up for sale, the Luedkes sold their home in Godfrey and moved to Alby Street so they could be closer to the mansion.

The struggle to restore the house has continued to be an uphill battle for them. They hope to eventually renovate it and open it as a bed-and-breakfast, but they were disappointed to learn that—contrary to the assurances that had received on the day of the auction—no grant money was available for the house from any federal, state, or local agencies. The house had been added to the National Register of Historic Places back in 1980, but that was the extent of the attention that it had received from historical groups. The Luedkes soon discovered that they were on their own, but they were not ready to give up on the old place. They have continued the fight, facing myriad problems with the city, and have made a valiant effort to make sure that the McPike Mansion remains a part of the city's present and future—not just its past.

But how did the mansion become known as such a haunted house?

There have been all manner of rumors and false stories started about the house, including that it has been the site of various murders and suicides over the years. Fortunately, such tales have no truth to them. Yes, there have been deaths in the house, as is the case with many old homes, but none have been sufficiently traumatic enough to seemingly cause the mysterious activity that has been reported there. In spite of this, ghost stories abound in this mansion, including many first-hand accounts from reliable people with absolutely no reason to lie. The mansion just seems to be "haunted by yesterday," as the events of the past have truly left an impression here that is relived in the present as more than one ghostly presence.

Sharyn Luedke came to believe the house was haunted almost from the beginning of her involvement with it. Her unusual encounters in the house carry much more weight than the claims of trespassers and curiosity-seekers that come to the house simply because it looks haunted. There have been hundreds of stories that have circulated about the mansion, from the chilling to the downright silly, but Sharyn's claims that the ghost of Paul Laichinger haunts the place seem to be the most credible. He is one of the few spirits alleged to haunt the mansion for which a real historical connection exists.

As mentioned earlier, Laichinger owned the house during the early part of the last century and died there in 1945. He was also preceded in death by his young son, who also may linger there. In an earlier part of this account, I briefly mentioned that a woman who had lived in the mansion during the time that it was a boarding house had contacted Sharyn. As a punishment for misbehaving, she and her sister often had to sit by themselves on a staircase outside of their apartment. On many occasions, the girls both heard the sound of a child running and playing upstairs—even though there were no other children living in the building.

As for Laichinger himself, he passed away from an illness that had been caused by years of heavy smoking. It is not uncommon for visitors to the house to smell strong whiffs of cigarette smoke, even though no smoking has been permitted in the structure in decades. Sharyn also told me that on one occasion, a group of people gathered at the house not only smelled the smoke but actually saw a cloud of it appear in the area above their heads.

Sharyn says that she had her first encounter with Laichinger's ghost about six weeks after she bought the house. She was on the property watering some plants and saw a man standing in the window, looking out toward where she was standing in the front yard. A chill came over her and she noted that the man, who then vanished, was wearing a striped shirt and a tie. Sharyn later obtained a photograph of Paul Laichinger wearing an identical outfit. She has since come to believe that it was his presence that she witnessed. Many people have told her that Laichinger had loved the house, and in some cases, those who pass on have returned to locations because they simply did not want to leave.

Another spirit in the house is thought to be a domestic servant that Sharyn dubbed "Sarah." She was little more than a presence with an assumed name until a man came by the house one day and presented the Luedkes with some books that he had removed from the house nearly two decades before. One of the books had the name "Sarah Wells" written inside it. Since that time, Sharyn has been touched (actually, hugged) by this spirit, and she and her husband have occasionally caught the scent of lilac on the third floor. They believe the odor is directly connected to this ghost and have been unable to come up with any other explanation as to why the smell so mysteriously comes and goes.

In the summer of 1999, one of the strangest and hardest to explain events occurred at the house. A video that was made at the time of the incident has since appeared on television and has yet to be debunked, even by skeptics and experts in special effects. One weekend that summer, René Kruse, a professor at California University in California, Pennsylvania, came to Alton to visit the McPike Mansion. Sharyn was taking her on a tour of the house and they descended down into the basement. As it happened, René was making a video of the tour and managed to capture what happened next on the tape.

As she turned a corner in the basement, an eerie white "mist" appeared and moved toward the small group that was with her. The mist, which was unlike anything that she had ever seen before, literally enveloped the group. René later described it to me as having what seemed like an "electrical charge" about it. It swirled all around them, which was seen on camera, and then would inexplicably dissipate and move off. René was able to follow the mist to several different locations in the basement, and as she would get near it, it would move and start to swirl around her. The mist was not being moved by air currents, as there was no outside air coming into the underground area, and instead seemed to move about as though it had intelligence behind it. This occurred several times before it vanished for good.

The entire incident was witnessed by those present and was also recorded on the videotape. The mist itself remains an absolute mystery, but the tape has been examined by everyone from videographers to debunkers and ghost researchers, and so far, no one has been able to provide information to adequately explain what it is or how it was able to behave in the manner that it did. A clip from the video was even shown on a television program and turned out to be one of the only segments that the experts were unable to duplicate and explain away.

Another weird incident occurred in the house in 2001. That summer, I had the chance to spend the night in the house, and an incident that occurred during my visit convinced me once and for all that something is haunting the place.

At one point over the weekend, a small group was gathered in the old McPike wine cellar. This vaulted and bricked room is located just below the level of the basement and has been the site of a number of eerie happenings over the years. This night turned out to be no exception.

Not long after everyone had gathered in the chamber, a friend's wife began to complain of being claustrophobic. Not sure of how to get out of the house from the basement, another friend offered to take her upstairs and outside so she could get some fresh air. The two ladies departed, and the group waited for the second woman to return. A few minutes later, sounds were clearly heard as it seemed she was coming back. Footsteps crossed the upstairs hall and traveled through the house, then descended the stairs to the basement. The steps were clearly heard as all of the basement stairs were crossed and then could also be heard as they walked across the basement floor. A few moments later, the metal door to the wine cellar scraped open. The bottom of the door barely cleared the stone floor of the basement, and as the door opened up, it made a squealing sound that could be heard on several recording devices running at the time. Everyone who was present turned to look as the door swung open—but no one came in. Thinking that she was perhaps trying to play a joke on the group, one of the group members walked over and peered out into the gloomy basement. He looked both ways but there was no one to see. "There's no one here," he said.

A few minutes later, the woman actually did come down the stairs, and when she was told about what had happened, she insisted that she had been outside the entire time. The other woman was able to confirm this and stated that no one had entered the house while they were out front. This added just one more mystery to the long line of strange events at the McPike Mansion that to this day remain unexplained.

It appears that there are more mysteries and questions about the McPike Mansion than there are real solutions. There have been dozens of paranormal investigations carried out there, as well as hundreds of stories told by ordinary people who never expected to find anything out of the ordinary about this crumbling old house. It is an eerie and mysterious place and yet a wonderful one at the same time. It is a part of Alton's local haunted history that we dare not lose and one that we can hopefully enjoy for many, many years to come.

Haunts of the Mineral Springs Hotel

The old Mineral Springs Hotel, located in the heart of Alton's historic downtown, is just one of the countless buildings in the city rumored to be haunted by ghosts from the past. There are many spirited tales connected to this building, but unfortunately, it is also a place where fiction mixes extensively with fact. That's not to say that the Mineral Springs is not haunted—far from it, in fact. This old hotel is a place where remnants of the past linger into the present in more ways than one. Even though no guests have stayed the night in the rooms in decades, you can almost expect to see them strolling through the former lobby. Many traces of the hotel still remain, including guest rooms that now house shops and restaurants, the once exquisite tile floors, and more. A visitor really does expect to see guests in period clothing walking up and down the corridors or lingering in the hotel bar.

And, according to some, they still do.

The Mineral Springs Hotel, the most spectacular hotel in the region, opened in 1914. Early advertising boasted that the hotel featured the "largest swimming pool in Illinois," mineral spring "cures," and the biggest table in the city of Alton, said to seat twenty-six people. It was constructed by August and Herman Luer, successful meat packers who originally intended to open an ice storage plant on the property in 1909. As workmen began drilling a well for an ice-making and cold storage facility, however, they discovered a natural spring under the ground. The water from the spring had a strong smell (it turned out to be high in sulfur content) and legend has it that the Luers declared it to have "medicinal qualities." The brothers decided to build a health spa on the site instead.

Construction was started in October 1913 with the building of a water bottling plant about five levels below the street in what became the lowest sub-basement of the building. The hotel was literally built on top of it, layer by layer, opening for business the following June. The finished structure was in an Italian Villa style, covered in beige stucco with a tile roof. The ornate interior contained terrazzo floors, marble staircases, decorated plaster cornices, and art glass throughout. It was elaborate and luxurious and an immediate success, especially after the two mineral pools opened on the lower levels. One of the pools was strictly for men, but the other pool was open to all guests and a number of receptions and parties were held there. This large pool became the biggest draw for the hotel, as the water was said to have caused "remarkable cures" for all sorts of ailments. Water was pumped into the pool from the spring, and it became a popular place for swimming lessons, water polo clubs, and for those seeking the healing powers of the mineral waters.

Thanks to some savvy advertising, water from the Mineral Springs was soon being shipped to customers as far away as Memphis and New Orleans. In July 1914, the hotel was bottling and selling more than a hundred bottles every day. Consumption of the water increased that year to 350 gallons weekly, and the hotel boasted that its curative power equaled that of water found in Hot Springs, Arkansas. The mineral water was extolled as a cure for headaches, colds, muscle aches, and even for alcoholism.

People began pouring into Alton to partake of the healing waters, and the hotel held its grand opening in September 1914. It was said that at one point, the swimming pool attracted more than three thousand people in one season. The hotel enjoyed its heyday throughout the late 1910s and the early 1920s. In 1918, Hollywood actress Marie Dressler spoke at the hotel on behalf of the Liberty Loan committee. A number of new rooms were added to the hotel in 1925, the same year that an orchestra was hired to play on Sunday afternoons and for dining in the evening.

August Luer sold the hotel in 1926, but it continued to thrive for many years afterward, finally beginning to deteriorate in the 1960s. Tourists and health fanatics stopped coming, and rooms that were once used for overnight guests began to be rented to transients on a weekly and even a monthly basis. In 1971, the Mineral Springs finally closed for good and was condemned because of general deterioration. The roof leaked in many spots and the ceiling had collapsed in others. In 1978, however, the building was developed as an antique mall featuring shops, offices, and restaurants.

Once the hotel reopened, stories started to be told about the place. Only these tales had nothing to do with "miracle cures" and the golden days of the hotel—they had to do with murder and ghosts. The Mineral Springs Hotel began to be regarded as a very haunted place.

Legends of the place claim there are several different ghosts that haunt the corridors and rooms of the Mineral Springs. One place in the building filled with more fancy than fact is the old basement swimming pool. At least one story frequently told about it is pure invention. This part of the hotel is haunted—perhaps the most haunted part of the place—but the haunting has nothing to do with the story that has made the rounds about a man who drowned there during the heyday of the Mineral Springs.

According to this story, the man was at a party with his wife back in the 1920s, and during an argument with her, he was accidentally knocked into the pool and drowned. In the years after, the man was said to be seen standing near the side of the pool or in other lower parts of the building. His ghost has been described as angry and brooding but impeccably dressed in black tie and tails. According to the legend, he is waiting here for the return of his wife's spirit so he can take his revenge on her for his death.

It's a great and scary story, but it's also not true. There is no record of an event like this ever happening and no real encounters with a man who lurks in the pool area.

However, that is not to say that ghosts do not linger in this eerie place. Apparitions have been seen around the old pool, disembodied footsteps have been heard, and more than once, witnesses have discovered a line of wet footprints that travel from the edge of the pool and vanish a few feet away. Eerily, there has been no water in the pool for decades!

The most famous ghost of the Mineral Springs is the legendary "Jasmine Lady." The accounts say that for many years she has haunted a staircase located a short distance from the former lobby. According to the hotel legend, this lady was once a guest at the hotel who had come here to take in the "healing waters" with her husband. While she was here, she became involved romantically with another guest and began an affair with him. One evening, while her husband was away, she took the other man up to her room with disastrous results. Her husband returned unexpectedly and caught the adulterous couple in the act. Needless to say, he was enraged. In the course of the violent encounter, she ran away from him and started down the steps. The stories vary as to whether the woman may have tripped on the stairs or whether her angry spouse pushed her down the staircase. In the end, it didn't matter, because somehow she fell, broke her neck, and was instantly killed. Her despondent husband then returned to their upstairs room and committed suicide.

Once again, however, history does not bear out the truth of this story. The only inkling that something resembling this occurred was in 1925, when a female guest did fall to her death on the staircase. It was ruled an accident; there was no evidence of foul play involved, and her husband certainly did not return to their room and take his own life. One might wonder how a story of adultery, possible murder, and suicide could grow out of this incident, but somehow it did.

Whatever the cause of the haunting, it seems very likely that a ghost does linger on and around the staircase. Over the years, when the hotel was still operating, staff members and guests caught glimpses of a woman's tragic fall down the stairs as her apparition replayed the terrible event over and over again. Stranger still, they also caught whiffs of a pungent jasmine scent on and near the staircase. Former owners and tenants of the hotel, including those who firmly stated that they did not believe in ghosts, were unable to explain the lingering smell of perfume around this staircase.

These are only two of the hauntings of the former Mineral Springs Hotel, and it's likely that these ghosts do not walk the corridors alone. Hotels are notorious for the ghosts that have been left behind. Imagine just how many people pass through a hotel in a single year. Then realize how many guests an old hotel might boast after decades in operation. It's not hard to imagine that there might be a ghost or two around—or perhaps a regular infestation in some instances.

The Mineral Springs Hotel seems to be no exception to this rule. It's a strange and mysterious location where guests from the past may have checked in, but apparently some never checked out.

The Ghosts of Grafton

Located almost at the exact point where the waters of the Mississippi and Illinois rivers meet is the town of Grafton. This small village came into existence thanks to one man, James Mason. He was a settler from Grafton, Massachusetts, who lived in Edwardsville and worked as a real estate agent. In 1818, he married the sister of one of the most prominent businessmen in St. Louis, Henry Von Phul, and it would be from this union that the town of Grafton, Illinois, would be born.

Around the time of Mason's marriage, he began joining in conferences with the governor of Illinois and a number of St. Louis businessmen. Their concern was the city of Alton, Illinois. At that time, Alton was actually growing faster than its rival city of St. Louis, and these men conspired together on ways to stop Alton from becoming the largest city in the region. Mason offered a solution. He would purchase the lands along the river where Grafton is now located and establish ferries across the Mississippi and the Missouri to St. Louis. He would also establish a road from Grafton to Carrolton, Illinois, that would allow easy access from Illinois to St. Louis, bypassing Alton altogether.

New businesses and riverboats soon made the small community a thriving one, and in 1832, Mason built four log cabins, and later a frame house, before passing away in St. Louis in 1834. His widow, who eventually remarried, plotted and named the town that was built here, calling it Grafton in honor of her late husband's birthplace. By 1836, Grafton was still growing. New businesses and stores were coming to town, warehouses were constructed for industry, and even a large wharf was built to accommodate traffic along the river.

Then in 1844, a terrible flood drove all of the merchants and residents from Grafton's business district. Many of them never returned, but the flood was actually a blessing in disguise because it ushered in Grafton's steamboat era. Thanks to the overflow of water from the rivers, the Grafton channel was now able to accommodate larger riverboats. These boats brought not only prosperity and commerce to the city, but excitement and violence, too.

The steamboat era was the most exciting time in the history of Grafton because it was also the heyday of the railroads in the city. The railroad came to Grafton in the 1880s, and at its peak, there were three rail lines that came into town. The riverboat period came to an end in the mid 1930s, and the last rail line into Grafton shut down in 1948, bringing an end to commerce and turning the place into a ghost town until the late 1960s, when the Great River Road was extended from Alton.

There are several ghostly legends that linger in the town of Grafton. During the height of the steamboat era, the boat-building and repair business also came to Grafton. The town became a center of operations for the Rippley Hardware Co., which built steel motors and dredge boats for use on the rivers. A number of barges were constructed by the Fleak Ship Co., which was also located in Grafton. The buildings that are now the Loading Dock and the Grafton Boatworks were constructed for the Rippley brothers during the company's heyday in 1892 when they entered into the boat business. In 1919, during World War I, the company produced one thousand lifeboats for use on Allied ships and employed as many as 125 men. In the 1920s, the Rippley company was purchased by Mid West Boat Co. and later by Everett Fry, who changed the name to the Grafton Boatworks.

According to some, these buildings are haunted today, although the identity of the spirits said to be present is unknown. They may be the spirits of men who were once employed there years ago, as witnesses claim to have heard the sounds of footsteps hurrying back and forth, along with metallic crashing sounds, as if some sort of boat-building is still going on.

Among the wooded bluffs above town was a place that those who lived in Grafton avoided. It was called the "Pest House" and was a quarantine area used to house those who suffered from contagious (and deadly) diseases like smallpox or cholera. The house was a one-room log cabin located deep in an area called Baby Hollow. Dozens of men, women, and children were buried in the woods here after dying from the diseases they had contracted. It was said that the only way that you could leave Baby Hollow was to recover and walk out of it under your own power—or to be buried in the surrounding forest. The stories say that very few people walked out of the hollow on their own. The Pest House was eventually razed in the early 1900s, but the legends of the place lingered long after. Stories circulated around Grafton that the ghosts of those who died in Baby Hollow were now haunting the woods near where the old house had been. Accounts told of cries in the night, moaning sounds, weeping, and even the occasional apparition. The stories were still being told within the last decade. Baby Hollow is now private property and trespassing is not allowed.

At the north edge of Grafton now stands a juvenile detention facility for the state of Illinois. Many years ago, this was the site of the River House, a place notorious for its role in local history. During the years before and after the Civil War, many bushwhackers, outlaws, thieves, and bandits (even, according to legend, Jesse James and his gang) escaped from Missouri and crossed the river to vanish into Illinois. The area around Grafton, with its hills, islands, forests, and caves, offered the perfect hiding place for those on the run.

It was at the River House where killers and thieves were often harbored from the law. It was just one of the twenty-six saloons that operated in Grafton in those days, and the atmosphere was so violent here that it was known by the nickname of the "Bloody Bucket." It was not unusual for bodies of hapless gamblers and innocent victims to be found in the woods around this blood-soaked establishment.

Many luckless travelers darkened the door of the place, having left the riverboats just a few steps away at Camden Landing. One incident took place after a number of steamboat passengers left their vessel to stretch their legs and have a drink at the River House. One of the passengers was a professional gambler, and after a few hands of cards, decided to stay behind at the tavern because the prospects at the tables looked good. When the other customers realized the man was a professional cardsharp, he was escorted outside and beaten with the butts of several pistols. Such behavior angered the captain of the riverboat, who had been delivering supplies to the tavern. When he began to voice his complaints to the manager of the River House, the manager responded by pulling out a gun and firing it over the captain's head. More gunfire then erupted from the woods around the tavern and from the windows of the River House itself. Needless to say, the captain, his passengers, and his crew quickly retreated to the boat. The occupants of the River House continued to fire at the steamship until it was out of sight.

Of course, those from the steamboat probably had no idea how lucky they were to escape from the place with their lives—for many did not. The River House had a reputation for the number of unsolved murders that had taken place there. One triple murder occurred over the payment for stolen horses. Three men from Grafton were delivering the horses to some Missouri outlaws and decided to argue over the amount of money being offered for them. The outlaws made no comment. They simply shot the three men and dumped their bodies into the Illinois River.

Over the years, dozens of other such incidents occurred, including when two men were hanged from the rafters in the upstairs sleeping quarters. It was said that when the River House was torn down in 1910, there were bloodstains found throughout the place— on the stairs, the walls, and splashed on the back door. When the wrecking crew came, they even found a noose still swinging from the rafters on the upper floor.

Not surprisingly, such violence gave birth to stories and legends of ghosts. The River House itself, which was abandoned for several of the last years of its existence, was said to be haunted by the spirits of the past. Those who were brave enough to wander inside of the empty shell of a building claimed to hear voices, strange sounds, and footsteps on the deserted upper floors. One man said that he was chased out of the hotel one day by the sounds of stomping feet—feet belonging to someone he could not see!

Perhaps the most famous haunted place in Grafton is the Ruebel Hotel. During Grafton's heyday of steamboats and railroads, the city was a rough and often rollicking place. In addition to the railroad and the river men who came to town, many respectable travelers who were in need of a decent place to spend the night passed through Grafton. Talk began to spread about the possibility of a grand hotel.

What followed was the Ruebel Hotel, which was built by Michael Ruebel in 1884. When it opened, it was the largest commercial hotel in Jersey County. It had thirty-two rooms with a bathhouse in the back, and it mainly played host to river travelers. Room rates at the time were $1 per day, while weekly rooms could be had for a rate of $8 and included three meals a day.

The hotel also boasted the finest saloon in town, at a time when twenty-six saloons operated in Grafton. Needless to say, this made the town a rowdy place, but with a population made up of mainly Irish and German quarry workers who were used to brawling and drinking contests, this number of saloons became a necessity. Because of its reputation on the river, the hotel was also frequently visited by river travelers and steamboat operators, further adding to the colorful atmosphere. The hotel thrived until 1912, when it was damaged by fire. It was quickly rebuilt, however, this time adding a restaurant on the first floor and a dance hall on the second. During World War II, the dance hall was turned into quarters for thirty Coast Guard men who were stationed in Grafton to provide protection for the river traffic.

As time went on, the rest of the world passed Grafton by. After two World Wars, the Great Depression, floods, the end of the steamboat era, and the closing of the local rail lines, the town slowly withered, and the Ruebel Hotel died along with it. By the 1980s, the building had become an abandoned derelict, its heyday long forgotten. Then, in 1996, the hotel was purchased by the Jeff Lorton family, who completely restored the place and opened it for business in the spring of 1997.

According to some staff members and a number of guests who have stayed here, the hotel is haunted. While most of the ghosts here are more than likely just residual images from the past, there does seem to be at least one with a personality, although just who she may be is unknown.

Hotels, especially older ones, are always ripe for a haunting. Literally hundreds of people pass through a hotel in any given year and are bound to leave a little piece of themselves behind. With a hotel like the Ruebel, which dates back more than a hundred years, there have been thousands of people who have stayed here.

Shortly after the Ruebel opened again, at least three guests and a hotel housekeeper reported encountering a ghost in the building. In April 1997, the three overnight guests told the owners the next morning they had spoken to the ghost of a little girl named "Abigail." Since then, a number of other folks who have spent the night in the hotel say they too have seen the young girl in the upstairs hallway and at the top of the stairway to the second floor.

"As many years as this place has been around, I'm sure that someone has died here, but none of us have seen anything," said Jeff Lorton. "I figure if I don't bother them, they won't bother me."

Hauntstown Treasure

Many ghostly tales have been told about Calhoun County, an area divided by the Mississippi and Illinois rivers. Tales and legends speak of the ghosts of abandoned houses and forgotten graveyards, ghost lights, and eerie sounds that pierce the night skies. One such story tells of an old cabin that was once located near a place with the unlikely name of "Hauntstown." According to the story, the cabin belonged to an old recluse named Jesse Barnes who, years before, had amassed a considerable fortune in the lumber business. It was said that he had owned several steamships and they made regular runs downstream to New Orleans.

Jesse was also said to have been an eccentric, especially after his wife died in childbirth years before, and he distrusted banks and bankers. Because of this, he kept all of his money hidden at his home near Hauntstown. Neighbors in the area often talked about Barnes and his elusive treasure, although none of them knew for sure where he kept the money hidden. The old hermit was not a very friendly man and rarely allowed anyone on his property.

Sometime prior to 1910, Jesse passed away, and the rumors once again began to circulate about his hidden fortune. The money had not been with the rest of his personal belongings, and most in the area were sure that it was still hidden somewhere on his property. One night, the Barnes cabin mysteriously burned to the ground. Many believe the fire may have been the work of looters, hoping to flush out the location of any gold coins secreted with the structure. Regardless, the blaze did not deter local folks from searching for the hidden loot.

Other rumors also began to spread. Those who ventured out to the old Barnes cabin to look for the gold began to tell of a ghost who haunted the place. Most believed this spirit was that of Jesse Barnes, still trying to hide his money. Were these stories true? Or were they merely the creation of treasure-hunters trying to keep other people away from the property? That much is unknown, but according to one story about a particular treasure hunt, it seems that supernatural forces may actually have been at work.

One night, a small group of people came from the local settlement of Batchtown to look for the treasure. One of them, a woman named Elizabeth, had recently been to see a Spiritualist medium. The medium had informed her that she was soon going to come into a large sum of money, which she would find hidden beneath a hearth stone for a fireplace. Excited, Elizabeth convinced three male companions to accompany her out to the site of the old Barnes cabin. She had heard the stories of the missing treasure and was sure this was the money she was due to discover.

They arrived at the wooded cabin site very late in the evening. As they drove back along the winding, dirt road through the forest, they noticed the flicker of lightning in the dark sky. A thunderstorm was quickly approaching, so they knew they had to work fast, or face being trapped in the woods at the end of a washed-out and muddy road.

Armed with shovels and a large lever, the group quickly got to work. They found the hearthstone amidst the ruins of the cabin; save for the crumbling chimney, it was one of the only remaining structures from the house. After about an hour, they had dug far enough beneath the stone to begin to raise it up from the ground. The stone slowly rose a few inches, and as Elizabeth bent down to peer into the dark hole, she heard the sound of a moaning voice that seemed to be coming from beneath the stone. She sprang backwards and collided with the men who were levering the stone. They fell to the ground and the hearthstone pitched sideways, uncovering the hole underneath it.

At that same moment, the sky overhead erupted with thunder and lightning and rain began to fall in sheets. The treasure-hunters reeled back from the uncovered pit and—well, no one knows what they saw after that. None of the four members of the group ever spoke about what they saw that night. Whether or not the treasure (or something worse) rested in that hole remains a mystery. What we do know is that they managed to get down the dirt road through the forest before the rain washed it out completely, and after arriving home, they were never heard from again. The last trace of Elizabeth is a letter that she sent her mother from New Orleans. She never returned to Batchtown again.

The following day, a neighbor who lived along a woods trail not far from the Barnes cabin decided to walk down to the old place. He was fairly sure that lightning had struck near the ruins of the cabin the night before and wanted to see what damage had been done. He later told, after hearing the story of the treasure-hunters, that when he arrived at the remains of the house, he saw nothing out of place. The hearthstone was in the same place it had been the last time he had seen it, and as far as he could tell, it had never been moved.

The neighbor also firmly stated that he did not believe in ghosts.

So, what had they seen that night? Was the stone really moved out of place? Or was the secret of the missing fortune covered over by supernatural forces? No one can really say for sure. Of course, if the story is true, then this means that a fortune in hidden treasure may still be lying out there in the woods near the former site of Hauntstown—just waiting for someone to find it.

The Diamond Island Mystery

The land along Illinois' rivers has long been plagued with weird stories and incidents that defy imagination. One of these strange tales involves the "fiery phantom" of Diamond Island, which was reported in the middle 1880s on a tiny island near Hardin, a small town between the Mississippi and Illinois rivers.

The first report of the spook actually came in 1885 when two young men were fishing along the river one night. Shortly after midnight, a bright ball of light suddenly appeared on the small island, which was directly in front of them on the river. The ball of light, described as a "fire ball," shot through the trees and then flew up into the air, where it hung suspended over the island. The two boys ran home and awakened their parents to tell them about the eerie event. They insisted that they had actually seen a face within the ball of fire.

Needless to say, their story was dismissed around town until other people, including a number of reputable town citizens, began to also report the strange light. "It was about the size of a barrel and there were definite features in it," said one local businessman. "I could see the shape of something fuzzy inside the fire."

Finally, in September 1888, a group of skeptical locals banded together for an all-night hunt for the island phantom. Armed with guns, knives, clubs, and pitchforks, they rowed out to the island in secrecy. They stayed as quiet as possible with the idea that if someone was hoaxing the weird events, they didn't want him to know they were there. The boats were hidden in the weeds along the riverbank, and the men quickly took cover at the edge of the trees. They were nervous, tense, and alert for any sign of the ghostly manifestation.

Suddenly, the entire end of the island where they were hidden was bathed in a glowing red-orange light. An inexplicable ball of flame rose out of the trees, swooped into the air, and then simply hung above the men's heads. Their frightened cries echoed out over the water, and they raised their weapons and began firing at the glowing object. The shotguns and rifles had no effect on the strange light, and instead of fleeing, it moved even closer to the men.

Finally, one of them shouted to "run" and they all scrambled for the boats. What happened next was even more terrifying.

Before the men could get to their boats, the fiery ball of light arced into the sky and landed inside the closest skiff. The boat plunged backward into the river and moved away from island. As it did so, the glowing light suddenly transformed into the shape of a small old man who was wearing a pair of denim overalls! He simply stood there in the boat for a few moments as it drifted out into the river, and then he was gone. The apparition seemed to catch fire and then, as a ball of light once again, it took off into the sky. It vanished quickly above the trees on the island.

The would-be ghost hunters were terrified and trembling. They could not believe what they had seen. Some of them shouted to the shore for help while others fell to their knees and prayed. The cries from the island awakened a local farmer, who managed to rescue them, even though one of their boats still remained moored on the island. "They were just too frightened to move," he later recalled. "One of the boys had to be carried on and off my rowboat."

The bizarre happenings continued on Diamond Island for several more months, much to the dismay of the local people. Then, like many other mysteries, the weird phenomena suddenly ceased without explanation. And Hardin's fiery phantom was never heard from again.

Secrets of the Miles Mausoleum

One of the strangest and most eerie landmarks of southwestern Illinois is an abandoned mausoleum that looks out from the edge of Eagle Cliff toward the distant Mississippi River. The view from this towering bluff is a breathtaking one, and to stand in the doorway of the crumbling burial structure, one has to wonder why the dead would choose to give up such a vantage point for eternity. Although abandoned many years ago, the mausoleum stands strangely intact about eight miles north of the small town of Valmeyer, at a place where Stephen W. Miles started a farm and established a grand estate like no other in the region.

Stephen Miles was one of the most prominent settlers of southwestern Illinois. Born in New York in 1795, he received a liberal education. Miles studied music and was an accomplished performer on the violin. As a veteran of the War of 1812, he received land in Monroe County, Illinois, and he came to the state in 1819. He led a large group of fellow settlers down the Ohio River on flatboats, and they landed near Cave-in-Rock. They brought along many head of livestock and wagons carrying farm equipment and household goods, but once they arrived in Illinois, they were lost. Trails leading from their landing place to Eagle Cliff were vague, remote, and hard to follow, but Miles carefully selected the better parts of the old trail, linked them with new pieces of road, and marked a route that was referred to for many years as Miles' Trace.

After establishing a home near Eagle Cliff, Miles began to prosper and soon owned several thousand acres of fertile farmland in the region. He bought much of the land at the government office in Kaskaskia, and other land came from his purchase of claims of those who had settled on land and then made improvements. Tradition has it that these settlers, in conjunction with Miles, would come into the region and file on land they claimed for military service. The men would then disappear, sometimes mysteriously, shortly after transferring their claims to Miles.

Today, only the abandoned mausoleum remains to remind us of the glory of the Miles estate. An inscription on the large marble panel to the right of the doorway informs visitors that it was built in 1858 by Stephen W. Miles, Esquire, the son of the elder Miles, as a memorial to the Miles family and their descendants. It was also stated that the mausoleum was to be cared for by the eldest son of each generation and to hold it "through this succession in trust for the above family." The bankruptcy of the younger Miles, however, brought this plan to an end. The vault, which had been built to hold fifty-six family members, once housed only eleven bodies, those of Miles, his two wives, and other descendants. According to local tradition, even Miles' mistress and some servants were buried in the tomb.

Back in the early 1960s, curiosity-seekers who managed to find the mausoleum where it was hidden in the forest found that vandals and grave-robbers had arrived first. Word spread, and even when Stephen's sister, Amanda Wheeler, died, she stated in her will that she was not to be buried in the mausoleum. She wanted to be buried in the surrounding cemetery and have a sturdy fence erected around her resting place.

According to reports, the vaults inside of the crypt had been torn apart, scattering marble and broken wood from the caskets onto the floor. Visitors found numerous bones with pieces of dried flesh still clinging to them, cloth from burial shrouds, bits of glass from the coffins, and other assorted debris. Jewelry that had been buried with the remains had apparently been the incentive for the destruction.

Believe it or not, things got worse. In the late 1960s, a cult group broke into the mausoleum and pulled the remaining bodies from the crypt. They defaced and destroyed the remaining vaults and then tossed the remains onto the ground outside. Attempting to "raise the dead," or so they later said, they burned the corpses of Miles and his descendants, desecrating the area forever. Is it any wonder that the mausoleum has gained a reputation over the years for being haunted?

Since that time, locals and members of the Miles Cemetery Association have cleaned up the mausoleum and the cemetery on the cliff. They have worked hard to preserve the site, where the father of the first governor of Illinois is buried, but they have been unable to discover just how many people are actually buried in the cemetery. The place is filled with unmarked graves, mostly due to vandalism over the years. Even so, in the daytime, this is a quiet and peaceful place. The problems still return after darkness falls, however, and even a dusk-to-dawn curfew sometimes fails to keep trouble away. The interior of the tomb is often marred by vandals' paint and by obscure messages that mean nothing to anyone other than those who left them.

This is a weird and spooky place, and even those who do not believe in ghosts or hauntings will admit that the cemetery has a mysterious air about it. A number of accounts tell of shadowy figures that have been spotted on the grounds of the graveyard, and weird whimpers, cries, and sobs that have been heard in the darkness. There are also tales of strange sounds that come from the mausoleum itself, including voices and anguished moans. Mysterious lights have often been reported coming from the interior of the mausoleum after dark. These lights have often been seen from the road that runs far below the cliff, but no one has ever been found inside the crypt or even in the surrounding cemetery.

The Millstadt Ax Murders

The small town of Millstadt is located just a few miles from Belleville, a long-established and prosperous southwestern Illinois city across the river from St. Louis. Millstadt has always been known as a quiet community. It was settled long ago by German immigrants who came to America to work hard, be industrious, and keep to themselves. It was a place where nothing bad could ever really happen—or at least that's what the residents there in the latter part of the 1800s believed. The murders that occurred on Saxtown Road, however, forever shattered that illusion. When a local German family was brutally slaughtered in 1874, it created a dark, unsolved mystery—and a haunting that still continues to be experienced today.

On March 19, 1874, Carl Steltzenreide, age 70; his son, Frederick, 35; Frederick's wife, Anna, 28; and their children, Carl, 3, and Anna, 8 months, were found brutally murdered in their home on Saxton Road, located outside of Millstadt. The grisly crime was discovered by a neighbor, Benjamin Schneider, who had arrived at the Steltzenreide home early that morning to collect some potato seeds from Carl Steltzenreide. As he approached the home, he found that the area was eerily still. The horses and cattle that were fenced in the front lot had not been watered or fed, and no one was taking care of the morning chores.

Schneider knocked on the front door, but no one answered. He called out and looked in the window, but it was too dark inside the house for him to see anything. Finally, he turned the knob and pushed the door open. As he stepped in, he looked down and saw the body of Frederick Steltzenreide lying in a large pool of blood on the floor. The young man had been savagely beaten, and his throat had been cut. Three of his fingers had been severed. Panicked, Schneider began looking for the other members of the family. He found Anna and her children lying on a bed. All of them had been bludgeoned to death, and Anna's throat had been cut. Her infant daughter, baby Anna, was lying across her chest, her small arms wrapped around her mother's neck. Her son, Carl, was found next to her. His facial features were unrecognizable because of the brutal blows that he had sustained to his head. All three of them had apparently been murdered as they slept. In a separate bedroom, Schneider found Carl Steltzenreide. He had been struck so many times, apparently with an ax, that he was nearly decapitated. His body was sprawled on the bloodstained floor, and it was later surmised that he had been roused from his bed by noises in the house and been struck down as he attempted to come to the aid of his family.

The only survivor of the carnage was the family's German shepherd, Monk. He was found lying on the floor next to Anna Steltzenreide's bed, keeping watch over the bodies of Anna and the children. Monk was known to be very protective of the family and downright vicious toward strangers. This fact would lead investigators to believe that the killer, or killers, was someone known to the family.

Schneider quickly left and summoned help. The authorities called to nearby Belleville for assistance, and several sheriff's deputies and detectives answered the call. Soon after arriving, Deputy Sheriff Hughes discovered footsteps leading away from the house. As they were examined, it was noted that the prints had been made by boots cobbled with heavy nails, making them very distinctive. Hughes also found indentions in the ground that looked as though they had been made by someone dragging a heavy ax. He followed the tracks for about a mile, and at the end of the trail, he found a pouch of partially chewed tobacco covered with blood. He deduced that the killer had been wounded during his attack on the family and had attempted to stem the bleeding with chewing tobacco, a popular folk remedy that was believed to draw the infection from a cut.

The footprints and the bloody tobacco pouch led the police to the home of Frederick Boeltz, the brother-in-law of Frederick Steltzenreide.

Boeltz was married to Anna Steltzenreide's sister, and there had been trouble between Boeltz and Frederick Steltzenreide because of $200 that Boeltz had borrowed and never repaid. Boeltz was friends with an itinerant farm worker named John Afken, who had once worked for the Steltzenreide family and who also harbored a grudge against Frederick. Afken was a large and powerful man who made his living as a "grubber," a backbreaking occupation that involved clearing trees and rocks from farm lots. He was considered an expert with an ax, as well as other hand tools, and was feared by many because of his quick temper. He also possessed another characteristic that was of interest to the investigators— he had a full head of light red hair. Carl Steltzenreide had died clutching a handful of hair that was exactly the same color.

Ladies from the Zion United Church of Christ in Millstadt prepared the bodies of the Steltzenreide family for burial. This gruesome task was carried out in the Steltzenreide barn, which still stands on the property today. The corpses were in such horrific condition that a number of the women became sick while washing them and had to be relieved. The killer had savaged the bodies so badly with his ax that the adults were nearly decapitated and the children were bloodied and pummeled beyond recognition. It was brutality like nothing these small-town folks had ever seen before.

The family was laid to rest on Sunday, March 22, at Frievogel Cemetery, located just a few miles from their home on Saxtown Road. The news of the horror spread across the region in newspaper accounts and even appeared on the front page of the *New York Times*. The terror and curiosity that gripped the area brought more than one thousand people to the Steltzenreides' funeral service.

Immediately after the burial, Deputy Hughes arrested Frederick Boeltz and John Afken on suspicion of murder. The two men were brought before a grand jury in April 1874, but the jury was unable to indict them. They believed there was insufficient evidence to connect them to the murders. Both suspects were released a week later.

Although the authorities had been unable to indict their main suspects in the case, the investigation into the two men's activities and motives did not come to an end. Investigators believed more strongly than ever that Boeltz was somehow involved in the murders based on the fact that the cash and valuables inside of the Steltzenreide house had been undisturbed. They believed there was a darker motive for the crime than mere robbery—and that Boeltz was definitely involved.

Just a few days before he was killed, on March 16, Frederick Steltzenreide confided to some friends and neighbors that he had just received a substantial inheritance from relatives in Germany. He was at an auction at the time he broke the news and was seen carrying a large willow basket covered with an oilcloth. Rumor had it that the basket contained the inheritance, which Frederick had collected at the bank just before attending the auction.

The Steltzenreide estate was reportedly worth several thousand dollars at the time of the murder. Investigators surmised that the wholesale slaughter of the family might have been an attempt to wipe out all of the immediate heirs to the estate. They believed that Frederick Boeltz, motivated by his dislike for Frederick Steltzenreide and his belief that he would inherit the money because of his marriage to Anna's sister, had hired John Afken to commit the murders. It was a viable theory behind the massacre, but the police were never able to make it stick.

Boeltz later brought suit against the Steltzenreide estate in an effort to collect whatever money he could. He was eventually awarded $400, and soon after, he and his family moved away from the area and vanished into history.

John Afken remained in the Millstadt area, and legend has it that he was often seen carrying a gold pocketwatch. When asked where he had gotten such an impressive timepiece, because it seemed much nicer than anything he could afford, Afken would only smile. Some whispered that the pocketwatch looked exactly like one that Carl Steltzenreide once owned.

The Steltzenreide home was torn down in August 1954, but the land where it once stood is said to be haunted. A former owner of a house that was later built on the property stated that he and his wife were often awakened by strange noises around the anniversary of the murders, March 19. They also both heard the sounds of doors opening and closing in the house, although nothing was ever found to be disturbed.

A tenant who moved into the house in the early 1990s also had chilling experiences, including hearing knocking on the front door of the house and footsteps going up and down the stairs to the basement. Startled by the sounds, he quickly checked the front door and the basement stairs but found no sign of visitors or intruders. The next day, he shared his story with the former owner, asking him about the anniversary of the Steltzenreide murders. The other man confirmed it for him—the ghostly happenings had taken place on March 19, the anniversary of the murders.

To this day, the slaughter of the Steltzenreide family remains unsolved. While many suspects have been suggested over the years, there is no clear answer to the mystery. The area where the house once stood along Saxtown Road has changed very little since 1874, and it's not hard to imagine the sheer terror of those who lived nearby after news of the murders began to spread. It's a lonely, isolated area, and if the stories are to be believed, it's also a haunted one.

But what ghosts still walk in this place? Are they the tragic spirits of the Steltzenreides, still mourning the fact that their deaths have never been avenged? Or do the phantom footsteps and spectral knockings signal the presence of the killer's wicked wraith, perhaps forced to remain here as a penance for the crime that he never answered to while among the living?

We may never really know, but for now, the haunting continues and the people of Millstadt continue to remember the day when horror visited their little town.

Southern
Illinois

Hauntings of the Old Slave House

The old house called Hickory Hill looks out over the rolling farmland of the southeast corner of the state like a dark bird of prey waiting to claim its next victim. The mansion on the hilltop near Equality has soaked up a terrifying history over the years and has been many things, from plantation house to tourist attraction to chamber of horrors for the men and women once brought here in chains. Thanks to that horrible era, Hickory Hill has long been known by its more familiar name, the "Old Slave House."

For decades, travelers have come from all over Illinois and beyond to see this mysterious and forbidding place. The secrets of slavery that were hidden here were given up many years ago, but there are other strange whispers about the place. These stories claim that the dead of Hickory Hill do not rest in peace and that this may the most haunted house in the state of Illinois.

Hickory Hill was the home of John Hart Crenshaw, a descendant of an old American family with ties to the founding of our country. Crenshaw himself has a notable spot in the history of Illinois, thanks to both his public and private deeds.

He was born in November 1797 in a house on the border of North and South Carolina. His family moved west and settled in New Madrid, Missouri, only to have their home destroyed by the great earthquake of 1811. A short time later, they moved to Saline County, Illinois, and started a farm on the east side of Eagle Mountain. There was a salt well on the farm called Half Moon Lick.

Not long after settling in Illinois, William Crenshaw died and left his eldest son, John, to provide for his mother and six brothers and sisters. By the time he was 18, he was already toiling in the crude salt refinery at Half Moon Lick.

Today, it is hard for us to understand the demand that existed for salt in times past. In those days, salt was often used as money or as barter material when purchasing goods and supplies. In the early 1800s, a large salt reservation was discovered in southern Illinois, and the land began to be leased out by the government. Individual operators rented tracts of land and hired laborers, usually poor white and black men, to work them.

In 1829, the government decided to sell off the salt lands to raise money for a new prison and other state improvements in Illinois. Individual operators were given the opportunity to purchase their holdings, and one man who did so was John Hart Crenshaw. He made a number of such purchases over the years and eventually owned several thousand acres of land. At that time, he also owned a sawmill and three salt furnaces for processing.

Eventually, Crenshaw became one of the most important and wealthiest men in southern Illinois. His fortunes were so great that at one time, he paid one-seventh of all of the taxes collected in the state. Despite his accomplishments, Crenshaw is best remembered today for Hickory Hill and his ties to Illinois slavery, kidnapping, and illegal slave trafficking—all in a state where slavery was not technically allowed by law.

Workers were always needed for the salt mines. The work was backbreaking, hot, and brutal, and attracted only the most desperate workers. Because of this, the Illinois government began to allow for slaves to be leased for one-year terms to work in the salt mines. The slaves became so essential to the mine operations that many owners, like John Hart Crenshaw, were not adverse to kidnapping free blacks and runaway slaves and pressing them into service. They also sold many African Americans into slavery. Night riders of the 1830s and 1840s were always on the lookout for escaped slaves, and they posted men along the Ohio River at night. Runaway slaves were captured and could be ransomed back to their masters or returned for a reward. They also kidnapped free men and their children and sold them in the South. The night riders created a "reverse Underground Railroad" where slaves were spirited away to the Southern plantations instead of to the Northern cities and freedom.

Local tradition has it that John Hart Crenshaw, who leased slaves to work the salt mines, kept a number of night riders in his employ to watch for escaped slaves. He used this as a profitable sideline to his legitimate businesses.

Crenshaw was a respected businessman and a pillar of the church and community. No one had any idea that he was holding illegal slaves or that he was suspected of kidnapping black families and selling them into slavery. They would have been even more surprised to learn that the slaves were being held captive in the barred chambers of the third-floor attic of Hickory Hill.

Hickory Hill was completed around 1841. It stands on a high hill overlooking the Saline River. The structure was built in the Classic Greek style of the time period and is three stories tall. Huge columns, cut from the hearts of individual pine trees, span the front of the house and support wide verandas. On the porch is a main entrance door, and above it, on the upper veranda, is another door that opens onto the balcony. Crenshaw furnished the interior of the house with original artwork and designs that had been imported from Europe. Each of the rooms—and there were thirteen on the first and second floors—were heated with separate fireplaces.

The house was certainly grand, but the most unusual additions to the place were not easily seen. Legend had it that there was once a tunnel that connected the basement to the Saline River, where slaves could be loaded and unloaded at night. In addition, another passageway, which was large enough to contain a wagon, was built into the rear of the house. It allowed the vehicles to actually enter into the house and, according to the stories, allowed slaves to be unloaded where they could not be seen from the outside. The back of the house is still marked by this carriage entrance today.

Located on the third floor of Hickory Hill are the infamous confines of the attic and proof that Crenshaw had something unusual in mind when he contracted the house to be built. The attic can still be reached today by a flight of narrow, well-worn stairs. They exit into a wide hallway, and there are about a dozen cell-like rooms with barred windows and flat, wooden bunks facing the corridor. Originally, the cells were even smaller, and there were more of them, but some were removed in the past. One can only imagine how small and cramped the cells must have been because even an average-sized visitor to the attic can scarcely turn around in the ones that remain. The corridor between the cells extends from one end of the room to the other. Windows at the ends provided the only ventilation, and during the summer months, the heat in the attic was unbearable. The windows also provided the only source of light. The slaves spent their time secured in their cells, chained to heavy metal rings. There are still scars on the wooden walls and floors today, and chains and heavy balls are kept on display.

After Crenshaw was indicted for kidnapping a free black woman and her children in 1842, rumors began to spread about his questionable business activities. One of his sawmills was burned down, and over the course of the next few years, his business holdings began to decline. In addition to several civil court actions against him, salt deposits were discovered in both Virginia and Ohio that proved to be more profitable than those in southern Illinois.

During the Civil War, Crenshaw sold Hickory Hill and moved to a new farmhouse closer to Equality. He continued farming but also diversified into lumber, railroads, and banks. He died on December 4, 1871 and was buried in Hickory Hill Cemetery, a lonely piece of ground just northeast of his former home.

Whether John Crenshaw rests in peace is unknown, but according to the tales of the area, many of his former captives most certainly do not. According to the accounts, "mysterious voices can be heard in that attic, sometimes moaning, sometimes singing the spirituals that comfort heavy hearts."

And those accounts are just the beginning.

In 1906, the Sisk family purchased Hickory Hill from a descendant of John Hart Crenshaw. It was already a notorious place in the local area, but it would soon become even more widely known.

To locals, the house was known more as the "Old Slave House" than as Hickory Hill, thanks to the stories surrounding the place. In the 1920s, the Sisks began to have visitors from outside the area. They would come to the door at just about any hour and request a tour of the place, having heard about it from a local waitress or gas station attendant as they were passing through. The Old Slave House, thanks to a savvy advertising campaign, became a destination point for so many travelers and tourists that the owners began charging an admission in 1930. For just a dime, or a nickel if you were a child, you could tour the place where "Slavery Existed in Illinois," as the road signs put it.

Shortly after the house became a tourist attraction, visitors began reporting that strange things were happening in the place. They complained of odd noises in the attic especially, noises that sounded like cries, whimpers, and even the rattling of chains. A number of people told of uncomfortable feelings in the slave quarters, such as sensations of intense fear, sadness, and of being watched. They also told of cold chills, being touched by invisible hands, and feeling unseen figures brush by them.

The rumored hauntings had little effect on tourist traffic, and if anything, the stories brought more people to the house. Other legends soon began to attach themselves to Hickory Hill. The most famous is the story that no one could spend the entire night in the attic. The story got started because of an incident involving a "ghost chaser" from Benton named Hickman Whittington, who planned to put the ghosts of the house to rest.

Years passed, and despite many attempts, no one managed to spend the entire night in the attic of the Old Slave House. Thrill seekers had a habit of running from the house long before daybreak. The practice was eventually ended because, as George Sisk informed me later, a small fire got started one night by an overturned lantern. After that, he turned down requests for late-night ghost hunting.

He only relented on one other occasion. In 1978, he allowed a reporter from Harrisburg named David Rodgers to spend the night in the attic as a Halloween stunt for a local television station. The reporter managed to beat out nearly 150 previous challengers and became the first person to spend the night in the slave quarters in more than a century. Rodgers later admitted that he was "queasy" going into the house and also said that his experience in the attic was anything but mundane. He heard many sounds that he could not identify, and later he would discover that his recorder picked up voices that he himself could not hear.

Stories from visitors and curiosity-seekers have continued to be told over the years, and the Old Slave House has been a frequent stopping place for ghost hunters, psychic investigators, and supernatural enthusiasts.

In 1996, the Old Slave House was closed down due to the declining health of Mr. and Mrs. Sisk. Although it looked as though the house might never reopen, it was finally purchased by the state of Illinois a little more than three years later. Plans are in the works to open the house again in the future as a state historic site.

Should you ever get the chance, mark Hickory Hill as a historic and haunted place to visit. If you climb those stairs to the attic, you will feel your stomach drop just a little and you might even be overwhelmed by sadness. Is it simply your imagination, or is there a feeling that tragedy still lingers in the house? No one can say for sure, but a visitor is guaranteed to find himself speaking softly in the gloomy attic of the old mansion. Voices often seem to be lowered in deference to the nameless people who once suffered in this place—and hushed so that nothing that still sleeps in this house is ever awakened.

Ghosts of Cairo

The now-faded city of Cairo is located at the southernmost tip of Illinois, at the convergence of the Ohio and Mississippi rivers. Once a place of glory and commerce, Cairo has become a shadow of its former self. There is no question, however, that it has earned a place in the annals of southern Illinois when it comes to both history and hauntings.

Illinois' southernmost point was first visited by Father Louis Hennepin, a French missionary and explorer, in March 1660. He and his party stayed for a very short time before continuing on down the Mississippi. He noted in his journals that "the banks of the river are so muddy and so full of rushes and reeds, that we had much to do to find a place to go ashore." In 1699, another French priest, Father Jean Francois de St. Cosme, visited the site for one night during the month of December. He also found the spot to be unremarkable and continued on his journey downriver. The site of Cairo was once again passed by during the explorations of Father Francois Regis in 1700. Another French explorer, Sieur Charles Juchereau de St. Denis, was slaughtered by Indians at the future site of Cairo while he and his men were preparing the hides of nearly thirteen thousand buffalo they had killed for shipment to France.

But not everyone ignored the promise of the location. Settlers soon began to arrive at this confluence of the rivers, and over the years, it grew into a bright and shining town, despite the opinion of British author Charles Dickens, who visited the town in the 1840s and referred to it as "a detestable morass" and "a grave uncheered by any gleam of promise." The city was chartered and laid out in 1837, and in 1840, work began on a levee, a shipyard, sawmills, an ironworks, a warehouse, and residential cottages.

In 1854, the U.S. Congress named Cairo an official Port of Entry, making it part of the collection district of New Orleans. A surveyor of customs was appointed to inspect and collect fees after goods had passed through the port of entry. A few years later, in 1859, it was decided that Cairo needed a Customs House, but no money was appropriated for this purpose before the Civil War broke out.

Cairo struggled as a river town for a number of years until the Illinois Central Railroad opened up commercial traffic for the city to Chicago. In 1859 alone, Cairo shipped six million pounds of cotton and wool to the north, along with seven thousand barrels of molasses and fifteen thousand hogshead of sugar. When the Civil War began, Cairo was found to be one of the most important pieces of real estate in the country. During the fall and winter of 1861 and 1862, both the Union and the Confederacy began to realize the city's strategic importance.

While most residents never really feared that Cairo would be invaded by the rebels, Governor Richard Yates was taking no chances and stated that he was "omitting no preparation to be ready in case an attempt was to be made." Yates ordered a contingent of soldiers and artillery to Cairo soon after Fort Sumter had surrendered. By June, Federal soldiers were in and around the city, as well as in Villa Ridge and Bird's Point, towns across the Mississippi and Ohio rivers in Missouri and Kentucky, respectively. In order to strengthen Cairo as a military camp and a naval base, Yates also sent seven thousand new guns, six thousand rifled muskets, five hundred rifles, and fourteen artillery batteries to the city in the autumn of 1861. These additions made Cairo a formidable place, and the entire city became an enormous military camp with a huge parade ground and clusters of barracks on every side. Military protocol became the order of the day for the entire city and dominated the lives of its citizens for years to come.

In spite of the advancements and the military buildup, Cairo was still at a disadvantage in many ways. Hemmed in by water on two sides, levees were built around the city, and while they protected Cairo from severe flooding, water still often managed to seep into the low, flat ground. There were no paved roads in those days, and so the entire area was almost always like a swamp. The only year-round access to the city was provided by the Illinois Central Railroad, which entered a causeway over the quagmire of water and mud north of town. Once within the city limits, the railroad split and ran in a loop along the levee and then joined again. Along this rail line came many divisions of soldiers that were destined to split the Confederacy by wreaking havoc all the way down to the Gulf of Mexico.

Cairo quickly gained the attention of the entire country, drawing many reporters to observe the military buildup. The *New York Times* referred to Cairo as "the Gibraltar of the West." Famous English novelist Anthony Trollope visited wartime Cairo in 1862 and wrote a dismal report on the city. He complained that "the inhabitants seemed to revel in dirt" and noted that the "sheds of soldiers are bad, comfortless, damp and cold." He also complained about the hotel accommodations there, especially the bathroom facilities.

After the war ended, the future still seemed bright for Cairo. Despite continued flooding throughout the remainder of the century, the city was still reveling in its Civil War glory. New homes were built, new businesses established, and the Customs House was finally built. It is believed that Stephen Douglas chose the location for the Customs House, construction of which was begun in 1867 and completed in 1872.

Sadly, though, things began to change in the late 1880s. It was at this time that politics brought about the end of Cairo's status as a port of entry. The Customs House was closed and all business of that sort was moved to Paducah, Kentucky. For Cairo, this brought about the decline of river business even before most other ports on the Mississippi and Ohio rivers. By the early 1900s, the railroad had all but replaced the rivers as the most efficient way to move goods and cargo. Thanks to the Illinois Central Railroad, Cairo was able to hang on longer than most towns, but soon railroads followed in the path of the riverboats, and by the 1950s, Cairo's final decline had begun.

A trip to this old river town today would shock many who have traveled here even in the last decade or so. Visitors are tragically greeted by many crumbling buildings and boarded-up windows, making the place look far too much like a forgotten and desolate city that has been cut off from the outside world. But all is not lost here. There are still many hidden—and haunted—jewels in Cairo. You just need to know where to find them.

Following the military expansion of Cairo, a fort was constructed at the apex of the heart-shaped city that consisted of a massive earthen mound fitted with three twenty-four-pound cannons and an eight-inch mortar. This placed the Union forces in full control of the rivers at their confluence. The earthwork was first named "Fort Prentiss," after Benjamin Mayberry Prentiss, who had served honorably during the Mexican War. The name was later changed to that of Fort Defiance. For many years before the war, the site was guarded by one lone cannon that was only used on special occasions. One sizable building, a whiskey distillery, was located here, but soldiers tore it down as they cleared the way for the fort.

When Federal troops began arriving in the region at the start of the war, they had an immediate dislike for the place, and in short time this dislike would grow into revulsion. Cairo's climate was humid; disease-carrying mosquitoes and rats were everywhere; and operators of taverns and brothels cheated and even robbed many of the men. Perhaps worst of all, though, were the periodic floods, which even the levees could not completely halt. These floods decimated the town, turning its streets and the soldiers' encampments into a sea of mud. The only benefit to the abominable living conditions at Cairo was it encouraged the soldiers to train harder for an invasion of the South.

In spite of the conditions, however, life at Camp Defiance was rigid but not intolerable. A regulation poster informed the troops that, after 8 P.M., there would be no "loud singing, no cheering or fir-ing arms." Soldiers were urged to attend Sabbath services "in an orderly and Christian-like manner." Apparently, food was no prob-lem. There were plenty of provisions, and locally grown fruit was plentiful. One soldier wrote to his wife that peaches were for sale every day in camp and that he had spent most of his money buy-ing fruit.

The fort was dismantled after the war ended, but the site was later taken over by the state of Illinois and turned into a park. It is within the grounds of the park that events from the past seem to be bleeding over into the present. According to local tradition, the ghosts of soldiers who once occupied these grounds are still being heard and experienced today. A number of witnesses claim that they have heard the sounds of men's voices and drumrolls being played in the darkness of the park at night. No explanation for these sounds has ever been adequately given.

Near Cairo is one of the most widely known burial grounds in southern Illinois, the Mound City National Cemetery. Located about six miles north of Cairo, it was created by an act of Congress in 1862 as a burying ground for the bodies of soldiers who had been scattered in several smaller graveyards around the immediate region and in Kentucky. The removal of the bodies took about two years, and the cemetery continued to grow throughout the years of the Civil War.

The grave markers here, as in all military cemeteries, are sim-ple and uniform in appearance. They have only slight differences to indicate the branch of military and the time of service. There are also graves of Confederate soldiers here, as well as one "Con-federate Spy" who remains nameless. There are also more than twenty-seven hundred Federal soldiers buried here who are also unknown. In addition to the men buried in the cemetery, there are also about fifty women, many of them nurses at the military hos-pital that was located in Mound City. There are also gravesites for many of the civilian workers from the hospital and shipyards in Mound City and Cairo.

Near the center of the cemetery is a large granite memorial that carries assorted legends and the names of many of the dead. A short way to the south of this prominent marker is a less orderly section of the burial ground. One stone in this section marks the grave of Brigadier General John B. Turchin, "the Mad Cossack," who was once an officer in the Army of the Russian Tsar. His checkered career in the American military tells a story of an efficient, but eccentric, officer. His wife, who accompanied him throughout the war, despite regulations against it, is buried beside him. Many believe it is the general's wife who haunts this cemetery.

Over the years, there have been many reports of a woman in white who wanders the grounds of the cemetery. She is most often seen near the section where General Turpin and his wife are buried. After the war ended, General Turpin went to live in southern Illinois' Washington County with his wife. They lived in fairly impoverished circumstances, but her devotion for him never faltered and she frequently visited his grave after his death. Some believe her ghost mourns here still—despite the fact that she joined him in death many years ago.

In addition to this lonesome ghost, there may be others here, as well. Visitors sometimes recount hearing unexplained noises on the ground and seeing mysterious lights. An old caretaker's house stood empty and abandoned on the grounds for many years, but people often claimed to see lights burning in the windows. During each of these incidents, the house proved to be unoccupied.

In the days when the steamships and riverboats were still journeying up and down the Mississippi and Ohio rivers and the city of Cairo was still a leading port at their confluence, there were many imposing mansions built along the magnolia-shaded streets of the city. In a portion of town that has been dubbed "Millionaires Row," the wealthiest of Cairo's citizens constructed massive mansions with which to place their money and influence on display. Even today, these magnificent homes loom over a city whose glory has long since passed. The residents who built these places have passed on—but have all of them left? A number of these old homes boast otherworldly occupants, but none are as active as the legendary mansion known as Magnolia Manor.

Without a doubt, the former Galigher House remains the most famous building in the city. Construction was started on the house in 1869, following the Civil War, and it was completed three years later. The man who erected this imposing brick structure was Charles A. Galigher, a leading citizen of Cairo during the war. Galigher was a milling merchant who had accumulated a fortune selling flour for hardtack to the government. After the house was completed, it was widely admired for its architecture and location. The walls were constructed of double brick with a ten-inch space between them to keep out the dampness of the river regions. A high white fence was built to surround the grounds, and a number of magnolia trees were planted in the yard.

The house became a social center during the 1870s, but the Galigher Mansion reached the peak of its fame in April 1880, when former president Ulysses S. Grant and his wife, Julia, were guests in the house for two days. This was not Grant's first visit to Cairo, nor was it the first time that he made the acquaintance of Charles Galigher. Through business transactions with the military during the Civil War, Galigher formed a friendship with General Grant, who had established a headquarters at the St. Charles Hotel in Cairo. As a guest of the Galighers, the Grants occupied the southeast bedroom on the second floor. The southwest bedroom was occupied by Mrs. Grant's packing cases of gifts and souvenirs that she had gathered on her recent world tour. Several receptions were held in the house during the Grants' visit, and afterward, they traveled north to Galena.

In the years that followed, the Galighers continued to welcome guests into the mansion among the magnolias. In 1914, the house was acquired by Peter T. Langan, a well-known lumber dealer in Cairo, and he and his wife continued the tradition of hospitality that had been established by the Galighers. After his death, the house was sold to Colonel and Mrs. Fain W. King, who occupied the house until 1952. At that time, the house was taken over by the Cairo Historical Association, and it became the group's initial restoration effort. Thanks to the amazing condition of the home, as well as the visit by the Grants, it was entered on the National Register of Historic Places in 1969 as "Magnolia Manor."

The mansion is open today for tours by the general public, and many unsuspecting visitors to the house have encountered the ghosts that are said to linger there. According to a number of reports that have been collected in recent years, tourists claim to have not only spotted ghosts dressed in period clothing who are often mistaken for reenactors, but to have also heard the sounds of whispers, voices, and footsteps in empty rooms of the house. One woman described in detail how she and her family were visiting Magnolia Mansion and were followed down a staircase by heavy footsteps. The steps were so insistent and seemed so impatient to get past her and her young daughter that the woman stopped and stepped aside to let them pass. She was startled when she realized there was no one behind her!

And it's not only visitors to the house who have strange encounters. Some of the staff members, volunteers, and former caretakers have had their own weird experiences. Several accounts tell of a young boy who has been seen in the mansion. One caretaker claimed he saw the boy, who looked to be between three or four, in the house on six different occasions over a two-year period. The boy is described as wearing a white shirt, dark pants, and suspenders, and having dark, tousled hair. He seems to be aware of the living people in the house, and when spotted, he runs away and vanishes into one of the rooms. A search of the room always reveals that he has disappeared.

In addition, doors have been seen to open and close by themselves, and there have been frequent problems with staff members attempting to open doors that seem to be locked. No matter how hard they push on them, the doors refuse to open, as if someone was holding them shut from the other side. Moments later, the door swings open, usually under its own power. Also, one staff member told of frequently walking into the bedrooms in the morning, after the house has been locked up for the night, and finding the impression of a sleeping form left on the bed. She described the shape as the perfect size of a person, but there was no way that anyone could have gotten into the place while she was away. Even when she checked with other staffers, all of them denied any knowledge of the eerie impressions.

So, is Magnolia Manor really haunted? That is up to the reader to decide, of course, but if you make it all of the way down to Cairo someday, be sure to put it on your list of places to visit. Haunted or not, it's a wonderful piece of Illinois history that has been remarkably preserved as a poignant reminder of a city that once was.

The Dug Hill "Booger"

A number of places in southern Illinois gained ghostly reputations in years past, in times when the land was more primitive and untamed. These were times when modern conveniences like electric lights, television, and paved roads had not yet intruded on the landscape of Egypt. Dug Hill is such a place. Many years ago, the road that cut through this hill was constructed so that settlers could pass from the Mississippi River to the interior regions. While it saw the frequent passing of many travelers, it was a still a secluded spot and one that was considered to be both dark and dangerous for those who used it.

Today, Dug Hill is located about five miles west of Jonesboro on State Highway 126. Unfortunately, the more sinister aspects of the passage have vanished, and the road bears little resemblance to its former appearance. Because of this, the ghost stories of Dug Hill have been largely forgotten, and few remember a time when it was one of the most haunted places in southern Illinois.

The stories vary as to how this area became so seemingly haunted. Most agree, however, that it involved an incident that took place during the closing days of the Civil War. The murder that occurred is believed to have given birth to the accounts of later years. Although reports of violence and robbery were common here, it was not until the bloody ambush of a provost marshal named Welch in April 1865 that a ghost was apparently left behind.

According to the legend, Welch arrested three deserters from the Union army one day and turned them over to the authorities in Jonesboro. A day or so later, word reached Illinois that the war had ended with General Lee's surrender in Virginia, so the deserters were released. They remained angry over their treatment by Welch and were determined to get their revenge on him.

Late that night, Welch passed through the cut alongside Dug Hill as he was riding home. He had no idea that the deserters were waiting for him there. They shot and killed him as he rode by and left his body lying in the road. Although Welch's body was found a short time later, no one was ever arrested for the crime and his murderers were never punished.

Soon after, travelers and local farmers began to report Welch's ghost on the old road. While some accounts stated that he was seen walking along the roadway in bloody clothing, imploring people to help him, his phantom was most commonly seen lying in the center of the dusty trail.

According to one account, a wagon driver was passing along Dug Hill Road one evening when he saw the body of a man lying facedown in the center of the road. He stopped his horses and climbed down to see if he could help. When he leaned down to try and turn the man over, his hands passed right through him. The teamster tried again to lift the body, and again, he only touched the dirt beneath it. Terrified, he ran back to his wagon. Cracking the whip, he drove the wagon forward and felt the distinct thump of the wheels passing over the spectral corpse! He looked back once and saw that the body had vanished.

Welch's ghost apparently was not the only haunt of Dug Hill. Another legend involves a spectral wagon that was often seen passing along the roadway. In one story, a farmer was riding along the road one night shortly after darkness had fallen. He was driving his team of horses, heading west, when the neck yoke came off one of the animals, forcing him to stop and replace it.

He was off the wagon when he heard a terrible sound approaching from behind him. It was late December and the road had been frozen hard, leaving ruts and grooves that caused wooden wagons to rattle and shake as they passed over them. The sound that he heard coming was that of an old wagon, being driven hard and fast on the nearly impassable road. A chill ran down the farmer's spine. The wagon was coming toward him much too fast on the darkened road. There was little room to pass on the narrow trail, and if the farmer could not warn the other driver or get out of the way, they would both be killed. He looked back up the road and yelled as loudly as he could into the darkness. He hoped the other driver could hear him over the racket, but if he did, there was no sign of it. The wagon kept coming toward him, growing louder as it drew closer.

The noise finally crested the hill, and the farmer looked up as he realized that the sound was no longer coming from the road, but from right above his head! There, coming over the hill, was a large pair of black horses, pulling a heavy wagon with sideboards. There was a man driving them, cracking the reins, but the farmer couldn't make out his features. The hooves of the horses seemed to pound the air and the wheels of the wagon spun as if they were on the ground.

The eerie apparition soared over the farmer's head, struck the crest of the next hill, and then kept going. The horrible sounds the wagon made echoed into the blackness until they finally faded away.

Another tale from Dug Hill involves what most of us would consider a mythical creature that has its roots in the nightmares of children. Many refer to this monster as the "boogeyman," but to early residents of Egypt, it was simply the "booger." Most would dismiss such a creature to the pages of fairy tales, knowing that no monster of this sort could possibly exist—or could it?

According to one old story, a man named Frank Corzine encountered a booger one night when he was riding over Dug Hill. The sun had just set on Corzine's journey, but he was in a great rush to make it to the local doctor's house. Corzine's wife had taken ill with cholera, and he needed the doctor to come and see what he could do for her.

He turned his horse down a narrow trail and saw the figure of a man appear at the edge of the woods. Corzine described the figure as being between eight and ten feet tall and wearing a white shirt, black pants, and a scarf that hung over his shoulders with both ends dangling in the front. When Corzine first spotted the manlike creature, it was about thirty feet away, but in an instant, it came to within inches of the rider.

Needless to say, Corzine was terrified by the mysterious figure, and his heels dug sharply into the sides of his horse. The animal bolted and broke into a run, snapping a strap on the saddle in the process. Corzine later claimed that no matter how fast the horse ran, the booger managed to keep pace with them.

They crossed the hill and Corzine rode straight to the doctor's house. By the time that Dr. Russell had appeared on the porch, the booger from the woods was gone. The doctor quickly realized that both the man and the horse were very frightened. Corzine was pale and trembling, and the horse was shaking, snorting, and stamping his feet on the dusty road. The doctor also knew what the visitor had seen.

Dr. Russell had also encountered the booger a few nights before at the same spot on the road. He questioned Corzine and found that his description of the creature matched what the doctor had seen. Fearful, he refused to go to Corzine's house that night and insisted that he would only cross the hill in the daylight. He soon had second thoughts, knowing that the sick woman could not be left alone until morning, so he woke up eight neighbors who lived nearby and told them to fetch their shotguns. The armed party escorted Corzine and Dr. Russell back over Dug Hill.

The monster didn't show itself again that night and may have never shown itself on Dug Hill again. If he did, no one ever spoke if it, for he vanished from history after that night.

Anna Bixby's Ghost Light

One of the greatest mysteries of southern Illinois involves a woman named Anna Bixby. There are so many stories and legends, and various versions of the legends, about this woman that it is impossible to know what to believe. According to the census records of southern Illinois, she was a real person, and it has been generally accepted that she discovered a cure for what was then called "milk sickness." Amazingly, she did so almost seventy years before the medical establishment acknowledged that the source of the sickness was the plant that Anna had discovered long before.

Anna Bixby was a doctor who lived years ago in southeastern Illinois. She was a talented midwife and healer who visited the sick, tended the wounded, and traveled around the area to help those who were ill. She likely had no real medical education and even more likely was unable to read or write, as would have been common at this time. Anna had already been a midwife in Tennessee when she came to Illinois with her husband, Isaac Hobbs. Anna's medical training came from her study of herbs and healing techniques, and she traveled widely to assist those in what would have been a wilderness at that time. When a strange disease began to break out in the region, killing both people and cattle, Anna was baffled. She watched, treated as best she could, observed the illness, and studied the habits of those who were stricken. As hard as she worked though, she was unable to stop the scourge.

The number of deaths increased alarmingly and whole herds of cattle were wiped out. The superstitious came to believe that the illness was caused by a poison being scattered by a witch. There was even talk of retaliation against various persons who were suspected. Anna did not believe that a witch was causing the plague and instead theorized that the cause of the illness was likely a plant the cattle were eating and then passing on through their milk. The milk cows themselves did not fall ill, but the other cattle and the people who drank their milk fell victim to the malady. Anna spread the word to the surrounding communities that they should refrain from drinking milk until after the frost in the autumn. Her warning saved many lives but did not save the young cattle on which the settlers depended. Greater tragedy had been avoided for the time being, but the sickness was sure to return in the spring. After her husband fell ill and died from the milk sickness, Anna was determined to solve the mystery of the disease.

She puzzled over the illness through the winter, and when spring came, she set off into the woods and fields to look for the plant that had caused so much misery. The solution to the problem came almost by accident when she chanced to meet in the woods an elderly Native American woman that the local people called Aunt Shawnee. She was also an herbalist and healer and showed Anna a plant that we now call "milkweed." It had caused the same symptoms in her tribe as the milk sickness did. The plant had killed many of the Indian cattle, and she told Anna that it was probably what she was looking for.

Anna again spread the word, and according to tradition, troops of men and boys prowled the woods, destroying the plant, for many years afterward. The plague was finally wiped out, and in 1928, almost seventy years later, medical scholars acknowledged Anna's find as the cause of the ailment. For this reason, she has long been considered something of a legend in southern Illinois as a healer and medical worker—but this was not the end of her story.

Anna's choice for a second husband was a regrettable one, a fact she discovered soon after she married Eson Bixby. The otherwise charming man was involved in a number of criminal enterprises, including thievery and counterfeiting. Bixby was no fool, though. He learned that Anna had amassed a small fortune over the years, so he decided to kill her and claim the money for his own.

The story goes that a rider came to the Bixby household late one night during a terrible thunderstorm. He called out to the house that someone needed Anna's medical skills, and of course, she immediately came out. She mounted the rider's second horse, and they rode into the woods. The trail was shrouded in darkness, thanks to the heavy storm clouds overhead, and Anna soon became disoriented and unsure of their route. At one point during the ride, however, she looked over when a flash of lightning illuminated the night and saw the identity of the mysterious rider—it was her husband Eson.

When he realized that she had discovered his identity, Bixby brought the horses to a halt, quickly bound her hands, and gagged her. It was obvious that he intended to kill her, and Anna began to panic. When she heard the jingle of chains being removed from his saddlebags, Anna became so frightened that she began to run, dashing into the dark woods. As she plunged into the forest, her fear became even stronger as she realized that she had no idea where she was. The storm continued to rage, sending rain lashing down on her and causing the wind to whip through the trees in a wild fury. Anna ran for some distance, and then suddenly the ground beneath her vanished. She tumbled over a large bluff and crashed to the ground far below. The fall broke the ropes that bound her hands but also broke some of her bones, seriously injuring her. Nevertheless, she managed to crawl a short distance to a fallen tree and slithered in behind it.

A few moments later, a light appeared in the darkness at the top of the bluff and Eson Bixby came into view carrying a burning torch. He climbed down from the top of the rocks and searched around for Anna, but he did not find her. After a few minutes, he returned to his horse and rode away.

Once he was gone, Anna began crawling and stumbling out of the forest. It took her until sunrise to find a nearby farmhouse, but when she reached it, she found herself at the doorstep of friends, only a few houses away from her own. They quickly took her in and she told them the story of what had happened.

Bixby was soon arrested and taken to the jail in Elizabethtown. He escaped, though, and vanished for a time. He was later captured again in Missouri, but once again, he escaped. This time, he disappeared for good and was never seen again.

Anna lived on in the Rock Creek community of Hardin County until the 1870s, and when she died, she was buried next to her first husband and only a simple "A" was inscribed on her tombstone. But the legend of Anna Bixby lives on.

The legend states that when Anna learned that her husband was a murderous thief, she hid her fortune away somewhere just before he attempted to do away with her. It is believed that the hiding place for the treasure was a cave beside Rock Creek in Hooven Hollow, which had once been the hiding place of an outlaw gang in the early 1800s.

The cave is still known today as Anna Bixby Cave, and it is along the bluff, in the vicinity of the cave, where people have reported seeing a strange light appear over the years. The large, glowing light moves in and out of the trees and among the rocks, vanishing and then reappearing without explanation. It is believed that the light may be that of Anna Bixby, still watching over the treasure that she hid away many years ago.

One of the most detailed accounts of the Bixby ghost light was collected by folklorist Charles Neely in 1938. The story of the spook light was told by Reverend E. N. Hall, a minister who once served the Rock Creek Church and who had a number of the brushes with the uncanny in this part of Hardin County. One evening in his younger days, Hall and a friend of his named Hobbs walked over to a nearby farm to escort two of the girls who lived there to church. When they got to the house, they found there were no lights on. It appeared that the girls had left without them, and the two young men stood around for a few moments, wondering what to do.

They stood at the edge of the yard as they talked and looked toward the darkened house. The house itself stood on a short knoll with a hollow that ran away from the gate to the left for about a hundred yards, then joined with another hollow that came back to the right side of the gate. Hobbs was looking eastward along the bluff when he saw what appeared to be a "ball of fire about the size of a washtub" going very fast along the east hollow.

At first, the young men thought that it might be someone on a horse carrying a lantern, but then realized that it was moving much too fast for that. The light followed the hollow to the left of the gate and along a small curve where one hollow met the other. It followed the opposite hollow and came right up the bank where the two men were standing. It paused, motionless, about thirty feet away from them and began to burn down smaller and smaller. Finally, it simply vanished.

The two young men decided not to go to church. They went directly to the farm where they had been working and went to bed. The next morning at the breakfast table, they told Mr. Patten, the farmer they had been working for, what they had both seen the night before. He laughed at them and said that it had just been a "mineral light" carried by the wind. He had no explanation though for how fast the light had moved or for the fact that there had been no wind the previous evening. He could also not explain why the light seemed to follow the two hollows and then stop in place and burn out.

Later, Hall had the chance to speak with the woman who owned the farm, a Mrs. Walton, and ask her what the light might have been. She then told him the story of Anna Bixby, who had owned the property before she had, and explained that to protect her money from her criminal husband, Anna had hidden her fortune in a cave located on the property. Mrs. Walton always believed that the spook light was the ghost of Anna Bixby checking to see that her money was still hidden away. She had seen the light herself on many occasions, always disappearing into the cave.

Hall asked her, if she knew so well where Anna's money was hidden, why she had never bothered to go and get it. "I would," Mrs. Walton answered, "if I thought that Granny Bixby wanted me to have it."

According to the stories, the treasure still remains in the cave. It is located today on private property near the Rock Creek community, a short distance from Cave-in-Rock. Travelers are advised that this fabled place can be dangerous for a variety of reasons, not the least of which is the unstable rocks around the cave entrance and the fact that the cool hollow is infested with rattlesnakes during the summer months. Regardless, the treasure is still hidden away here and the ghost light still watches over it, even after all these years.

The Headless Horseman of Lakey's Creek

For nearly 150 years, the small town of McLeansboro has been haunted by a headless rider. The grim apparition appears on a concrete bridge that spans the murky waters of Lakey's Creek. While the identity of this spectral rider has long been known in the area, only a few people are aware of why this phantom continues to ride today.

The creek that the headless rider crosses was named after an early settler to this community named Lakey. After coming here, he began building a small cabin near the creek, just off a road that connected Mt. Vernon to Carmi. Lakey made quick work of the cabin, although he often could be found stopping his work and chatting with travelers and neighbors who passed by. This was what he was reportedly doing on the last evening that he was seen alive. A few neighbors later recalled riding by and stopping to talk with Lakey, who had completed the walls of his home and was now cutting clapboards for the roof.

The next morning, a neighbor from the settlement stopped to drop off some extra eggs for Lakey. He called out, but after receiving no answer, he looked around the back of the house and found a gruesome sight. Lakey's bloody and headless body was lying next to a tree stump in the yard. His head had rolled a few feet away and was pressed against the murder weapon—Lakey's own ax.

News of the horror quickly spread and settlers came to examine the scene. The local sheriff was dispatched, but he was as bewildered as everyone else. Lakey had been a friendly man, with no known enemies and no hidden wealth to speak of. There was also nothing to suggest that Lakey had struggled with anyone. The killer, whoever it might have been, was never found. Lakey was buried next to his unfinished cabin, but he would not stay in his grave for long.

One night, a short time after Lakey's funeral, two men who lived on the west side of McLeansboro were walking near the cabin. Suddenly they spotted a headless figure on a large, black horse. The specter appeared alongside the creek and followed along with them as they walked. Neither of the men spoke, as they were too afraid to say anything, and the rider was also silent. As the men headed down into the shallow crossing of the stream, the rider also turned. They waded out into the middle of the creek, and as they did, the horseman turned left, passed downstream, and then inexplicably vanished into a deep pool near the crossing.

The two men hurried home, and while they hesitated to tell anyone what they had seen, they soon found that it didn't matter. Other locals also began seeing the rider. Two nights later, a small group of travelers from the western side of the state spotted the rider and told others about it. The horseman began to be seen on a regular basis, giving birth to an eerie legend. Locals believed the ghost was that of Lakey himself, searching for the man who killed him. They said that his ghost followed the travelers until he could be sure that they were not the man he was looking for.

The rider continued to join travelers as they crossed the creek but would always turn and vanish as they reached the other side. As time passed, the stream crossing was replaced with a bridge, and the stories changed to say that the rider now would appear on the creek bank, cross the bridge to the center of the water, and then vanish.

Many years have passed since then, and the legend of Lakey's ghost is largely forgotten. Perhaps the pace of modern life has rendered the ghost and his phantom steed somewhat obsolete. Despite the fact that it is seldom told, the story has never been completely lost, leading some to speculate that perhaps Lakey is still out there. Perhaps he still seeks the justice, or the vengeance, that he never found.

Do travelers still encounter the ghost as they cross the old bridge over Lakey's Creek? Perhaps not in the way that they used to, but many area residents will assure you that both Lakey and his legend live on. Some still say that it is not uncommon for people walking near the bridge to hear odd sounds coming from the roadway. They claim these sounds are the clip-clop of horse's hooves on the pavement but that the horse that walks there is never seen. Could it be Lakey out on a midnight ride?

Haunts of the Fife Opera House

The Fife Opera House in the small town of Palestine is a place of history—and some say many ghosts, as well. It was part of the town's thriving business district for many years, but when it became the scene of a mysterious suicide in 1935, it began to gain a ghostly reputation.

The old town of Palestine is located along the Wabash River on the eastern edge of the state. It is a place with a long history in Illinois, and the town, which took its name from the pages of the Bible, has the oldest continuous charter in the state. A French trapper named John LaMotte founded it in 1678, and the settlement has been occupied ever since. Thanks to its strategic location on the river, it was the site of two forts during the War of 1812 and later became Crawford County's first government seat.

These days, Palestine's historic business district features a collection of restored shops and historic buildings, as well as the magnificent Fife Opera House. The building has been undergoing a massive restoration over the past few years, and as the work continues, it has also started to gain a reputation as one of the most haunted places in the area.

David Fife began construction on the grand opera house in 1898 and finished it three years later. Prior to the opening of the opera house, local residents found their entertainment at the Rising Sun Tavern, which Fife purchased in 1894 and converted into a hardware store and harness shop. The top floor, which had once held a hotel, was taken over by an area newspaper. By 1898, Fife's business had outgrown the smaller building, so he decided to raze it and build a new structure on the site. When the new structure opened in 1901, there was a hardware store located on the first floor and the second floor was dominated by the theater, which boasted seating for seven hundred patrons. Here, customers could enjoy the latest entertainment while seated in red leather seats and in front of backdrops that had been hand-painted in Chicago.

On May 21, 1901, electric lamps all over Palestine dimmed as David Fife switched on the lights for the first time at his new opera house. The first performance was held in September of that year, and shows continued until May 1912, when the stage went dark for good.

In addition to the hardware store and opera house, Fife used the building for other business ventures, including a funeral business that was run from the back portion of the second floor. Fife, who graduated from the Indianapolis School of Embalming, operated his undertaking business until 1926. He then sold it to Goodwine & Goodwine, who remained in the building for some time after.

Fife died in 1942, and his wife, Alta, operated the hardware store and also leased out the huge upstairs auditorium to a number of businesses. In 1951, she sold the building to Kent Phillips and Jim Goodwine (from the funeral business), and not long after, Goodwine bought out his partner and continued to operate the hardware, and now furniture, store. He used the second floor as storage. Goodwine became the sole owner of the funeral business in 1980 and moved out of the Fife building. In 1989, the opera house was purchased by the Palestine Preservation Projects Society, and they began the enormous task of restoring the building to its former glory.

The opera house has not always been considered haunted. Reports of ghostly activity began soon after the restoration project was started. This is often the case with old buildings, although no one can say why with any certainty. It is thought that perhaps construction and renovation can disturb the atmosphere—and the ghosts—of a building. This may be the case at the Fife Opera House.

Some believe that at least one ghost was already present here, although dormant, thanks to the years of inactivity in the building. On April 29, 1935, Harold Fife, the nephew of David, was working upstairs on the second floor of the building. It was an otherwise ordinary day, or so the other employees in the building thought, until they heard a single gunshot from upstairs. When the staff ran to see what had happened, they discovered the body of Harold Fife in a pool of blood on the floor. He had died from a self-inflicted gunshot to the head. He had given no warning of being depressed, and to this day, the reasons for Harold's suicide remain a mystery. Perhaps this is why his ghost walks in this place.

Over the past decade and a half, many reliable witnesses have told of strange happenings in the building. Reports and rumors have circulated about ghostly figures and phantom footsteps that have been heard crossing the floor on the upper level. Heavy steps have often been heard pounding overhead, but when those present go upstairs to see who might be in the auditorium, the place is always found to be empty. Many have heard the footsteps, as well as eerie voices and, on one occasion, the cracking sound of a single gunshot.

Does history repeat itself over and over again in this building? Perhaps—theaters have long been considered a place where events from the past record themselves on the atmosphere and then reverberate again and again over time. The Fife Opera House is a place that has seen more than its share of tragedy, triumph, and heartbreak over the years, and perhaps these events merely replay themselves as time goes by—leaving a haunting for the next generation to experience.

The Last Woman Hanged in Illinois

There are incidents in the history of any region that the local residents would rather forget than honor. Among these incidents were the public hangings that drew curious crowds of onlookers who often purchased tickets for the spectacle of watching a man die. Most small towns, and even larger cities, are somewhat embarrassed today about how such events were handled in days gone by and are quick, whenever possible, to sweep the memories of them under the proverbial rug. In some cases, however, when tragedy was mixed together with death, the stories and impressions left behind are not so easily forgotten—and they do not quickly fade away.

In May 1845, Elizabeth "Betsy" Reed earned an infamous place in Illinois history as the first—and only—woman to be hanged in the state. The story of the strange events surrounding her execution began in the summer of 1844 in a place called Purgatory Swamp. It was a rural, backwoods area at the time that Elizabeth and her husband, Leonard Reed, lived there. They resided in a log cabin located about eight miles south of Palestine and about one-half mile north of Heathsville. The old cabin has been gone for many years, and Purgatory Swamp is long forgotten, but in 1844, nearly everyone who could read a newspaper in Illinois knew exactly where it was.

During the hot days of that summer, Leonard Reed became ill. A neighbor girl, Eveline Deal, was called to the cabin to help care for Reed. She would later testify that she was present when a doctor came to call on the sick man. After a brief examination, the doctor announced that Reed was too sick to survive. After the doctor had left the cabin, Deal claimed that she saw Elizabeth pour some sort of white powder into her husband's sassafras tea. Elizabeth explained to the young girl that it was "medicine." Before the doctor returned the following day, August 15, Leonard Reed was dead.

At the time of the funeral, Elizabeth seemed to be a grieving widow. It was not until later that her behavior became suspect, perhaps after Eveline Deal mentioned the "medicine" that Reed had slipped into the dead man's tea. Suspicion soon fell on Elizabeth, and rumors began to spread that someone should look into the death of Leonard Reed; it might not have been a simple fever that killed him after all.

At that time, Elizabeth Reed was thought of as a strange woman with a "very peculiar and hardened disposition." Her unusual behavior, even before her husband's death, led many to question whether something was wrong with her. Legend has it that locals considered her to be a witch, and there is no doubt that she made an interesting spectacle on occasions when she came into town. Elizabeth is believed to have had some sort of facial disfigurement and always wore a white cap or white band over her head. Attached to the band was a veil, which she was never seen without, hiding her features and causing area tongues to wag. It was no surprise that Elizabeth was accused of murdering her husband and even less of a surprise that most people were quick to believe that she committed the crime.

The whispers, rumors, and speculation spread, and eventually, the Crawford County sheriff was forced into launching an investigation. There was little to suggest that Reed had actually committed any crime, except for the account from Eveline Deal, and so the investigation was started more to settle the unrest in the community than because any evidence existed of wrongdoing. As it turned out, however, the investigation would reveal that Elizabeth was deeply involved in her husband's death.

A search of the Reed cabin turned up a piece of brown paper that matched the description of the paper that Elizabeth told Eveline Deal contained her husband's "medicine." Sheriff Thorn was able to trace the paper to a druggist in Russellville, who identified it as the same type of paper he used to package various types of medicine. In addition, it was also the same type of paper in which he had wrapped a quantity of arsenic for Elizabeth Reed! To make matters worse for Elizabeth, several witnesses verified that they had seen her in Russellville while she was making her purchase from the druggist. Several of them also stated that she had been wearing a disguise at the time, which is why they remembered her. No description was ever given of this "disguise" in the court records, and so it has been surmised that it may have been her customary scarf and veil. Such an odd ensemble would have appeared to be a "disguise" to those not familiar with her eccentric garb.

Although such scant evidence would not be enough to convict anyone of homicide today, in those times it was enough to get Elizabeth arrested and charged with her husband's murder. She was placed in the county jail in Palestine in August 1844, and shortly after her incarceration, the wooden jail mysteriously burned to the ground. This further fueled the speculation that Reed was a witch, especially since there seemed to be no cause for the blaze. The structure was never rebuilt, and the county seat was relocated to Robinson a short time later. Elizabeth, meanwhile, was moved to a loft above the sheriff's home and fastened with a chain to a sturdy bed. She remained there for several weeks while preparations were made for her trial.

A grand jury found the evidence against her to be enough to charge her with murder in September, and a change of venue was requested and approved. Elizabeth was transported to Lawrenceville in Lawrence County for her trial, which was finally held in April 1845.

The trial lasted only a few days and ended with Elizabeth being found guilty of murder. She was sentenced to hang on May 23 and returned to the jail to await her execution. According to some stories, the governor of Illinois, Thomas Ford, offered to revoke the execution if Reed would make a full confession about what she had done. It has been said that she did indeed confess to a clergyman who came to Lawrence County to comfort her. The confession was also apparently printed in a small pamphlet, which was not distributed until after her death. The sentence was not commuted, however, perhaps because most local residents saw her in the same way as the prosecuting attorney in the case. He stated that Elizabeth Reed was "not having the fear of God before her eyes, but being moved by the Devil."

A local resident would later recall, "The execution day dawned bright and balmy." People from all over the state and from Indiana came to Lawrence County to witness the death sentence being carried out. By some estimates, the crowd of curiosity-seekers swelled to nearly twenty thousand people. Elizabeth left the jail and rode to the site of her hanging in the back of a wagon, sitting atop her coffin. A friend who had been giving her religious instruction in jail was at her side. Reed had been baptized after her conviction and had found the Lord while chained to the bed in the loft above the sheriff's home. She came to her execution dressed in a long white robe, and as the wagon approached the site where the execution was to be carried out, onlookers were startled to hear her praying loudly and singing hymns at the top of her lungs.

Elizabeth was led onto the gallows and stood as Reverend John Sneed preached her funeral sermon. She loudly commented on everything the preacher said, and her enthusiastic responses were the only sound that was heard at the scene. The crowd stood watching in absolute silence.

When the sermon ended, Elizabeth stepped bravely onto the trapdoor, and a black hood was placed over her head, followed by a noose. Sheriff Thorn had tried in vain to find someone else to hold the rope that would send Reed into the afterlife, but he was finally forced to do the honors himself. Just after noon, he cut the rope and the trap dropped under her feet. Reed plunged down through the opening and "revolved several times, but did not struggle much," according to an eyewitness account. When it was over, her body was taken down and buried in a shallow grave directly beneath the gallows. She did not remain there for long, though. Relatives soon dug up her remains and placed them next to those of her husband in Baker Cemetery, just outside of Heathsville.

Those who visit the small graveyard today can find the graves of Elizabeth and Leonard Reed under an unobtrusive marker in the southwest corner of the grounds. The stone is a simple one, bearing the names of both. Below Leonard's name are the words "killed by murder" and beneath Elizabeth's, the stone bears the inscription "killed by hanging." Even the most jaded visitor to the cemetery admits to feeling a little unsettled to read these peculiar memorials written so plainly, side by side. It's no surprise that, over the years, locals have reported hearing a woman weeping in this small, darkened graveyard and seeing the apparition of a lady in white flitting among the stones.

Still Doing Time in Thebes

Located in the old river town of Thebes is a place that was once known as the "most formidable jail in Illinois," a collection of stone cells under the old courthouse in town that once housed famous prisoners and common criminals alike. At some point over its long history, a prisoner was incarcerated there who simply never left, making this old jail an impossible place to escape from—even after death.

The historic town of Thebes sleeps peacefully along the banks of the Mississippi River about forty miles northwest of Cairo. Built on high ground, it has rarely been inundated by the river, as many flood areas have been, and for this reason much of its history has been preserved. Thebes was first chartered by President Andrew Jackson to Franklin G. Hughes and Joseph Chandler in March 1846.

Before Cairo became a city of importance, Thebes served as the seat of Alexander County, although it was not the region's first choice. When the county was first established in 1819, five county commissioners were given the task of choosing a "permanent seat of justice," and they chose the long-vanished village of America. America seemed to be a good choice, and it grew rapidly. Several hundred people came there to live, build homes, and start businesses—then misfortune arrived. Business failures, a shifting of the river channel, several fires, and even an epidemic combined to dim the hopes of the town, and within a decade, the place was deserted.

A vote was taken to move the county seat, and in 1833, a new site was chosen for the "permanent seat of justice"—well, actually, two or three sites were chosen. In one report, the site was a vague location about three miles east and two miles north of the present-day town of Unity. The name of Vernon was chosen for the new village, but it never came to be. Another report adds to the confusion, picking the new site as a tract of land "located in the southwest half of the southeast quarter and north end of Section 36." This one did not work out either. Finally, David Hailman and his wife donated twenty acres of land to be used for a county seat that was not mentioned in any of the reports. This tract was described as "beginning at the three white oaks at the northwest corner of section 6."

Located near Unity, the county building combined a jail and courthouse and was built on the land given by the Hailman family. It was constructed of logs, weather-boarded, and served for a number of years, but it was never considered a "permanent" site. In 1843, two prisoners set fire to the building as part of their escape plan and the courthouse was destroyed. Plans were immediately made to move the county seat from Unity, and this time, Thebes was chosen.

The first court term held here was in 1845, under the shade of a large elm tree. A courthouse was constructed the following year. The old courthouse was built over a two-year period between 1846 and 1848. The shingles were made from native timber, and the walls were plastered, inside and out, with local products. The building had the honor of being known as the most secure jail in Illinois. The cells had three-foot-thick stone walls with a vaulted stone ceiling. Narrow windows were crisscrossed with heavy iron bars, and with a stone floor and double doors of heavy iron, it was a truly formidable place. In fact, local legend has it that famed slave Dred Scott was held here for a time while awaiting his court case for freedom.

In addition to Dred Scott, several Illinois notables walked the floors of the old courthouse. General John A. Logan once argued a lawsuit there, and he also appeared in Thebes to speak on behalf of the Union during the trying early days of 1861. Logan faced a potentially unfriendly crowd in this pro-southern region, but he managed to win many local men over to his cause. In addition, Abraham Lincoln also appeared here during his days of riding the law circuit.

As time passed and Thebes lost prominence in the region, the old courthouse was abandoned. Over the years, it was used as a church, a school, by fraternal orders, as a point for political gatherings, and for community purposes. During its times of complete abandonment, it was a favorite place for local boys to break into and wander about. It later years, it became the Thebes City Hall and the local library, and it is now a historic site that is open for public tours.

In a place where so much history has occurred, it's no surprise that a few stories of hauntings emerge from this stately building at the top of the hill. Visitors claim to have experienced strange sounds, footsteps in empty parts of the building, and mysterious cold spots that have no explanation. One report tells of a visitor who was touring the building one day and encountered a man in shackles in one of the basement jail cells. Surprised, but believing that it was a reenactor playing a prisoner from the courthouse's past, he started to speak to the man—only to see the spectral prisoner vanish before his eyes. Did a former resident of Illinois' most secure jail remain behind in the building?

Perhaps, and he may not be the only one who has stayed behind. Other reports claim to have spotted semitransparent figures in other parts of the building, perhaps still trying cases and arguing the law in a different time and space from the present.

Lingering Spirits of the Hundley House

Although more than eighty years have passed since two murders were committed in a historic home in Carbondale, those who have lived and worked in the place have come to believe that the spirits of the dead still linger within its walls. Such stories are spread about myriad allegedly haunted houses in the state of Illinois, but few of them have seen the kind of carnage and violence that occurred in the Hundley House in December 1928.

John Charles Hundley was a prominent wealthy citizen of Carbondale at the time of his death. He had been the mayor of the city in 1907–08 and enjoyed many friendships and business acquaintances throughout the area. But Hundley's life had not always been perfect. In fact, in 1893, he had committed murder. In that incident, Hundley had killed a music teacher in town but was acquitted by a jury after pleading the "unwritten law," meaning that he had murdered the man who had been sleeping with his wife. The incident led to him divorcing his wife, which caused bitter feelings between him and his son, Victor. Although the problems between them had supposedly been settled years before the elder Hundley's death, some witnesses would later claim that the quarrel continued. This led to Victor becoming the chief suspect in the murder of his father.

Hundley remarried a few years after his divorce, and in 1915, he and his second wife, Luella, purchased a lot at the corner of Maple and Main streets and constructed what became their sprawling and luxurious home.

Luella Hundley was the daughter of Ruffin Harrison, one of the founders of the city of Herrin and the owner of numerous coal mines in the region. She was also the sister of George Harrison, president of Herrin's First National Bank. She was said to have been an accomplished musician and very involved in local charity work. Perhaps for these reasons, she was regarded as having no enemies, which made her murder all the more puzzling.

The lives of the Hundleys were destroyed just before midnight on Wednesday, December 12, 1928. Investigators believed that Mr. Hundley was murdered first. His body was found in an upstairs bedroom, dressed only in a nightshirt and socks. He had been shot six times from behind with a .45-caliber revolver. Mrs. Hundley was killed downstairs. She had been shot twice in the back of the head and once in the heart. She had been shot in a rear stairway, up which she had apparently started to climb in order to aid her husband. Her body had rolled into the kitchen, and a pencil was resting next to her left hand. An unfinished letter on the table in an adjoining room was mute evidence of what she was doing when she was alarmed by the shots that killed her husband.

According to newspaper reports, neighbors across the street who heard the shots being fired called the police, who arrived at the scene of the crime within minutes. The next morning, Chief of Police Joe Montgomery told the press that robbery seemed to be the most likely motive for the murders, even though the house was not disturbed when officers arrived. The only evidence that pointed to a robbery of the house, which contained valuable artwork, expensive furnishings, and a large amount of cash, was the discovery of an empty pocketbook on the floor near Luella Hundley's body. Neighbors told police that they believed the purse was kept in a writing desk downstairs. Because most of the valuables in the house appeared to be untouched, though, the police soon began to believe that there were other, darker motives for the crime.

On the morning of December 13, police investigators thoroughly searched the Hundley House. Tracking dogs were brought in and placed on the trail of the killer, and four times, the dogs led their handlers straight to the home of John Charles Hundley's son Victor, a prominent coal dealer in the city. Investigators believed that the killer might have been known to Mrs. Hundley because it appeared that she had opened the door and let him into the house, as she would have done, even at that late hour, for her stepson.

Victor also seemed to have a motive for the murders. At an inquest that was held that afternoon, Joab Goodall, a friend of the Hundleys and the last person to see them alive, testified that the elder Hundley had recently told him that he planned to make a new will and disinherit Victor "because he was no good." A bitter feud had long existed between father and son, and though allegedly patched up, it had possibly flared into existence again. If this was the case, then Victor Hundley stood to lose a great amount of money if his father changed his will. His father's estate was worth more than $350,000, but Victor would have been left with only his trust fund, which amounted to less than $15,000.

Goodall also told the coroner's jury that the Hundleys had been in excellent spirits when he visited with them on the night of their murders. They were planning a motor trip to their winter home in Florida, and they planned to leave on Sunday. Goodall left the Hundley home around 8 P.M. on Wednesday evening and stated that Mrs. Hundley had locked the rear door behind him. Officers who arrived at the house four hours later found this door unlocked.

Another neighbor, Olga Kasper, who lived next door to the Hundleys, testified at the inquest that she had heard the fatal shots fired and had seen the lights in the house turned off immediately after. She said she heard someone running past her home, coming from the direction of the Hundley house and toward Victor's house, a short time later.

Investigators from the Jackson County sheriff's office searched the route described by Mrs. Kasper and followed it to Victor Hundley's home, which was just two hundred yards away. Along the path, officers found several slips of paper that were presumed to have been lost in flight. One paper, dated December 5, was a notice of the termination of partnership of Mr. and Mrs. J. C. Hundley with Victor Hundley in his coal business. Another paper was a bank deposit slip, the back of which bore notes that figured out the interest on a loan that amounted to $532. The note was in Luella's handwriting, and at the top of the paper was written "Vic."

Victor Hundley was brought in for questioning and subjected to seven hours of interrogation by Sheriff William Flanigan and his investigators. His house was also searched, and a bloodstained khaki shirt was discovered. Hundley claimed that he had been wearing the shirt when he was told about the crime. Police officers awakened him and told him that his father and stepmother had been murdered and asked him to come to the house. While he was wearing the shirt, Hundley said, he had picked up the body of his stepmother. According to investigators, Hundley had never touched the body, so the blood had to have come from somewhere else. Suddenly, Victor recalled that he had been wearing the shirt while quail hunting and that was where the blood had come from.

Victor denied that there was any current trouble between him and his father. He told investigators that on Wednesday night, he had been home all evening, reading and playing with his son. He had gone to bed early and was awakened by the police. Hundley also admitted that he owned a .45-caliber revolver, but he claimed that he had recently loaned it to his father. A search of both of the Hundley's houses failed to turn up the gun. To this day, it has never been recovered.

After hours of exhaustive questioning, Victor broke into tears and cried out, "Oh my God! This is terrible!" He again swore that he had nothing to do with the murders. He was taken home but was placed under house arrest as the investigation continued.

On December 15, immediately following the funeral of the Hundleys, Victor was arrested for their murders. Although the coroner's jury was unable to name the killer, the state's attorney, Fletcher Lewis, believed that he could prove that Victor was guilty in a court of law. Unfortunately, it wouldn't work out that way, and on December 31, Lewis was forced to let Victor go. He filed a motion during Hundley's preliminary to dismiss the case due to insufficient evidence. The judge sustained the disappointed prosecutor's motion.

Lewis made a statement to reporters after the hearing. "While the facts and circumstances learned from the investigation amply justified the holding of Victor Hundley and the filing of a complaint charging him with murder . . . I have decided to prosecute this particular case no further," he said.

Then he added, "I feel quite sure that the atrociousness of this crime will compel the conscience of the person who committed it to someday make public his guilt."

But Lewis was wrong. No one ever came forward, and the killers of J. C. and Luella Hundley were never found. The case languished in limbo for a time and then was relegated to the "unsolved" section of the city's law enforcement files. There were many who believed that Victor Hundley had gotten away with murder, but they could never prove it. Victor never spoke of the crimes again, and he continued to live in the Carbondale area for the rest of his life. Eight decades later, the murders of Carbondale's former mayor and his wife remain unsolved.

And perhaps for that very reason, many have come to believe that their spirits do not rest in peace.

The Hundley mansion at the corner of Maple and Main streets remained empty for two years after the murders. The only physical reminder of the horrific crimes that occurred there was a bullet hole in a wall near where Luella's body had been found, but the memories of that night remained in the minds of the townspeople.

The house remained vacant until 1930, when it was purchased by Edwin William Vogler Sr. He bought the house and all of its contents from the Hundley estate. It remained in the Vogler family until 1972, when it was sold to a family named Simonds, who converted the huge residence into a gift shop with apartments upstairs. In 2000, it was sold to Victoria Sprehe, who ran the gift shop for five years before selling it to spend more time with her young son.

Rumors that date back many years claim that the Hundleys still haunt this house. A number of the past owners and tenants in the building have had strange encounters that they are unable to explain. One former resident told of loud knocking sounds that reverberated in her room at night and the faint sound of the downstairs piano as the keys tinkled by themselves. Her family also recalled hearing footsteps going up and down the stairs, as if perhaps the killer of the Hundleys was doomed to repeat his walk to J. C. Hundley's bedroom again and again.

Former owner Victoria Sprehe said that whenever she was alone in the house, lights would turn on by themselves, as if someone were watching over her. She said that she believed that Luella's ghost followed her home from work on at least one occasion. Walking into the empty house, she heard pots and pans clanging and noticed that lights were on in the kitchen. She noted, however, "It's not like a scary presence. It's a very peaceful vibe."

Perhaps it's not a scary presence, but it could be unnerving. Sprehe was sometimes bothered by a door that opened by itself and by footsteps that she heard walking on the stairs—the same stairs where a previous family also reported disembodied steps. Tenants who lived in apartments on the upper floor also told stories of the creaking stairs and what definitely seemed to be the sound of boots, or heavy shoes, clomping on the wooden risers. One tenant laughed and stated that this was only the sound of the old house settling, but then lost his grin when he admitted that he had never heard of a house that settled in just that way.

Victoria Sprehe's daughter, Nina Bucciarelli, also recounted odd incidents in the house, like the front porch swing that would move by itself, even when there was no wind. Sprehe's husband had also noticed this odd occurrence. Nina had her own explanation for the swing's strange movement. "At night, if you drive by the porch swing, it's just swinging away. I think Mr. and Mrs. Hundley still like to swing at night," she said.

And perhaps she's right, because if the stories of the past decades are to be believed, the Hundleys have not yet departed from the house they called their own—and the place where their lives were taken away too soon.

Central Illinois

Railroad Ghosts of Central Illinois

The railroads first came to central Illinois in the 1850s, completely changing the way of life for those who lived in what were little more than farm communities. With the coming of the railroads, the outside world was now open to these simple folk. All at once, goods from the East could be purchased in local stores, and products from the prairie, like grain and cattle, could be shipped to expanding markets all over the country.

One of the greatest railroad hubs in central Illinois was the city of Decatur. All of the major rail lines that came through Illinois had headquarters and rail service through this small Midwestern town. The arrival of the railroad in Decatur in 1854 changed the future of the city forever. The first railroad to establish service in Decatur was the Great Western Line, which became part of the Norfolk & Western Railroad in later years. There were also a number of other rail services to Decatur, but the greatest of these were most likely the Wabash and the Illinois Central.

The first Wabash roundhouse was built in Decatur in 1869 and had eight stalls. The Wabash shops were moved to Decatur in 1884 and operations here expanded rapidly. Decatur became the hub of all of the railroad's operations, and in 1925, it had a peak employment of thirty-five hundred men, making it the largest employer in the city. Eventually, the railroad died out in the city, and the Wabash merged with Norfolk & Western in 1964. A heavy loss in passenger service was cited as the main reason for the merger, and most of the service was finally abandoned. At its peak, the Wabash Railroad operated twenty-five passenger trains out of Decatur every day.

The second rail service to come to the city was the Illinois Central, which arrived here in October 1854. A union station was built in 1856 at the southeast corner of the intersection of the Illinois Central and Wabash lines. This building served until 1903, when both companies built their own stations. The old union station included the Central House hotel, which offered sleeping quarters, offices, and a dining room. Abraham Lincoln stayed the night at the hotel while attending the Republican convention here in 1860.

The new Illinois Central Station was built in 1900 and was the loading point for twenty-seven daily passenger trains. Decatur was once the main stop between Chicago and St. Louis, but eventually the passenger service died out and the station was razed in 1951, leaving only memories behind.

The old train stations were once located just north of Eldorado Street in Decatur. Today, this area is a forgotten place, although it was once one of the busiest parts of the city. Now, only the distant rumble of freight cars can be heard here, providing a remembrance of what once was.

During the day, this was a stopping place for passengers who were riding the trains and passing through the city. During the heyday of the railroad in Decatur, hundreds of people came here every single day, possibly heading for a city as near as Chicago or possibly traveling the first link to a final destination on the other side of America. Besides the two train stations, the Wabash and the Illinois Central, there were a number of hotels, restaurants, and businesses located here, all hoping for the prosperity delivered with each train that arrived in the city.

But that was in the daylight hours.

After darkness fell, this area, known as the Levee District, was considered to be one of the most dangerous parts of the city and the hub of Decatur's most illicit activities. The Levee District extended from Water Street on the west to Wabash Street on the north, and ended at the Illinois Central tracks. The place became a magnet for crime and criminals over the years and was known for its collection of saloons, gambling houses, and brothels. The old Levee is deserted today. The saloons, restaurants, hotels, and stores have vanished, and little remains save for empty buildings, a few remnants of stone, and a lot of memories.

It has been many years since passengers have been able to leave Decatur by railroad, but freight trains still use the aging tracks every day. Late at night, in some parts of the city, one can hear the rolling, booming sounds of the cars as they rumble along the tracks or the lonely whistle of the engine as it rides along through the darkness. The railroads are not completely forgotten in Decatur—and neither are the railroad's ghosts.

One of central Illinois' railroad ghost stories concerns the phantom of a young girl who was reportedly seen inside of the Wabash station during the years when it was still in operation. Back in those days, the building was a still a hub of activity, and passengers came and went all day long and into the night. It would be during these nighttime shifts that staff members and railroad workers would encounter the eerie woman in white who was seen sitting on a bench in the station.

According to the legends, this young lady had once been married to a man who went off to fight in World War I in 1918. After many months of fighting, she received a letter from him stating that he was coming home. Eagerly, she went down to the train station on the scheduled date of his arrival to meet the train. She waited all afternoon, watching the passengers disembark from each train, but her husband did not appear. She returned home disappointed but came back the next day, thinking that perhaps he had been delayed. Another day passed and then another, until finally, an entire week had gone by. Still, there was no sign of him. Then, a telegram arrived the following afternoon. Her husband had been killed in a bus accident in New York, on his way to the train that would have taken him home. Distraught, the young woman swallowed a bottle of pills and committed suicide. She had been unable to cope with the loss of her true love. As the years passed, those who worked and even passed through the Wabash station reported the sight of a lovely young woman, still waiting expectantly on a bench in the station.

She was seen many times over the years and was heard occasionally as her heels tapped on the polished floors. Others claimed to smell her perfume when the ghost was nearby, still waiting for her lost love to return. Today, the Wabash station has been turned into an antique mall, but this phantom of the past still lingers behind—and she may not be the only ghost in the building. The owners of the antique mall, as well as tenants and customers, claim to have seen spectral shapes in the hallways, been touched by unseen hands, and have had problems keeping merchandise from being broken in a section of the building where prisoners were kept as they waited to be loaded onto trains.

The events of the past may be a distant memory at the old Wabash station—but they don't seem ready to be forgotten just yet.

Another of Decatur's railroad ghost stories involves a mysterious light that is seen bobbing along through the site of the old Wabash rail yards, a mostly deserted area that was once filled with tracks, machine shops, warehouses, and the Wabash roundhouse. The light has been spotted countless times throughout the years as it moves back and forth and follows the lines of the old railroad tracks for some distance before suddenly blinking out.

There have been a couple of different explanations for why the light appears here. One of them is a folk legend of some endurance, which claims the light is the lantern of a railroad worker who was beheaded during an accident in the rail yards many years ago. He is now looking for his missing head, the stories say. While a check of old newspaper accounts does reveal numerous injuries in the Wabash yards in the early 1900s, I believe that the ghost light can be more credibly explained by a real event from the rail yard's past.

In October 1935, one of the most sensational unsolved murders in local history took place just north of the Wabash Station. On a chilly evening of that year, former Decatur police chief Omer Davenport was brutally slain by unknown assailants. At the time of his death, Davenport was on duty as a special patrolman for the Wabash railroad.

Davenport was probably one of the most well-liked and respected men in the city. He had distinguished himself in the military and had become the commanding officer of the 130th Infantry regiment of the Illinois National Guard. After serving during World War I, he returned to Decatur and became the chief of police for three years. He was the youngest chief to ever serve, taking over the position at the age of twenty-six. Davenport left the police department in 1927 and became a special patrolman for the railroad—a job that would eventually get him killed.

On the morning of October 8, the Wabash Passenger Train No. 17 arrived in Decatur from Chicago, and Davenport was nearby as it pulled to a stop just west of Morgan Street. In the dim light, he saw two men jump from the train and dodge behind a flagman's shack. Davenport started in their direction to investigate, but before he could get very far, both of them pulled out revolvers and began firing in his direction. One bullet struck him in the leg and the other in the neck. He fell beside the tracks, bleeding badly, while the two men climbed onto the nearest passing freight train and disappeared.

Other patrol officers began searching the area, and after a phone call, the Decatur police force also joined in the hunt. The description of the two men was sketchy, but the police had other clues to work with. The gun that killed Davenport had been stolen the night before from the home of Isaiah Taylor, who also reported that a number of other items had been taken. Some of these items were later found near the scene of Davenport's shooting.

Police detectives searched the area, and officers from all over the city and county worked overtime on the case. The night shift worked all the way through the next day as they scoured the city for leads. The local highways, railroad yards, and freight cars were searched, and one group of officers walked along the line from the Wabash yard to a town several miles away in hopes that some lead might be found. Trains were stopped and cars searched. Trucks were stopped on the highways, and deputies went to nearby towns to search the railroad depots. The state police aided in the search and broadcast the description of the suspects all over Illinois.

Meanwhile, Omer Davenport had been rushed to the nearby Wabash Employees Hospital, which was located on East Grand Avenue, a short distance from the station. He was still alive when he arrived there but began to fail a short time later. The doctors, who initially felt that he might recover, now began to offer a poor prognosis. The bullet that had struck his throat had worked itself into one of his lungs. It was causing serious complications, and if they tried to operate, they were convinced that it would kill him. He died later that night.

A few days later, the manhunt began to slow down. Detectives traveled as far as St. Louis and Chicago in pursuit of some sort of lead, but they found nothing. A reward was offered by the railroad in exchange for information about the killers, but it was never paid. Whoever the two men were, they vanished into history, leaving behind no clues as to their identities.

Omer Davenport was buried with full military honors, but many believe he has never rested in peace. For years after his death, there were those who believed that his ghost haunted the Wabash Employees Hospital where he died. There were many reports of a man fitting his description who was seen walking the hallways and vanishing without explanation.

The hospital closed down in 1972 and was used for a time as a community health improvement center before being abandoned. During its final years of operation, staff members spoke of the ghost of a man who wandered the building as if lost and then faded from sight. Could this have been the lingering spirit of Omer Davenport? The old hospital was demolished in 1996, leaving that question unanswered.

But what about the other haunting connected to the railroad detective?

This brings us back to the mysterious light that appears behind the old Wabash station, almost exactly where Davenport was shot in 1935. Many Wabash workers, railroad men, and police officers who worked in the area became convinced that the eerie light is the ghost of Omer Davenport that roams the rail yard. Thanks to his untimely death—and the fact that his killers were never brought to justice—it is believed that the light is actually the flashlight of the slain patrolman as he wanders the line, hoping to find some clue to the identities of the men who took his life.

Another story of a railroad ghost in central Illinois caused such a sensation during its first appearance that hundreds of people showed up just to get a glimpse of it. The phantom was known for years as the "Forsyth Ghost." She appeared along a stretch of tracks in Forsyth, Illinois, a small town located north of Decatur.

On January 25, 1871, a young woman who was walking along the railroad tracks at night was killed by a speeding Illinois Central train called the "Diamond Special." The train was heading south to Decatur when it struck the woman, pulling her along the tracks and tearing away all of her clothing except for her corset and her underskirt. The train finally screeched to a halt, and rescuers managed to free the girl from the tangle of the engine. She was horribly mangled by the force of the train and covered with blood. The woman, a few breaths away from death, still managed to whisper a dire warning to the engineer of the train. She vowed that she would come for him and take her revenge. She told him she would return from the grave in twenty years, which was her exact age on the day he had killed her.

The vow apparently proved true. The engineer continued working that same line for the next two decades, and as the train thundered along the tracks near Forsyth in 1891, he was still driving the same locomotive. Suddenly, at the exact spot of the accident, a woman appeared on the side of the tracks. The engineer would later claim in interviews and published reports that she had "long streaming hair and eyes like balls of fire." The mysterious woman was also nearly naked, wearing nothing more than a brief corset and a tattered scrap of an underskirt.

The engineer was so shocked by the sight of this creature that he slammed on the air brakes. Passengers were thrown from their seats and cases were strewn all about the baggage car. The train stopped, and several men jumped off and tried to approach the woman. When they got near her, she inexplicably vanished. Strange screams and cries were heard in the darkness, and the passengers hurried back to the train.

For several nights after, the ghost appeared along the route. The story of the weird specter began to spread, especially after it was featured in a small, local newspaper called the *Forsyth World*. The following night, townspeople, farmers, and even Decatur residents began lining the tracks, hoping to catch a glimpse of the ghost. Even though the creature failed to appear on schedule, the curiosity-seekers refused to leave. They came back each night, and the crowd increased in number each evening.

Finally, the railroad tried to nip the story in the bud. They never denied the existence of the ghost but instead criticized the newspaper for publicizing her appearances. They blamed the news stories and claimed the paper was responsible for "immense crowds who broke down fences and nearly trampled the track out of existence."

Needless to say, the "Diamond Special" was rerouted to another line, and the ghost of the young woman was never seen again.

Remnants of the Past in the Loomis House

Resting silently on Carlinville's town square is a crumbling, old building known as the Loomis House. This grand old hotel, where time stands still, looks out over the idyllic square, the preserved buildings of the town, and of course, toward Carlinville's most famous landmark, the "Million Dollar Courthouse." The Loomis House was named for its founder, Judge Thaddeus Loomis, during a time when his name garnered great respect in the city—a time before the construction of the opulent courthouse and the scandal that followed, and before his namesake hotel became known as one of the most haunted places in the region.

Thaddeus Loomis was born in New York and came to Illinois with his family when he was a young boy. In addition to helping his family on the farm, Loomis studied hard and eventually enrolled in Illinois College at Jacksonville; he then studied law at the University of Kentucky in Louisville. He graduated in 1849 and returned home for a short time before, like many young men of the era, traveling to California to take part in the legendary gold rush. He spent five years in the gold fields of California before coming back to Illinois and buying a farm near Carlinville. For the next six years, he farmed and also managed to build a small fortune cutting timber for the Chicago & Alton Railroad and speculating in real estate.

In 1861, Loomis entered the world of politics. The Democratic Party nominated him as a county judge, and he was elected to the seat in November. During his tenure, he managed to pay off a staggering county debt, for which he was widely acclaimed. This accomplishment, though, was soon to be forgotten in light of the scandal that accompanied his involvement in the new courthouse.

Macoupin County had been created in 1829 after hard work on the part of state senator Thomas Carlin. His efforts were rewarded with the founding of a town named in his honor, and Carlinville became the county seat. The first courthouse, a simple log cabin, was constructed in 1830 and served the area for nearly thirty-five years before the county decided in 1865 that a new courthouse was needed. At that time, Judge Loomis was up for reelection, and everyone knew that a vote for Loomis was a vote for the new courthouse, as he was solidly behind the project. Loomis handily won the election and unveiled his plans for the new building.

Architect Elijah Meyers created the plans for the courthouse, as well as for a new jail. Construction began in 1867 and lasted through the winter of 1869–70, with Loomis playing a central role in the project. As construction was winding down, Loomis began building the hotel that he would name for himself on the Carlinville square, a short distance from the courthouse construction site.

Almost immediately, charges of corruption were hurled at Judge Loomis and his associates, and the story of the Macoupin County courthouse became a phenomenon in Illinois history. To finance the construction of the courthouse, a bond totaling $50,000 was issued on a ten-year plan that would pay a 10 percent interest rate, but this amount of money barely paid for the foundation. By January 1869, the construction cost was $400,000 over budget and the building was still not finished. More bonds were issued, and taxes rose higher and higher until a "courthouse tax" of 50 cents was levied on every $100 of real estate and personal property. Taxpayers bitterly fought back, but their outcry fell on deaf ears. When the courthouse was officially completed in 1870, the final cost was $1,342,226.31—more than $18 million in today's dollars!

The expense to taxpayers had been devastating and became a major scandal. Most of the blame fell on Judge Loomis and George H. Holliday, who was a county clerk at that time. Judge Loomis was officially cleared of all blame, but the guilt or innocence of Holliday will never be known. According to local legend, Holliday hopped a Chicago & Alton train one night and was never heard from again. The courthouse expenses have never been fully explained. Most believe that some of the project money likely disappeared with Holliday—or vanished into the brick and mortar of the Loomis House hotel.

Despite the lingering questions, Loomis managed to escape from the scandal with his reputation mostly intact. He retreated to his new hotel and devoted himself to making it a landmark for Carlinville. Over the next eleven years, the Loomis House played host to traveling actors, politicians, salesmen, and leisure travelers. Business boomed until 1881, when the hotel's bar owner, William Siemens, was convicted of violating Illinois liquor laws, and the tavern was closed down. Suddenly unable to meet the mortgage payments, Loomis was forced to turn the hotel over to the banking firm of Chester and Dubois, who held the paper on the property. Chester and Dubois was already on the edge of financial ruin, thanks to their handling of the courthouse bonds, and within a few months, the firm folded. The hotel was sold to William Robertson, a wealthy farmer and the bank's largest creditor.

Robertson was a strict Prohibitionist and vowed that liquor would never again be served in the Loomis House. Soon after he bought the place, Robertson died, and the hotel was left to his family, who shared his views on alcohol. It took six months for them to reopen, but without liquor, the business suffered. Eventually, the business was put up for sale and was purchased by a Decatur man named Simonson. He believed the name "Loomis House" had given the place an "unsavory reputation," thanks to the scandal over the courthouse, so he changed the name to the grand-sounding St. George Hotel. He then proceeded to outfit the place with all of the latest luxuries.

Simonson remained the owner of the hotel until 1909, when he sold it to Theodore C. Loeur, a druggist who operated a pharmacy on the first floor. Loeur's nephew took over the pharmacy, and the place became a fixture on the Carlinville square. In 1953, the building was sold to the Elks Club, and they continued to operate it as the Elks Hotel for nearly two more decades. During their time in the building, the old roof began to leak, and the resulting water damage forced the Elks to finally sell the place to Alex and Fern Perardi in 1975. They changed the name of the place back to the Loomis House and reopened the bar, which was dubbed the St. George Room, but by this time, the hotel was simply too far gone to operate anymore. The Perardis closed the top two floors and converted the second floor into a restaurant that operated for almost ten more years. Soon after the restaurant opened, occupants of the building learned that they were sharing the place with ghosts.

Over the years, many strange encounters in the building have been linked to the hotel's ghosts. A number of places in the building are believed to be haunted by spirits from the past, including the main stairs that reach the restaurant on the second floor. During the time that the Elks Club was using the building as a hotel, an unfortunate gentleman stumbled down the steps, broke his neck, and died. This occurred in 1960, and yet almost fifty years later, visitors have reported an unexplainable uneasy feeling near the staircase. Others claim that they have seen a shadowy figure on the steps, which disappears when confronted. Could it be the ghost of this luckless hotel resident?

Staff members at the restaurant that operated here in the 1970s were the first people to report mysterious apparitions in the hotel. One waitress was working on a few odd jobs before opening up for the day when she walked out of the kitchen to see a man standing in the center of the dining room. She was just about to tell the man that he had come in too early to get anything to eat when he turned abruptly away from her and started to quickly walk. About halfway across the room, he vanished!

The waitress never described the man she saw, but another person did. Bill was a regular at the second-floor bar, and one evening he looked up from his stool and noticed a man standing in the corner. He later described the man as being very pale, oddly dressed, and looking very ill at ease. The man's clothing looked like it had come from the early 1900s, and he wore a full, white beard. Bill was just starting to point out the man to his friends when suddenly the unusual figure turned and vanished into a brick wall. Needless to say, Bill was stunned, and when asked what he had been trying to get their attention about, he shrugged the whole thing off. He feared that his friends might tease him about it, but he did tell Fern Perardi, who would remember it in the years to come. She came to believe that the specter, based on the man's description, was none other than the hotel's original owner, Judge Loomis.

And if he does haunt the place, many have wondered if he walks the halls here alone. There have been many other encounters in the stairwells, former bathrooms, and guest rooms of the building. There is no question that it is an eerie place and one where events from the place seem to linger into the present.

Ghost of the Greene County Hanging Tree

The story of the "hanging tree," and the phantom that haunts it, has been told in Greene County for more than a century. The strange tale of murder and the macabre was recounted for misbehaving children as a bedtime story; it involved a traveling body used to frighten wrongdoers as it hung from a post at the railroad station. It remains today as one of Illinois' strangest tales of crime and a lingering ghost.

Dr. Charles MacCauliffe was the only physician in the small town of Wrights in 1879. While a respected and generally well-liked man, his sterling personality traits did not save him from death at the end of a rope after he committed murder. MacCauliffe and his brother-in-law, a local man named James Heavener, were drinking one evening in the town's only saloon and, at some point, got into a heated argument. Obviously fueled by too many drinks, the fight became so intense that Dr. MacCauliffe went behind the bar, grabbed a shotgun that the owner kept there, and fired both barrels into Heavener's chest. His brother-in-law was instantly killed, and when he saw what he had done, the doctor panicked, threw the shotgun on the floor, and ran from the saloon. He left Heavener on the floor in a growing pool of his own blood.

As MacCauliffe ran, a group of men who witnessed the murder chased after him. They quickly found the doctor hiding in a neighborhood barn, took him into custody, and delivered him to the town constable. Wrights was not large enough to have its own jail, so after some discussion, the constable and several of the men decided to take Dr. MacCauliffe to nearby Carrollton. They loaded him onto a wagon and started out into the night.

Not far from town, the wagon rolled past a large oak tree located at the edge of Hickory Grove Cemetery, and as the men looked up into the leaves and branches, they decided that they would hang the doctor right then and there. With the full approval of the constable, they tied a rope around MacCauliffe's neck and stood him up in the back of the wagon. Ignoring his pleas for mercy, one of the men slapped the horse on the hindquarters and it jerked forward, pulling the wagon out from under the struggling doctor's feet. He hung there, his feet kicking and his body twitching, as he slowly strangled to death.

Later on, the constable and some of the other men in the lynching party told people that a mob of men had surprised them, took the doctor away, and hanged him from the cemetery oak tree. Of course, most folks knew this was not the case because, after the hanging, all of the men involved had gone home to bed. If the doctor really had been taken away from them, they would have scoured the countryside for his abductors. Even though no one believed their story, no arrests were ever attempted for the doctor's murder.

Most of the local people found out about the lynching the next morning. A group of children was walking along the road near the cemetery and saw MacCauliffe's body still hanging there, gently twisting in the breeze. They became frightened and ran home to tell their parents. Several adults went back to the cemetery and cut down the corpse. There was a lot of discussion about what to do with the body. At some point, it was loaded on a wagon and taken to the railroad station in town. With the rope still knotted about its neck, the corpse was hoisted up on a pole and left on display as a warning to passersby about what happened to lawbreakers in Wrights.

The body became quite an attraction, and people traveled from nearby towns to get a look at it. The late Vera Harr, a resident of Carrollton, recalled, "My mother was born that year and grandma wasn't allowed to see the body for fear that the baby would be marked for life."

Finally, after several days, the corpse was cut down and buried in an unmarked grave in the southeast corner of Hickory Grove Cemetery. The doctor was laid to rest with no ceremony whatsoever, and no one was present at his burial, save for the two men who dug the grave. However, a local farmer, John W. Flowers, decided that Mac-Cauliffe's grave should be marked.

From the nearby woods, Flowers dug up a small cedar tree and planted it next to the doctor's grave. He also used some cement and creek sand and created a small, stone monument. Using the metal nameplate from the door of the doctor's office in Wrights, he embedded it in the wet cement. The plate read simply, "Doctor MacCauliffe." Below it, he scratched out the words, "Died 1879." The plate is still readable today, but the lettering that was cut into the stone is barely legible.

Later, a marker was also placed on the old "hanging tree," telling the story of the murder and the lynching that occurred. Unfortunately, the tree blew down in a storm a few years ago, bringing at least one eerie story to an end.

For decades, legends told in Greene County advised against walking the road beneath the "hanging tree" at night. It was said that on certain nights, the ghostly figure of Dr. MacCauliffe could still be seen hanging from the twisting branches overhead. As he swayed in the wind, his body twisted until trespassers could see his face. If his eyes opened, the legend stated, then you were bound to die within the next year. It was a warning of death that most superstitious local residents went out of their way to avoid.

The Ghost of Mary Hawkins

One of the most famous ghosts in Illinois is the specter that haunts the women's dorm known as Pemberton Hall at Eastern Illinois University in Charleston. This building has a long and rich history that is filled with tradition—and tales of ghosts.

Pemberton Hall was the first college building in Illinois to provide on-campus housing for women. It may also be the first such building to become haunted. The past decades have provided literally hundreds of tales of strange events, ghostly apparitions, and frightening tales about the dorm. For more than eighty years, women living in the hall claim to have encountered the ghost, or ghosts, and have reported the spirit playing the piano and scratching on the walls of the building's abandoned fourth floor.

The haunting began with a murder that allegedly took place one winter's night in the early 1900s. According to the story, a student was attacked in the fourth-floor music room of the hall and left for dead. She managed to make it down the stairs to the door of a hall counselor before she died.

As the years have passed, residents of Pemberton Hall say they have heard this event from the past repeating itself in the building. They recall the dragging sounds heard near the stairs that lead to the upper floor and the sounds of scratching on doors and walls. Most disconcerting, though, are the bloody footprints that have appeared in the corridor, only to vanish moments later. Many believe the ghost of the murdered young woman has returned to haunt Pemberton Hall. But she is not the most famous spirit who wanders these halls.

The counselor who discovered the murdered girl was named Mary Hawkins. She was a young woman herself, barely older than the ladies she had been hired to assist. She was a very attractive woman with a bright disposition that quickly made her a favorite among the residents of Pemberton Hall. However, the effect of the murder on Mary's personality was devastating. She became haunted by the death of the young woman, and students spoke of seeing her pacing the hallways at all hours of the night, unable to sleep and tormented by horrible visions and guilt. Finally, unable to cope with her depression and the nightmares that accompanied it, Mary was institutionalized and later committed suicide.

Shortly after her death, the residents of Pemberton Hall started to report some rather strange occurrences in the building, and these spooky events continue today. They believe the incidents can be explained as the ghost of Mary Hawkins, still making her rounds and checking in on the young women who live in the building. Perhaps her spirit is unable to rest after losing one of the women in her care and she still roams the hall, watching out for them and protecting them from harm. Her ghost is said to glide through the rooms, locking and unlocking doors, turning off radios and televisions, and generally keeping track of things that go on here.

Throughout the decades, residents have reported hearing the sounds of whispers in the building, especially on the fourth floor. One student, who lived in Pemberton Hall in 1976, recalled the problems that the resident advisors had with the furniture in one of the lounges. It seemed that all of the furniture in this room was often found to be overturned, or at the very least, rearranged.

Some claim they have witnessed the apparition of a woman in the corridors of the dorm and have come to believe that it is that of Mary. There are also reports of her opening doors and peering into rooms, as if checking to see if the occupants are asleep.

In recent years, the majority of weird reports have centered on the fourth floor. Even though no one ever goes up there, this has not stopped residents from reporting the sound of footsteps pacing overhead and the strains of faint piano music filtering down from the upper floor. The floor remains darkened and closed off and is empty save for old furniture and the dust of decades. It has been abandoned by students and visitors alike, although there is still a piano stored in the music room. Is this where the music comes from? If so, one has to wonder if the music that emanates from it these days is of our world or the next.

The Weird Happenings of Hell Hollow

The first settler to build a home near Decatur, in the heart of the Illinois prairie, was William Downing, a fur trapper and honey gatherer who erected a log cabin in 1820. More settlers arrived in the years that followed, and by 1829, the settlement had officially become a town. It was named after the naval hero, Stephen Decatur, who had been noted for his spectacular feats of bravery during the wars with the Barbary pirates in the early 1800s. The population in the immediate area had swelled to nearly six hundred people by this time. A delegation from the new town traveled to the state capital in Vandalia, where a declaration was passed that formed Macon County. Decatur was named the county seat.

The hardships and trials of early life in Decatur were much like those in other frontier settlements. Most of the settlers lived outside the village in log cabins, spread out in the forest and along the river. Most of them were traders or farmers, and malaria and other diseases often shortened their lives. While funerals were common, they reached a peak during the terrible winter of 1830, which is still remembered as the "Deep Snow."

Many died from the bitter cold and fierce storms, but that winter also gave birth to one of the greatest legends of the Decatur area—a legend of death, depravity, and cannibalism in an area known today as "Hell Hollow." In later years, this area would be considered "cursed" or "tainted" as it had become known to attract the worst elements of the city. It has been a hideout for outlaws, a "hobo jungle," and more. In the 1930s, it would realize its greatest infamy when it was connected to a vicious series of unsolved murders.

More than a century before those events would make Hell Hollow infamous, though, another incident occurred that would forever mark this area. Many believe that it could explain why the hollow has attracted such a dark element over the years. On the other hand, some believe the land here was already sour and that evil has festered in this area for many, many years.

According to the legend, the wooded area that would someday be Hell Hollow was once the location of a small settlement. It was the most secluded of the outposts surrounding the village of Decatur and was in an area that most of the local settlers avoided. They came here only for the purpose of burying the dead. The hills above this narrow valley were part of an Indian burial ground that was soon taken over by the settlers. In later years, it would become Greenwood Cemetery, but in those days, the pioneers seldom visited and it was held in superstitious awe.

In the late 1820s, a group of settlers constructed cabins in the valley west of the burying grounds. They survived here for a few years, until the bitter winter of 1830. Snow fell throughout the winter, alternating with sleet and ice, and it killed off the livestock and game that the pioneers did not quickly eat. Many settlers died in the bitter cold, and the snow and storms gave birth to strange legends in Hell Hollow.

The lack of food struck there the hardest. The tiny collection of cabins was cut off from the rest of the settlers in the area. At first, wild game approached the cabins without fear. Food was so scarce that the animals hoped for handouts of grain, but they were instead captured and ended up in the stew kettle. As the cold months wore on, the deer, turkey, squirrels, and prairie chickens all but disappeared, and soon the stores of flour and dried meat followed suit. The outlook was growing grim, and there was a good chance that the settlers would starve to death long before spring arrived. They survived on what they had and could forage, boiling the bark from the trees into a bitter soup, and then eating portions of shoe leather and rawhide to stay alive. Finally, the legends say, there were no other choices left to them. They had no option but to turn to the only food supply still available—each other.

In the early months of the winter, one of the older members of the community had passed away, and the body had been stored in an outbuilding so that he could be buried when the ground thawed. This was the first of two corpses that the settlers were forced to eat that terrible winter.

When the weather finally broke and contact with the outside could be achieved again, the bodies were secretly buried on the hill and the cannibals were sworn to secrecy. No one was ever to know under what conditions the community had survived. A few months passed, and the settlers from the small community were never heard from again. Someone had apparently discovered their horrible secret, and they vanished from the area without a trace.

The legend has been passed along for many years, and while it may have been the first bizarre event to take place in Hell Hollow, it would certainly not be the last.

At some point in the mid 1800s, the hollow became the territory of a gang that the local populace called the "Biscuit-Necks." They specialized in extortion and robbery and used the woods south of the cemetery as their base of operations. One night, a lynch mob from town captured the gang here. The crime for which they were pursued remains unknown today, but it is believed to have been the robbery of a store, during which the owner was killed. The authorities had failed to find the killers, so a vigilante group took up the chase. After the gang was captured, they were hanged right on the spot. As a message to other criminals operating in the area, the vigilantes left the bodies of the "Biscuit-Necks" hanging there in Hell Hollow, swaying in the wind. They were left that way until the corpses finally succumbed to the elements and the carrion birds.

Years passed, and the edge of the hollow became known as a "hobo jungle," where transients and small-time criminals camped and lived. The railroad tracks passed close to this area, and it was convenient for the hoboes to hop a freight train from one town to the next. It was during this period, in the spring of 1930, that a caretaker from Greenwood Cemetery named Mel Savage was murdered at the edge of the woods. His murder was never solved.

Even as the city of Decatur grew up around it, the hollow still managed to span several hundred acres. It remained a rough part of the city made up of wooded areas and poor, rundown neighborhoods of shacks and dilapidated houses. The region spanned what is now the area around South Main Street to as far west as present-day Lincoln Park. In the days before Lake Decatur was formed, this region sprawled in all directions and was known as a place where criminals could find shelter from the law. The area also spawned two dilapidated housing areas called "Coaltown" and "Oklahoma," which were little more than collections of shacks, shanties, brothels, and makeshift gambling parlors.

To make matters worse, in 1936, a series of Chicago newspaper articles pinpointed Hell Hollow as the hideout for a gang of grave robbers and killers who committed a number of murders in Decatur. The gang, which was dubbed the "Hounds of Hell Hollow," supposedly "ruled the south end of the city with shotgun and whipping post." They often met in Greenwood Cemetery, robbed graves, and sold bootleg liquor. Even though Decatur officials hotly denied the stories, there was an element of truth to them. They cleverly blended fact with fiction and mixed in real stories and events to give the tale credibility. Needless to say, the articles did little to enhance the reputation of Hell Hollow.

The size of Hell Hollow continued to shrink as the years went on. Coaltown was eventually destroyed and turned into a park and a housing addition, the acres of woods and brush were cleared away, and finally, only a small valley remained just west of Greenwood Cemetery. This was the original location of the hollow, the site of cannibalism and murder, and the center for the strange activity that has continued to radiate outward from the region.

For a long time, this area remained a thick forest of trees and undergrowth through which a narrow gravel road twisted and turned. This became known as simply "Hell Hollow," the last reminder of the violence of years gone by, but the legend was not quite dead yet. The "Hounds" eventually became a forgotten story of the past, but the Hollow soon earned a new notoriety with teenagers as a spooky place for a romantic rendezvous. A new collection of stories started to be told about crazed killers with hooks for hands and horrifying murders that usually involved teenagers in parked cars.

But not all of the stories could be passed off as mere folklore. Occasionally, the unexplained was still encountered in Hell Hollow—and continues to be encountered there today.

One particular story involved a couple who had gone down to the hollow for a romantic interlude one night and were surprised to hear and feel what seemed to be open hands slamming down on the trunk of their car. Thinking that someone was playing a trick on them, the young man jumped out of the car and looked around. To his surprise, no one was there. He heard a movement over to his left and turned to see the tall grass alongside the road being pushed aside, as if some invisible presence was passing through it. When he quickly returned to the car, something caught his eye. There, on the dusty trunk, were the clear impressions of handprints, even though he had seen no one standing behind the car.

The hollow remained a popular and spooky place for some time. In the late 1980s, the road that ended in Hell Hollow was closed off, and city crews cut and cleared away the thick growth of trees that once filled the valley. Another roadway that passed through the area, running from South Main Street along the Sangamon River, remained open until just a few years ago. It offered the only remaining access to Hell Hollow, and thanks to this, it was also plagued with dark incidents and unexplained happenings. In the mid 1990s, two young men were executed here by drug dealers, and since that time, their phantom cries have been reported on occasion—adding to the list of ghosts that are still said to be encountered in this area.

Strange things continue to happen in Hell Hollow today, as if some sort of weird and frightening energy still lingers there. The valley is no longer accessible by road, but a walking trail was cut through the forest a few years ago, offering those with a curiosity about the macabre to still walk the same ground that both killers and victims walked in years gone by.

Decatur's Common Burial Grounds

The land the city of Decatur now occupies was largely untamed prairie until the 1820s. During the years when the Native Americans lived and hunted the lands of central Illinois, a number of tribes settled around the Decatur area, although strangely, none of the villages were located within the future city limits. When the first settlers arrived, they would find the land had been abandoned by the Native Americans. Rather than live on the land, they instead used it for their burial grounds. Legend holds that the Native Americans believed the land was more closely connected to the next world, thus making it a perfect place to bury the dead and ensure their safe and easy passage to the world beyond. And perhaps they were right—for the city of Decatur seems to have an inordinate number of hauntings.

Decatur's poor luck continued when it came to building on top of cemeteries. Besides the Indian burial sites, sketchy records exist today that say there were once a number of private and family cemeteries scattered throughout Decatur. Most of these sites have been forgotten over the years. Early burial records in the city were largely nonexistent, and many of the forgotten graves were marked with primitive wooden planks that deteriorated in a few short years.

It is not really surprising that many of these tiny graveyards faded from memory within a generation or two, but what of the secrets left behind by Decatur's first "official" cemetery, the Common Burial Grounds? The cemetery was started for early Decatur residents in 1833 and was located in an area that is today bordered by Oakland, West Main, and West Wood streets. It was as large as several acres, and although no records were ever kept as to the number of burials there, estimates say that the number of bodies interred on the grounds was in the thousands.

The cemetery was open for use until 1885. With no records being kept, residents were asked to mark all of the graves as best they could, which usually meant a wooden marker or crude stone. It was finally closed down due to both overcrowding and its location within the city limits. When it had been started in 1833, the burial ground had been located far out on the prairie, west of the city at the time. By the 1880s, though, Decatur had grown much larger, and the cemetery was impeding progress to the west. Workmen were brought in to carry out exhumations of all the graves at the site, and the bodies were supposed to be moved to other cemeteries that had since been established in the area.

The problematic exhumations took more than three years to carry out. No one had any idea just how many people had been buried in the graveyard over the years, thanks to unmarked graves, poor records, and lost grave markers and stones. The city pushed the move ahead, and the workmen were advised to do the best they could with what information they had. By the end of the third year, most of the land in the area had been sold off for the construction of new homes and businesses, and everyone was anxious for the exhumations to come to an end.

The first major construction work was a required extension of West Main Street, which would allow the transport of building materials to the far west side. In 1895, while work crews were excavating for the extension, they began discovering dozens of skeletons, casket remains, and pieces of tombstones that had been left behind by the exhumation workers. Workmen were brought in to scour the area again for more missing remains, and over the course of the next nine months, hundreds of additional bodies were removed.

Soon after, construction began on many of the buildings in the area. Unfortunately, the grisly finds continued with every new foundation and basement that was dug. For years after, new construction brought to light skulls, bones, and pieces of wooden coffins.

In 1935, a building on West Wood Street had its basement lowered, and a broken wooden box containing a complete skeleton was found beneath the dirt. Later that same year, a man working in his backyard found four skulls and three long bones in the spot where he planned to put a vegetable patch. This convinced him to find another location for his garden. A popular restaurant in the area called the Blue Mill was the subject of rumors about strange discoveries on the grounds. In 1930, the dirt-floored crawlspace of the restaurant was lowered to make room for an actual basement. When this occurred, six skeletons in wooden boxes were found beneath the dirt floor, but they were left in place as concrete was poured over them.

There were no clues as to just how many bodies had been left behind, although people seemed to have a casual attitude about it at the time. According to recollections from children and grandchildren today, most home owners simply boxed up the remains that they discovered and stored them in a backyard shed, or simply reburied them. No one gave much thought to the discoveries—until the hauntings began.

Thanks to the lost cemetery, the entire area where it once stood has been plagued with hauntings and ghost sightings and has perhaps more alleged haunted houses than any other part of the city. Reports have included knocking sounds, footsteps, doors that open and close, water faucets that turn on by themselves, toilets that flush without assistance, apparitions that have been seen standing in yards, running down hallways, and disappearing into walls, and much more. The hauntings continue to this day, and recent accounts tell of eerie voices and a man in a striped shirt who walks the same path through a house on West Main Street over and over again.

And houses are not the only structures here that are haunted. Many nearby businesses also have their own ghosts. In addition to apparitions that have been seen in two local drinking establishments, bar owners and staff members also tell of chairs that move by themselves, barstools that fall over with no explanation, objects that vanish and show up in other places, and glasses and bottles that move around at night while no one is in the building. The Blue Mill, once located at Wood and Oakland streets, was said to be haunted, likely due to the bones that were disturbed in the basement in 1930. In later years, staff members often spoke of bizarre events that occurred downstairs, including lights that inexplicably shut off and kitchen items that moved around, and most of them were afraid to go into the basement alone.

In 2002, the Blue Mill was torn down, and a new complex of restaurants and shops was built on the site. As excavations began on a new parking lot, more bones and pieces of skeletons were unearthed on the property as the occupants of the long-ago cemeteries were again brought to the surface. Most of the site was soon paved over, but a visit to the location will reveal one part of the lot where the paving suddenly stops, leaving an oddly shaped parking lot. An archaeologist from the state of Illinois discovered more than 133 sets of human remains on the site, and for this reason, the parking lot was never completed.

The odd-shaped lot is a very visible reminder of the events of the past, a counterpart to the ethereal reminders that still linger in the buildings located nearby—ghosts from the Common Burial Grounds.

The Greenwood Cemetery Ghost Lights

Ghost lights, or spook lights as they are often called, have long been a part of anomalous history in Illinois. Such a light is best defined as being a luminous phenomenon that, because of the way it behaves, its location, and its regular manifestation, is put into a separate category from ball lightning or such supernatural phenomena as ghosts. Most spook lights, however, especially those that appear regularly over a period of time and in one location, tend to take on a supernatural air. Legends tend to grow around them concerning strange deaths, and most often, a beheading for which a ghost returns looking for the severed head. The spook light is most often said to be the light of a lantern that the spirit carries to assist him in the search.

Spook lights appear in many places around the state, and while most of them have an eerie legend or two attached to their appearance, few explanations can be reached as to why they appear. In the instances when the lights have been thoroughly investigated, the results have been inconclusive at best, and disappointing at worst. In some cases, the mysterious lights turn out to be nothing more than the headlights of cars on distant highways or reflections of stars and lights that refract though layers of different air temperatures. But that's not always the case.

There are a number of locations in Illinois where spook lights manage to escape such explanations. These are locations where reports of the lights date back to well before the advent of the automobile and where claims of artificial lights in the distance just don't hold up. These are lights that serious researchers have been unable to debunk. And while it is the opinion of many with an interest in such things that spook lights are a natural part of our world for which we do not yet have an explanation, the most compelling ones still remain unsolved.

One location that has long eluded explanation is a ridge of small hills on the southern side of Greenwood Cemetery in Decatur—a place with more than its share of supernatural happenings.

The beginnings of Greenwood Cemetery have remained a mystery for more than 150 years. No record exists to say when the first burials took place in the plot of land that would someday be Greenwood. It was not the city's first official burial ground, but the Native Americans who lived here first used it as a burial site, as did the early settlers. The only trace they left behind was the large number of unmarked graves scattered about the present-day grounds. During the 1820s, it is believed that local settlers used this area as a burial site, and legend has it that even a few runaway slaves who did not survive their quest for freedom were buried on the grounds under the cover of night.

The Greenwood Cemetery Association was organized in March 1857, and the cemetery was incorporated into the city of Decatur.

By 1900, Greenwood had become the most fashionable place in Decatur in which to be buried. It had also become quite popular as a recreational park, and it was not uncommon to see noontime visitors enjoying their lunch on the grassy hills. Unfortunately, by the 1920s, the cemetery was bankrupt and could no longer be maintained. It was allowed to revert back to nature, and it wasn't long before the cemetery began to resemble a forgotten graveyard with overgrown brush, fallen branches, and tipped and broken gravestones. Hundreds of graves were left unattended and allowed to fall into disrepair. The stories and legends that would "haunt" Greenwood for years to come had taken root in the desolate conditions that existed in the oldest section of the graveyard. Tales of wandering spirits and glowing apparitions began to be told about the cemetery, and decay and decline came close to bringing about the destruction of the place. The cemetery became a forgotten spot in Decatur, remembered only as a spooky novelty.

At this point, the cemetery was nearly in ruins. The roads had become partially covered mud and cinder tracks so deeply rutted that they were no longer passable. The oaks, which had added beauty to the cemetery, had now become its greatest curse. Leaves, which had not been raked away in years, were knee-deep in some places. Fallen branches from the trees littered the grounds, which were overgrown and tangled with weeds and brush. Water, time, and vandals had wreaked havoc on Greenwood's grave markers. Years of rain, harsh weather, and a lack of care had caused many stones to fall at angles; many more were simply lost altogether. Others lay broken and damaged beyond repair, having given up the fight with the elements.

In 1957, however, ownership and operation of the cemetery was taken over by the city of Decatur, and township crews have since maintained it. Despite this, the place has not lost its eerie reputation, and the stories of ghosts and the unexplained still mingle with fact and fiction, contributing to a strangeness that is unparalleled by any other location in the haunted heart of Illinois.

There are many ghost stories that plague the history of Greenwood Cemetery, including that of a bride who committed suicide when her fiancée was murdered and who now haunts a lonely hill within the cemetery; Confederate prisoners who perished aboard a train that was passing through the city and who were buried on a hillside, only to restlessly haunt the area; a phantom woman who appears on a staircase; and more.

As mentioned, the "lost years" of Greenwood seem to have spawned most of the eerie tales of the place. The story of Greenwood's most famous resident ghost, the "Greenwood Bride," begins around 1926 and concerns a young couple engaged to be married. The young man was a reckless fellow and a bootlegger, and his future bride's family greatly disapproved of him. One summer night, the couple decided not to wait any longer to get married and made plans to elope. They would meet just after midnight, as soon as the young man could deliver one last shipment of whiskey and have enough money for their wedding trip. Unfortunately, he was delivering the bottles of whiskey when he was murdered. The killers, rival businessmen, dumped his body into the Sangamon River, where two fishermen found it the next morning. In a fit of grief, his fiancée committed suicide, and after her death, her grieving parents found the wedding dress that she planned to wear. Her body was laid to rest in her bridal gown in Greenwood Cemetery, but she does not rest there in peace. As time has passed, dozens of credible witnesses have reported encountering the Greenwood Bride on that hill in the cemetery. They claim the ghost of a woman in a glowing bridal gown has been seen weaving among the tombstones. She walks with her head down and with a scrap of cloth gripped tightly in her hand. Occasionally, she raises it to her face, as if wiping away tears.

Located on the edge of the forest that makes up Greenwood's northwest corner is an old burial plot that sits upon a small hill. This is the plot of a family named "Barrackman," and if you approach this piece of land from the east, walking along the cemetery's narrow roads, you will find a set of stone steps that lead to the top of a grassy hill. There are four rounded stones here, marking the burial sites of the family. Little is known about the Barrackmans, other than that four members of the family are buried in Greenwood. No records exist about who they were, when they may have lived here, or even about what they may have accomplished in life. We simply know their names—father, mother, son, and his wife—as they are inscribed on the identical tombstones. As mentioned, two of the stones bear the names of the Barrackman women, and although no one really knows for sure, it may be one of these two women who still haunts this burial plot.

According to many accounts collected over the years from dozens of people who never knew one another, a visitor who remains in the cemetery as the sun is going down may be treated to an eerie, and breathtaking, sight. According to the story, the visitor is directed to the Barrackman staircase as dusk falls on the graveyard. It is said that a semitransparent woman in a long dress appears on the stone steps. She sits there on the staircase with her head bowed and appears to be weeping, although she has never been heard to make a sound. Those who do get the chance to see her never see her for long. She always inexplicably vanishes as the sun dips below the horizon. She has never been seen in the daylight hours and never after dark—only just at sunset.

Located on a high, desolate hill in the far southwest corner of Greenwood Cemetery is a collection of identical stone markers inscribed with the names of the local men who served, and some who died, during the brutal days of the Civil War. But not all of the men buried here served under the Stars and Stripes of the Union army. There are a number of dark secrets buried here.

During the years of the Civil War, a great many trains passed through the city of Decatur. It was on a direct line of the Illinois Central Railroad, which ran deep into the South. The line continued north and connected to a railroad that went to Chicago. Here, it reached Camp Douglas, a prison for Confederates who were captured in battle. Many trains traveled north carrying Union troops bound for Decatur and beyond. Soldiers aboard these trains were often wounded, sick, or dying. Occasionally, deceased soldiers were taken from the trains and buried in Greenwood Cemetery, which was very close to the train tracks. In 1863, a prison train holding Southern prisoners pulled into Decatur. It was filled with more than a hundred prisoners, and many of them had contracted yellow fever in the diseased swamps of the South.

The Union officers in charge of the train had attempted to separate the Confederates who had died in transit, but to no avail. Many of the other men were close to death from the infectious disease, and it was hard to tell which men were alive and which were not. The bodies were removed from the train and taken to Greenwood Cemetery. Here they were unloaded and stacked at the base of a hill in the southwest corner of the graveyard. This location was possibly the least desirable spot in the cemetery. The hill was so steep that many of the gravediggers had trouble keeping their balance. It was the last place that anyone would want to be buried.

The men hastily dug shallow graves and tossed the bodies of the Confederates inside. It has been said that without a doctor present, no one could have known just how many of the soldiers had actually died from yellow fever—were all of those buried here actually dead? Many say they were not, and that some of them were accidentally buried alive, and this is why the area is the most haunted section of Greenwood.

Reports from eight decades have revealed unexplainable tales of ghosts and strange energy lingering around this hill. Visitors who have come here, many of them knowing nothing about the bizarre history of this place, have told of hearing voices, strange sounds, footsteps in the grass, whispers, and cries of torment; some even claim to have been touched or pushed by unseen hands. There are also the reports of the soldiers themselves returning from the other side of the grave. Accounts have been revealed over the years that tell of visitors to the cemetery actually seeing men in uniform walking among the tombstones—men who are strangely transparent.

Of all of the ghostly events to occur here, though, the most enduring mystery of the cemetery is likely the oldest. The story involves the ghost lights that appear on the south side of the burial grounds. These small globes of light have been reported here for many decades and are still reported today. While there is no logical explanation for what they are, or why they appear here, the lore of the cemetery tells a strange and tragic story.

The legend tells of a flood in 1910 that wiped out a portion of the cemetery. The Sangamon River, located just south of the cemetery, had been dammed in the late 1800s and was often prone to floods. During that particularly wet spring, the river overflowed its banks and washed into the lower sections of the cemetery. Tombstones were knocked over, and the surging water even managed to wash graves away and force buried caskets to the surface. Many of them went careening downstream on the swollen river.

Once the water receded, it took many days to find the battered remains of the coffins that had been washed down the river, and many were never found at all. For some time after, farmers and fishermen were startled to find caskets, and even corpses, washing up on riverbanks some miles away. There were many questions as to the identities of the bodies, so many of them were buried again in unmarked and common graves. These new graves were placed on higher ground on the southern hills of Greenwood.

Since that time, the mysterious lights have appeared on these hills. The stories say that the lights are the spirits of those whose bodies washed away in the flood. Their wandering ghosts are now doomed to search forever for the place where their remains are buried.

Dozens of trustworthy witnesses have claimed to see the spook lights on the hill, moving in and out among the old, weathered stones. The mystery of the lights has managed to elude all those who have attempted to solve it. Many have tried to pass them off as reflections from cars passing over the lake—but what of sightings that date back to before Lake Decatur ever existed? In those days, a covered bridge over the Sangamon River took travelers along the old county highway, and for many years, not a single automobile crossed it, as motorcars had not yet come to Decatur.

Whether the cause is natural or supernatural, the lights can still be seen along the edge of the graveyard today. Want to see them for yourself? Seek out the south hills of Greenwood some night by finding the gravel parking lot that is located across the road from the cemetery fence. Here, you can sit and observe the hills. You have to have a lot of patience, and you may even have to make more than one trip, but eventually, you will probably be lucky enough to see the ghost lights.

The Owner Who Never Left His Theater

The first real movie theater to open in Decatur, aside from a handful of storefront nickelodeons, was the Avon, which was officially started in November 1916. The Avon was a unique place in that it was a large, grand theater constructed for showing moving pictures only. There was nothing else like it in central Illinois at the time, and to most, the theater was a folly. It could never succeed, people thought, because they believed that moving pictures were simply a passing fad that would never last.

Over the years, the American film industry has defied the odds and has endured. Fortunately, even after a number of near disasters, the same can be said for the Avon. After a bright beginning, a number of rough spots, and years of success, the theater was closed down and abandoned, and most feared that it would be lost. Although scheduled for demolition several times, the Avon has managed to endure as a thriving, independent theater—and as a very haunted place.

The original owner of the Avon Theater was a man named James Allman, who envisioned the place as an upscale movie house, the likes of which had never before been seen in the area. He paid more than $25,000 to have the theater built; then he decorated it with original artwork and paintings, installed huge pipe organs, and furnished it so lavishly that he hoped even the upper class residents of the city, who disdained moving pictures as cheap entertainment for the masses, would not be able to stay away. The theater opened to standing-room-only crowds, but within six months, Allman had lost his entire investment and was forced to sell out to a Chicago theater chain, which was also unable to make the Avon a success.

The Avon limped along for a number of years, and then in 1926, it was purchased by four Greek immigrants who owned a candy store across the street at the Empress Theater. The Constanopoulos brothers—Angelo, Gust, Christian, and Theodore—purchased several theaters in the area, but the Avon became their crown jewel. Gust became most involved with the Avon and worked there, mostly seven days a week, until his death in 1965. After he died, his brothers decided to leave the movie theater business, so they sold the Avon to a theater chain based in Springfield.

The Avon remained in business until 1985, when it became the last of Decatur's downtown theaters to close. For the next several years, the theater remained dark and empty, save for a few attempts to revive the place with live music and an attempt to attract the low-budget crowd with second- and third-run bargain films. Interest waned and eventually died out.

In 1999, the Avon opened once again, this time as an independent and art film theater, showing alternative films and limited-release features that in the past would never have been seen in Decatur. The Avon began to thrive again and today is open seven days a week, competing against theater chains with first-run films and original entertainment.

The stories of at least one restless ghost at the Avon go back to the 1960s. Staff members at the time began reporting the presence of a thin, older man with glasses and a bald head wandering through the theater, especially in a private hallway above the lobby where the theater's offices were located. They also spoke of hearing footsteps, laughter, applause, and voices coming from the auditorium after it had emptied for the night. The sounds of people walking about in empty rooms and hallways were common, as were the feelings of being watched and being touched by ghostly hands. Theater patrons also told of seeing shadowy figures in the seats, apparently watching the film, which were there one moment and gone the next.

In 1995, Skip Huston, the Avon's current owner, came face-to-face with the thin, balding ghost who had been reportedly haunting the theater since the 1960s. Skip was in the theater one rainy afternoon, working in an office off the private hallway upstairs. He heard noises that sounded like footsteps in the hall outside of the room, but when he looked to see who was there, the corridor was always empty. He eventually heard another strange noise and reflexively turned around—but this time, he found that he was not alone. A man stood in the doorway of the room. He was thin, bald, and wearing glasses, and he looked around the room as if he did not see Skip standing there at all. Skip later reported that the man looked completely solid. Thinking that an intruder was in the building, he started to speak and tell the man that he had to leave, but the man suddenly turned and walked away down the hall. Skip followed him to the door, but all he saw was an empty hallway—the man was gone.

As time passed, Skip told the story of meeting the ghost to a number of people—many involved in local theater—and some of them said that his description of the apparition in the hallway sounded just like the ghost that so many other people had seen. A few years later, research uncovered a photograph of the Constanopoulos brothers, and Skip identified Gust as the man he had seen in the hallway that day. Apparently, the owner of the Avon during its heyday had simply never left the place!

In early 2005, I began working out of an upstairs office at the Avon, and on one chilly afternoon in March, I was behind my desk, talking to a friend of mine on the telephone. As I was sitting there, I happened to glance up and see someone walk past the door of the room, which was standing wide open. I couldn't see who this person was; I just caught a quick look at them as they walked down the hallway.

Assuming that it was Chris Barnett, the theater projectionist who I often bumped into at the theater during the day, I put down the telephone and got up to speak to him. I left my friend on hold and told her that I would be right back. I quickly opened the door and leaned out to see who was there but saw no movement—except for the door of the room next to the office. It was softly clicking shut, and I guessed that Chris had gone into the room. I had gotten up too quickly for him to have gone anywhere else, and the door that led downstairs to the lobby was shut tight. I walked down the corridor a few steps and opened the door of the next room to say hello. But the room was empty.

I suddenly realized that whoever had been walking down the hallway was not among the living! I hurried back into the office, picked up the telephone again, and told my friend what had happened. She gasped. "What are you going to do?"

"I'm closing the door to the office," I quickly replied. "That way, if any more ghosts walk by, I won't see them."

Does Gust Constanopoulos still watch over the Avon Theater? I believe that he does, but don't just take my word for it. Experience the Avon Theater for yourself. There is a very good chance that the place might make a believer out of you!

Lingering Ghosts of the Lincoln Theater

There is an old adage that says "every good theater has a ghost." Some theaters, however, seem to have more than their share of restless spirits. The Lincoln Theater in Decatur is just such a place. There have been stories of hauntings there since the late 1920s, and based on the sheer number of accounts, the building is apparently teeming with ghosts. Where do they all come from? Are they all staff members that remained behind after death, so devoted to the place that they simply refused to leave? Are they stagehands who died in the theater, causing their souls to linger there? Or, as in the case of the Lincoln, are they ghosts that were already on the site even before the theater was built?

The heyday of the Lincoln Theater was launched with great fanfare in October 1916. The theater opened with a standing-room-only crowd of Decatur's finest citizens, dressed in black tie and formal wear and eager to see the new, glorious theater about which they had heard so much. The first program to be presented was George M. Cohan's stage comedy *Hit the Trail Holliday*, starring Frank Otto. The audience loved the show and raved about the spectacular design of the theater, from its private seating boxes and massive ivory-colored columns to the 1,346 seats, all of which offered a splendid view and wonderful acoustics. Also new to Decatur was the mezzanine seating, which ran just below the balcony and offered seats that were only slightly above the level of the stage.

In those early years, the main emphasis at the Lincoln was onstage shows and vaudeville acts. Many famous stars appeared here, including Ethel Barrymore, Al Jolson, Ed Wynn, Jeanette Mac-Donald, and many others. Audiences also thrilled to such attractions as a sparring exhibition by Jack Dempsey, not long after his famous fight with Georges Carpentier.

In February 1926, the theater hired a twelve-member orchestra to provide music for all stage productions and the silent films that were starting to gain popularity. Vaudeville still remained the most popular attraction the theater had to offer, however, and the orchestra's leader brought a young, unknown comedian named Bob Hope to the Lincoln in 1926 to show Decatur how to dance the Charleston. Hope was just starting his career in those days, and he would return often during the 1920s to appear in vaudeville shows and comedy productions.

Moving pictures continued to increase in popularity in the city, and Decatur was demanding more and more films to take the place of stage shows. In April 1928, the first "talkies" came to Decatur and played at the Empress Theater. The Lincoln began showing them fourteen months later at the close of the vaudeville season. This would herald the end of the vaudeville days at the Lincoln, and perhaps in the entire city. Sound equipment was installed in the theater for films, making silent movies obsolete, and bandleader Billy Gail and his orchestra were promptly dismissed.

The theater operated steadily for many years but closed down for good in December 1980. After that, the Lincoln was closed for nearly a decade, only opening occasionally for live music and a handful of events. By 1990, the building had deteriorated badly and was suffering from neglect. It had been abandoned by everyone except for the bats and pigeons that had taken up residence in the auditorium.

Thankfully, the Lincoln came to the attention of a restoration group, and some life has been brought back to the old place. A grant awarded to the theater in 2006 greatly helped in the restorations, and the theater has seen more life in recent years than it has in the last few decades.

The recent renovations have seemed to "stir up the ghosts" in the Lincoln; stories have circulated about the theater being haunted since at least the 1920s. A staff member who worked there in that year stated that they were already telling ghost stories about the Lincoln, even at that time. Reports by witnesses from those early days of film in the theater have suggested that a multitude of spirits may linger in the Lincoln, from apparitions in the balcony to mysterious figures on the stage. As the years have passed, dozens of witnesses have reported strange sounds, voices, and footsteps in the otherwise empty theater—sounds that cannot be explained away as simply the theater's acoustics. They have also reported whispers, strange voices, and shadowy shapes that cannot be easily explained away.

In addition to the sightings, many of the supernatural encounters have been up close and personal. Many have experienced inexplicable cold chills in certain spots in the building. Others claim to have been touched by unseen hands, and some have been pushed, pinched, or had their hair pulled and their clothing tugged. Witnesses have reported feeling the backs of their seats kicked, only to turn and find there is no one behind them. Others have mentioned seeing theater seats in the auditorium actually raise and lower by themselves, as if an unseen audience was watching the proceedings onstage.

Other supernatural incidents have occurred around what may be the most haunted spot in the theater—a metal, spiral staircase located in the back corner of the stage. Many witnesses claim to have had unearthly encounters on and around the staircase. For example, in 1994, an entertainer who was performing in a traveling production reported that he saw a man lurking on this staircase. He was in the back corner changing his costume when he heard a voice whispering to him. When he looked up, he saw a shadowy figure on the steps. He was unable to describe the figure, but he was convinced that it was a man. He complained about the presence to a nearby theater staff member, but when they checked the staircase, they found it empty. Strangely, the actor had no idea about the legends of the Lincoln, nor that the staircase was rumored to be haunted.

Several years ago, I had my own encounter with ghosts at the Lincoln Theater. I was in the theater one afternoon with a reporter and a cameraman from a local television station. After completing an interview about the history and hauntings of the place, I decided to join the cameraman for a trip up the spiral staircase. He took his camera along, hoping to film the theater's stage from this vantage point. We rounded the staircase and reached the top, then stood talking for a few moments. What happened next was enough to convince the cameraman, a skeptic about the existence of ghosts, that the Lincoln Theater was haunted.

We had climbed the spiral staircase and left the reporter down on the stage by herself. We weren't surprised to soon hear the sound of her footsteps as she followed us up the stairs. Her hard-soled shoes made a distinctive sound as they echoed on the metal steps. Realizing that we had the only portable light, and the staircase was quite dark, the cameraman leaned over the railing with his camera light so that the reporter would be able to see. Just as he did this, from out on the stage, we heard the sound of a voice calling to us. We looked and saw the reporter standing in the middle of the stage—dozens of feet from the base of the steps and much too far away to have been climbing the staircase just moments before.

We suddenly realized the footsteps on the staircase had not belonged to the reporter. Whose footsteps were they? We had no idea, but the cameraman, who had not believed in ghosts just moments before, hurried down from the staircase and left the theater. He refused to come back inside after his unnerving encounter.

But who are the ghosts that haunt the Lincoln Theater—and why do there seem to be so many of them?

The site where the Lincoln Theater now stands was once occupied by the Decatur Arcade Hotel, a downtown rooming house built in 1904. In April 1915, a spectacular fire broke out and destroyed the hotel, damaging several of the surrounding structures. The blaze was believed to have started because of some oily rags left near the boiler of the hotel. A night watchman discovered them smoldering and tried to put them out, but he was driven back by the thick smoke that began churning out of the basement. The blaze quickly spread, and although all of the fire equipment in the city arrived on the scene within minutes, smoke was soon billowing from the lower windows.

The blaze swept through the hotel, burning fast and hot. The firefighters began pumping water into the building, but within ten minutes, the blaze had entered the walls and was eating through the roof of the hotel. With no hope left for the hotel, the fire crews turned their attentions to saving the nearby buildings, which included the YMCA, the First Presbyterian Church, and the Odd Fellows building. All of them were saved, but when the north wall of the hotel collapsed, it struck a furniture warehouse with a tremendous crash and a loud explosion. The warehouse was only saved because its heavy firewall refused to give in.

Two men were identified as victims of the fire, an engineer and a traveling salesman, but there were thought to be many others. Only the remains of the two men were found after the fire, but more than two dozen guests were never found at all. They may have escaped, but it's more widely believed that their bodies were completely destroyed by the fire and the ruins of the Decatur Arcade Hotel became their final resting place. The hotel was never rebuilt, and the Lincoln Theater was later built directly on the site.

It is believed that this may explain the myriad spirits lingering in the Lincoln Theater. The restless souls of those who perished in the flames of the hotel fire now walk the dark corners of the building, perhaps looking for peace after all these years.

The Mad Gasser of Mattoon

There is no greater phantom attacker in the history of the unexplained than the legendary "Mad Gasser of Mattoon," a bizarre figure who wreaked havoc in the small Illinois town in 1944. This creature turned out to be so elusive that law enforcement officials eventually declared him nonexistent, despite dozens of eyewitness reports and actual physical evidence that was left behind at the scene of some attacks.

This mysterious black-clad figure, who came and went without warning, left little in the way of clues, and for some reason, sprayed a paralyzing gas into the windows of unsuspecting residents. The gas he used was never identified.

Perhaps what makes this mystery so great is the fact that the central figure in the Mad Gasser case is such a puzzle. Who (or what) attacked the unsuspecting citizens of Illinois? Was it a mad scientist carrying out some secret experiments? A government agency? A visitor from another planet? No one will ever know for sure, but whoever the Gasser was, he vanished as mysteriously as he arrived, leaving no clues to his identity.

Mattoon, located in the southeastern part of central Illinois, is a fairly typical Midwestern town. The strange events that took place here in 1944, however, were anything but typical. These events would place the small city under the scrutiny of the entire nation and would one day become a textbook case of what authorities and psychologists called "mass hysteria." But was it really?

The whirlwind of events began in the early morning hours of August 31. A Mattoon man was startled out of a deep sleep and complained to his wife that he felt sick. He questioned her about leaving the gas on in the kitchen because his symptoms seemed very similar to gas exposure. The woman tried to get out of bed and check the pilot light on the stove, but found to her surprise that she could not move. Just minutes later, according to published reports, a woman in a neighboring home also tried to get out of bed and discovered that she, too, was paralyzed.

The next evening, a woman named Mrs. Bert Kearney was awakened by a peculiar smell in her bedroom. The odor was sweet and overpowering, and as it grew stronger, she began to feel a peculiar prickling feeling in her legs and lower body. As she tried to get out of bed, she realized that her limbs were paralyzed. She began screaming and, drawing the attention of her neighbors, was able to alert the police. The following day, she would complain of having burned lips and a parched mouth and throat from exposure to the gas. A hasty search of the yard by police officers and her shaken neighbors revealed nothing. But that would not be the last strange event to occur at this particular house . . .

Later on that evening, around midnight, Bert Kearney returned home from work, completely unaware of what had happened in his home that night. As he turned into his driveway, he spotted a man lurking near the house that would later fit the descriptions of the Mad Gasser. The stranger, according to Kearney, was tall and dressed in dark clothing and a tight-fitting black cap. He was standing near a window when Kearney spotted him, and the odd man ran away. Kearney pursued the tall man but was unable to catch up with him.

These events soon became public knowledge, and panic gripped the town. The story was badly handled by the authorities, and the local newspaper reported the Kearney case, and subsequent others, in a wildly sensational manner. Many believe the newspaper is the culprit behind the "gasser hysteria." Years later, the newspaper would be blamed for everything that happened in the case and for manufacturing the scare. The frightened citizens, according to these skeptics, took leave of their senses and began to imagine that a "mad gasser" was wreaking havoc in the town. This particular approach has been considered by many to be the simple explanation for the affair, but it certainly does not eliminate all of the evidence that something very bizarre happened in Mattoon.

By the morning of September 5, the Mattoon Police Department had received reports of four more gas attacks. The details in each of these "attacks" were eerily similar, even though none of the witnesses had compared notes or had time to check their stories. The newspapers had published a skewed version of the events; the subsequent reports were not only almost identical, but were accurate as to what had actually occurred. In each of the cases, the victims complained of a sickeningly sweet odor that caused them to become sick and slightly paralyzed for up to thirty minutes at a time.

Late on the night of September 5, the first real clues in the case were discovered. They were found at the home of Carl and Beulah Cordes, but what these clues meant has yet to be discovered. The Cordeses were returning home late that evening when they found a white cloth lying on their porch. Mrs. Cordes picked it up and noticed a strange smell coming from it. She held it up close to her nose and felt immediately nauseated and light-headed. She nearly fainted, and her husband had to help her inside the house. Within minutes, she was seized with a severe allergic reaction. Her lips and face began to swell, and her mouth began to bleed. The symptoms began to subside in about two hours, but needless to say, she was terrified. Carl Cordes called the police, and officers came out to investigate. They took the cloth into evidence, along with a skeleton key and an empty tube of lipstick found on the porch. They decided the prowler had probably been trying to break into the house but had failed.

The police surmised that the cloth was connected to the other gas attacks. It should be noted, however, that the odor on the cloth caused different symptoms in Mrs. Cordes than in the other victims. She did become sick to her stomach, but there were no sensations of paralysis. This incident is also different because if this was the Gasser at work, then it is the only time when he actually tried to gain access to the home of his victims. Could his intentions in this incident have been different?

The Gasser attacked again that same night, but he was back to his old tricks and sprayed his gas into an open window. There would only be one other report that even hinted that the attacker tried to break into the house. The woman in this instance claimed that a "person" in dark clothing tried to force open her front door. Was it really the Mad Gasser?

The attacks continued, and Mattoon residents began reporting fleeting glimpses of the Gasser, always describing him as a tall, thin man in dark clothes and wearing a tight black cap. More attacks were reported, and the harried police force tried to respond to the mysterious crimes that left no clues behind. Eventually, the authorities even summoned two FBI agents from Springfield to look into the case, but their presence did nothing to discourage the strange reports. Panic was widespread, and rumors began to circulate that the attacker was an escapee from an insane asylum or a German spy who was testing some sort of poisonous gas.

Armed citizens took to the streets, organizing watches and patrols to thwart any further attacks, but several occurred anyway. The gas attacks were becoming more frequent, and the attacker was leaving behind evidence such as footprints and sliced window screens. This evidence would become particularly interesting after the revelations of the authorities in the days to come.

A local citizens' "vigilance group" did manage to arrest one suspect, but after he passed a polygraph test, he was released. Local businessmen announced that they would be holding a mass protest rally on Saturday, September 10 to put more pressure on the already pressured Mattoon police force. Now that the Gasser was becoming

more than a threat to public safety, he was becoming a political lia-
bility and a blot on the public image of the city.

The Gasser, apparently not impressed with armed vigilantes
and newspaper diatribes, resumed his attacks. The first residence
to be attacked was that of Mrs. Violet Driskell and her daughter,
Ramona. They awoke late in the evening to hear someone removing the storm sash from their bedroom window. They hurried out
of bed and tried to run outside for help, but the fumes overcame
Ramona and she vomited. Her mother stated that she saw a man
running away from the house.

A short time later that night, the Gasser sprayed fumes into the
partially opened window of a room where Mrs. Russell Bailey,
Katherine Tuzzo, Mrs. Genevieve Haskell, and her young son were
sleeping. At another home, Miss Frances Smith, the principal of the
Columbian Grade School, and her sister, Maxine, were also overwhelmed with gas and fell ill. They began choking as they were
awakened and felt partial paralysis in their legs and arms. They also
said that the sweet odor began to fill the room "as a thin, blue
vapor." They heard a buzzing noise from outside and believed that
it was the Gasser's "spraying apparatus" in operation.

By September 10, Mad Gasser paranoia had peaked. FBI agents
were trying to track down the type of gas being used in the attacks,
and the police force was trying to not only find the Gasser, but also
to keep the armed citizens off the streets. Neither law enforcement
agency was having much luck with these tasks. By the following
Saturday night, several dozen well-armed farmers from the surrounding area had joined the patrols in Mattoon. In spite of this, six
attacks took place anyway, including the three just mentioned.
Another couple, Mr. and Mrs. Stewart B. Scott, returned to their
farm on the edge of Mattoon late in the evening to find the house
filled with sweet-smelling gas.

This period seemed to mark a turning point in the case. The
idea of the gas attacks moving from the city of Mattoon to the
country outside of it had pushed the scales of official acceptance in
the wrong direction. In the words of Thomas V. Wright, the City
Commissioner of Public Health: "There is no doubt that a gas
maniac exists and has made a number of attacks. But many of the

reported attacks are nothing more than hysteria. Fear of the gas man is entirely out of proportion to the menace of the relatively harmless gas he is spraying. The whole town is sick with hysteria and last night it spread out into the country."

At this point, newspaper accounts of the affair began to take on a more skeptical tone, and despite claims by victims and material evidence left behind, the police began to dismiss new reports of attacks and suggested that local residents were merely imagining things. The episode had gone so far that it was really the only thing left for them to do. The Gasser, if he existed at all, could not be caught, identified, or tracked down. They started to believe that if they ignored the problem, it would just go away. After all, if the man were real, how could he have possibly escaped detection for so long?

Psychology experts opined that the women of Mattoon had dreamed up the Mad Gasser as a desperate cry for attention, as many of their husbands were overseas fighting in the war. This theory ignored the fact that many victims and witnesses were men and that this so-called "fantasy" was leaving behind evidence of his existence.

On the night of September 11, the police received a number of phone calls, but after half-hearted attempts to investigate, dismissed all of them as false alarms. Just days before, a crime specialist with the State Department of Public Safety named Richard T. Piper told reporters, "This is one of the strangest cases I have ever encountered in my years of police work." But new calls were now only worthy of perfunctory examination. This was in spite of the fact that a doctor who appeared on the scene shortly after one of the evening's attacks stated that there had been a "peculiar odor" in the room. The officials were just no longer interested.

The Mattoon police chief issued what he felt was the final statement on the gas attacks on September 12. He stated that large quantities of carbon tetrachloride gas were used at the local Atlas Diesel Engine Co. and that this gas must be causing the reported cases of illness and paralysis. It could be carried throughout the town on the wind and could have left the stains that were found on the rag at one of the homes. As for the Mad Gasser himself, well, he was simply a figment of their imaginations. The whole case, he said "was a mistake from beginning to end."

Not surprisingly, a spokesman for the Atlas Diesel Engine plant was quick to deny the allegations that his company had caused the concern in town, maintaining that the only use for that gas in the plant was in their fire extinguishers, and any similar gases used at the plant caused no ill effects in the air. Besides that, why hadn't this gas ever caused problems in the city before? And how exactly was this gas cutting the window screens on Mattoon homes before causing nausea and paralysis?

The official explanation also failed to cover just how so many identical descriptions of the Gasser had been reported to the police. It also neglected to explain how different witnesses managed to report seeing a man of the Gasser's description fleeing the scene of an attack, even when the witness had no idea that an attack had taken place!

The last Gasser attack took place on September 13, and while it was the last appearance of the attacker in Mattoon, it was also possibly the strangest appearance. It occurred at the home of Mrs. Bertha Bench and her son, Orville. They described the attacker as a woman dressed in man's clothing who sprayed gas into a bedroom window. The next morning, footprints that appeared to have been made by a woman's high-heeled shoes were found in the dirt below the window.

After this night, the Mad Gasser of Mattoon was never seen or heard from again.

The real story behind what happened in Mattoon is still unknown, and it's unlikely that we will ever know what was behind these strange events. It is certain that something did take place there, however strange, and theories abound as to what it may have been. Was the Mad Gasser real? If so, who was he?

Stories have suggested that Mattoon's Gasser was anything from a mad scientist to an ape-man. Researchers today have their own theories, some of which are just as wild. Could he have been some sort of extraterrestrial visitor using a paralyzing agent to further a hidden agenda? Could he have been some sort of odd inventor testing a new apparatus? Interestingly, I was sent a letter in 2002 from a woman who explained to me that her father grew up in Mattoon during the time the gas attacks were taking place. He told her that there had been two sisters living in town at the time who had an allegedly insane brother. A number of people in town believed that he was the Gasser, so his sisters locked him in the basement until they could find a mental institution to put him in. After they locked him away, her father told her, the gas attacks stopped.

Or could the Gasser have been an agent of our own government, who came to an obscure Midwestern town to test some military gas that could potentially be used in the war effort? It might be telling that once national attention came to Mattoon, the authorities began a policy of complete denial, and the attacks suddenly ceased. Coincidence?

Whoever or whatever he was, the Mad Gasser has vanished into time and, real or imagined, is only a memory in the world of the unknown. Perhaps he was never here at all—perhaps he was, as Donald M. Johnson wrote in the 1954 issue of the *Journal of Abnormal and Social Psychology*, simply a "shadowy manifestation of some unimaginable unknown."

But was he really? How do we explain the sightings of the Mad Gasser that were made by people who did not even know the creature was alleged to exist? Or identical sightings from independent witnesses who could not have possibly known that others had just spotted the same figure? Was the Gasser, as some have suggested, a visitor from a dimension outside of our own, thus explaining his ability to appear or disappear at will? Was he a creature so outside the realm of our imaginations that we will never be able to comprehend his motives or understand the reason why he came to Mattoon?

Could the Mad Gasser have been some sort of mysterious presence that could pass from one dimension to another, coming and going without explanation? Could this solution to the mystery explain the appearance of the Mad Gasser? And perhaps more chilling is this question: If this he was a supernatural presence, where might he turn up next?

School Spirits at Illinois College

School spirits are not all that uncommon on the prairies of central Illinois. There are a number of schools and universities that boast haunted dorms and spirit-infested theaters, but few of these halls of learning can compare with the number of ghosts alleged to wander the campus of Illinois College. There is a very good chance that it just may be the most haunted school in the state!

Illinois College was founded in 1829 by Reverend John M. Ellis, a Presbyterian minister who felt a "seminary of learning" was needed in the new frontier state of Illinois. His plans came to the attention of a group of Congregational students at Yale University. Seven of them came westward to help establish the college. It became one of the first institutes for higher learning in Illinois, and the first two men to graduate from an in-state college were Richard Yates, who became the Civil War governor of Illinois and later a U.S. senator, and Jonathan Edward Spilman, the man who composed the now-familiar music to Robert Burns' immortal poem, "Flow Gently, Sweet Afton." Both men received their baccalaureate degrees from Illinois College in 1835.

Nine students met for the first class, held on January 4, 1830. Julian Sturtevant, the first instructor and the second president, reported, "We had come there that morning to open a fountain for future generations to drink at." Shortly after, Edward Beecher left the Park Street Church in Boston, Massachusetts, to serve the new college as its first president. He created a strong college and retained close intellectual ties with New England. His brother, Henry Ward Beecher, preached and lectured at Illinois College, and his sister, Harriet Beecher Stowe, was an occasional visitor. His brother, Thomas, graduated from Illinois College in 1843. Ralph Waldo Emerson, Mark Twain, Horace Greeley, and Wendell Phillips were among the visitors and lecturers in the early years.

In 1843 and 1845, two of the college's seven literary societies were formed. Possibly unique in the Midwest today, the societies have continued in their roles as centers for debate and criticism. Abraham Lincoln was one of many speakers appearing on the campus under the sponsorship of a literary society.

Illinois College also became heavily involved with the abolitionist movement as President Beecher took a very active role. At one point, a group of students was indicted by a grand jury for harboring runaway slaves. Illinois College was also a well-known station on the Underground Railroad, and a number of tunnels can still be found under the college leading to the Smith and Fayerweather houses on the campus.

In the years following the Civil War, graduates contributed with distinction to the national scene. Among these was William Jennings Bryan, who within fifteen years after graduating was the Democratic candidate for the U.S. presidency in the 1896 race against William McKinley. He continued with a prominent role in politics even after losing the election.

There were many other famous and prominent graduates of the school over the years, and it has maintained an outstanding scholarly program. Not surprisingly, it has also maintained close ties to the supernatural world. Like with many other historic spots in Illinois, the events of the past have certainly left their mark on Illinois College. Many of these events still come back to "haunt" students and faculty members today, and there are many who have encountered the ghosts of yesterday face-to-face.

Built in 1829, Beecher Hall is one place where strange events have been reported. This two-level building is now used as a meeting hall for two of the school's literary societies, Sigma Pi and Phi Alpha. The Sigs meet on the upper floor and the Phis meet in the lower part of the building. The majority of the encounters here seem to involve the groups who frequent the upper floor. The most commonly reported events are ghostly footsteps that can be distinctly heard in one room, always coming from another. If the witness follows the sound, then the footsteps will suddenly be heard in the other room instead.

Years ago, this was a medical building, and cadavers were stored on the upper floor. Some believe that this may explain the ghostly activity. Legend has it that the students here were not actually supposed to have the cadavers secreted away in the building. They were so dedicated to collecting medical knowledge, however, that they stole them from local hospitals and cemeteries, introducing the art of "body snatching" to Illinois College. The corpses were hidden in the attic until the stench of decaying flesh alerted college officials to their presence.

Other legends claim that the ghost in the building is that of Williams Jennings Bryan, returning to haunt his old school. He was a member of Sigma Pi and was often in the building during his years at Illinois College. There are others who say that it might be Abraham Lincoln's ghost instead. He was an honorary Phi Alpha, and although he did not attend the school, he did speak at Beecher Hall on occasion. In addition, William Berry (Lincoln's law partner at New Salem), William H. Herndon (his law partner), and Ann Rutledge's brother, David, all attended Illinois College.

Another allegedly haunted spot on campus is the David A. Smith House, which was built in 1854. Today, the structure is home to three of the women's literary societies: the Gamma Deltas, the Chi Betas, and the women of Sigma Phi Epsilon. There is a parlor for all of them, but the Deltas use a room on the main floor while the Betas and the Sig Phis have rooms on the second floor. All of the groups use the attic, but there is also a dining room, a kitchen, and an apartment at the back of the house.

There are several versions of the historic legend concerning the ghost in this house, but all of them claim that she is Effie Smith, the daughter of the original owner. As the story goes, a young man from the town was courting Effie and they became engaged. When he proposed to her, he gave her a diamond ring, and she was said to have scratched it against her bedroom window to see if the diamond was real. When she realized that it was, she etched her signature into the glass, and her name remained for many years afterward. The window has recently been removed and this small and unusual piece of history has been lost.

The story then begins to take different paths. In one version, David Smith was very disapproving of his daughter's new fiancé, so he literally locked Effie into a closet one day when the man came calling. Fearful of the father's wrath, the young man hid himself in a small room that was only accessible from the attic. For some reason, he nailed himself in to escape from David Smith and later died there. According to students who have been in the attic, the nails are still visible there today, nailed from the other side of the door. When Effie learned of her lover's cruel fate, she threw herself from an upstairs window and died in the fall.

In the second version of the story, Effie's young man went off to fight in the Civil War. Every day, Effie climbed up to the attic and watched for him to return. When she later learned that he had been killed in battle, she committed suicide by, once again, jumping out of the window. Yet another variation of the legend has Effie being jilted by her lover, so she committed suicide. Regardless of what happened, the story stands that she killed herself and has since returned to haunt the house.

Effie's rocking chair is still located in the attic, and the stories say that if you move the chair away from the window (where it sits, facing out), leave the attic and then return later, the chair will have returned to its original position. This window is located in a storage area for the Chi Beta society, and every year, they frequently test the chair and discover that the story is true. One young woman even walked into the room one day and the door suddenly slammed closed behind her. It is also not uncommon for cold air to suddenly fill this room, even though for years, the windows were painted shut. It was said that an icy cold wind would often come from the window that had Effie's name etched on the glass.

Another reportedly ghostly location is Whipple Hall, which was constructed in 1882. The spectral occupant of this place is known only as the "Gray Ghost." The upper part of the building serves as a meeting hall for the Eta Sigma chapter of the Alpha Phi Omega society, a national service fraternity, and as the location of the security office. The lower part of Whipple is the meeting hall of the Pi Pi Rho literary society. The basement of the building is only accessible from the outside and is divided in half. One side of it was a classroom when this was Whipple Academy, a college prep school.

Perhaps the most famous sighting on campus of the "Gray Ghost" occurred to a girl who was leaving a Pi Pi Rho party one night and had to retrieve something from the Alpha Phi Omega hall. She had been drinking (but later insisted that she was not drunk) before she started climbing the curved staircase. As she reached the middle of the curve of the stairs, she looked up to the top landing and saw a man standing there. He was dressed all in gray, and she quickly realized that he was not a security officer. As she peered into the shadows, she realized something else—that he had no face! She began screaming and ran back down the staircase and out of the building. Due to the noise of the party, no one heard her, and the revelers wouldn't learn of the strange experience until later.

A room located on the third floor of Illinois College's Ellis Hall is also rumored to be infested with ghosts. According to reports, no one lives there if they don't have to. Rumor has it that a girl hanged herself in the closet there around 1986 after not getting a bid from a literary society. It is said that doors open and close on their own, appliances and radios turn on and off, and windows have a habit of going up and down under their own power. Or at least that's one version of the story . . .

Other students and alumni of Illinois College claim that the girl who haunts Room 303 was actually a young woman named "Gail" who died of natural causes in the room. Apparently, Gail's parents were aware that she was terminally ill when she went to school, but since attending college had always been her dream, they allowed her to go anyway. She died while living in Ellis Hall, and a small plaque is mounted on the door of the room in her memory. It is said that her ghost is a mischievous one, opening doors and hiding things. Local legend has it that third-floor residents have often said that if they lose anything, they will ask out loud for Gail to return it. The missing item is usually found a short time later.

A former student of the college, who lived for two years in Ellis Hall, wrote to tell me of experiences she had while living below the "haunted room." She said that she often heard knocking sounds coming from the other side of the wall, even though there was nothing there. It was the outer wall of the building and there were no trees nearby.

There are other supposedly haunted places, too, but stories from some of these sites are much sketchier. One of them is Fayerweather House, a residence hall for women. It has been said that windows and doors operate on their own and that lights turn on and off without explanation. Legend has it that a girl hanged herself in the house, committing suicide in the closet of Room 5, which is located on the stairway landing between the first and second floors of the house. "Susie," as she has been called, is noisy and can often be heard walking around the house, opening doors in the middle of the night and scratching on walls. One correspondent informed me that Susie was once blamed for the violent removal of a clothing rod from the wall. They could never explain how this had happened.

The stories also maintain that although the attic of the Fayerweather House has been fully converted into dorm rooms, they are never used. It has been said that the rooms were closed when too many strange things started to happen to the students who lived there. One of my correspondents had a sister who lived in Fayerweather and told her of doors slamming and lights turning on and off, as well as objects flying about the rooms.

Another site is Sturtevant Hall, one of the most famous spots on campus. Recent stories say that a ghostly young man in a Civil War–era uniform is sometimes seen here. In addition, it is nearly impossible to find someone who will spend the night in the north tower of the building, claiming the strange noises that haunt the place will drive anyone away. Before it was made into classrooms, the building housed the Pi Pi Rho literary society. Members of the society still maintain that toilets in the hall often flushed by themselves.

Crampton Hall, built in 1873, is also believed to be home to a ghost. The residence was built to house sixty-nine men and was named in honor of Rufus C. Crampton, a former professor and president of the college. According to the story, there was a male student who left a party one night and was found hanged in his closet. Rumors still state that he was hanged in a way that he could not have done himself. His former room is now believed to be haunted.

And apparently closets in Crampton Hall are as mysterious as the stories that revolve around them. One student told me of three residents who were waiting on a fourth friend to get ready so they could all go somewhere together. Finally, they tired of waiting and went to check on him, only to find that he was hanging upside down in the closet, stark naked, and so frightened that he was almost incoherent. The student went on to say that he lived in this building for one semester and "would never live there again." One night, he fell asleep with his lights on but was awakened by a noise. When he looked up, he saw a man standing there looking at him. The man quickly turned and vanished into the closet.

Another resident haunt can be found in the McGaw Building. It has been reported that you will never find anyone alone in the auditorium of this performing arts building at night. The place is allegedly haunted by the ghost of a man wearing clothing from the 1940s. He is usually seen out of the corners of the eyes of those who are onstage.

Rammelkamp Chapel allegedly has a haunted basement. Some of the students tell stories of classroom doors that open and then slam shut, sometimes in the middle of lectures. The classrooms are located on both sides of a long hall, and by looking out the door of one of them, a person can see into the classroom across the hall. One day, during a class, a student reportedly became quite upset when she looked across the hall and spotted a woman in white in the adjoining classroom. This would not have been so strange if the woman had not vanished right in front of her eyes!

The English Country House on the Illinois Prairie

No location is more out of place on the prairies of central Illinois than the Robert Allerton estate. To wander the vast estate is almost like taking a trip through another world. It boasts original artwork, exquisite gardens, miles of hiking trails, a Chinese pavilion, sunken gardens, statuary such as the impressive Sun-Singer, the Centaur, the avenue of Chinese musicians, and the fearsome Fu-Dogs—and of course, the forty-room manor house that serves as the centerpiece of the estate.

But who was Robert Allerton, and what drove him to carve this strange place from the Illinois prairie? And what of the ghost who allegedly walks here? Are the stories of her presence really true?

According to staff members and guests of the estate, they are very true—but who is she, and why does her spirit linger at the Allerton House?

Robert Henry Allerton was born in March 1873, the only son of a wealthy Chicago businessman named Samuel Waters Allerton. The elder Allerton was a self-made millionaire who had amassed a fortune through real estate, banking, and a variety of other enterprises. Robert grew up as a privileged young man on fashionable Prairie Avenue in Chicago with neighbors like the Marshall Fields, the Pullmans, and the Kimballs. He wanted for nothing and yet he was an unhappy child. His mother died in 1880, just five days before Robert's seventh birthday, leaving a void in his life. Two years later, however, his father married Agnes Thompson and she became Robert's stepmother, mentor, and friend. She encouraged his interests in music, literature, art, and gardening.

As Robert grew older, he studied at the Art Institute and then attended the Allen Academy and the Harvard School in Chicago. His father sent him to a prep school in New Hampshire in the company of his friend, Frederic Clay Bartlett. After attending school for two years, the two young men decided not to go on to college, but to go to Europe and study art instead. Needless to say, Samuel Allerton was not pleased.

Regardless, Robert spent the next five years studying art in Munich and Paris. He was admitted to the Royal Academy of Bavaria and to the Acadamie Julian, and then at the age of twenty-four, Robert ended his budding career as an artist. One afternoon, he returned home and destroyed every painting he had ever created. What prompted this remains a mystery, because he never gave up art altogether, remaining a collector and patron of the arts for the rest of his life.

He returned home to Chicago in 1897 and announced to his father that he wanted to become a farmer. Samuel was pleased with this, feeling that it would encourage his son's "health, vitality, and character." He had given Robert 280 acres of land in Piatt County when his son was younger, and he now gave him money to build a house on the land. He also put him in charge of managing other family holdings in downstate Illinois. Robert named his

Piatt County holdings "The Farms," and by 1914, he had increased the size of the estate to about 12,000 acres.

Robert decided that he needed a house to serve as the center of the estate. This would be no mere farmhouse, but a mansion where Robert could feel comfortable in the rural setting. There, he would store his large art collection and would create a place of beauty for himself and his friends to enjoy.

In October 1898, Robert journeyed to England with his friend John Borie, an architect he had met in Paris. The two men spent the winter visiting English country houses and landscaped gardens, looking for the perfect design for the Illinois house. The following spring, they returned to America, their plans for the house complete.

Construction was finished in 1900, and the house remains an eclectic mix of styles, including British and American Colonial. The house also had a formal pool, and a small lake was created nearby. Robert and Borie designed landscaped gardens that bordered on the woods and open fields. Borie also designed a walled vegetable garden, the gatehouse, and a series of greenhouses. Robert designed much of the grounds. He created additional formal gardens and an amphitheater he called the "Sunken Gardens." He built a bridge over the Sangamon River, connected the stables to the house by way of a marble walkway, and constructed the "House in the Woods" on the property in 1917.

Meanwhile, Robert began setting up a very profitable farming system that would more than support his lifestyle. He hired excellent farm managers and worked in partnership with area farmers. In addition to work, he also continued to travel and to collect books and works of art.

Robert's father died in 1914, and Robert gained a number of new responsibilities as part of his large inheritance. He became an executive board member of banks and businesses in the Chicago area, forcing him to spend more time in the city. While in Chicago, he became involved with a number of clubs and civic organizations, including the Art Institute and the Chicago Civic Opera.

He divided his time between Chicago and the Farms and continued to make improvements and manage affairs. Whenever possible, he also entertained his artist friends, who enjoyed the seclusion of the rural estate. A frequent visitor to the country was his stepmother and friend, Agnes, who brought with her a young woman named Ellen Emmett Rand. Robert and Ellen were said to have formed a romantic attachment, and most referred to them as being "unofficially engaged." For some unknown reason, though, they would never marry.

In the 1920s, Robert became closely involved with the University of Illinois, where he served on several boards and established landscaping and architecture scholarships. Once each year, he invited graduating students to a reception at the Farms. In 1922, he attended a "Dad's Day" dinner at the Zeta Psi House in Champaign. It was there where he met a young architecture student named John Wyatt Gregg. The student had lost both of his parents, and since Robert had no children, the two of them were paired for the day. They became friends and developed a father-son relationship that would last for the rest of Robert's life.

After John graduated, he went to work for architect David Adler, a close friend of Robert's. Due to the stock market crash in 1929, however, there was little work for the young man. Finally, in 1931, he came to live at the Farms and became Robert's personal architect and protégé. He also became Robert's legally adopted son a number of years later.

During the 1930s, Robert and John made several trips to Europe, the Far East, and the Pacific Islands. They purchased artwork for the house and created new additions for the estate. Robert's tastes had changed from Edwardian to Oriental, and his new interests began to appear in landscaped gardens on the farm, along with the Fu-Dog Trail and the House of Golden Buddhas.

The two men entertained often, hosting a large garden party each spring. Guests were given Roman togas and Japanese kimonos so they would feel comfortable in the peaceful surroundings. The old conservatory of the house was turned into a costume room, and guests were free to come and go as they liked.

In 1937, Robert and John visited Hawaii on their way to Australia and fell in love with the tropical climate. By the next autumn, Robert had purchased 125 acres of land and started construction on a new house and gardens. By 1938, he had moved from Illinois to Hawaii and incorporated much of the artwork from the Farms into the new house. Furniture, books, and art from the Illinois house were either moved, sold, or given away. The house was largely abandoned, and Robert would not live there again during his lifetime. In 1946, he donated the Farms to the University of Illinois with the stipulation that it remain as a wildlife and plant preserve, an education center, and a public park.

By this time, the estate in Hawaii had become known as a showplace for tropical plants, and Robert became an honorary member of the Honolulu Garden Club and a generous benefactor of the art museum. He gave money for a library and a new wing that contained more than two hundred pieces of Oriental art. He also donated money to fund the Pacific Tropical Botanical Garden, which was established in 1964.

Robert Allerton died that same year, on December 22, at the age of ninety-one. At his request, his body was cremated and his ashes were scattered on the outgoing tide.

So who haunts the Allerton House today? The restless spirit here is not Robert, returning to his once-beloved home, but that of a woman who has been described as wearing a white dress. No one knows when the haunting began, but in recent years, there have been a number of strange encounters.

The estate today remains under the care of the University of Illinois. The manor house, Evergreen Lodge, the Gate House, and the House in the Woods are all used as guest facilities for the conference center and are normally closed to the public. Staff members and guests in the main house, however, sometimes get more than they bargained for when working or attending a conference.

One former staff member who encountered the "woman in white" once served as the night manager at the house. When he came to work there, he was the first employee to be given a bedroom in the house. On the day that he arrived, the room was not ready, so he was given the master bedroom to sleep in that night. It would be in this room where he would have his first encounter with the resident ghost.

The staff member was sound asleep in the early morning hours when he was awakened by a terrible sensation of cold and energy. The energy came over him like a wave and jolted him awake. He described it as sliding over and then off his body, and he sensed it move away toward the adjoining bedroom.

This would be the first time he encountered the ghost, but it was not the last. On another occasion, he was surprised to feel a small hand touching the back of his own. He looked down and saw the filmy image of a woman's hand and the cuff of a startlingly white dress. He could see and feel the hand, but beyond it, the image faded away into nothingness. Then, the hand itself vanished. After that, he truly began to believe that the Allerton house was haunted.

And he would not be the only person to feel this way. Guests and other staff members at the house have reported hearing phantom footsteps in the empty hallways and the sounds of someone descending the stairs. They would often look to see who was there and find no one.

On several occasions, individuals reported the ghostly image of a woman in a white, old-fashioned dress wandering through the hallways and in the bedrooms. Perhaps the most amazing encounter came when two ladies were sharing a bedroom one night during a conference. They later learned, by comparing notes, that both of them were restless during the night. Each of them tossed and turned, and both of them separately reported a chilling sight. At different times, each of them saw a woman in a white dress sitting in a chair on the far side of the room. The woman was looking in the mirror and adjusting her hat, then pulling on formal, white gloves. She remained there for several moments and then inexplicably vanished.

But who is the lovely ghost that lingers here? Several people connected to the house believe that it may be the spirit of Ellen Emmett Rand, Robert Allerton's one-time fiancée. Ellen was a frequent visitor to the house during a period prior to the 1920s, often traveling from Chicago in the company of Robert's stepmother. She was an artist in her own right and was the only woman ever linked romantically to Robert. Everyone always assumed the two of them would marry, but for some reason, they never did. Later, Ellen would marry another man, and Robert would stay single throughout his entire life, preferring only the company of John and his many friends.

Many believe that perhaps Ellen's heart was broken when she learned that Robert never planned to marry her, and perhaps this revelation led to a falling-out that would leave Robert single and turn Ellen to another man. Although she perhaps considered Robert her one true love, it was a marriage that was never meant to be.

If this is true, it might explain why Ellen's ghost has returned to haunt the house. Perhaps she is still reliving the wonderful days when she, Robert, and their artist friends gathered at the estate to laugh, create, and live extravagantly. In her world, it may still be those gilded days after the Great War, when art, literature, and beauty were still the passions of this golden circle of friends. It was a time when everything seemed right with the world, and for Ellen, perhaps it is still that time. Perhaps she has chosen to return to those days in a house where she knew happiness—becoming a true spirit of another place and time.

The Ghost of Peggy Van Noy

One of the strangest criminal cases in the history of central Illinois occurred in the prairie regions of Menard County in 1826 and involved a murderer named Nathaniel Van Noy. The story of the events surrounding his life and death created a legend of brutal homicide, postmortem experiments, and ghosts.

According to author John Winterbauer, the lives of the early pioneers in central Illinois were sometimes disturbed by events of such magnitude that they were used to mark time. He states that the murder of Peggy Van Noy was just such an event. For years afterward, residents would recall events (like births and deaths), often starting with the phrase, "two years before Van Noy was hanged . . ." or something very similar. The circumstances around the murder were so strange and so shocking that few local residents ever forgot them.

Nathaniel Van Noy and his wife, Peggy, came to Illinois around 1820 and began homesteading a small tract of land that came to be known as the Van Noy Settlement. The area was about five miles west of present-day Athens, in Menard County. The property was made up of forest and carved-out farmland and was traversed by the road that ran from Springfield to Beardstown. This was the main artery of travel through the area. Thanks to the amount of traffic that could be found on the road on any given day, it was a prime location for Van Noy's blacksmith shop, which he constructed on the north side of the thoroughfare. The shop catered to locals and travelers alike and was soon doing a brisk business. Across the road from the shop, he constructed a large, comfortable cabin for himself and his wife.

The Van Noys' existence seemed peaceful and happy, aside from the fact that Nathaniel spent little time at home with his wife. Although he had established a good trade, he began closing down the shop without warning and departing on lengthy trips. The blacksmith would be gone for long periods of time, and when he returned, he always had plenty of money, even though his business was sometimes closed for weeks at a time.

Van Noy's frequent closures did not seem bother his neighbors very much, and he still managed to get work done whenever he happened to be home. On August 27, 1826, however, a local man and his young daughter came to the shop and found the place to be deserted. They walked across the road to the Van Noy cabin to see when the blacksmith might be returning and knocked on the door. There was no answer from inside, so the neighbor peered in—only to be shocked by a horrible sight. Peggy Van Noy was lying on the floor of the cabin in a large pool of blood. He pushed open the door and searched frantically for Nathaniel, worried that the couple had been murdered by passing travelers on the Springfield road. A quick search revealed that the blacksmith was not in the house.

The man sent his daughter back through the forest to summon help, and a number of local men soon arrived to await the return of Van Noy. At first, they were concerned that he would be grief-stricken by his wife's death, but while they waited, they made a shocking discovery that cast suspicion on Van Noy as having a hand in his wife's death. Hours passed as they waited at the cabin, and at some time during the vigil, the men discovered the secret of Van Noy's wealth and the reason behind his many extended absences. Hidden on the property were all the implements needed for a sophisticated counterfeiting operation. It would later be revealed that Van Noy would make up a batch of phony currency and then travel to distant towns to "push" it on unknowing storeowners and businesses. Counterfeiting was one of the most lucrative criminal enterprises in Illinois at the time, and Nathaniel Van Noy would turn out to be one of the most prominent operatives in the region.

Van Noy finally returned home late that night. When he arrived, he was immediately seized by the waiting men. He was visibly agitated and claimed that he had spent the day stalking a deer that he had wounded while hunting. When questioned about his wife's death, he claimed that he was innocent and tried to shift the blame to a group of Native Americans who lived nearby. The men were not convinced, so they turned Van Noy over to Sheriff John Taylor.

Judge John Sawyer immediately called a special session of the Sangamon County Circuit Court, and a grand jury was sworn in to hear the case. Despite very little evidence of Van Noy's guilt, the jury decided it was enough and ordered that the blacksmith be tried for his wife's murder.

The trial of Nathaniel Van Noy began on August 28, just one day after his wife had been found murdered. There is no record of testimony given at the trial, but whatever was said and done, the jury was convinced and took only one day to find him guilty. Van Noy was sentenced to be hanged for his crime, and he was removed to the Sangamon County Jail to await his execution.

There would be little to make this story unusual—it seemed a simple case of murder—if not for the visitor that Van Noy received while he was incarcerated at the county jail. A Springfield doctor named Addison Philleo came to see Van Noy one day in his cell, and the two of them made a strange, unsettling bargain. Dr. Philleo believed that he had created a device that, if applied to a corpse just after death, could reanimate the body. The doctor was convinced that this device would work and apparently convinced Van Noy of it, as well. He literally sold his body to Dr. Philleo with the belief that he would be brought back to life shortly after he was hanged.

On November 20, the day of Van Noy's execution, a crowd formed around the jail. Large numbers of men, women, and children arrived in Springfield and gathered to witness the hanging at a hollow just north of the present-day state capitol building. A rumble went through the crowd when Van Noy appeared. He was driven to the execution site in a wagon, which was stopped beneath two posts. A noose was tightened around his neck, and then the horses were whipped. They jerked forward, pulling the wagon out from beneath his dangling feet. Van Noy slowly strangled to death, his body twitching and shaking for several minutes until he finally became still.

Van Noy's body was left hanging for five hours before being cut down. Apparently, Sheriff Taylor had heard about the dead man's deal with Dr. Philleo and was determined not to allow him access to the fresh corpse—just in case his reanimation device actually worked. Dr. Philleo, his experiment ruined, began to conduct an autopsy on the corpse right on the spot. The onlookers were so disturbed and disgusted by the proceedings that law officers forced him to move to a nearby building to finish his work. Unfortunately, he was forced to abandon his work when he realized that Van Noy had simply been left hanging too long. There is no record that he ever attempted to use the device again.

Nathaniel Van Noy's story did not end with his hanging in November 1826. One of the last statements he made claimed that he had buried a large quantity of gold beneath a tree that stood near his cabin on the Springfield road. Many neighbors and treasure-hunters searched for the gold, but to this day, it has never been found.

Soon, though, even the lure of treasure was not enough to get people to trespass on Van Noy's former land. It became a place to be feared by travelers on the roadway and by settlers who lived nearby. A number of memoirs penned by area pioneers recalled how horses were always spooked when they passed by the Van Noy cabin, perhaps disturbed by the ghosts that lurked there. The house remained standing until the 1850s, some say long after, and it was always regarded as a haunted place—and to some, it still is. Even after the house was torn down, stories circulated that the spirit of Peggy Van Noy wandered the fields where the Van Noy Settlement was once located.

One story was told by a traveler who journeyed past the house late one night. He was startled to hear the sound of a woman's bloodcurdling screams coming from inside. The man, who was not aware of the house's violent past, hurried into the building to see if someone needed help. After a few minutes of searching and calling out to anyone who might be inside, he realized that the cabin was abandoned. When he reached the Hall Tavern in Athens, he told his story, and several locals gathered there recounted the tale of Peggy Van Noy's murder.

Other travelers reported the spectral form of a woman, believed to be Peggy Van Noy, floating through the woods. Stories of this female phantom—and at least one other ghost—continued for many years. One such tale involved an Athens man named Alexander Hale who, along with two friends, went out to the Van Noy farm one night, looking for the gold that was allegedly buried on the property. They searched the property as thoroughly as darkness and lantern light would allow, but after several hours, gave up without finding anything.

As they prepared to leave, one of the young men pointed out an unusual glow coming from deeper in the woods. Believing that it might be the lantern light of a rival treasure-hunting party, they decided to sneak up on them and try to scare them away. They crept quietly through the trees, getting closer and closer to the strange light. Suddenly, one of the men hurried ahead, jumped out from behind a tree, and came face-to-face with the eerie glow. He stumbled into a clearing and saw a man glaring at him. The translucent figure was not holding a lantern—the glow was actually emanating from the figure itself! The specter raised a threatening hand, and the treasure-hunter immediately turned and ran, colliding with his companions who were several steps behind. Sensing his panic, they allowed themselves to be pulled along with him as he ran headlong toward the road.

The young man's companions, not having seen the ghost, were skeptical of their friend's story. He breathlessly recounted what he had seen while standing in the roadway near the house. Intrigued, Hale and the third man wanted to go back and take another look, but their frightened friend was adamantly opposed to the idea. They finally relented and accompanied their shaken confederate back to Athens.

The next day, Hale and the other man returned to the Van Noy property to collect the tools they had left behind the night before. They also wandered into the woods to look for any sign of the mysterious "glowing man" that their friend had so colorfully described. Finding no sign of any ghost, they returned home, and no further mention was ever made between them of the haunted farm or the missing treasure.

Oddly enough, the following year, Alexander Hale, in partnership with John Overstreet, constructed a large, brick flour mill in Athens at a cost of nearly $11,000. This was no small amount of money in 1856, and no record shows where the funds for the project actually came from. Of course, there was a lot of speculation at the time (as there is today) about the source of the money, but it's unlikely that we will ever know.

The Four–Legged Ghost of Villa Kathrine

Those traveling along Illinois' Great River Road may be shocked when they reach the old town of Quincy and see what appears to be a small Moorish castle overlooking the Mississippi. The house is not a figment of their imagination but a real-life castle created by an eccentric millionaire named George Metz, who abandoned the place after the death of his only companion—his dog, Bingo. Although Metz loved the house, he has not returned here in death. The same cannot be said for Bingo, who continues to linger here, many decades after his passing.

Villa Kathrine was built in 1900 as a virtual museum for the exotic furnishings collected by Metz during his world travels. The son of a wealthy Quincy businessman, William Metz, George was so rich that he never worked a day in life. When he came into his fortune, he decided to travel the world instead. His love for the world's wonders made Metz himself something of a wonder to the small-town folks in his hometown. Reporters wrote speculative tales about Villa Kathrine, which was named for his mother, and townspeople gossiped about the castle's mysterious owner.

According to legend, Metz's wanderings were motivated by his lifelong dream to find the perfect home. He found it in the centuries-old Villa Ben Ahben in Algiers. He later stated that he was struck by the golden color of the exterior and the large domes, and he became obsessed with creating his own version of the place in Quincy. He also wanted to purchase suitable furnishings for the house and claimed to spend the next two years wandering North Africa with the "secretive Moors," haggling with caravan trains. He bought thousands of items and pieces of furniture for the villa, including crescents for his domes, antique door knockers, divans, Egyptian lamps, and much more. During this time, he designed, sketched, and discarded ideas for the house, and then he returned to Quincy to make his dreams come true.

Needless to say, he had a tough time finding a sympathetic architect to build the "perfect house" in his hometown. He finally found a young man named George Behrensmeyer, who took on Villa Kathrine as his first commission. Together they found a site for the house on a bluff that looked down on the Mississippi River and toward the homes and buildings of the city. Working from Metz's drawings, Behrensmeyer began designs for the dream castle. He scaled the place down so that it would rest securely on the bluff, and then in 1900, the brick and stucco walls of Villa Kathrine began to rise.

Locals whispered about the unusual house from the very beginning. According to legend, Metz built the house while in mourning over a lost love. The stories had it that he met a "fair-haired, blue-eyed" woman in Germany, and together they had discovered the beauty of Villa Ben Ahben. Metz planned to bring his love home with him to his villa on the banks of the Mississippi, but his bliss was short-lived. Sadly, she refused to come to Quincy, and a broken-hearted Metz retired to a reclusive life in the newly completed villa. Metz's refusal to deny or confirm the story fueled the gossip and speculation ran rampant, but little record about Metz's world travels remain except as it related to the house. As history would have it, the villa on the hill created—and devoured—the man.

The finished castle evoked images of Moorish homes in North Africa and Spain, but at its heart, Villa Kathrine was a modest, two-story home. However, a one-story side wing, the two square towers, several porches, and the numerous setbacks and projections gave it an exotic, castlelike outline. The villa's unique square south tower was decorated on all sides with a diamond pattern, with inlaid, carved lattice woodwork. Another tower was topped by a Muslim minaret with swirling red and white stripes and a silver dome. It was a miniature replica of a dome on the famous Mosque of Thais in Tunisia. The north tower also had a dome topped with a Muslim crescent that Metz found in an ancient ruin in northern Africa.

An unusual variety of windows, including rounded and pointed arches, keyhole shapes, and diamonds, added to the villa's exotic appearance. The larger windows were also fitted with grilles in Moorish patterns. A terrace surrounded the front entrance, and one could reach the door through a Moorish arch. Over the front door was a tile that held a relief cast of a woman's hand adorned with a wedding ring and holding a dove. Some believe that it was a cast of the hand of Metz's lost love, but we will never know for sure. The wooden door was ornamented with antique brass door trimmings brought from an old house in Algiers.

The inside of the building continued the Moorish theme. Heavy wooden beams crossed the ceiling, and keyhole niches were fitted into the walls. Shelves of exotic pottery, carved chairs and tables, wall hangings, and rugs added greatly to the feel of the rooms. Inside the front door was the drawing room, and up a short flight of steps and through glass doors was the interior court. The court was surrounded by a gallery supported by eight pointed arches that were embraced by spiral pillars. The pillars are copies of those in the Court of Dolls in Seville, Spain. Around the center court, on both floors, were small square rooms that bordered a central pool. Above the pool, the villa's atrium was open to the roof, where a winter glass cover would be replaced by a summer awning. The walls of the court appear to be covered in black-and-white tiles, but this is only an illusion. For some reason, Metz had the walls painted to look like tile, an odd, money-saving gesture that stands out amidst the wealth of the house. Metz furnished the court with chairs, rugs, settees, and stools, and oil lamps dimly lit the area. In the dining room, however, he hung a huge chandelier that once graced the salon of a luxurious Mississippi River showboat. The dining room and smoking room were decorated with rugs, art objects, tapestries, and trophies he had collected in the East.

The stairs ascended from the court into the upper levels and the north tower. The court is surrounded by a decorative rail and around it is an upstairs gallery where the bedrooms were located. Entry to the summer dining room was gained from the north tower's stairs. Metz often dined there on summer nights, enjoying the cool air and the view of the passing boats on the river.

Metz lived at Villa Kathrine as a bachelor for twelve years. He was not a total recluse, though. On September 30, 1904, Albert Hastings and Pansy Darnell, an old family friend of Metz, were married at Villa Kathrine with Metz playing the wedding march on his pipe organ.

Despite friends who often dined with him, however, his only constant companion in the house was his beloved dog, Bingo. Brought over from Demark by Metz after one of his trips, Bingo was a 212-pound Great Dane that was rumored to be the largest dog in America. Metz had a special addition built off the kitchen for the dog. When Bingo died, he was buried on the grounds of the estate. Faced with the loss of his longtime friend, a cloud descended over Metz's dream, plunging him into a terrible depression.

Out of fear for his safety, mostly based on his age and his inability to climb stairs and care for the house, Metz's relatives urged him to sell the place. Finally, in 1912, he agreed.

One day, a visiting couple who professed a great interest in the house prevailed on him to sell to them. Their enthusiasm convinced

Metz that they would be ideal occupants for the villa, and he sold the house and all of its furnishings to them. Little did he know that the buyers were actually agents for the railroad who planned to tear down the house and build a railroad yard on the site. Word got out, and vandals descended on the mysterious house and carried off the decorations and the furniture, turning the place into a ruin.

Metz returned to the house one time, in 1913, with a reporter from St. Louis. The house was overrun with vermin and birds, the tinted walls were stained and destroyed, and what little furniture remained was shredded. He left it, vowing "never to return to this ruin again." Nineteen years later, Metz did come back for one final visit, returning this time with a reporter from Decatur to find the villa crumbling with decay. "I wish this place were mine again," he said, "I'd tear it down."

George Metz never lost his love for views of the Mississippi River. After leaving Villa Kathrine, he lived in a succession of apartments with a wide view of the river, first at the Hotel Newcomb, then on the second floor of a house, and finally at the Lincoln Douglas Hotel. He spent most of his spare time feeding the birds and squirrels in Quincy's parks. Poor health finally brought him to St. Vincent Hospital, where he died from pneumonia in 1937.

Villa Kathrine survived the treachery of the Alton-Quincy Interurban Railroad, and it passed into the lives of decades of owners, renters, caretakers, and finally, the Quincy Park District. After years of decay and vandalism, the castle has at last been saved and restored for generations of people to marvel over—and to wonder about.

It seems impossible for such a wonderful house to exist without at least one ghost story connected to its history, and it's no surprise that Villa Kathrine does have one resident ghost. As mentioned, it's the spirit of Bingo that seems to have lingered here. Perhaps it was George Metz's enduring affection for the dog that kept him from passing on to the other side, but whatever the reason, staff members at the house have often reported hearing the clicking of Bingo's toenails on the tile floors of the house. This canine phantom creates one more mystery of Villa Kathrine—one that merely adds to the lore of the house.

Abraham Lincoln's
Haunted House

There is no question that the most famous former resident of Illinois is Abraham Lincoln, our nation's sixteenth president and one of the most revered figures in American history. Lincoln believed wholeheartedly in the supernatural, and his connections with the unknown were maintained throughout his life, and some say, beyond it. He believed in prophetic dreams, dabbled in Spiritualism, and was admittedly haunted by the spirit of his dead son. Is it any wonder that he is one of America's favorite ghosts?

But is it the ghost of Abraham Lincoln that reportedly still lingers in his former home in Springfield? Is it Mary Lincoln, returning to one of the few places in life that she knew happiness? Or is it, as I believe, the ghost of another occupant of the house entirely?

Abraham Lincoln was a frontier lawyer who had come to the city of Springfield to earn a living. His new wife, Mary, insisted that they have a good home in which to raise their children, and by 1844, Lincoln was able to purchase a one-and-a-half story cottage at the corner of Eighth and Jackson streets, not far from Lincoln's law office in the downtown district. The Lincolns lived in the house from a period shortly after their son Robert was born until they moved to Washington in 1861.

The house was originally built in 1839 by a Reverend Dresser and was designed in the Greek Revival style. When Lincoln purchased the home, it was still a small cottage. It had been constructed with pine exterior boards, walnut interiors, and oak flooring; wooden pegs and handmade nails held everything together. In 1850, Lincoln improved the exterior of the property by having a brick wall constructed and adding a fence along Jackson Street, but nothing major was done to the house until 1856. In that year, the house was enlarged to a full two stories, adding new rooms and much-needed space.

Today, the house is presented in much the same way as it looked during the Lincoln years. It is now owned and operated by the National Park Service, but they are not thrilled that the house has gained notoriety as a "haunted" site. They have always publicly maintained that no ghosts walk here, although many of the witnesses to the strange events have been former employees and tour guides of the house.

There is no question that the house has clear connections to supernatural history, dating back to Election Day in 1860, when Abraham Lincoln won the election for President of the United States. After a long day spent with his friends and a midnight celebration at the telegraph office when the final election results came in, Lincoln returned home during the early morning hours. He went into his bedroom for some much-needed rest and collapsed onto a settee. Near the couch was a large bureau with a mirror on it, and Lincoln started for a moment at his reflection in the glass. His face appeared angular, thin, and tired. Several of his friends suggested that he grow a beard, which would hide the narrowness of his face and give him a more "presidential" appearance. Lincoln pondered this for a moment and then experienced what many would term a "vision"—an odd vision that Lincoln would later believe had prophetic meaning.

He saw that in the mirror, his face appeared to have two separate, yet distinct, images. The tip of one nose was about three inches away from the other one. The vision vanished but appeared again a few moments later. It was clearer this time, and Lincoln realized that one of the faces was actually much paler than the other was, almost with the coloring of death. The vision disappeared again, and Lincoln dismissed the whole thing to the excitement of the hour and his lack of sleep.

The next day, he told Mary of the strange vision, and he talked about it to friends for several years to come. Mary believed she knew the significance of the vision. The healthy face was her husband's "real" face and indicated that he would serve his first term as president. The pale, ghostly image of the second face, however, was a sign that he would be elected to a second term—but would not live to see its conclusion.

Long after the Lincolns left the house, stories began to circulate about the apparition of a woman seen there. Many passed this off to wishful thinking, but in more than one circumstance, the image was spotted by multiple witnesses.

A number of years ago, a local newspaper interviewed some current and former staff members of the house, all of whom claimed to have had brushes with the supernatural. At that time, a woman named Shirlee Laughlin was employed at the house as a custodian. She claimed that her superiors were very unhappy with what they termed her "vivid imagination." But were the events she experienced really all in her mind? In her interview, Laughlin claimed to have experienced ghosts in the house on many occasions. "I don't see the images as such," she said, "I see things happening."

Among the things she witnessed were toys and furniture that moved about the house from one room to another, unlit candles that mysteriously burned down, and Lincoln's favorite rocking chair rocking back and forth under its own power. "At times, that rocking chair rocks," she stated, "and you can feel the wind rushing down the hall, even though the windows are shut tight."

Laughlin also recounted an occurrence that took place while she was rearranging furniture in Mary Lincoln's former bedroom. Besides being a custodian, she was also an expert on historic home restoration and would often attempt to recreate the layout of the household furniture as it looked when the Lincolns lived in the house.

She was in the bedroom alone one afternoon when someone tapped her on the shoulder. She looked around the room, but there was no one there. She decided to leave the furniture the way she had found it.

Another former guide said that she was on duty at the front door one afternoon when she heard the sound of music being played on the piano that used to be in the parlor. She turned to stop whoever had touched it and found that no one was in the room. Another ranger who worked in the house recalled several occasions when strange feelings, and the touch of invisible hands, caused her to close up the house quickly on some evenings.

And again, she wasn't alone either. One ranger told of one late afternoon when she was in the front parlor by herself. There was a display there of some of the items that could commonly be found in households of the period, including some children's toys. As she was standing in the room, she caught a movement out of the corner of her eye. When she looked, she saw a small toy as it rolled across the floor on its own. She didn't stay in the room very long.

Staff members are not the only ones to have odd encounters. A number of tourists have also noticed things that are a bit out of the ordinary, such as hearing voices in otherwise empty rooms, hearing the rustle of what sounds like a period dress passing by them in the hallway, experiencing unexplainable cold spots, and most common, seeing the rocking chair as it gently moves back and forth.

One tourist, an attorney from Virginia, even wrote the staff after he returned home to tell them of his own strange sighting. He claimed to see a woman standing in the parlor of the house who abruptly vanished. The tourist had enough time to recognize the woman and he believed her to be Mary Lincoln.

But was the ghost really Mary? For those who believe the house is indeed haunted, they believe the ghost is not actually one of the Lincoln family, but rather a later occupant of the house, Mrs. Lucian A. Tilton. Mrs. Tilton and her husband, the president of the Great Western Railway, had rented the home from the Lincoln family when they left for Washington in 1861. After the president's assassination, however, his body was placed on display in the house when he was returned to Springfield. Mrs. Tilton had been constantly plagued by visitors during the four years that she lived in the house, prior to 1865. They estimated that at least sixty-five thousand people had visited the home and asked to take a tour of it, ringing the bell and knocking on the door day and night.

Needless to say, Mrs. Tilton was worried about what might happen to the house during the Lincoln funeral, but she was a kindhearted person and had already resolved herself to the fact that she was going to allow people to take grass from the yard, flowers from her garden, or leaves from the trees. She had no idea what was coming—by the end of the funeral services, her lawn and gardens had been stripped, paint had been scraped from her house, and bricks had been carried away from her retaining wall as souvenirs.

The Tiltons moved out of the Lincoln home in 1869, but some believe that Mrs. Tilton has never left it. There are those that believe the ghost who lingers here, and who has been seen on many occasions cleaning and straightening the house, is the beleaguered Mrs. Tilton, still worried over the disruptions that continually marked her brief tenancy in this famous home.

Stealing Abraham Lincoln

After President Abraham Lincoln was assassinated in April 1865, his body traveled west from Washington, spending several weeks visiting towns and cities along a circuitous route. His funeral service in Springfield did not take place until May 4, and it followed a parade route from the former Lincoln home to Oak Ridge Cemetery, on the far edge of the city. But it would be many years before Lincoln was allowed to rest in peace. His tomb has long been a place of mystery, intrigue, speculation, bizarre history, and some say, a haunting.

But if Abraham Lincoln's tomb is actually haunted, then it is likely because of a crime that was carried out here in 1876, an attempted theft that would cause Lincoln's body to be hidden in one place after another for the next two decades. Lincoln was finally laid to rest in 1901, but the disturbance that shattered his peace got its start many years before with the arrest of a counterfeiter named Benjamin Boyd.

Following the assassination of President Lincoln, his body was returned to Springfield to rest in a grave in a remote, wooded cemetery called Oak Ridge. The cemetery had been started around 1860, and it mostly consisted of woods and unbroken forest. In fact, not until after Lincoln was buried there was much done in the way of improvement, adding roads, iron gates, and a caretaker's residence. Lincoln himself had chosen the rural graveyard as his final resting place, but city leaders insisted that he be buried elsewhere. Officials actually began construction on a large and elaborate monument in downtown Springfield for the president's tomb, and Mary Lincoln was infuriated that they ignored her husband's wishes. She began to make immediate plans to have Lincoln moved to Chicago, and city officials quickly surrendered. Lincoln was moved to Oak

Ridge Cemetery, and the city of Springfield ended up constructing the new state capitol building on the site they had planned for Lincoln's tomb.

Once the dust had settled, Lincoln was taken to the temporary receiving vault in the cemetery and placed there with his sons, Willie, who had died during the presidency, and Eddie, who had died many years before. Willie's body had accompanied his father's from Washington, while Eddie's had been exhumed and brought over from another cemetery. A short time later, a temporary vault was built for Lincoln, and on December 21, he was placed inside. Six of Lincoln's friends wanted to be sure the body was safe, so a plumber's assistant named Leon P. Hopkins made an opening in the lead box for them to peer inside. All was well, and Lincoln and his sons were allowed a temporary rest. Hopkins stated in a newspaper story of the time, "I was the last man to look upon the face of Abraham Lincoln." Of course, he had no idea at the time just how many others would look upon the president's face in the years to come.

Construction on a permanent tomb for Lincoln lasted more than five years, and on September 19, 1871, the caskets of Lincoln and his sons were removed from the hillside crypt and taken to the catacomb of the new tomb. The plumber, Leon P. Hopkins, opened the coffin once more and the same six friends peered again at the president's face. There were several crypts waiting for Lincoln and his sons, although one of them had already been filled. Lincoln's son Tad had died in Chicago a short time before, and his body had already been placed in the nearly finished monument.

During the move, it was noticed that Lincoln's mahogany coffin was beginning to deteriorate, so his friends brought in a new iron coffin, to which the inner coffin of lead, containing Lincoln's body, was transferred. The dead president was laid to rest again, for another three years, as the workmen toiled away outside.

On October 9, 1874, Lincoln was moved again. This time, his body was placed inside a marble sarcophagus in the center of the semicircular catacomb. A few days later, the monument was finally dedicated. The citizens of Springfield seemed content with the final resting place of their beloved Abraham Lincoln. But then a threat arose that no one could have ever predicted—a plot to steal the body and hold it for ransom! This event became one of the strangest stories in the annals of Illinois crime and may be the source of the many ghostly and mysterious legends connected with Lincoln's tomb.

The events began with the arrest of Benjamin Boyd, a petty criminal who had, by 1875, established himself as one of the most skilled engravers of counterfeit currency plates in the country. Boyd had been doggedly pursued by Captain Patrick D. Tyrell of the Chicago office of the U.S. Secret Service for eight months before he was finally captured in Fulton, Illinois, on October 20. Following his trial, Boyd was sentenced to a term of ten years at the Joliet Penitentiary.

Shortly after Boyd's arrest, the strange events concerning the body of Abraham Lincoln began in Lincoln, Illinois. The city was a staging point for a successful gang of counterfeiters run by James "Big Jim" Kneally. The place was an ideal refuge for Kneally's "shovers," pleasant-looking fellows who traveled around the country and passed, or shoved, bogus money to merchants. It's been said that, around this time, at least half of the currency being used in Logan County was counterfeit. Following Boyd's arrest in the spring of 1876, business took a downturn for the Kneally Gang. With their master engraver in prison, the gang's supply of money was dwindling fast. Things were looking desperate when Kneally seized on a gruesome plan. He would have his men kidnap a famous person and, for a ransom, negotiate for the release of Benjamin Boyd from Joliet prison. Kneally found the perfect candidate as his kidnapping victim: Abraham Lincoln, or at least his famous corpse.

Kneally placed Thomas J. Sharp in charge of assembling the gang and leading the operation. Sharp was the editor of the local *Sharp's Daily Statesman* newspaper and a valued member of the counterfeiting gang. Meanwhile, Kneally returned to St. Louis, where he owned a legitimate livery business, so that he could be far away from suspicion as events unfolded and have an airtight alibi. In June, the plan was hammered together at Robert Splain's saloon in Lincoln. Five of the gang members were sent to Springfield to open a saloon that could be used as a base of operations.

This new place was soon established as a tavern and dance hall on Jefferson Street, the site of Springfield's infamous Levee District, a lawless section of town where all manner of vice flourished. Splain served as the bartender while the rest of the gang loitered there as customers. They made frequent visits to the Lincoln Tomb at Oak Ridge, where they found the custodian, John C. Power, more than happy to answer questions about the building. On one occasion, he innocently let slip that there was no guard at the tomb during the night. This clinched the last details of the plan, which involved stealing the body and spiriting it away out of town. It would be buried about two miles north of the city, under a Sangamon River bridge, and then the men would scatter and wait for Kneally to negotiate the ransom. They chose the night of July 3, 1876, to carry out their plan.

The Springfield saloon was up and running by the middle of June, leaving the men with several weeks of nothing to do but sit around the tavern, drink, and wait. One night, one of the men got very drunk and spilled the details of the plan to a prostitute who worked at a nearby "parlor house." He told her to look for a little extra excitement in the city on Independence Day. He and his companions planned to be stealing Lincoln's body while the rest of the city was celebrating the holiday. The story was too good to keep, and the woman passed it along to several other people, including the city's chief of police, Abner Wilkinson, although no record exists as to how these two knew one another. The story spread rapidly and Kneally's men disappeared.

Kneally didn't give up on the plan, however. He simply went looking for more competent help. He moved his base of operations to a tavern called the Hub at 294 West Madison Street in Chicago. Kneally's man there was named Terence Mullen, and he operated a secret headquarters for the gang in the back room of the tavern. One of Kneally's operatives, Jack Hughes, came into the Hub in August and learned that a big job was in the works. Kneally wanted to steal Lincoln's corpse as soon as possible. Hughes and Mullen had no desire to do this by themselves, so they brought another man into the mix. His name was Jim Morrissey, and he had a reputation for being one of the most skilled grave robbers in

Chicago. They decided he would be perfect for the job. Unknown to the gang, "Morrissey" was actually a Secret Service operative named Lewis Swegles. He had a minor criminal background and had served time for horse stealing. When released, he went to work as an undercover agent for Captain Patrick Tyrell. When he heard what was happening with the counterfeit gang, he posed as a grave robber.

In 1876, grave robbery was still a national horror and would remain that way for some years to come. Illinois, like most other states, had no laws against the stealing of bodies. It did, however, have a statute that prevented selling the bodies that were taken. Needless to say, this put medical schools into dire need. They often had to depend on "ghouls," or grave robbers, to provide fresh corpses for their anatomy classes. These "ghouls" had become the terror of communities, and friends and relatives of bereaved families some-times patrolled graveyards for several nights after a funeral, with shotguns in hand.

Swegles, pretending to be Jim Morrissey, came into the Hub and discussed the methods of grave robbery with the other two men. The three of them quickly devised a plan. They would approach the Lincoln monument under the cover of night and pry open the mar-ble sarcophagus. They would then place the casket in a wagon and drive northward to the Indiana sand dunes. This area was still remote enough to provide a suitable hiding place for however long was needed. Swegles, being the most experienced of the group, agreed to everything about the plan except for the number of men needed. He believed the actual theft would be harder than they thought and wanted to bring in a famous criminal friend of his to help them. The man's name was Billy Brown, and he could handle the wagon while the others pillaged the tomb. The other two men readily agreed.

On November 5, Mullens and Hughes met with Swegles in his Chicago home for a final conference. They agreed the perfect night for the robbery would be the night of the upcoming presidential election. The city would be packed with people and they would be in downtown Springfield very late, waiting near the telegraph and political offices for news. Oak Ridge Cemetery, more than two miles away and out in the woods, would be deserted, and the men could work for hours without being disturbed. It would also be a perfect night to carry the body away, as the roads would be crowded with wagons and people returning home from election celebrations. One more wagon would not be noticed.

The men agreed and decided to leave for Springfield on the next evening's train. Swegles promised to have Billy Brown meet them at the train but felt it was best if he didn't sit with them. He thought that four men might attract too much attention. Hughes and Mullen conceded that this was a good idea, but they wanted to at least get a look at Brown. Swegles instructed them to stay in their seats and he would have Brown walk past them to the rear car. As the train was pulling away from the station, a man passed by the two of them and casually nodded his head at them. This was the mysterious fourth man. Brown, after examination, disappeared into the back coach. Hughes and Mullen agreed that he looked fit for the job.

While they were discussing his merits, Billy Brown was hanging onto the back steps of the train and waiting for it to slow down at a crossing on the outskirts of Chicago. At that point, he slipped off the train and headed back into the city. "Billy Brown" was actually Agent Nealy of the U.S. Secret Service.

As Nealy was slipping off the train, more agents were taking his place. At the same time the conspirators were steaming toward Springfield, Tyrell and half a dozen operatives were riding in a coach just one car ahead of them. They were also joined on the train by a contingent of Pinkerton detectives, who had been hired by Robert Lincoln after he got word of the plot to steal his father's body. The detectives were led by Elmer Washburne, one of Robert Lincoln's law partners.

A plan was formed between Washburne and Tyrell. Swegles would accompany the grave robbers to Springfield, and while assisting in the robbery, would signal the detectives, who would be hiding in another part of the monument. They would then capture Mullen and Hughes in the act.

When they arrived in Springfield, Tyrell contacted John Todd Stuart, Robert's cousin and the head of the new Lincoln National Monument Association, which cared for the tomb. He advised Stuart of the plan, and together, they contacted the custodian of the site. The detectives would hide in the museum side of the monument with the custodian. This area was called Memorial Hall, and it was located on the opposite side of the structure from the catacomb. They would wait there for the signal from Swegles, and then they would rush forward and capture the robbers.

The first Pinkerton agent arrived just after nightfall. He carried with him a note for John Power, the custodian, which instructed him to put out the lights and wait for the others to arrive. The two men crouched in the darkness until the other men came inside. Tyrell and his men explored the place with their flashlights. Behind the Memorial Hall was a damp, dark labyrinth that wound through the foundations of the monument to a rear wall of the catacomb, where Lincoln was entombed. Against this wall, in the blackness, Tyrell stationed a detective to wait and listen for sounds of the grave robbers. Tyrell then returned to the Museum Room to wait with the others. Their wait was over as darkness fell outside.

A lantern flashed outside the door and sounds could be heard as the grave robbers worked at the lock. Almost immediately, Mullen broke the saw blade that he was using on the lock, and so they settled in while he resorted to the long and tedious task of fil- ing the lock away. After some time, Mullen finally removed the lock and opened the door to the burial chamber. Before them, in the dim light, they saw the marble sarcophagus of President Lincoln. Now all they had to do was to remove the lid and carry away the coffin, which turned out to be much harder than they had anticipated. The stone was too heavy to move, so they used an ax to break open the top, then moved the lid aside and looked into it. Swegles was given the lantern and was stationed nearby to illuminate the work area. Left with no other option, he complied, although he was supposed to light a match at the door to alert the Secret Service agents that it was time to act. Meanwhile, Mullen and Hughes lifted out the heavy casket. Once this was completed, Mullen told Swegles to go and have the wagon moved around. He had assured Mullen and Hughes that Billy Brown had it waiting in a ravine below the hill.

Swegles raced around to the Memorial Hall, gave the signal to the detectives, and then ran outside. Tyrell whispered to his men and, with drawn revolvers, they rushed out and around the monument to the catacomb. When they arrived, they found the lid to the sarcophagus was moved aside and Lincoln's casket was on the floor—but the grave robbers were gone!

The detectives scattered outside to search the place. Tyrell ran outside and around the base of the monument, where he saw two men near one of the statues. He whipped up his pistol and fired at them. A shot answered and they fought it out in a hail of gunfire, dodging around the monument. Suddenly, one of the men at whom he was shooting called out Tyrell's name—he was firing at his own agents!

Mullen and Hughes had casually walked away from the tomb to await the return of Swegles, Brown, and the wagon. They never suspected the whole thing had been a trap. They had only wanted to get some air and moved into the shadows where they wouldn't be seen in case someone wandered by. After a few minutes, they saw movement at the door to the tomb and had started back, thinking that Swegles had returned. They heard the pistol shots and saw a number of men around the monument. They took off running past the ravine and vanished into the night. Assuming that Swegles had been captured, they fled back to Chicago, only to be elated when they found him waiting for them at the Hub tavern. He had returned with the horses, he told them, but found the gang gone. He had come back to Chicago, not knowing what else to do, to await word of what had happened. Thrilled with their good fortune, the would-be grave robbers spent the night in drunken celebration.

The story of the attempted grave robbery appeared in the newspaper following the presidential election, but it was greeted with stunned disbelief. In fact, only one paper, the *Chicago Tribune*, would even print the story because every other newspaper in the state was sure that it was not true. To the general public, the story had to be false, and most believed that it had been hoaxed for some bizarre political agenda. Most people would not believe that the Secret Service and Pinkerton agents would be stupid enough to have gathered all in one room where they could see and hear nothing, and then wait for the criminals to act. The Democrats in Congress charged that the Republicans had hoaxed the whole thing so that it would look like the Democrats had violated the grave of a Republican hero, and in this way, sway the results of the election. To put it bluntly, no one believed that Lincoln's grave had been, or ever could be, robbed!

The doubters became believers on November 18 when Mullen and Hughes were captured. The newspapers printed the story the following day, and America realized the story that had appeared a short time before had actually been true. Disbelief turned into horror. Letters poured into the papers, laying the guilt at the feet of everyone from the Democrats and the Southern sympathizers to the mysterious John Wilkes Booth Fund.

The people of Illinois were especially outraged, and punishment for the two men would have been severe—if the law had allowed it. After their arrest, the conspirators were placed under heavy guard in the Springfield jail, and on November 20, a special grand jury was convened in Springfield and returned a bill against Mullen and Hughes for attempted larceny and conspiring to commit an unlawful act. There was nothing else with which they could be charged. Grave robbery was not a crime in Illinois, and the prosecution, bolstered by Chicago lawyers dispatched by Robert Lincoln, could find no grounds to charge them with anything other than the minor crimes of larceny and conspiracy. Ironically, the charge was not even for conspiring to steal President Lincoln's body. It was actually for planning to steal his coffin, which was the property of the Lincoln National Monument Association.

The public was aghast at the idea that these men would get off so lightly, even though the grand jury had returned a quick indictment. Continuances and changes of venue dragged the case along to May 1877, when it finally came to trial. The prosecution asked the jury to sentence the men to the maximum term allowed, which was five years in prison. On the first ballot, two jurors wanted the maximum; two of them wanted a two-year sentence; four others asked for varying sentences; and four others even voted for acquittal. After a few more ballots, Mullen and Hughes were incarcerated for a one-year stay in Joliet.

And Abraham Lincoln was once more left to rest peacefully in his grave, at least for a while.

It was not long before the story of the Lincoln grave robbery became a hotly denied rumor, or at best, a fading legend. The custodians of the site simply decided that it was something they did not wish to talk about. Of course, as the story began to be denied, the people who had some recollection of the tale created their own truth in myths and conspiracies. The problem in this case, however, was that many of these "conspiracies" happened to be grounded in the truth.

Hundreds of people came to see the Lincoln burial site, and many of them were not afraid to ask about the stories that were being spread about the tomb. From 1876 to 1878, custodian John C. Power gave rather evasive answers to anyone who prodded him for details about the grave robbery. He was terrified of one question in particular, which seemed to be the one most often asked: Was he sure that Lincoln's body had been returned safely to the sarcophagus after the grave robbers removed it?

Power was terrified of that question for one reason—at that time, Lincoln's grave was completely empty!

On the morning after the election of November 1876, when John T. Stuart of the Lincoln National Monument Association learned what had occurred in the tomb with the would-be robbers, he rushed out to the site. He was not able to rest after the incident, fearing that the grave robbers, who had not been caught at that time, would return to finish their ghoulish handiwork. So he contacted the custodian and told him that they must take the body from the crypt and hide it elsewhere in the building. Together, they decided the best place to store it would be in the cavern of passages that lay between the Memorial Hall and the catacomb.

That afternoon, Adam Johnson, a Springfield marbleworker, and some of his men lifted Lincoln's casket from the sarcophagus. They covered it with a blanket and then cemented the lid back into place. Later that night, Johnson, Power, and three members of the Memorial Association stole out to the monument and carried the five-hundred-pound coffin around the base of the obelisk, through Memorial Hall, and into the dark labyrinth. They placed the coffin near some boards that had been left behind in the construction. The following day, Johnson built a new outer coffin while Power set to work digging a grave below the dirt floor. It was slow work because it had to be done between visitors to the site, and Power also had a problem with water seeping into the hole. He finally gave up and simply covered the coffin with the leftover boards and wood.

For the next two years, Lincoln lay beneath a pile of debris in the labyrinth, while visitors from all over the world wept and mourned over the sarcophagus at the other end of the monument. More and more of these visitors asked questions about the theft, questions full of suspicion, as if they knew something they really had no way of knowing.

In the summer and fall of 1877, the legend took another turn. Workmen arrived at the monument to erect the naval and infantry groups of statuary on the corners of the upper deck. Their work would take them into the labyrinth, where Power feared they would discover the coffin. The scandal would be incredible, so Power made a quick decision. He called the workmen together and, swearing them to secrecy, showed them the coffin. They promised to keep the secret, but within days everyone in Springfield seemed to know that Lincoln's body was not where it was supposed to be. Soon, the story was spreading all over the country.

Power was now in a panic. The body had to be more securely hidden, and in order to do that, he needed more help. Power contacted two of his friends, Major Gustavas Dana and General Jasper Reece, and explained the situation. These men brought three others, Edward Johnson, Joseph Lindley, and James McNeill, to meet with Power.

On the night of November 18, the six men began digging a grave for Lincoln at the far end of the labyrinth. Cramped and cold, and stifled by stale air, they gave up around midnight with the coffin just barely covered and traces of their activity very evident. Power promised to finish the work the next day. These six men, sobered by the responsibility that faced them, decided to form a brotherhood to guard the secret of the tomb. They brought in three younger men, Noble Wiggins, Horace Chapin, and Clinton Conkling, to help in the task. They called themselves the Lincoln Guard of Honor and had badges made for their lapels.

After the funeral of Mary Lincoln, John T. Stuart told the Guard of Honor that Robert Lincoln wanted to have his mother's body hidden away with his father's. So, late on the night of July 21, the men slipped into the monument and moved Mary's double-leaded casket, burying it in the labyrinth next to Lincoln's.

Visitors to the tomb increased as the years went by, all of them paying their respects to the two empty crypts. Years later, Power would complain that questions about Lincoln's empty grave were asked of him nearly every day. Finally, in 1886, the Lincoln National Monument Association decided that it was time to provide a new tomb for Lincoln in the catacomb. A new and stronger crypt of brick and mortar was designed and made ready.

The press was kept outside as the Guard of Honor, and others who shared the secret of the tomb, brought the Lincoln caskets out of the labyrinth. Eighteen persons who had known Lincoln in life filed past the casket, looking into a square hole that had been cut into the lead coffin. Strangely, Lincoln had changed very little. His face was darker after twenty-two years, but he still had the same sad features these people had always known. The last man to identify the corpse was Leon P. Hopkins, the same man who had closed the casket years before. He soldered the square back over the hole, thinking once again that he would be the last person to ever look upon the face of Abraham Lincoln.

The Guard of Honor lifted Lincoln's casket and placed it next to Mary's smaller one. The two of them were taken into the catacomb and lowered into the new brick-and-mortar vault. Here, they would sleep for all time.

"All time" lasted for about thirteen more years. In 1899, Illinois legislators decided the monument was to be torn down and a new one built from the foundations. It seemed that the present structure was settling unevenly, cracking around the "eternal" vault of the president.

There was once again the question of what to do with the bodies of the Lincoln family. The Guard of Honor came up with a clever plan. During the fifteen months needed for construction, the Lincolns would be secretly buried in a multiple grave a few feet away from the foundations of the tomb. As the old structure was torn down, tons of stone and dirt would be heaped onto the grave site both to disguise and protect it. When the new monument was finished, the grave would be uncovered again.

When the new building was completed, the bodies were exhumed once more. In the top section of the grave were the coffins belonging to the Lincoln sons and to a grandson, also named Abraham. The former president and Mary were buried on the bottom level, so safely hidden that one side of the temporary vault had to be battered away to reach them.

Lincoln's coffin was the last to be moved, and it was close to sunset when a steam engine finally hoisted it up out of the ground. The protective outer box was removed, and six construction workers lifted the coffin onto their shoulders and took it into the catacomb. The other members of the family had been placed in their crypts, and Lincoln's casket was placed into a white marble sarcophagus.

The group dispersed after switching on the new electric burglar alarm. This device connected the monument to the caretaker's house, which was a few hundred feet away. As up-to-date as this device was, it still did not satisfy the fears of Robert Lincoln, who was sure that his father's body would be snatched again if care were not taken. He stayed in constant contact with the Guard of Honor, who were still working to ensure the safety of the Lincoln remains, and made a trip to Springfield every month or so after the new monument was completed. Something just wasn't right. Even though the alarm worked perfectly, he could not give up the idea that the robbery might be repeated.

He journeyed to Springfield and brought with him his own set of security plans. He met with officials and gave them explicit directions on what he wanted done. The construction company was to break a hole in the tile floor of the monument and place his father's casket at a depth of ten feet. The coffin would then be encased in a cage of steel bars, and the hole would be filled with concrete, making the president's final resting place into a solid block of stone.

On September 26, 1901, a group assembled to make the final arrangements for Lincoln's last burial. A discussion quickly turned into a heated debate. The question that concerned them was whether or not Lincoln's coffin should be opened and the body viewed one last time. Most felt this would be a wise precaution, especially in light of the continuing stories about Lincoln not being in the tomb. The men of the Guard of Honor were all for laying the tales to rest at last, but Robert was decidedly against opening the casket again, feeling that there was no need to further invade his father's privacy. In the end, practicality won out, and Leon P. Hopkins was sent for to chisel out an opening in the lead coffin. The casket was placed on two sawhorses in the still-unfinished Memorial Hall. The room was described as hot and poorly lighted, as newspapers had been pasted over the windows to keep out the stares of the curious.

A piece of the coffin was cut out and lifted away. According to diaries, a "strong and reeking odor" filled the room, but the group pressed close to the opening anyway. The face of the president was covered with a fine powder made from white chalk. It had been applied in 1865 before the last burial service. It seemed that Lincoln's face had turned inexplicably black in Pennsylvania, and after that, a constant covering of chalk was kept on his face. Lincoln's features were said to be completely recognizable. The casket's headrest had fallen away, and his head was thrown back slightly, revealing his still perfectly trimmed beard. His small black tie and dark hair were still as they were in life, although his eyebrows had vanished. The broadcloth suit that he had worn to his second inauguration was covered with small patches of yellow mold, and the American flag clutched in his lifeless hands was now in tatters.

There was no question, according to those present, that this was Abraham Lincoln and that he was placed in the underground vault. The casket was sealed back up again by Leon Hopkins, making his claim of years ago true. Hopkins was the last person to look upon the face of Lincoln.

The casket was then lowered down into the cage of steel, and two tons of cement was poured over it, forever encasing the president's body in stone.

That should have been the end of it, but as with all lingering mysteries, a few questions still remain. The strangest are perhaps these: Does the body of Abraham Lincoln really lie beneath the concrete in the catacomb? Or was the last visit from Robert Lincoln part of some elaborate ruse to throw off any further attempts to steal the president's body? Did Robert, as some rumors have suggested, arrange with the Guard of Honor to have his father's body hidden in a different location entirely?

Most historians would agree that Lincoln's body is safely encased in the concrete of the crypt, but let's look at this with a conspiratorial eye for a moment. Whose word do we have for the fact that Lincoln's body is where it is said to be? We only have the statement of Lincoln's son, Robert, his friends, and of course, the Guard of Honor. But weren't these the same individuals who allowed visitors to the monument to grieve before an empty sarcophagus, while the president's body was actually hidden in the labyrinth beneath a few inches of dirt? It's interesting to consider, but it's unlikely that we will ever know, one way or another.

And what of the stories that claim Lincoln's ghost still walks the tomb?

Many have reported that he, or some other spirit here, does not rest in peace. Many tourists, staff members, and historians have had some unsettling impressions that aren't easily laughed away. Usually these encounters have been reported as the sound of ceaseless pacing, tapping footsteps on the tile floors, whispers and quiet voices, and the sounds of someone crying or weeping in the corridors.

Is it Abraham Lincoln? Most likely, it's not. In fact, it's unlikely that the tomb is even "haunted" in the traditional sense of what we think of when we consider a place to be haunted by ghosts. If there are strange things occurring here (and based on the hundreds of mysterious reports and encounters, there seem to be), it's most likely that they are "echoes" of events from the past still making themselves known today. Are the weeping sounds simply "memories" of the millions of grief-stricken people who have visited this site? Are the voices, banging sounds, and restless tapping a "residue" of the dark events that occurred here in 1876?

Many paranormal researchers, especially those well versed in the history of President Lincoln, believe this to be the case. Residual hauntings like those reported at the Lincoln tomb are not ghosts in the truest sense of the word. They are actually memories or events that have somehow become impressed upon the atmosphere of a location. These events then replay themselves like a recording when conditions are right. The haunting at Lincoln's tomb may be just this kind of manifestation. There have been literally millions of people who have passed through this monument between 1871 and the present, including friends of the Lincolns and mourning admirers of the president. If we also factor in the drama of the opening and reopening of the grave and the wide range of emotion that has been expressed on this stone structure, then conditions are certainly ripe for something unusual to happen. The attempted grave robbery in 1876 had likely left a bigger impression behind than any other event in the tomb's history. The fear and excitement of that emotionally charged evening may have been etched on the atmosphere of this place in the same way that Leon Hopkins' chisel carved its way into the lead of Lincoln's casket.

So does the ghost of Abraham Lincoln haunt his burial site? Probably not, nor does any other "spirit" likely linger in the tomb. What does linger behind is the residual energy of more than a century of grief and pain experienced by millions of mourners, the fear and excitement of the grave robbers, and the paranoia of the men who were sworn to protect the president's remains at all costs.

Legends of Voorhies Castle

When several generations of people who grew up on the central Illinois prairie were asked to name the most haunted house in the region, one dwelling always came to mind—Voorhies Castle. This lonely and isolated old house was the stuff from which decades of legends were born, from mysterious deaths and strange disappearances to haunted happenings and myriad ghosts. The "castle" became a wonderfully spooky place to visit for legions of area teenagers, all hoping to see a ghost. But few of them actually knew the real story behind the building—and subsequent abandoning—of the house. If they had, they might have found the place to be even scarier!

The story of Voorhies Castle began in 1867 when a Swedish immigrant named Nels Larson arrived in America. He settled near Galesburg, Illinois, and went to work for a local farmer, soon earning a reputation as a hard and efficient worker. Larson saved every dollar he made, and within a short time, he moved south and settled in Piatt County, near the town of Bement. Here, he went to work for a local farmer and landowner named William Voorhies.

Voorhies himself had returned to America in 1868. During the Civil War, he studied medicine in Germany, then returned to his home state of Kentucky and married Ellen Duncan of Lexington. Two years later, he gave up practicing medicine and moved north to Illinois. He purchased three sections of prairie land in Piatt County and set aside a parcel for a homestead. He soon found the land to be rich and productive, and he had a fine two-story home built with a wide veranda on three sides. Although prosperous, Voorhies discovered that he had more land than he could handle, so he began selling off small parcels to upstanding and hardworking men in the area. Nels Larson would purchase one of these parcels of land in 1885.

Before that time came, however, Nels Larson started out with very little. Even after going to work for William Voorhies, he only earned $30 a month in the summer and $40 a month in the fall and winter. He also had to give back $9 each month for room and board and provide his own clothing. He lived frugally and saved all of the money he could. Finally, in 1872, he spent $325 for a good team of horses and went into debt for a harness, plows, and a wagon. He rented sixty acres of land from Voorhies and set out on his own. Later, he bought a large parcel of property from his former employer near the small town of Voorhies. Also in 1872, Larson sent for his fiancée, Johannah Nilson, who was still living in Sweden at that time. Later that same year, they were married.

Larson continued to buy more land and lease other parcels. He now had a number of farmers working for him, renting his property in exchange for a portion of the proceeds from the harvest. In addition to his own farm, he was a partial owner in many others. The small town of Voorhies, which Larson owned, was also growing, consisting of small businesses and tenant homes that Larson's farmers rented. The town also contained a church, a general store, a grain elevator, a corn crib, and several barns. There was also a barber shop, a jeweler, a blacksmith, and a postmaster. At the post office, a license was granted for the sale of postal money orders, and locals could purchase tickets for travel on the Wabash Railroad line that passed through town. The rail station was also useful for the loading and unloading of grain and cattle. The grain elevator was added to the town in 1897 and was operated by Larson's son, George, who was also the postmaster.

There was no question that Larson was now the most powerful and wealthy landowner in the area, but he certainly wasn't liked by everyone. It was often stated that he expected more from his workers than most were willing to give, and some have described him as a "tyrant." A worker could be fired for the slightest infraction, often at Larson's whim. One night, the local general store was burned to the ground at a loss of more than $1,600. Although it was clearly a case of arson, Larson refused to allow an investigation and simply rebuilt the place, hiring a security guard to watch over the new building. There were other cases of vandalism, too, possibly by disgruntled employees, which ended in the burning of cattle guards and small structures. Larson chose to ignore them.

The greatest animosity toward Larson probably came from his son, George, who was born in 1873. He was a graduate of both Bement High School and Brown Business College in Decatur but could never get out from under his father's control. He always admitted that he was afraid of his father, and for this reason, he stayed in Voorhies to act as postmaster and handle the running of the grain elevator.

In 1903, George began courting a local girl named Naomi Shasteen. His parents disapproved of her and stated that she was only after the Larson family money. Nevertheless, the two of them were married in June of that year. They took a wedding trip to Chicago and then settled into a small cottage that was built just west of the Larsons' main house. This arrangement was not a good one, and dissension quickly grew, building toward a confrontation that took place one morning on the sidewalk between the two houses. Naomi, who was accustomed to gentlemen stepping off the sidewalk and allowing her to pass, refused to step off when ordered to do so by Nels Larson. He demanded that the young woman move out of his way, but she refused. Infuriated, he screamed at her, leaving the girl in tears. Shortly after, George constructed a house for him and his wife a quarter mile away, across the railroad tracks from Voorhies.

On the other hand, Larson's daughter, Ellen, was the pride of his life and his spoiled princess. Ellen was born in August 1880, and after graduating from Bement High School in 1901, stayed at home in the now-completed "castle." She had a room tucked between the twin towers of the house, which was richly decorated and furnished with whatever the young woman desired. She reigned over the house and grounds, flirting with being an artist and rising late in the day. Her life in Voorhies was pleasant and filled with good memories, unlike her brother's sad life. Ellen later married James Lamb, a doctor from Cerro Gordo.

By 1900, Larson was firmly entrenched as the "ruler" of his vast domain, consisting of tenants, farms, land, various businesses, and even an entire village. He had lived in several houses around the area, but now decided he needed a manor house from which to oversee his property. This house, later dubbed "Voorhies Castle," would be patterned after a chalet in his native Sweden. Larson contacted a Chicago architect to draw up plans to his specifications. A contractor was then hired, and construction began in the summer of 1900.

The house was a strange mixture of styles and eccentricities. When first completed, the towers on the corners of the house were three stories high, looming one floor higher than the rest of the structure. Larson had thought they would be desirable vantage points from which to view his land holdings and a suitable place for his office. When completed, however, they looked so strange that Larson reluctantly ordered the third floor of each tower removed. He was forced to rely on the front porch alone, with a frontage of sixty feet and a double platform swing, from which to look out on the fields and village.

The front door of the house was extra wide and commonly called a "casket door," as it allowed access for both coffin and pallbearers in the days when funerals were held in the homes of the deceased. The door was flanked by large windows that, like those in the rest of the house, were wider than normal for the time period. Each was designed with a large pane in the lower sash and a series of smaller ones in the top sash. Either lace curtains or velvet draperies hung from the windows, depending on the room.

Inside the house was a large reception hall fitted with an oak fireplace. The mantel was carved with an amaranth leaf, bleeding heart flowers, and lion's heads. Larson had brought an artist from Sweden especially for the purpose of hand-carving this fireplace, along with two others in the house. Sliding pocket doors that led to the adjoining rooms were fitted into each doorway.

The west parlor contained a cherry wood fireplace. It was also decorated with a large fern that was kept near the south window. The fern was so long that it stood on a round, wooden pillar so that its fronds did not touch the floor. This parlor led into the west tower, and the doorway was adorned with wooden scrollwork. The ceiling was papered and decorated with clouds and stars. It was in this room where Larson conducted most of his business affairs.

On the opposite side of the reception hall was the east parlor, where Ellen's piano was kept. This room was designed for lady visitors, and it contained emerald-colored furniture, scrolled doorways, a bookcase secretary, and even a "fainting couch" for the lady whose corset stays might be too tight.

The house also boasted indoor plumbing and a bathroom with all of the latest innovations. It was located between the east parlor and the back room, which served as Johannah's sewing room and as an extra bedroom. The bed was a foldaway device, and an oak dresser, a washstand, and a walnut bureau were also kept here. A heavy safe was kept hidden in the closet, and the walls were undecorated except for a large map of Illinois.

The dining room, located on the first floor, also boasted a beautiful parquet floor designed of maple, mahogany, birch, oak, and sycamore pieces. There was also a marble-topped sideboard and a dining room table that could be extended to seat twenty-four people. In the corner of the room was a gold-colored couch where Larson napped each day following his lunch. The telephone and the doorbell, both battery-operated devices, were mounted on the wall of the dining room.

The kitchen was small but filled to capacity. It had a tiled floor, a drop-leaf table and chairs, a high cupboard, a stove, a sink, and a water heater. The kitchen was further cramped by the five doors that exited off of it—leading to the basement, the upstairs, the back porch, the dining room, and to a small pantry lined from floor to ceiling with shelves and cupboards.

The largest of the upstairs chambers was the master bedroom, which extended across the east end of the house. It was dominated by a huge rosewood bed and dresser that had to be moved into position before the house could be completed. The bedroom furniture had been acquired as part of a settlement between Larson and William Voorhies, the details of which have never been revealed. The tower room adjacent to this bedroom offered the best view of the land, and it has been said that Larson looked out over his holdings every morning after he rose from bed.

Only the finest materials were used in the construction of the house, which delayed its completion until 1904. On many occasions, Larson would return entire loads of lumber to the warehouse after discovering a few boards with knots in them.

The most eccentric addition to the estate was a clock tower barn that Larson had built in 1910. The stories say that Larson had a fascination, or perhaps an obsession, with clocks. They could be found all over the house, from the large grandfather clock in the reception area to the small timepieces scattered on the top of the wooden trunk in his bedroom. He constructed a large barn that could contain a clock tower. He ordered a Seth Thomas clock from a jeweler in Monticello and began construction on the new building. The work on the barn took almost five years to complete, even longer than it took to build the house. The new structure had to be equipped with a sixty-eight-foot tall tower and had to be given enough support to hold the nearly two-ton clock mechanism.

Legend states that the clock mysteriously struck thirteen times at the moment of Nels Larson's death, as though the man and the machine were somehow connected. The stories went on to add that the clock continued this odd activity for five decades, ringing out on the anniversary of its owner's passing. The clock tower remained an odd landmark on the prairie until the summer of 1976, when it was destroyed by a tornado. It has been said that the now phantom clock continues to chime each March 29, at the very hour that Nels Larson passed from this world to the next.

The strange legends of the house began while the Larsons were still living there. The most mysterious event occurred in 1914 when Johannah died. Many have speculated that she had a heart attack on the staircase, but the real cause of her death remains a mystery to this day. One of the field hands had gone to the house one afternoon to find her lying in a crumpled heap on the floor. Nels Larson was so stunned by this event that he left the house that night and went to Ellen's home in Cerro Gordo—never to return. All of the clothing, furniture, and even his personal belongings were left behind. He never returned to the house, abandoning everything that had been left there. The house seemed trapped in time with clothing in the closets, the table still set for dinner, Johannah's apron hanging over the back of a chair, and food still sitting on the cold stove.

Johannah was gone—but did she ever really leave the house? Legends stated that on certain nights, an eerie light could be seen coming from the east tower of the house. Those who were brave enough to venture onto the property claimed to see Johannah framed in the window of the room.

Nels Larson died in 1923, and his will specified that the house should remain in the family. The problem was that no one in the family wanted to live there because the house had no electricity. It was abandoned and remembered only by time and the elements.

Ellen and her husband had four children, but her heart developed a complication with the fourth pregnancy. After that, she was often confined to bed and was only allowed to leave the house occasionally for the evening or for a Sunday afternoon drive. She withdrew more and more into seclusion, only visited by a few friends. During her infrequent day trips, she usually visited the empty "castle" and disappeared inside, where she remained for hours. Perhaps she was trying to recapture a little of the life she once knew there. Ellen passed away in 1955, just four months after the death of her husband.

Over the years, a number of tenants moved into the house, but none stayed for long. It's likely that they were chased away by the deteriorating conditions of the house more so than by the ghosts. However, the rapid succession of tenants and the spooky atmosphere of the place combined to give the Castle a ghostly reputation. The stories grew and were embellished as the years went by. It was said that someone died of fright in the house, and the imprint of his or her body was still pressed into a couch in the living room. There was also said to be a pillar in the west parlor—which once held a large fern—that would inexplicably spin around under its own power. Reports said it spun so much that it eventually wore down into a circular area on the floor.

In 1967, the grandchildren of Nels Larson donated the Castle to the Illinois Pioneer Heritage Center in Monticello. The center opened the house as a tourist attraction, reportedly drawing up to thirty thousand visitors each year. They came to view the unique architecture of the place and soak up some of the ghostly ambiance. Unfortunately, the house became simply too expensive to take care of and was closed down once again.

The Castle was empty with only caretakers to watch over it on occasion. These caretakers claimed the lights in the house refused to stay off and the windows would often open on their own. Another caretaker reported eerie sounds inside the house, such as footsteps on the stairs and piano keys clinking in the darkness. He finally quit working there after he was startled one night by a shadowy figure in the east tower. He was convinced that he had seen a ghost.

The odd stories about the house never seemed to stop, and it became a favorite "haunt" for late-night curiosity-seekers. Many of them claimed to have bizarre experiences and brushes with the supernatural. Many spoke of apparitions, glowing balls of light, sounds like whispers and ghostly footsteps that had no explanation, flashlights that suddenly stopped working, and more.

The notoriety of the house began to fade by the mid 1970s. In 1972, Voorhies Castle was purchased by Milton and Sue Streenz, a Bloomington couple who set to work restoring the place. Over the course of the next six years, they repainted the entire house and did some extensive remodeling. They replaced 138 windowpanes and even added seven truckloads of flowers and trees to the estate. The couple remained in the house for the next six years, but in June 1978, Voorhies Castle was once again auctioned off. The elderly couple sadly admitted they were no longer able to keep up with the physical work needed to maintain the old mansion.

The house was eventually sold, but over the course of the next few years, it was frequently vacant and began to deteriorate again. The decay of the mansion became the biggest problem that all of the new owners and tenants would face—along with fending off the sightseers, for whom the ghostly landmark was still an attraction. Several of the more recent owners have made valiant attempts to restore the house and have done everything possible to discourage visitors from coming to the house. The most recent owners (as of this writing) have done further restoration and do occasionally open up the house for tours. Unauthorized visitors are still unwelcome, however.

The many legends of Voorhies Castle are as haunting as the house has always been said to be, leaving a number of unanswered questions. Is it possible that the haunting has somehow just faded away over the years? Many believe this to be the case. But what if whatever was there still remains? What if it is just resting now, and waiting for some night, perhaps in the distant future, to begin its haunting again?

Northern
Illinois

Spirits of Starved Rock

Starved Rock, located near Utica, is regarded as one of the greatest natural wonders of the state of Illinois. Long before it gained its infamous name, the huge outcropping was the site of Fort St. Louis, a sanctuary constructed by the famous French explorer LaSalle and his adventurous companion, Henri de Tonty. The rock rose more than 120 feet from the currents of the Illinois River below and offered only sandstone cliffs and shadowy crevices as ways of obtaining the summit. Here, the French established an outpost, and goods like hatchets, traps, kettles, and blankets were traded for buffalo and beaver skins.

As Fort St. Louis grew atop the towering rock in 1683, Tonty and LaSalle roamed the region. The Indians brought furs to the rock and pelts were stored in new warehouses. The settlement grew, and soon, more than twenty thousand Native Americans were living and trading near the fort. The tribes gathered here were at peace, and it looked as though LaSalle's commercial enterprise would be a great success. A political setback, however, caused LaSalle to lose his support in France, and his supplies from the north were cut off. He left Fort St. Louis and began to seek out a new trade route to the south, journeying down the Illinois to the Mississippi.

Henri de Tonty remained behind at the rock, and for ten years, between two dangerous journeys, the fort would remain his home. Here, he counseled with the chiefs, sent agents to outlying tribes, and conducted trade with Canada. Tonty was by turns an Indian fighter, a diplomat, a businessman, and an independent frontiersman operating with only frail lines of communication in a rough region larger than all of France. He survived attacks from the rampaging Iroquois Indians, as well as political and financial attacks by jealous rivals. When he learned that his friend LaSalle had vanished while exploring the regions along the southern part of the Mississippi, Tonty went in search of him. Two years passed before he learned LaSalle's fate—killed by his own rebellious men and his bones picked clean by wolves in Texas. Weary from his journey and wasted by fever, he returned to Fort St. Louis in September 1690.

By the following year, the decade of trading at Fort St. Louis had badly depleted the game in the region, so Tonty moved his headquarters to Lake Peoria. More political problems eventually drove him out of the region, and he traveled south to Mobile, Alabama. He died of disease in September 1704 and was buried far from the Illinois country that he had so bravely conquered. Or was he?

According to some of the Native Americans who knew and respected the explorer, Tonty returned to the rock to die—many years after his reported death at Mobile. They said that he came as a white-haired old man with a staff in his hand, groping his way along the twisting path to the summit. It became a local belief that the spirit of Tonty still haunts the rock on nights when the moon appears over the river and silvers the wild and vanished country he once knew.

After Tonty's departure, the fort was abandoned and fell into ruin. Within a few years, though, the rock itself became the scene of death and tragedy and finally earned the name by which it is known today.

Long before the French explorers came to the region, Native American hunters and wanderers inhabited the area. They were the sole occupants of the land, with their small villages scattered across the prairie and nestled close to the rivers and water sources.

When the French encountered these Indians at the mouth of the Des Moines River, the Indians referred to themselves as the "Illiniwek." This was actually interpreted to mean "the men," which was how these Native Americans referred to their tribe. This designation was used to separate them from the Iroquois Indians, who were their mortal enemies and who they referred to as "animals." From that time on, they became known as the "Illinois" confederation, and it would be from this band that the state would later take its name. The confederation was made up of several tribes who had banded together for the purpose of defense. They held a large portion of the state, which they shared with several other tribes, including the powerful Kickapoo Indians.

In the latter years of the 1600s, the Illiniwek were nearly wiped out by the rampaging Iroquois and Fox Indians, and their numbers grew smaller. They were constantly beaten and harassed by their enemies, and the arrival of the white settlers ruined their hunting grounds, bringing the Illiniwek occupation to an end.

Prior to that, the Illiniwek battled courageously against the other tribes' attacks. The Fox, in particular, had staged a series of bloody skirmishes against the Illiniwek. By the last months of 1721, the fighting between them had grown so intense that the Fox allied with other tribes and pursued the struggling Illiniwek to the Illinois River. They sought safety atop the same rock where LaSalle and Tonty had constructed Fort St. Louis years before. At first, the fortress seemed a safe refuge from the Fox, Winnebago, and Sauk tribes below, but they soon realized they were trapped—there was no way to escape from the rock. Their enemy waited below them, and at their back was a steep drop to the rocky banks and swirling waters of the Illinois River.

The Illiniwek began to slowly waste from sickness, cold, and most of all, from hunger. Most of those who tried to escape were killed after jumping from the edge of the cliff. A few of the more daring warriors attempted to flee through the forest, only to be struck down and slaughtered by those laying siege below. Others who were captured were horrifically burned at the stake.

No one really knows how long the Illiniwek were trapped on the summit that came to be known as Starved Rock. A number of accounts say that at least a dozen of them escaped through the woods or by the river. They took shelter with friendly tribes or with French trappers. Others told stories of miraculous escapes and of a mysterious snow that fell one night and covered the tracks of the desperate Illiniwek, giving them just enough time to escape. When they were gone, they left nothing behind at the old fort save for items they could not carry and the bodies of the dead.

By the end of the ordeal, the once great Illiniwek confederation had collapsed to less than a hundred persons. Eventually, they were all sent to a reservation in Kansas. It is believed that not a single descendant of the Illiniwek nation still lives today. They were completely wiped out by the events at Starved Rock and vanished forever—or did they?

According to legend, spirits of some of the desperate Illiniwek still roam the woods near the base of Starved Rock. Those who died while trying to escape have lingered here, and reports claim that the sounds of cries and screams are sometimes heard in the forest.

In March 1960, the violence of the past returned to Starved Rock with the discovery of the bludgeoned bodies of three women from Riverside, Illinois. The land around LaSalle's fortress had been turned into a state park years before, and on March 14, the women's bloody corpses were found in one of the park's fabulous box canyons. The murders sent the entire Illinois River Valley into a panic and left a lingering taint on the park that is still felt to this day.

The three middle-aged women, Mildred Lindquist, Lillian Oetting, and Frances Murphy, had come for a four-day, late-winter holiday at Starved Rock Park. They had lunch on the day of their arrival and then went for a hike on the snow-covered trails. Eventually, they came to the dead end of St. Louis Canyon, where steep, rocky walls framed a majestic, frozen waterfall. The three women were only one mile from the lodge. After admiring the beauty of the scene and taking some photographs, the three ladies turned to leave the canyon—and came face-to-face with a horror that would stun the entire nation.

When it was discovered that the women were missing, a search of the park found their bodies in St. Louis Canyon. The three mutilated women were laying side-by-side, partially covered with snow. They were on their backs, under a small ledge, and their lower clothing had been torn away and their legs spread open. Each of them had been beaten viciously about the head, and two of the bodies were tied together with heavy white twine. They were covered with blood, and their exposed legs were blackened with bruises. A frozen tree limb was found nearby, covered with blood, and investigators realized that it had been the murder weapon. A trail of gore also led them to speculate that the women had been killed deeper in the canyon, and then their bodies had been dragged and positioned under the rock ledge.

The investigation went on for months, and hundreds of possible suspects were questioned and released. Eventually, a match was found between the twine that had been used to bind the victims and the twine used in the kitchens of the Starved Rock Lodge. This led detectives to a former dishwasher at the lodge named Chester Weger, who failed a lie detector test and later confessed to the murders. He took investigators to St. Louis Canyon and reenacted the crimes—only to retract his confession later on, claiming that he had been coerced and fed information by the police. A jury didn't believe his denials, and he was sentenced to life in prison. Weger has been denied parole two dozen times since 1972, and most feel that he belongs securely behind bars.

In the minds of some people, however, there are questions about the case that remain unanswered. Many feel that the evidence used to convict Weger would not stand up in court today. His prosecution largely turned out to be based on his confession, which predated Miranda warnings that are required today. Weger has appealed his case several times, but each appeal has been denied. He continues to maintain that he was framed for the murders. But all of the law enforcement officials in the case, until the day each of them died, insisted that Weger had confessed. They firmly believed that he had committed the murders and perpetrated one of the most heinous acts in the already-bloody history of Starved Rock.

Tragically, the story does not end there.

Many believe that these horrific acts are still being experienced today in the depths of Starved Rock's St. Louis Canyon. In recent years, long after the murders here were consigned to the historic annals of crime, hikers and outdoor enthusiasts have told of strange happenings in the beautiful canyon. According to many of them, eerie cries and unearthly groans are not uncommon in this place. One hiker reported that she was in the canyon alone one day and heard the sound of women screaming. Startled, she hurried ahead and ran into the back wall of the canyon to see if someone had been hurt. There was no one there at the time. "I was so unnerved by this that I left right away. There was just this feeling of dread that came over me that I couldn't shake. It felt horrible," she later recalled with a shudder.

Some who have broken park rules and dared to venture into the canyon at night also claim to have been assaulted by screams, strange sounds, and feelings of terror. Are these events merely overactive imaginations at work, or does the land where blood was spilled at Starved Rock still cry out after all these years? Many believe that it does. This is a place where violence and death have been common for centuries and where memories of the past do not yet want to sleep.

Ghosts of the Bartonville Asylum

If spirits are truly the personalities of those who once lived, then wouldn't these spirits reflect whatever turmoil might have plagued them in life? And if hauntings can sometimes be the effects of trauma being imprinted on the atmosphere of a place, then wouldn't places where terror and insanity were commonplace be especially prone to these hauntings? As an answer to both of these questions, I need point no further than to the strange events that have plagued the old State Mental Hospital in Bartonville, a small town near Peoria, for many years.

In its final years of operations, after the last patients had departed, staff members in the building started to report some odd occurrences. In more recent years, the building has been the site of frequent excursion by vandals, trespassers, and curiosity-seekers, many of whom claim to have had their own weird encounters in the place.

But what macabre history is behind this now crumbling building? There are many tales to tell about this sad and forlorn place. It is a strange story filled with social reform, insanity, and yes, even ghosts.

Prior to 1900, mental health care barely existed. In those days, anyone suffering from a mental disorder was simply locked away from society in an asylum. Many of these hospitals were filthy places of confinement where patients were often left in straitjackets, locked in restraint chairs, or even placed in crates or cages if they were especially disturbed. Many of them spent every day in shackles and chains, and even the so-called "treatments" were barbaric.

Not surprisingly, such techniques brought little success, and patients rarely improved. In the days before psychiatry and medication, most mental patients spent their entire lives locked up inside asylums. Things began to change around 1905, when new laws were passed and psychiatry began to promote the fact that the mentally ill could actually be helped, not just locked away and forgotten.

One man who was a leader in this social reform was Dr. George A. Zeller, who became the first superintendent of the Bartonville asylum in 1898. He served in the Spanish-American War, worked as the Illinois State Alienist, and then served at Bartonville until his death in 1938. He is remembered today as one of the most influential mental health care providers in Illinois history.

Construction was completed at the Bartonville asylum in 1902 and opened under the leadership of Dr. Zeller. It was called the Peoria State Hospital, named for the closest large town. The hospital implemented what was called the "cottage system," and thirty-three different buildings were used to house patients. There was also a dorm for the nursing staff, a store, a powerhouse, and a domestic building with a laundry, bakery, and kitchen. Dr. Zeller also supervised the creation of cemeteries, where the bodies of unknown patients could be buried. The burial grounds eventually grew to include four different graveyards, although the oldest cemetery would mark the location of the first ghost story to ever be associated with the hospital.

And this is no mere rumor or folktale, but a documented account of a supernatural event. The teller of the tale was Dr. George A. Zeller himself!

Shortly after organizing the cemeteries for the hospital, Dr. Zeller put together a burial corps to deal with the disposal of deceased patients' bodies. The corps consisted of a staff member and several of the patients. Although the patients were disturbed, all of them were competent enough to take part in the digging of graves. Of all the gravediggers, the most unusual man, according to Dr. Zeller, was a fellow called "A. Bookbinder."

This man had been sent to the hospital from a county poorhouse. He had suffered a mental breakdown while working in a printing house in Chicago, and his illness had left him incapable of coherent speech. The officer who had taken him into custody had noted in his report that the man had been employed as "a bookbinder." A court clerk inadvertently listed this as the man's name, and he was sent to the hospital as A. Bookbinder.

Dr. Zeller described the man as being strong and healthy, although completely uncommunicative. He was attached to the burial corps, and soon, attendants realized that "Bookbinder" was especially suited to the work. Ordinarily, as the coffin was lowered at the end of the funeral, the gravedigger would stand back out of the way until the service ended. Nearly every patient at the hospital was unknown to the staff, so services were performed out of respect for the deceased and not because of some personal attachment. Because of this, everyone was surprised during the first internment attended by Bookbinder when he removed his cap and began to weep loudly for the dead man.

"The first few times he did this," Dr. Zeller wrote, "his emotion became contagious and there were many moist eyes at the graveside, but when at each succeeding burial, his feelings overcame him, it was realized that Old Book possessed a mania that manifested itself in uncontrollable grief."

It was soon learned that Bookbinder had no favorites among the dead. He would do the same thing at each service, and as his grief reached its peak, he would go and lean against an old elm tree that stood in the center of the cemetery and sob loudly.

Time passed, and eventually Bookbinder also passed away. Word spread among the employees, and because Book was well liked, everyone decided they would attend his funeral. Dr. Zeller wrote that more than a hundred uniformed nurses attended, along with male staff members and several hundred patients.

Dr. Zeller officiated at the service. Bookbinder's casket was placed on two crossbeams above his empty grave, and four men stood by to lower it into the ground at the end of the service. As the last hymn was sung, the men grabbed hold of the ropes. "The men stooped forward," Dr. Zeller wrote, "and with a powerful, muscular effort, prepared to lift the coffin, in order to permit the removal of the crossbeams and allow it to gently descend into the grave. At a given signal, they heaved away the ropes, and the next instant, all four lay on their backs. For the coffin, instead of offering resistance, bounded into the air like an eggshell, as if it were empty!"

Needless to say, the spectators were a little shocked at this turn of events, and the nurses were reported to have shrieked, half of them running away and the other half coming closer to the grave to see what was happening.

"In the midst of the commotion," Dr. Zeller continued, "a wailing voice was heard and every eye turned toward the Graveyard Elm from whence it emanated. Every man and woman stood transfixed, for there, just as had always been the case, stood Old Book, weeping and moaning with an earnestness that outrivaled anything he had ever shown before." Dr. Zeller was amazed at what he observed, but had no doubt that he was actually seeing it. "I, along with the other bystanders, stood transfixed at the sight of this apparition . . . it was broad daylight and there could be no deception."

After a few moments, the doctor summoned some men to remove the lid of the coffin, convinced that it must be empty and Old Book could not be inside of it. As soon as the lid was lifted, the wailing sound came to an end. Inside of the casket lay the body of Old Book, unquestionably dead. It was said that every eye in the cemetery looked upon the still corpse and then over to the elm tree in the center of the burial ground. The specter had vanished!

"It was awful, but it was real," Dr. Zeller concluded. "I saw it, one hundred nurses saw it, and three hundred spectators saw it." If it was anything other the ghost of Old Book, Dr. Zeller had no idea what it could have been.

A few days after the funeral, the graveyard elm began to wither. In spite of efforts to save it, the tree declined over the next year and then died. Later, after the dead limbs had dropped, workmen tried to remove the rest of the tree, but stopped after the first cut of the ax caused the tree to emanate what was said to be "an agonized, despairing cry of pain." After that, Dr. Zeller suggested that the tree be burned; however, as soon as the flames started around the tree base, the workers quickly put them out. They later told Dr. Zeller they had heard a sobbing and crying sound coming from it.

The tree eventually fell down in a storm, taking with it the lingering memories of a mournful man known as Bookbinder.

After Dr. Zeller's death, the hospital remained in use for many years, adding buildings, patients, and care facilities for children and tuberculosis patients. The asylum was finally closed down in 1972 and remained empty for a number of years before being sold at auction in 1980.

Even though the site is private property, it has not stopped vandals and would-be ghost hunters from going inside of the place. Many of these curiosity-seekers, drawn to the building because of its legends and ghosts, claim to have encountered some pretty frightening things here, from unexplained sounds to full-blown apparitions. Some might even say that many of the former patients are still around!

So, is the old hospital really haunted? Scores of people who have visited the place certainly think so. The reader must agree that the place certainly has the potential for a haunting, even without the story of A. Bookbinder and the graveyard elm. The atmosphere of the place alone is more than enough to justify the reports of apparitions and strange energy. The impressions of the past would certainly be strong in a building where mentally ill people were housed and where "psychic disturbances" would be common. There is also the matter of conscious spirits, as hospitals have long been places where the spirits of the dead are said to linger. Besides that, some would say that the hospital was the only home many of the patients knew, and they are going to stay where they were the most comfortable.

"The place is full of spirits" has been said on more than one occasion, and I wouldn't be surprised if this proclamation is right!

The House with No Square Corners

Near the tiny town of Bull Valley is perhaps one of the strangest houses in northern Illinois. It was originally located far off the beaten path and today remains secluded along a quiet and mostly deserted country highway. George and Sylvia Stickney built this English country house in the mid 1800s. They chose such an isolated place for the peace and quiet, as well as for their spiritualistic activities. Both of them were said to be accomplished mediums, and they planned to host parties and séances for their friends.

The house itself was very unusual in its design. It was two stories high, although the second floor was reserved for a ballroom that ran the entire length of the building. During the Civil War, the house also served as quarters for Federal soldiers and was home to the first piano in McHenry County. But this was not why the house gained its fame, or rather its notoriety.

As devout practitioners of Spiritualism, the Stickneys insisted on adding distinctive features into the design of the house. These features, they assured the architect, would assist them when holding séances and gatherings at the property. They specified that the house should have no square corners in it. Spirits, they explained, have a tendency to get stuck in these corners, which could have dire results.

According to legend, though, one corner of a room accidentally ended up with a 90-degree measurement. How this could have happened is unknown. Perhaps the architect either forgot or was unable to complete the room with anything but a right angle. This single corner would give rise to an eerie legend of the house.

The stories say that it was in this corner where George Stickney was discovered one day. He was slumped to the floor, dead from apparent heart failure, although no visible signs suggested a cause of death. Was he right about the square corners? Could an angry ghost, summoned by a séance, have been trapped in the corner?

After the death of her husband, Sylvia Stickney lived on in the house and gained considerable fame as a spirit medium. The upstairs ballroom was converted into a large séance chamber, and people came from far and wide to contact the spirits.

Time passed, and despite the séances and the mysterious death of George Stickney, no one considered the house to be haunted until the late 1970s. It was at this time that a real estate listing for the house was printed, which seemed to show a woman in a white gown pulling aside a curtain and peering out. The photographer who took the picture said that no one was in the house at the time.

The house eventually sold, and the next owners claimed to experience nothing unusual in the place. They stayed on for several years but moved out when their plans to restore the mansion didn't pan out. Their occupancy left nothing to suggest that they were bothered by ghosts, and apparently, neither are the owners today. The local police department uses a portion of the restored house as their headquarters and claims nothing out of the ordinary. The official word is that, while the house was badly treated by vandals, it is not, nor was it ever, haunted.

So, who knows? Some area residents dispute the final word from the authorities. They say that ghostly things have been going on in the Stickney Mansion for many years and continue to go on today, whether the local police officers want to admit it or not. What is the truth? No one seems to be able to say, and the ghosts, if there are any here, are certainly not talking!

Echoes from the Past at Vishnu Springs

Hidden away in a secluded valley along the Lamoine River in McDonough County is a secret place—a place long forgotten by the outside world. Once considered a magical valley, it was visited by those seeking peace, serenity, and the healing waters of the springs. Today, it is an abandoned village where no homes, streets, or residents remain. Only a once stately, three-story hotel remains here as testimony to days gone by.

But while Illinois history has forgotten Vishnu Springs, Vishnu Springs has not forgotten the events that once took place here. It lingers behind as a ghostly echo from the past.

The shady valley was always the place that attracted early pioneers of the region. They used the quiet spot as a place to picnic, and it was not long before many residents of nearby Colchester began to realize that the water in the valley was different from the drinking water found elsewhere. All that is remembered today is that the springwater was said to have a peculiar salt content, seven medicinal properties, and an especially appealing taste. People began coming from near and far to sample the water, hauling away jugs of it from the springs. Doctors allegedly sent their patients here on crutches, and they walked away without them.

By the 1880s, the owner of the property, Darius Hicks, began to realize its potential. Hicks came from a local wealthy family, and he and his brother managed the family land. It was on one of these sections of land that he became acquainted with the rich mineral springs that would become Vishnu. He was toiling in the fields one hot summer day and wandered into the shady valley for a drink of water. Almost immediately, he fell under the spell of the place. He later began marketing and selling the water.

He named the place Vishnu after reading about the 1861 discovery of Angkor, an abandoned city perfectly preserved for three hundred years by vegetation growing out of the Krishna River. Vishnu was a Hindu god whose earthly incarnation was the river that had covered Angkor.

By 1889, Hicks became quite aware of what the springs had to offer, but he also realized that he would reap the benefits of them at a price. Nearly three thousand people came to attend a camp meeting at Vishnu, trampling down an entire field of Hicks's corn and frightening a prize bull so badly that he disappeared. Hicks now had to choose whether to farm the land or develop it. Instead of farming, he chose to build a town. The first new building was the Capitol Hotel, which would offer rooms for those who came to the health resort. Hicks publicized the springs, and soon, land was purchased and other projects followed.

By the following spring, Vishnu had three stores, a restaurant, a livery stable and blacksmith, and a photo gallery. Hicks organized the "Vishnu Transfer Line" that made trips from Colchester to the new resort. For the cost of 75 cents, a passenger could be transported to Vishnu, have dinner, and then be transported back.

Although local newspapers reported that Vishnu was an idyllic "boomtown," there was an undercurrent of trouble at the springs.

Hicks evidently did not get along well with his developer, Charles K. Way, and there was talk of dividing the community into two parts. Way eventually developed land southeast of the hotel. The resort also became known for the sale and consumption of illegal alcohol (Colchester and the county were both dry at that time). Drinking on the grounds of the resort led to occasional fights.

Meanwhile, despite the drinking and violence, Hicks continued to develop the resort as a place of peace and healing. A new organ was installed in the hotel parlor, and the building boasted a number of other improvements, such as running water and an elevator to reach the third-floor ballroom. Amusements were added for the resort travelers, such as a real horse–powered carousel, and the lawn around the hotel was fitted with swings, hammocks, a croquet grounds, a picnic area, and a large pond that was dubbed "Lake Vishnu" and stocked with goldfish. Hicks also built a racetrack and established a park, both of which were not in the valley but on a nearby hill. He also promoted and arranged for cultural activities like dances, band concerts, and holiday celebrations.

While Hicks worked to create a viable community at the springs, his personal life was filled with problems. In 1889, Hicks had married for a second time, this time to Hattie Rush of Missouri, one of the many pilgrims who had traveled to Vishnu in search of healing waters. She had also been married before and had children of her own, including a twelve-year-old daughter named Maud. Hattie suffered from Bright's Disease and was plagued with heart trouble. She died in 1896 at the age of only forty.

Whether his marriage to Hattie had been happy or not, Hicks then went on to do something that would scandalize those in the region for some years to come—he married his stepdaughter. Maud became the third Mrs. Hicks in September 1897 in a private, civil ceremony at the McDonough County courthouse. She was only twenty years old at the time. Although the marriage was not actually incestuous, it was seen as improper, and Hicks was shunned by the more conservative members of the community. In 1898, Maud gave birth to a son, and in 1903, she gave her husband a daughter. In just two years, though, Maud would be dead, and a curse would settle over the struggling community of Vishnu Springs.

In 1903, two events occurred that led to the final decline of Vishnu. One warm summer day, the owner of the children's carousel was crushed to death when his shirt sleeve somehow became caught in the gears. When it stopped that day, it never ran again.

Later that same year, Maud Hicks gave birth to another daughter, but both she and the child died during the delivery. Maud's death was a tremendous shock to Darius Hicks. He certainly never dreamed that his wife, who was twenty-seven years younger than he was, would precede him to the grave. On the day following Maud's funeral, he took his young son and turned his back on Vishnu, never to return. But his troubles were not yet over.

After leaving Vishnu, Hicks bought a farm a short distance away and took up residence there. He hired a housekeeper named Nellie Darrah, a widow, who was needed to help care for Hicks's two young children. In the years that followed, Nellie became a mother figure to the children and became romantically involved with Hicks. By the winter of 1908, Nellie had become pregnant and confronted Hicks, demanding that he marry her. He refused, and she subsequently sought an abortion. The procedure did not go well and required that she be hospitalized.

While in the hospital, Nellie contacted Hicks and threatened to publicize their entire affair. Hicks never replied to her threats, but he did shoot himself in the head with a .32-caliber rifle. He died at the age of fifty-eight.

The death of Darius Hicks sounded a death knell for Vishnu Springs. He had been the main promoter of the town and had remained involved in the business of his hotel, even after moving away. Hicks's death sent the community into a decline from which it never recovered.

The hotel and the town, now under indifferent management, began to attract gamblers, thieves, and criminals. On one occasion, a huge quantity of counterfeit half-dollars, which looked like the real thing but were made from pewter, were seized here. There were other stories of lawbreakers captured at Vishnu, and legend has it that some of their loot remains hidden in the caves surrounding the valley.

The property was eventually sold and left to decay. By the 1920s, Vishnu was nothing more than a legend-haunted ghost town, abandoned and forgotten in the secluded valley. Vandals stole valuable hotel furnishings and broke out the windows of the buildings and the old hotel.

By the 1930s, the hotel had decayed into little more than a shell, and the owner, a local banker, lost all his property during the Depression. It seemed the "curse" that plagued Vishnu was continuing to wreak havoc.

In 1935, a restoration effort was started by Ira Post. He bought the hotel and 220 acres around it, restored the building, and hired a caretaker. He opened the former resort as a picnic grounds, and though it met with a limited amount of success, Vishnu would never again be a community. Post and his family lived at the hotel for weeks at a time, overseeing the work that was being done. He died in 1951, and while the hotel was occasionally rented in the years after, the grounds became overgrown and unkempt. Soon, it was once more completely abandoned.

In the early 1970s, Vishnu Springs saw life again as a sort of commune for a group of Western Illinois University graduates and their friends. They turned the hotel into their home and sacrificed their professional careers to live with nature. Earning enough money to pay the rent and the expensive winter heating bills, the group gardened and raised livestock to make ends meet, occasionally hosting music festivals and parties. They, too, eventually left, and Vishnu was once again deserted.

As the years have passed, the old hotel has continued to deteriorate, and today it is little more than a crumbling shadow of its former self. Despite the interest of local societies and historic groups, the valley remained private property until the death of the last member of the Post family. Since that time, the status of the land has remained in limbo, and the ultimate fate of Vishnu remains a mystery.

And perhaps it is this very mystery, as well as the site's isolation, that has been the source of the legends that have come to be told here. As the town fell into ruin and the houses collapsed and were covered with weeds and brush, those who ventured into Vishnu came away with strange and perplexing tales. The accounts spoke of a woman in black who roamed through the abandoned streets. Who this woman may have been is unknown, but she was said to vanish without a trace when approached. Visitors also told of sounds from Vishnu's past echoing into the present. They were the sounds of voices, laughter, and music, as if the glory days of Vishnu were still being enjoyed in a world just beyond our own.

And apparently, the sounds of everyday life continue here as well. One witness told me of visiting the hotel and hearing the sound of someone pounding on metal coming from outside. It would not be until I showed him an old map of Vishnu that he realized the sounds were coming from the direction of the old livery barn and blacksmith shop. No trace of this building remains today, and no hammers and anvils can be found among the ruins of Vishnu.

Is Vishnu Springs a haunted place? Perhaps not in the traditional sense, as aside from the legendary woman in black, there are no ghostly apparitions to be found wandering in the darkness. Nevertheless, how do we explain the eerie sounds that have been reported by several generations of visitors to this quiet place? Can they be anything but echoes of a time gone by?

So yes, Vishnu is haunted by the ghosts of the past, and it remains a part of Illinois history that most have forgotten. If you go there, be careful how you step in Vishnu and leave nothing of what you bring with you behind. Years ago, Ira Post's niece and daughter erected a sign at the entrance to Vishnu, and although the sign is now gone, the sentiment behind it remains.

The sign read in part: "Vishnu Springs was preserved as planned by Ira Post. The spring water of the wonderful world of nature is left to enjoy . . . the springs should be left as nature provided it. Take care of it all and then all will be benefited in the years to come. Ira Post died in 1951. The wishes expressed here were his. Help us to see that his wishes are carried out."

School Spirits at Channing Elementary

The Channing Memorial Elementary School was built in 1968 in Elgin. What should have been an ordinary construction project turned macabre when a number of skeletons that belonged to Elgin's earliest residents turned up during the excavation of the new school's basement. The construction crew quickly discovered that the site had once been the city's first cemetery—and that a number of the residents had been left behind.

Bluff City Cemetery was located on the same hill as the school from 1845 to 1945. In the 1940s, city planners decided to move the burial ground and replace it with an athletic field. This area was later turned into a park, and in the 1960s, the site was chosen for the location of Channing Elementary School. The remains from the cemetery had all been moved in the late 1940s, or so it was thought. Unfortunately, the early records had not been complete; quite a number of the graves were unmarked, and as it turned out, left behind in the move.

As construction began on the new school, workers made a gruesome discovery. Caskets and loose bones were uncovered, and horrified officials called for their immediate removal. Most don't believe, however, that all of the bodies have been removed, even after a second attempt. Rumors persist that the construction workers made only a half-hearted attempt at the job, and worse, were disrespectful of the remains. It was not uncommon for pranksters on the site to put bones into their buddy's lunchbox or for a man to go to his car at the end of the day to find a skeleton propped behind the wheel.

Ever since the school opened, some staff members and many of the children who attend here have come to believe that the disturbed dead beneath their feet do not rest in peace. And although the children's ghostly stories were dismissed in the past, as the years went by, teachers, parents, and staff members began to have their own unsettling encounters within the walls of the modern brick building. The presences that walk through the school are not hampered by doors, separate floors, or solid walls—and no one seems to be immune to their effect.

Reports have filtered out about an elevator that goes from floor to floor by itself, without ever being summoned by the call button, and of a huge wooden door that operates by a hydraulic device and yet manages to open and slam shut under its own power. Staff and visitors also tell of hearing footsteps pounding across the roof. One night custodian, Ricky Bell, even called the police after hearing these sounds. When officers came to investigate, they found no one in (or on) the building.

The building's chief custodian, Joe Gutierrez, once reported that he heard his name being called when he was alone on the third floor, and he and others have also reported the sounds of laughter coming from empty classrooms. On the occasion that he heard his name being called, he went to investigate but found nothing from the direction of the voice. However, he then heard a loud sound coming from the room that he had been working in and reentered it to find that a ceiling panel he had moved was now shifted back into its original position. There had been no one else in the room! Eerie laughter has plagued many of the night workers in the school, who have also reported seeing shadowy figures in the hallways. One custodian was so frightened by the laughter he heard one night that he locked himself in the principal's office and called Gutierrez at home, actually weeping over the telephone and begging him to come back to the school and help him.

A former principal named Clark White, along with several of the teachers, also reported hearing what seemed to be scratching and clawing coming from inside the walls of the school. Some dismiss this as being nothing more than "squirrels in the wall," but others are not so sure. The sheer number of reports, dating back more than three decades, seems to give some credibility to the idea that something strange is going on at Channing Elementary. What that "something" might be remains to be seen, but one thing is sure—few people want to stay around there at night to find out.

The Ghost of Orval Cobb

Knox College, located in Galesburg, has a long history on the Illinois prairie. It was founded in 1837 as a manual arts college and has a place in state history as one of the only physical locations where debates between Abraham Lincoln and Stephen Douglas took place. The historic debates occurred in 1858 at the Old Main on Knox's campus. A platform was constructed outside of two windows of the building and the candidates were forced to crawl out of them to appear before the crowd below.

With a history that dates back so many years, Knox College is bound to have its share of macabre stories. One such story tells of a student who committed suicide by hanging himself outside of a window several years ago. Students and passersby allowed the boy to hang there all night long, assuming that the dangling figure was merely an effigy in the spirit of the Halloween season. They discovered the next morning they were wrong. There are also stories of haunted dorm rooms, sorority houses, and apartments, but one story of Knox College stands out among the rest.

This secret story of the college comes from a house located just off campus. The house has been in the Godsil family for many years, and I first learned about their resident ghost in the mid 1990s. I had the opportunity to visit with them soon after, and this large Catholic family welcomed me into their home. Anyone who has ever wondered how it would be possible to make a ghost a part of the family needs only to meet the Godsil family to understand. This happy, busy, and loving family had enough room for ten children, more than two dozen grandchildren, a great-grandchild—and one very hard-to-miss ghost.

The story of Orval Cobb, the resident ghost, began in the house in 1943, but the Godsil family first moved into the house on December 31, 1964. The dwelling had previously been used as an apartment house, so with its many rooms, it was just right for the large family to occupy. Shortly after they took up residence, they began to notice they were not in the house alone. The older children seemed to notice things first, and they planned to keep the ghostly activity a secret from their younger siblings.

But before long, everyone had a story to tell, even their father, who had been skeptical about anything strange going on for some time. One afternoon, while he was in the house alone, he went down to the basement to do some work. He heard the sound of someone walking through the house above his head, and assuming one of the kids had come home, he went upstairs to look. He found that no one else was there. Thinking the sound must have just been the old house settling, he went back downstairs. The footsteps soon started again. He searched the house once more and found no one. Almost against his will, he was now a believer.

The footsteps weren't the only thing the family noticed, but they were the most frequent. They described them as "heavy," and they heard them tromping around the house on dozens of occasions. They traveled through the hallway, into the rooms, up and down the stairs, and just about everywhere else in the house.

They also sensed the presence of someone standing inside the rooms on many occasions and had the feeling that someone might be just over their shoulder. The girls in the family also reported never feeling alone while taking a shower, as if they had caught the interest of a healthy young man. The ghost also had the habit of knocking on doors and doing other things to get attention, such as causing items to disappear and then later putting them in strange places. Several members of the family also caught glimpses of a shadowy figure around corners, in reflections, just past doorways, and out of the corner of the eye. He was frequently seen in a small parlor located just off the dining room.

The ghost never did anything destructive or unfriendly to anyone in the house, and in fact, seemed to like the family and enjoyed being part of the hustle and bustle of daily life with the large group. But sometimes he was still frightening. This was the main reason that the Godsils chose to try and discover just who the ghost in the house might be—and why he was haunting their house on West Street.

They began by searching the old files of the library and the archives of the college, following one single lead. Someone told them that a Knox student had died at the house many years ago. The boy's name had been Orval Cobb, and he had been a freshman at Knox College in 1943. He was from St. Charles, Illinois, and most high school friends remembered him as a bright, fun-loving youth who had been an honor student and well-liked by his classmates.

Unfortunately, when Orval came to Knox, he enrolled as a chemistry major and soon found that he was in over his head. His grades plunged and despair began to set in. He felt overwhelmed by his classes, and some say he may have feared being drafted into the military, too.

Finally, on the eve of a big chemistry test, Orval committed suicide, leaving a poem and a letter behind, detailing why he felt that he was a failure and had no reason to go on. Ironically, Orval stole a mixture of potassium cyanide from the chemistry lab with which to do the deed. His body was discovered by his roommate, William Bartlett, who told the authorities that he had come into his room on Monday night and seen Orval in bed, apparently sleeping. He knew that his friend had a test the next day, so he assumed that he had been up late studying and didn't try wake him up until about an hour before class on Tuesday morning. When he tried to wake his friend, he realized that Orval had been dead for many hours.

The coroner stated that traces of poison were found in a test tube beside Orval's bed. He had dissolved a cyanide tablet in water and then had swallowed the mixture. The poison stopped his heart immediately. On his desk, propped up against a reading lamp, was the tragic letter he had written to his parents:

Dear Mom and Dad,

I hope that you will not take this to heart. I am trying to save you much later heartbreak. I can see now that I will never be a son to be proud of. I am going to be just another mediocre person. Knowing what that means, I can't take the sadness it will cause.

Please understand. You have both done so much for me that I can never repay you the way I am; never to my own satisfaction. To make you proud of me has been my ambition.

I am failing. To fail is something that I cannot swallow. I could not go on being a failure and knowing how it would hurt you both. This end is the best for us all. My love to you both. May your remaining years be pleasant and cheerful without me. A failure never brings happiness to anyone. My love to Vi, Min and the Millers. All my love to the dearest people on earth.

Orv

In addition to the letter, Orval also left behind a morbid poem by Charles Hanson Towne entitled "Of One Self-Slain." He also left two brief notes to his roommates telling them of his determination to take his own life and thanking them for the friendship they had always shown him. Orval died in the front upstairs room of the house, later used as a bedroom by the Godsil family.

After learning all of this, the Godsils were sure they had discovered the identity of the ghost, and it appeared they were right. The haunting continued to go on for many years, and the family came to accept Orval as their own, even visiting his former home, and his grave, in St. Charles. They truly made this ghost a welcome member of the family.

You have to admit, it is ironic the way that it has all turned out. Orval Cobb took his own life because he believed that he was a failure and an outsider, and because he felt that his life was not worth living. It wasn't until he was dead for more than fifty years that he seemed to finally find his place.

The Body on the Railroad Tracks

Until the minute the coroner arrived on the scene, the engineer of the Joliet & Eastern freight train was sure that he had killed the woman who was sprawled in a tangled, bloody heap alongside the railroad tracks. His locomotive had struck her as it cut through the darkness underneath a viaduct a half mile north of Wayne. The time was 8:22 P.M. on Friday, September 26, 1913.

The story of this mysterious woman would create a sensation in northern Illinois and would involve dance halls, ex-husbands, and a prison convict before all was said and done. It would also become a piece of a puzzle that involved as many as two dozen murdered women—and a lingering ghost.

Du Page County Coroner Hopf and Sheriff Kuhn were soon on the scene. After Hopf had examined the body, he made an announcement that, although reassuring to the train's engineer, was ominous to the sheriff. The woman had been dead for some time before the train had stuck her. She had been shot in the head and then placed on the tracks to make it look like an accident.

Even in the light of the investigator's lanterns, and after being struck by the locomotive, the features of the dead woman gave evidence that she had been more than ordinarily attractive. She had auburn hair and looked to be about thirty-five years old. She wore a smart blue suit, white gloves, and expensive red shoes. Near the body was a red purse that Kuhn searched to see if he could find any clue to her identity. It contained a handkerchief, face powder, a comb, and a visiting card bearing the name "Mildred Allison." A small change purse held a few coins but no bills.

The fact that Mildred Allison was the woman's name seemed to be corroborated by the gold bracelet on her left wrist. It bore the inscription "W.H.A. to M.A." Another discovery on the rail bed, however, offered conflicting information. The sheriff found a letter, torn into several pieces, which the investigators were able to reconstruct well enough to learn that the salutation read, "Dear Mrs. Rexroat." Aside from its proximity to the body, there was nothing to suggest that the letter was connected to the victim. Nevertheless, the police collected the fragments for further study.

The body was taken to the morgue, and then Sheriff Kuhn began to make local inquiries about the victim. Newspaper reporters from Chicago, about thirty miles to the east, soon got wind of the story, and details began appearing in their daily publications. By mid-morning of the following day, the police were contacted by the agent at the Wayne station of the Aurora, Elgin & Chicago interurban electric railroad. He was certain he had seen the dead woman before.

The rail agent told the police that on the night of September 26, the woman, carrying a small rattan suitcase, had gotten off the 7:25 P.M. train from Chicago. She was accompanied by a man who the agent described as wearing glasses, of medium height, clean-shaven, with wavy hair, and carefully dressed. The two had left the Elgin station and headed toward the nearby tracks of the Joliet & Eastern. An hour later, the man returned, alone. He was now carrying the rattan suitcase. Before he boarded the 8:30 Chicago-bound Elgin train, he presented a return ticket to Chicago for a refund.

When the sheriff had completed the restoration of the letter fragments, he realized that, if connected to the victim, the note indicated her occupation. The message, dated September 23 and signed by John Zook, appeared to be a reply to Mrs. Rexroat concerning the rental of a hall for dance classes. Zook had informed his correspondent that the hall could be engaged for $10 per night, including light, heat, and janitor service. The envelope in which the letter was mailed could not be found, and Zook's address was not on the single sheet of reconstructed paper.

While Kuhn was pondering the whereabouts of Zook—for there was no one by that name in the area around Wayne—a report came in that strengthened the supposition that the victim had been a dancer, and in turn, the likely recipient of the letter. Early that morning, a trackwalker for the Elgin rail line stumbled across a pink dancing gown and a pair of pink slippers. The garments, which were in fresh condition, were of the exact size of the victim. They had been found on the right side of the rail bed, suggesting they had been tossed from a Chicago-bound train.

At noon, John J. Halpin, the Chicago Chief of Detectives, telephoned Kuhn and told him that a man named William H. Allison had just come into headquarters and stated that he was afraid the dead woman might be his former wife. Allison told Halpin that he had once given her a bracelet that matched the description of the one the dead woman was wearing. Allison asked if the body could be moved to Chicago so that he could take charge of the funeral arrangements.

Kuhn agreed, but he told Halpin that he was taking the first train to Chicago to talk with Allison himself. Halpin set up an interview room, where William Allison tearfully identified the dead woman as his former wife, Mildred. He told a sad story of their marriage. The two had gotten married seventeen years before, when Mildred was eighteen years old. For some time, they got along well, but several years before, Mildred had started frequenting dance halls, cafés, and other nightspots. This eventually brought an end to their marriage. They lived apart for months, and then, in May 1913, they divorced. Allison claimed that he had had no contact with Mildred since that time and only knew that she had been living in the home of friends, Mr. and Mrs. Victor Johnson, on Eggleston Avenue in Chicago. He was also aware that she had become a dance teacher.

As for the puzzling salutation of "Mrs. Rexroat" and the identity of Zook, Allison declared that he was completely in the dark. He also knew of no one who might have any reason to kill his ex-wife, although, as the officers who heard the story also realized, there had been a number of men in her life.

The Rexroat angle of the story was solved after a visit to the Johnson house. Here, Kuhn and Halpin interviewed Mrs. Johnson, who confirmed Mildred's residence with the family and provided additional information about Mildred's life, including the fact that William Allison had not been her last husband. Since their divorce, she had married a farmer from Macomb named Everett Rexroat. The month before, however, Mildred had left her second husband and come to live with the Johnsons. At present, she had taken a job as a dance instructor at the Club Felicia, in the Chicago Loop.

The officers obtained a description of Everett Rexroat from Mrs. Johnson and realized that, in general, it fit the man who had been seen with Mildred in Wayne. The only exception was that Rexroat did not wear eyeglasses.

Mrs. Johnson described the last time she had seen her friend. "Mildred left the house late yesterday afternoon. Earlier, she got a phone call. The connection was bad and she became impatient. She handed the phone to me and said, 'See if you can figure out what he's talking about.' I took the call. It was a man who wanted Mildred to meet him in time to catch the 6:28 to Wayne, where he had a dancing class for her all arranged. No, he didn't tell me his name, although, of course, Mildred seemed to know who it was."

Mrs. Johnson added that she did not know a John Zook, but she did recall Mildred leaving the house the day before carrying a rattan suitcase. She also remembered her wearing a large diamond ring that had been a gift from Everett Rexroat. The ring had not been found with her body. This piece of information, combined with the fact that no money had been found in her purse, suggested that Mildred had been killed during a robbery. Apparently, the police thought, the killer had lured her to a deserted spot on the railroad tracks under the pretext of having arranged a dance class in Wayne.

Kuhn and Halpin left the Johnson home and returned to police headquarters, where they immediately put a call through to the sheriff's office in McDonough County, of which Macomb—about two hundred miles southwest of Chicago—was the county seat. They asked that Rexroat be informed of his wife's death and, if he was in Macomb, that he be escorted to Chicago.

Then, Kuhn and Halpin went to Club Felicia. The nightspot, a publicly patronized dance hall, was well into the swing of its evening activity. The owner acknowledged Mildred's recent employment there but stated that he didn't know her very well and knew nothing of her habits, friends, or outside activities. He did recall, though, that one man who had been in lately seemed to monopolize all of her time. The owner didn't know his name but described him as being a "natty dresser," having wavy hair, and wearing eyeglasses.

It was almost the exact same description of the mysterious man who had been seen by the railroad agent on the night that Mildred had been killed.

On the afternoon of Sunday, September 28, Everett Rexroat arrived in Chicago. When asked to identify the body of his wife, he complied, but when he did so, he showed little emotion. Halpin noticed his lack of grief and asked him about it.

Rexroat replied, "You think it odd? Well, maybe you'd change your mind if you knew what our life together was like."

He explained that he had met Mildred in October 1912, when he came to Chicago to study the garage business. He fell in love with her and, soon after the New Year, asked her to marry him. He was shocked when she told him that she was already married. She explained that she had not been living with her husband, however, and agreed to seek a divorce. After she obtained it, they were married on May 26 in Crown Point, Indiana. Until July 31, they had lived in Chicago, but then Rexroat's father wrote to him and told him that help was needed on the family farm. He asked that Rexroat and his new wife come back to live in Macomb. Farm life appalled Mildred, and soon after they arrived, she made it very clear that she missed the lights of Chicago. She couldn't wait to get back to them, she often told her husband.

The incident that finally precipitated her departure involved an itinerant photographer who stopped by the farm to take pictures. After he left, Mildred expressed great admiration for him. The next day, August 26, she left Macomb and never returned. Rexroat stated that he had heard nothing from her since that time, although he did receive a letter from a man who represented himself as a Chicago attorney, who declared that Mildred was in a maternity hospital and demanded money for her care. Rexroat had ignored the letter, and later destroyed it, recognizing it as an attempt to perpetrate a fraud.

Kuhn asked him if the name "Zook" meant anything to him, and Rexroat immediately recognized it. "He lives in Bushnell, fifteen miles from Macomb, and owns a lot of real estate, including a hall which he rents out. Mildred met him while she was living on the farm and thought, I guess, the hall would be a good place to give dance lessons," he said.

Rexroat admitted giving Mildred the diamond ring and told Halpin that he had paid $350 for it. Halpin asked him where he had been on the night of his wife's murder, and he said that he had been playing cards with several friends, whom he named, in Macomb.

Halpin asked if he had been around the Club Felicia lately, but Rexroat claimed that he had never heard of the place. When it was explained that his wife had been working there, he seemed puzzled. He said, "When she left Macomb, she told me that she was going back to work at Sans Souci Park. That's where I first met her."

Halpin started two inquiries in McDonough County through its local officers; first, to look into Rexroat's alibi, and next, to talk with John Zook. Both of these tasks turned out to be unnecessary after Halpin and Kuhn paid a visit to Sans Souci Park. They learned that

Mildred had worked in the dance hall during the 1912 season and had returned for the last few days of August 1913. On these last occasions, she had often been accompanied by a wavy-haired man who wore eyeglasses. She had introduced him to several of the other girls who worked there.

Halpin asked one of the dancers, "What was his name?"

"Henry Spencer," she replied.

Ironically, Detective Halpin knew exactly who Henry Spencer was, and in fact, the man had come to him just a few weeks before looking for help in finding a job. Spencer was on parole from Joliet Prison for robbery, and Halpin assisted him in finding some employment, but the ex-convict didn't last at the position for long.

With this new information, Halpin and Kuhn rushed back to police headquarters and obtained Spencer's file. The man had been in and out of Illinois jails since his youth, and a frequently recurring charge was for molestation of women and fraud. Within hours, those who had seen Mildred's companion at Club Felicia, Sans Souci Park, and the Wayne train station positively identified Spencer's photograph as the man they had seen.

Now that the investigators knew the identity of the man last seen with Mildred, they had to find him. In Spencer's file, it noted that he had lived for a time with a woman who occupied an apartment on Michigan Avenue, so Halpin and Kuhn called on her. They found her to be surprisingly cooperative, but quickly understood why after she went on for several minutes about Spencer's faithless ways and the inconsiderate way in which he treated her. Hell hath no fury, the investigators knew, like a woman scorned.

She reported that she had last seen Spencer the previous Friday night, when he had been very anxious and nervous. She recalled that he had come to her apartment with a small rattan suitcase from which, in her presence, he had removed a single shell from a revolver and thrown it out the window.

Halpin, now certain that Spencer was the killer, ordered the woman to say nothing of their visit and set up a twenty-four-hour-a-day detail to keep watch on the apartment. For six days, this surveillance yielded nothing; but then, on Saturday, October 4, Spencer was arrested as he walked into his girlfriend's building.

At police headquarters, he first denied any knowledge of Mildred Allison and claimed he knew nothing about her death. When he realized the strength of the case against him, though, he changed his story and offered a full confession—and then some.

According to Spencer, he had met Mildred at Sans Souci Park. A relationship developed as the two of them began telling each other their troubles, although Spencer said he always thought of Mildred as "easy pickings." He told the investigators, "The day I killed her, she met me at the Aurora & Elgin station. We bought tickets to Wayne, and on the way out, we talked about our love affair. We were to be married. After I killed her, I caught a train back to Chicago and threw her dancing clothes out the window. I kept the suitcase and gave the ring to another girl."

Spencer freely admitted that he had murdered Mildred Allison, but he then went on to shock the detectives by telling them that he had also killed two dozen other women in Illinois and the Midwest! It was subsequently proven that much of this "confession" was sheer imagination, but it was also probable that he told the truth in describing his responsibility for at least six of these murders.

One consistent thread ran through his revelations: an almost maniacal hatred of women. He told Detective Halpin, "Sometimes you can trust a living man—never a living woman. I hate them all—all of them. It seems as if I could look into their lying little brains and watch them scheming against me. So, I pat them on the cheek, call them sweet names—and kill them."

Although prosecutors had a number of charges for which to try Spencer, they chose his last, and perhaps his most cold-blooded: the murder of Mildred Allison Rexroat. On November 14, 1913, in the Du Page County courthouse at Wheaton, Henry Spencer was found guilty and sentenced to hang. The court's pronouncement was carried out on July 31, 1914.

The hanging of Henry Spencer should have brought an end to this sensational case from northern Illinois' past, but unfortunately, it did not. According to stories and sightings that have occurred over the course of almost the last century, the ghost of Mildred Allison has never rested in peace. For many years, railroad engineers, brakemen, and other employees claimed that they often glimpsed the image of a woman standing alongside the railroad tracks about a half mile from Wayne, at the exact spot where Mildred's body was found. She was often spotted looking forlornly at the train as it passed by. Often, the crew would not realize there was something not quite right about the woman until the train had passed—and the auburn-haired beauty had simply disappeared.

One night in the summer of 1938, a locomotive engineer actually stopped the train because he thought he saw a woman lying across the tracks near the old viaduct outside of Wayne. He brought the train to a halt, and crew members checked the tracks, but could find nothing. The engineer was sure about what he had seen. He told his fellow employees, "She was wearing a white dress and was lying across the road bed. I was sure that we were going to run over her!" The engineer had no knowledge that a murder had occurred nearby and knew nothing of the story of Mildred Allison.

In recent times, reports of Mildred's lingering ghost have been few, perhaps because of the decline of the railroad, which was just about the only thing that brought people to this lonely stretch of countryside. We have to wonder if she lingers here still. Does she still walk along the railroad tracks, lost and confused over a life destroyed so many years ago? Perhaps she does, and should you ever journey out along this largely forgotten rail line, have a kind thought for this tortured soul and remember her the way she used to be.

The Macomb Poltergeist

The word "poltergeist" actually means "noisy ghost" when translated from German, and for many years, researchers believed that these noisy ghosts were causing the phenomena reported in cases of a violent and destructive nature. The variety of activity connected with poltergeist cases includes knocking and pounding sounds, disturbance of stationary objects, doors slamming shut, and usually violent, physical actions by sometimes heavy objects. Despite what some believe, many cases like this have nothing to do with ghosts.

The most widely accepted theory in many "poltergeist-like" cases is that the activity is not caused by a ghost, but by a person in the household. This person is usually an adolescent girl who is troubled emotionally. It is thought that she is unconsciously manipulating the items in the house by "psychokinesis," the power to move things using energy generated in the mind. It is unknown why this ability seems to appear in females around the age of puberty, but it has been documented to occur. Most of these disturbances are short-lived because the conditions that cause them to occur often pass quickly. The living person, or "agent" as he or she is called, subconsciously vents their repressed anger or frustration in ways that science has yet to explain.

But not all poltergeist cases involve the mere movement of objects. In some cases, the bizarre energy that is expended comes in other forms—such as the creation of fire.

Over the years, I have become acquainted with a number of both professional and volunteer firemen, who explain that they always try to be certain a fire is totally extinguished before leaving the scene. The image of a department can be badly tarnished if its men have to return to a scene because they missed some smoldering spot that causes the building to burst back into flames. For just this reason, there are a few cases when firefighters have been forced to return to a scene a second time, but rarely do they have to come back a third or fourth time. In these latter cases, the fires have almost always been in warehouses and factories where combustible materials were present and almost never in a private home.

But some fires are different. They obey a different set of physical laws that we are only beginning to comprehend. The origin of such fires is not only bizarre—it's also terrifying.

One of the most famous fire-starter cases in American history took place in Illinois in 1948, galvanizing the residents of the small town of Macomb. The case became so well known that it appeared in almost every newspaper in the country, often on the front page. The case of the "Macomb Poltergeist" created a mystery that remains unsolved to this day.

In the summer of 1948, a disturbed teenager named Wanet McNeill was forced to live with her father after her parents' bitter divorce. The girl and her father moved to a farm that belonged to an uncle, Charles Willey, located just south of town. The situation with her father and mother had plunged Wanet into a deep depression. She had been uprooted from her home, school, and friends, and she didn't understand what had occurred between her parents in the divorce. She was very unhappy about being forced to live on the farm, which was very rural compared with her former home in Bloomington, and her emotions were running very high. Soon, those emotions took a dangerous turn, and it is believed that in the weeks following her arrival, Wanet somehow managed to start fires all over her uncle's farm. She didn't use a box of matches and oily rags—instead, the fires seemed to be caused by a force from Wanet's mind. She had no idea that she was causing the phenomenon to take place. The kinetic energy in her body inexplicably caused an eruption of power that ignited combustible material all over the house and property.

The mysterious fires began on August 7. The farm where the events took place was located about twelve miles outside of Macomb. The residents of the farm included Charles Willey, his wife, his brother-in-law (Wanet's father), Arthur McNeil, and McNeil's two children, Arthur Jr., 8, and Wanet, who had recently turned 13. As mentioned, McNeil and his wife had recently divorced, and contrary to the standard of the day, he had received custody of the children. His former wife was living in Bloomington, where Wanet wanted to be. There is no information available as to what had caused the marriage to end or what may have occurred that would have given McNeil custody of the children. Whatever the situation had been, it had apparently been a volatile one that caused a horrible family situation, which the McNeils brought with them to Macomb.

The first fire began not as a blaze but as a small brown spot that appeared on the wallpaper in the living room of the Willey farmhouse. That first spot was followed by another and then another. The spots would appear, spread out several inches as they smoldered, and then, when the spots became hot enough, they would burst into flames. The brown spots occurred day after day, leaving the family confused and befuddled. They searched for some cause for the fires, thinking that perhaps wiring in the walls was going bad, but they could find no reason behind them. Willey called on several of his neighbors to investigate, but they were as mystified as he was. Many of them stayed on the property, however, crowding into the house and even sleeping on the floor in an attempt to help keep watch over the situation. Pans and buckets were filled with water and placed all over the house, and each time one of the small fires broke out, it was quickly doused.

In spite of this, fires materialized right in front of the startled witnesses. As word spread, more people came to see what was going on and offer assistance if possible. Volunteers stood by with hoses and with buckets of water to put out the blazes. They were quick to extinguish them, but no one could come up with a reason as to why they were occurring at all. The fire chief from Macomb, Fred Wilson, was called in to investigate. He was just as perplexed as everyone else, but he did have some ideas that he believed could help the situation. Wilson directed the family to strip the wallpaper from every wall in the house. Since the brown spots were burning on the wallpaper, he surmised that perhaps it was something in the paper or the glue that held it in place that might be causing the fires to appear. The paper was quickly torn down, but then dozens of witnesses, including Chief Wilson, watched as the anomalous brown spots appeared on the bare plaster and again burst into flames. And then, a new development occurred as small fires began to appear on the ceiling as well.

"The whole thing is so screwy and fantastic that I'm almost ashamed to talk about it," Wilson said. "Yet we have the word of at least a dozen reputable witnesses that say they saw mysterious brown spots smolder suddenly on the walls and ceilings of the home and then burst into flames."

In the days that followed, fires also appeared outside of the house on the front porch. Curtains were ignited in several of the rooms, an ironing board burst into flame, and a cloth that was lying on a bed burned so hot that it turned into ash. In a bizarre turn, the bed beneath the scorched cloth was untouched. According to witnesses, the quilt that covered the bed was not even warm. Later on, the bed itself was completely engulfed by flames—but the floor beneath it, as well as a nearby rug, was not burned at all.

Chief Wilson was still convinced that the wallpaper in the house was somehow to blame for the fires. He had never seen anything like what was happening on the Willey farm before, and this small-town firefighter was searching for some sort of explanation that made sense. He sent a sample of the paper to the National Fire Underwriters Laboratory, but they reported that the wallpaper had been coated only with flour paste, which was a flame retardant, and that no flammable compound was present in the material. They had no explanation for what could be causing the fires in the house.

Because of the damage being done in the house, Charles Willey (understandably) contacted his insurance company. After receiving the report, the company immediately sent investigators to the farm, looking for any evidence that Willey, or a member of the family, was starting the fires in an attempt to commit fraud. They could find nothing to suggest that the fires were caused by arson and could provide no explanation for the blazes.

The insurance investigators were not alone. Chief Wilson contacted Deputy State Fire Marshal John Burgard, who then came to the Willey farm. He was also confused by the strange events. "Nobody has ever heard of anything like this," he announced to the press, "but I saw it with my own eyes."

In the week that followed, more than two hundred fires broke out at the house, an average of nearly thirty each day. Finally, on Saturday, August 14, one of the blazes raged out of control, and before the Macomb Fire Department could be summoned with trucks, the entire Willey farmhouse was consumed. Charles Willey drove posts into the ground and made a tent shelter for he and his wife, while McNeil and the children moved into the garage. The next day, while the Willeys were milking cows in the barnyard, the barn burst into flames and destroyed the building. Willey, already distraught, was now shattered. He had only $1,000 insurance on the house and $400 on the barn. Neither policy would come close to replacing the buildings. To make matters worse, at this point, the insurance company was still unwilling to pay even those small amounts. Their investigators were still perplexed about the cause of the fires but believed that further investigations might reveal the source.

Two days later, on Tuesday, several fires broke out on the walls of the milk house, which was being used as a kitchen and dining room for the family. On Thursday morning, there were two more fires; in another incident, a box filled with newspapers was found burning in the chicken house. A few minutes later, Mrs. Willey opened a cupboard door in the milk house and discovered more newspapers smoldering on a shelf inside. There had been no one else in the building, and the cabinet had not been opened. There was no logical reason for the newspapers to have caught fire.

Later that day, at about 6:00 P.M., the farm's second barn caught fire. The blaze burned so hot that the entire building was destroyed in less than a half hour. Firefighters who arrived on the scene were unable to get close to the inferno. A company that sold fire extinguishers was on hand with equipment, but it did little good. An employee of the company stated that "it was the most intense heat that I've ever felt."

Only six small outhouses remained on the farm, so the family escaped to a nearby vacant house. Regardless, the fires continued. The United States Air Force even got involved in the mystery. They suggested that the fires could be caused by some sort of directed radiation, presumably from the Russians, but could offer no further assistance. Lewis Gust, the chief technician at Wright Field, Ohio, sent an expert to the farm to test for "very high frequencies and short waves." He thought the fires might be related to several unsolved airplane fires in which radiation was suspected of playing a part. The Russians were believed to be the culprits. "We can't afford to take any chances," he told reporters. "We must test anything, even if it sounds a bit far-fetched. Suppose you had material that could be ignited by radio and wanted to test it for sabotage value. Wouldn't you pick some out-of-the-way place like the Willey farm to make the test?"

Gust explained that scientists believed that powerful, high-frequency—or extremely short—radio waves could cause fires to start. For example, radar waves set off photographic flash bulbs inside of airplanes that were in flight. An interview with an unnamed scientist in Chicago confirmed these theories and agreed that radioactivity or radio waves could cause "such disturbances," but he added that it was "highly unlikely because there had been no other reactions in the area." If Russian spies were shooting radio waves at the Willey farm, it would have been impossible, the scientist noted, to direct them in such a way that no other homes or farms near Macomb would be affected.

By the end of the following week, the farm was swarming with spectators, curiosity-seekers, official and self-appointed investigators, and reporters. More than a thousand people came to the farm on August 22 alone! Theorists and curiosity-seekers posed their own theories and explanations. They ran the gamut from fly spray to radio waves, underground gas pockets, flying saucers, and more. The authorities had a more down-to-earth explanation in mind. They suspected arson. They realized that they could not solve the riddle as to how fires could appear before the eyes of reliable witnesses, but things were getting out of hand on the Willey farm. An explanation needed to be discovered, and quickly.

Two investigators noted that there seemed to be a difference between the fires in the house and the later blazes. Professor John J. Ahern, from the Illinois Institute of Technology, suggested that combustible gases inside of the walls might have caused the house fires, while those fires that destroyed the barns seemed to spring from "other causes." State Fire Marshal John Craig said that the burning of the house "looked like an accident" but that the barn fires might have been "touched off by an arsonist." This was enough for some of the officials involved. They overlooked the mysterious nature of the fires and heard only the fact that some of the fires might have been started by arson. There was no conclusive evidence of this, but the case had to be closed as soon as possible.

On August 30, the mystery was publicly announced "solved." The arsonist, according to officials, was Wanet McNeil, the slight, red-haired niece of Charles Willey. They claimed that she was starting the fires with kitchen matches when no one was looking, ignoring the witness reports of fires that sprang up from nowhere, including on the ceiling. Apparently, this little girl possessed some pretty amazing skills, along with a seemingly endless supply of matches.

According to Deputy Fire Marshal Burgard, there had been a minor fire at the farmhouse where the family had moved after the other buildings had been destroyed. He had placed a box of matches in a certain position, and the box had been moved. Wanet was nearby—but she was never seen touching the box or holding a match. This didn't matter, however. Burgard and State Attorney Keith Scott had taken Wanet aside for an hour's worth of "intense questioning." After that, she had allegedly confessed. She stated that she was unhappy, didn't like the farm, wanted to see her mother, and most telling, that she didn't have pretty clothes. The mystery was solved! This was in spite of the fact that witnesses to the fires had seen them appear on walls, floors, and furniture, all when Wanet was not even in the room.

This explanation pleased the authorities, but not all of the reporters who were present seemed convinced. The hundreds of paranormal investigators who have examined the case over the years have not been reassured either. One columnist from a Peoria newspaper, who had covered the case from the beginning, stated quite frankly that he did not believe the so-called "confession." Neither did noted researcher of the unexplained Vincent Gaddis, who wrote about the case. He was convinced the case was a perfect example of poltergeist phenomena.

He noted that many poltergeist cases made it necessary to figuratively—and sometimes actually—slap little girls into "confession." In many cases, there is no doubt about the paranormal nature of these manifestations, and yet there is a general prejudice against real mystery. Perhaps it is a fear of the unknown that demands explanation. And so, no matter how incredible the phenomenon, no matter how impossible it would be for a person to produce the phenomenon by trickery, we have "confessions." The agent—not realizing consciously that she is causing the phenomenon—seems at times to have a sense of guilt, or perhaps even some small awareness, of her part in the matter. Such agents can be pressured into a confession, despite the fact that the events could not have been caused by normal means.

Irritated investigators and worried parents occasionally use force to get confessions, and the history of poltergeist manifestations is riddled with examples of boys being whipped and girls slapped. In other cases, the agent may be told to either reproduce the phenomenon by paranormal means or confess that it was fraudulent. Frantic, some may resort to crude trickery, only to be caught, or may simply make a false confession. According to experts, these false confessions occur much more commonly than people outside the field of psychology realize. Dr. Ian Stevenson, from the University of Virginia School of Medicine, stated that "a vague impression of guilt about something often suffices to motivate a false confession. Innocent persons have frequently confessed to serious crimes like murder, sometimes implicating innocent persons as accomplices . . ."

For just this reason, confessions in poltergeist cases are often worthless unless they can include an explanation that is reasonable, practical, and fits the known facts. In the case of the "Macomb Fire Starter," the confession certainly didn't fit the facts, but by the time it came, people were too worried, tired, and traumatized to care.

What really happened on the Willey Farm? We will probably never know because the story just went away after that. Wanet was taken to Chicago for examination at the Illinois Juvenile Hospital, but a psychiatrist, Dr. Sophie Schroeder, found her to be mentally normal. "She's a nice little kid caught in the middle of a broken home," she reported. Wanet was later turned over to her grandmother and spent the rest of her teenage years untroubled by mysterious brown spots that appeared, spread, and burst into flames.

The insurance company paid Willey for the damage done to his home and farm, and the farmhouse was later rebuilt. Arthur McNeil and his son moved back in with the Willeys for a time before eventually moving out of state.

Fire officials abandoned the case after the "confession" cleared up the mystery for them, but privately, many of those involved continued to question what really occurred on the Willey farm. Fire Chief Fred Wilson talked about the case for quite some time; when he later retired from his position, he remained convinced that something unexplainable had taken place.

The reporters who descended on the Willey farm all received closure for the stories, whether they believed the conclusion or not, and the general public was given a solution that could not have possibly been the truth. Not surprisingly, the case is still listed as "unexplained" today.

Hauntings of the Joliet Penitentiary

The Joliet Penitentiary was meant to be the last stop for many of the thieves, killers, and desperate criminals who found themselves locked behind the prison's ominous walls. It was not designed to be a place of hope or rehabilitation, but instead was a place of punishment for the men who chose to ignore the laws of society. The Joliet Penitentiary broke the bodies and minds of scores of criminals over the years of its operation, and for many of those who perished there, the prison became their permanent home. There was no escape, these luckless souls discovered, even after death.

For more than forty years, from Illinois' statehood in 1818 to around 1858, there was only one state penitentiary in Illinois, located in the Mississippi River town of Alton. The prison was completed in 1833 but soon deteriorated beyond repair, which was a major concern as the state's population was growing rapidly, as was the crime rate. During his inaugural speech in 1853, newly elected Governor Joel Mattson, a Joliet native, spoke out for the need of a prison in northern Illinois. By the mid 1800s, the population center of the state had shifted from southwestern Illinois toward the expanding city of Chicago. In 1857, spurred by scandals involving the horrific conditions of the Alton prison, the Illinois legislature finally approved a commission to scout for locations for the new penitentiary.

Governor Mattson's friend, Nelson Elwood, a former mayor of Joliet, was appointed to the Board of Penitentiary Commissioners. Elwood convinced the members of the board to build a prison at a site that was then two miles north of the city of Joliet. The location boasted a freshwater spring and proximity to railroads, the Illinois and Michigan Canal, and the city of Chicago. But the greatest argument in favor of the site was the limestone deposits located under the fifteen-acre location. The deposits were so deep that no inmate could escape by tunneling out through them.

Construction on the penitentiary began in 1858. The workforce consisted of fifty-three prisoners that had been transferred from Alton. They lived in makeshift barracks while they mined the Joliet-Lemont limestone quarry, located just across the road from the building site. Local private contractors supervised the construction and the prisoners. Quarry drilling was done entirely by hand, and the huge blocks were hauled by mule cart to the road. A conveyor belt was later built to transport rocks to the surface. As work progressed, more prisoners were transferred to Joliet and assigned to work on the construction. There was no shortage of stone or labor, and in 1859, the first building was completed. It had taken just twelve months for the prisoners to construct their own place of confinement. By then, the Alton prison had been completely shut down, and all of the state prisoners had been sent to Joliet.

The Joliet Penitentiary contained 1,100 cells—900 for the general population, 100 for solitary confinement, and 100 to house female inmates. At the time it was finished, it was the largest prison in the United States and was adopted as an architectural model for penitentiaries around the world, including Leavenworth and the Isle of Pines in Cuba.

Prisoners were housed in two-man cells that were six by nine feet, with no electricity, plumbing, or running water. Each cell had a pitcher for fresh water and a bucket for waste. The stone walls of the cells were eight inches thick with only the door and a small ventilation hole for openings. The cellblocks were built running the length of the middle of the long row house, away from any natural light. The cells were grim, confined, dimly lighted chambers that offered little hope for the men incarcerated in them.

Life in the new penitentiary was harsh and sometimes brutal. The plan for the Joliet prison was based on the dreaded Auburn System, which was created in Auburn, New York, in the early 1800s. The inmates at Joliet passed their days under a strict regime of silence, but were allowed to speak in quiet voices to their cellmates during the evening hours. Contact with the outside world was severely limited, and no recreational activities were offered.

Prisoners moved from place to place within the prison using a "lockstep" formation, which was a sort of side-step shuffle with one hand on the shoulder of the man in front of them. Inmates' heads had to be turned in the direction of the guards, who watched for any lip movement that signaled when someone was talking. The lockstep formation also made it easier for one guard to watch over a larger number of prisoners. Floggings, stocks, and extensive time in solitary confinement were common punishments for those who broke the rules. The inmates wore striped uniforms year-round. Men who were deemed to be escape risks were shackled in irons.

Convict labor, under constant discipline, allowed the Joliet Penitentiary to initiate factory-style working conditions at a profit. Lucrative contracts were sold to the highest private bidder, who then sold the products manufactured in the prison on the open market. Under the constant scrutiny of the guards, the prisoners were put to work producing an array of goods: rattan furniture, shoes, brooms, chairs, wheelbarrows, horse collars, and dressed limestone. The prison was also self-sufficient in most aspects of daily life. It had a thriving bakery, a tailor shop, a hospital, and a library, which was administered by the prison chaplain.

A prisoner's day began at 6:00 A.M. when he was marched into the prison yard to empty his waste bucket into the sewage ditch. He then marched into the kitchen, then back to his cell for a breakfast of hash, bread, and coffee. When the dining hall was completed in 1907, prisoners were allowed to eat communally, but in silence. Prisoners in solitary confinement received a daily ration of two ounces of bread and water.

The prison buildings were impossible to keep warm in the winter and very hard to keep clean, which made it a breeding ground for lice, rats, and various diseases. Tuberculosis, pneumonia, and typhoid were the main causes of death among inmates. Unclaimed bodies were buried in a pauper's graveyard, called Monkey Hill, near the prison on Woodruff Street.

The strict silence, unsanitary conditions, forced labor, and harsh punishments gave the Joliet Penitentiary a reputation as the last possible place that a man wanted to end up.

Prison reform was first introduced at Joliet in 1913 with the appointment of Edmund Allen as the warden. By 1915, the striped uniforms and the lockstep formation were gone, and the rule of silence ended. Prisoners were allowed recreation privileges, and a baseball diamond was built. Warden Allen also started an honor farm on twenty-two hundred acres four miles north of the prison. Prisoners were allowed to work in the fields and on the farm as a reward for good conduct.

Ironically, Warden Allen, who lived in an apartment on the prison grounds with his wife, Odette, experienced personal tragedy, possibly at the hands of one of the trusted inmates. On June 19, 1915, Warden Allen and his wife planned to leave on a trip to West Baden, Indiana. Mrs. Allen's dressmaker had not quite finished two of her dresses, and Odette persuaded her husband to go ahead and leave without her. Early the next morning, a fire broke out in the Warden's apartment. When the prison fire department responded, they discovered Mrs. Allen dead and her bed engulfed in flames. The fire was ruled as arson, and a trusty, "Chicken Joe" Campbell, who had been Mrs. Allen's servant, was charged with the crime. Campbell was tried, convicted, and sentenced to death, despite the fact that the evidence against him was purely circumstantial. At Warden Allen's request, Gov. Edward Dunne commuted his sentenced to life imprisonment.

Construction on a new prison, called Stateville, began in 1916 on the land where the honor farm was located. It was originally intended to replace the older prison, but the national crime sprees of the 1920s and 1930s kept the old Joliet Penitentiary open for more than eighty years.

During its time in operation, the prison housed some of the most infamous and deadly criminals in Illinois history. Some of them were already well-known when they walked through the front gates, but others gained their infamy inside the walls.

The first execution at the prison took place during the Civil War years, in the spring of 1864. George Chase, a convicted horse thief, attempted to escape from the penitentiary. When Deputy Warden Joseph Clark confronted him, Chase attacked him with a club and hit him so hard in the head that he killed the officer. Chase was recaptured, charged with murder, and sentenced to hang—turning a short sentence for stealing horses into the death penalty. Chase was hanged a short time later and became the first inmate to be executed at Joliet.

Famous Chicago gangster George "Bugs" Moran served three terms for robbery at Joliet between 1910 and 1923. After the murder of his crime mentor Dion O'Banion in 1926, Moran became the leader of Chicago's North Side bootleggers. His time in power lasted until 1929, when seven of his men were slaughtered by the Capone gang in the St. Valentine's Day Massacre. Moran turned to a life of petty crime and died in Leavenworth in 1957.

Frank McErlane was considered one of the most vicious gunmen in Chicago, and before being sent to Joliet, was credited with killing nine men, two women, and a dog. Arrested for his part in the murder of an Oak Park police officer in 1916, he served one year at Joliet before trying to escape. He was caught and served another two years for the attempt. Later, shortly after the start of Prohibition, McErlane began running a gang with partner Joseph "Polack Joe" Saltis on Chicago's South Side. Later, they allied with the Capone gang against the South Side O'Donnell Brothers. During the war with the O'Donnells, McErlane introduced the Thompson machine gun to Chicago, and with it, killed at least fifteen men during the Beer Wars. McErlane was suspected to have taken part in the St. Valentine's Day Massacre, and he suffered serious wounds during a gun battle with George Moran in 1930. While recovering, Moran sent two gunmen to kill him, but McErlane pulled a revolver from underneath his pillow and began firing, driving off the surprised gangsters. McErlane was wounded in the gunfight, suffering two wounds in his injured leg and one in his arm, but he recovered. In 1932, he became ill with pneumonia and died within days.

Nathan Leopold and Richard Loeb, two college students from wealthy families, were sentenced to life imprisonment at Joliet in 1924 after kidnapping and murdering fourteen-year-old Bobby Franks. They had been attempting to pull off the "perfect crime."

Warden John L. Whitman was firm in his assertion that the young men received the same treatment as the other prisoners, but his claims were nowhere near the truth. Leopold and Loeb lived in luxury compared with the rest of the inmates. Each enjoyed a private cell, books, a desk, a filing cabinet, and even pet birds. They also showered away from the other prisoners and took their meals, which were prepared to order, in the officers' lounge. Leopold was allowed to keep a flower garden. They were also permitted any number of unsupervised visitors and were allowed to keep their own gardens. The doors to their cells were usually left open, and they had passes to visit one another at any time. Loeb was stabbed to death by another inmate in 1936. Leopold was eventually released in 1958, after pleas to the prison board by poet Carl Sandburg. He moved to Puerto Rico and died in 1971.

George "Baby Face" Nelson also served time at Joliet. In July 1931, he was convicted of robbing the Itasca State bank and sentenced to one year to life at Joliet Penitentiary. He served two months before being sent to stand trial for another bank robbery. He was under armed guard when, on his way back to Joliet, he escaped and went back to robbing banks with the Dillinger gang.

Another famous inmate was Daniel L. McGeoghagen, a racketeer, Prohibition beermaker, and skilled safecracker. The McGeoghagen gang attempted to loot three hundred safe deposit boxes in 1947, but when things went wrong, they ended up taking seven people hostage. A gun battle with the police ensued, leaving two people dead and two wounded. McGeoghagen was captured, tried, and sentenced to fifteen to twenty years at Joliet. He was paroled in 1958.

In 2001, the Joliet State Penitentiary was closed down. The crumbling old prison had finally been deemed unfit for habitation, and all of the prisoners were moved out. As many who came to the penitentiary were soon to discover, however, the prison may have been abandoned, but it was certainly not empty.

The first mention of ghosts connected with the old penitentiary was not so much a story about the prison being haunted, but rather about one of the inmates. That man's name was Adolph Luetgert, Chicago's "Sausage King." Luetgert was a German meatpacker who was charged with killing his wife, Louisa, in May 1897. The two of them had a stormy marriage, so when Louisa disappeared, detectives feared the worst and searched the sausage factory located next door to the Luetgert home. In one of the vats in the basement, human bone fragments and a ring bearing Louisa's initials were found, and Luetgert was arrested.

His first trial ended with a hung jury on October 21 after the jurors failed to agree on a suitable punishment. Some argued for the death penalty, while others voted for life in prison. Only one of the jurors thought that Luetgert might be innocent. A second trial was held, and on February 9, 1898, Luetgert was convicted and sentenced to a life term at Joliet. He was taken away, still maintaining his innocence and claiming that he would receive another trial. He was placed in charge of meats in the prison's cold-storage warehouse, and officials described him as a model inmate.

By 1899, though, Luetgert began to speak less and less and often quarreled with the other convicts. He soon became a shadow of his former self, fighting with other inmates for no reason and often babbling incoherently in his cell at night. But was he talking to himself—or to someone else?

According to legend, Luetgert began to claim that he was talking to Louisa in his cell at night. His dead wife had returned to haunt him, intent on having revenge for her murder. Was she really haunting him, or was the "ghost" just the figment of a rapidly deteriorating mind? Based on the fact that residents of his former neighborhood also began reporting seeing Louisa's ghost, one has to wonder if Luetgert was seeing her ghost because he was mentally ill—or if the ghost had driven him insane.

Luetgert died in 1900, likely from heart trouble. The coroner who conducted the autopsy also reported that his liver was greatly enlarged and in such a condition of degeneration that "mental strain would have caused his death at any time."

Perhaps Louisa really did visit him after all . . .

In 1932, the Joliet Penitentiary gained statewide attention, and great notoriety, for a strange ghostly phenomenon that was allegedly occurring at Monkey Hill, the old pauper's burial ground on the property.

In the 1930s, the prison maintained a large field behind the compound for grazing cattle, as well as a limestone quarry that served to provide the prisoners with hard labor. Nearby was the pauper's graveyard where the unclaimed dead were buried. The graveyard was a desolate place largely ignored by those who lived nearby. It probably would have never been talked about at all, if not for the fact that an unexplained voice began to be heard in the cemetery in July 1932.

On July 16, the night of a full moon, a woman named Mrs. Dudek was standing in her backyard, which adjoined the potter's field. As she was enjoying the cool night air on that summer evening, she began to hear a beautiful baritone voice singing what sounded like Latin hymns from a Catholic mass. She called to her daughter, Genevieve, and the two of them took a flashlight and pointed it in the direction the voice was coming from. They saw nothing there.

The next evening, Mrs. Dudek's son, Stanley, and her husband, George, both of whom had been away the night before, also heard the singing. They searched the cemetery but found no one. They were unable to determine where the sound was coming from. News of the voice spread through the neighborhood, and those who came to listen to what the Dudeks claimed to hear went away stunned. They quickly realized that the voice was not coming from someone's loud radio. It was a ghost, they said—a ghost in the old prison cemetery!

News of what was assumed to be a specter in the potter's field spread throughout Joliet, and soon, people from all over town were coming to hear the Latin hymns. Lines of cars filled Woodruff Road and then turned into the prison field, where neighborhood boys directed them to parking places. The procession began early in the evening each night because the voice began to sing around midnight.

After about ten days of this, the enigmatic voice was heard about all over the Chicago area. Curiosity-seekers came from the city, from Indiana, and from the nearby cities of Plainfield, Lockport, Aurora, and Rockdale. The story was picked up in the local newspapers, then in Chicago and Indiana, and finally, across the country. The people of Joliet had a genuine mystery on their hands.

People soon began to come from as far away as Missouri, Wisconsin, and Kentucky to hear the singing. According to the local newspaper, a man named Joshua Jones from Sickles Center, Missouri, was sent by a local contingent from his town. "Folks in my town read about this in the newspapers, but they won't believe it until they hear it from me," Jones told a reporter.

The visitors to the old cemetery originally numbered in the hundreds, and the groups of thrill seekers soon began to grow into the thousands. From the beginning, the tourists attempted to uncover the source of the "ghostly" sounds, or at least the whereabouts of the person pretending to be a ghost. Whenever the singing began, the searchers rushed into the field, looking behind bushes, in trees, and even below ground for any hidden caverns. They looked for wires, loud speakers, and concealed microphones, but found nothing. In spite of this, the singing persisted night after night, and each night it was the same—the low, mournful calling of Latin hymns.

The skeptics who came in search of a reasonable answer just went away confused. People soon began to accept the genuineness of the phenomenon, as all attempts to prove it as a hoax had failed. Each night, thousands of people drove to the field and climbed the hill to what had once been a lonely graveyard. They sat on the flat gravestones, spread their blankets in the grass, and brought along picnic baskets and thermoses of coffee. The crowds waited expectantly for the eerie voice and, for a time, were never disappointed.

The voice eventually began to miss its nightly performance, however. And when it did come, it was sometimes as late as 4:00 A.M., several hours after it had originally started. The faithful stayed and waited for it, though, huddled in blankets and sleeping in the chilly air of the early morning hours. They claimed the voice was offended by those who came only for thrills. It waited for the quiet, attentive listeners, who received a performance of prayerful hymns.

Even the most devoted, however, still searched for an explanation for the voice. Was it some sort of heavenly visitor? The ghost of a deceased prisoner? No one knew, but in late July, officials at the prison announced that they had an explanation for the singer. They claimed that it was merely an Irish-German prisoner, a trusty named William Lalon Chrysler, who was singing in joy about his upcoming parole. Chrysler had been convicted of larceny and had served four years of his term before becoming eligible for parole. Toward the end of his sentence, he had been placed in charge of late-night inspection of the water pumps at the nearby quarry. It was said that the "mysterious" singing was Chrysler intoning Lithuanian folk songs in English to relieve the monotony down in the depths of the quarry. The prison officials reported that the bare stone walls of the quarry were a perfect sounding board for enhancing and throwing his voice to the hilltop, which was more than a quarter mile away. They added that if there were a wind from the north, it would sound as though the voice was right inside the cemetery, where the crowds had gathered. There was nothing supernatural about the voice, they said—it was merely a trick of sound and the wind. The case was closed.

Many people went away convinced that this "official" story was the final word on the subject, but others were not so sure. Many believed that the prison officials were more concerned about getting rid of the crowds than with solving the mystery of the voice. For the entire month of July, thousands of people had encroached on the prison's property. The barbed-wire fence that had surrounded the prison field was broken down, and the cow pasture had been turned into a parking lot.

To make matters worse, Joliet police officers were unable to deal with the massive numbers of people who came to hear the voice. Local criminals began preying on the tourists, picking pockets and breaking into cars, while some of the less savory neighborhood youths began a car parking racket that extorted money from those who parked in the field. They began threatening motorists with broken windshields if they didn't pay protection money to keep their autos safe. The situation had become a far cry from the first days of the phenomenon, when neighborhood children were helping to direct traffic.

Since the prison officials were unable to stop the voice from being heard, they discredited it instead. William Chrysler provided the perfect solution. He was assigned to the sump pumps at the quarry, so he was outside, and he was due for parole at any time, which meant that he wouldn't chance offending prison officials by denying that his voice was the one heard singing. The officials named Chrysler as the unexplained voice, and they closed off the fields to trespassers for good.

The Joliet singer had been given an official solution, but did the explanation really measure up to the facts in the case? Not everyone thought so in 1932, and not everyone today does either. In the official version of the "facts," Chrysler was at the bottom of a quarry when he sang, and his voice was transported to a hilltop about a quarter mile away. He had to have had a light with him in the bottom of the quarry, because it was otherwise pitch dark, and yet no one who searched the area reported seeing a light.

Another problem with the story is how Chrysler's voice could have been heard over such a distance. The "quarry as a sounding board" theory makes sense, but it is unlikely that the sound could carry anywhere other than inside the quarry and to a short distance around it. No one who searched the area ever reported hearing the singing coming from the quarry, which means that Chrysler would have had to have been purposely hoaxing the crowds using ventriloquism. Magicians and ventriloquists who were interviewed in 1932, however, stated that this would have been a very difficult, if not impossible, trick, especially for someone with none of the necessary skills. Chrysler readily admitted that he had never been trained in magic or in the art of throwing his voice.

And finally, strangest of all, why did no one ever report hearing the sump pumps at the quarry? According to the official story, Chrysler was out in the field because he was manning these pumps, singing to himself. If this was the case, then how could his voice have been heard, but not the much louder sounds of the mechanical pumps?

Even with these lingering questions, though, it must be admitted that the singing voice was never heard again after Chrysler's "confession" and the closing of the field. Was the whole thing really a hoax? Or was it simply that the voice was no longer heard singing because people stopped coming to listen for it? One has to wonder what a visitor might hear today if he happened to be on that field some summer night near midnight.

After the Joliet Penitentiary closed in 2001, questions remained as to what would become of the old building. It sat empty for the next several years and then, interestingly, became the setting for the 2005–09 Fox television series *Prison Break*. Standing in as the fictional "Fox River Penitentiary," the Joliet Prison became the setting for the first season of this innovative television show. In the series, actor Wentworth Miller played Michael Scofield, a structural engineer who gets himself thrown into prison to try and save his brother, Lincoln Burrowes (played by Dominic Purcell), who was framed for murder and is scheduled for execution. Scofield has the blueprints for the prison cleverly disguised in the tattoos on his body and has created an elaborate plan to help his brother escape—which, of course, goes awry along the way.

Shortly after the large cast arrived for filming at Joliet, they began to realize there was something not quite right about the old prison. Lane Garrison, the actor who played "Tweener," a young convict on the show, stated that standing in the shadow of the prison walls made it easier for him to get into his character. He recalled, "My first day here, I walked through those gates and a change happened. You see the walls and the razor wire, and you feel the history here. It's not a positive place. We do some stuff in [John Wayne] Gacy's cell, which is really scary."

Rockmund Dunbar, who played the inmate called "C-Note," was usually the most creeped out of the cast and referred to the prison as "stagnant." He often refused to walk around in the cellblocks by himself. "You're expecting something to come around the corner and grab you. I don't go into the cells. I just don't want to get locked in there."

He was also the first cast member to admit that he believed the prison was haunted. "There were stories of neighbors who called, saying 'stop the prisoners from singing over there'—and the prison was closed!" he said.

Perhaps the one cast member to talk most openly about his strange experiences and haunted happenings at Joliet was Dominic Purcell, who played the ill-fated Lincoln Burrowes. Purcell's office on the set was John Wayne Gacy's former cell, which Purcell said was not a nice place, and "a little creepy." He added, "If I let my imagination run away with me, I can start to pick up on some stuff. I don't like to spend too much time in there, knowing that one of the world's most notorious serial killers was lying on the same bunk that I'm lying on. It ain't a comfortable feeling."

Purcell confessed that many members of the cast and crew believed that the spirits of former prisoners still lingered at Joliet. He described one weird incident that he personally experienced. "I had something touch me on the neck. I looked around and thought, 'It's weird,' and blew it off and didn't think about it too much. Then, in the afternoon, one of the other actors came to me and said 'Did you just touch me on the shoulder?' No . . . Then I went back to my little thing and said 'Hmmm,' and the crew was starting to talk about the weird stuff that's going on. Some said the prison's known to have been haunted for a long time," he said.

Purcell, like Lane Garrison, admitted that it was easy to get into character after setting foot inside the prison's walls, but when the time came to wrap up filming for the day, he was always ready to leave. "I am always relieved to leave, always. You never want to hang out there by yourself. The corridors are long, so far, and you get creeped out exploring. There's a section in the yard where they used to do hangings, and you can see the foundations of what they used to use.

That place left a brutal impression on me. It ain't a place for the faint-hearted," he concluded.

Today, the Joliet Penitentiary still stands, slowly crumbling as the years pass by. What will become of this old place? Many locals consider it an eyesore and embarrassment, but still others see it as an important place in Illinois history. It's been a target for the wrecking ball and been named as a possible historic site, but for now, its future remains a mystery.

Do the ghosts of the past still linger in this place, trapped here in time as they were trapped in the cells that once held them? Many believe this to be the case, leading them to wonder what will happen to these mournful spirits if the prison that holds them is lost. Only time will tell . . .

Fred Vanucci's "One-Way Ride"

On the morning of May 31, 1938, the bound and bullet-ridden body of a man who was later identified as Fred Vanucci was discovered lying along a country road outside Crete, a tiny Illinois town just south of Chicago. The police and prosecutors announced that he had been the victim of a "one-way ride," and his killers were never found.

The case, along with Fred Vanucci himself, has been largely forgotten over the years, which was why people were so puzzled when an eerie light began appearing along a five-mile stretch of rural roadway in the early 1940s. Was the light somehow connected to Vanucci and his one-way ride? Those who remembered his tragic story came to believe so.

Fred Vanucci was born in the Illinois Valley region in 1907, and during the dry days of Prohibition, became a well-known bootlegger in the area. He had a number of run-ins with the law in those days, but it was not until he expanded his operations into extortion that he got into real trouble.

In May 1930, Vanucci and two associates, Ralph Scalla and Thomas Walsh, came to the home of Phillip Oliver, a small-time bootlegger who lived in Streator. Vanucci convinced Oliver that he and his friends were corrupt Prohibition agents, and they further enhanced the story by showing him fake badges. They demanded that he pay them $1,500 or they were going to have him arrested on liquor charges. Oliver's brother, James, and his brother-in-law, Joseph Persong, were both present at the time and genuinely believed the incident to be a law enforcement shakedown. Phillip Oliver paid them $900 on the spot, and he made arrangements to deliver the rest of the money to them in Chicago the following week.

At some point after Vanucci, Scalla, and Walsh left the house, Oliver came to the realization that he had been duped. Strangely, the bootlegger took his story to Streator Police Chief Thomas Mottershaw, which implied a rather cozy relationship between a law enforcement official and a lawbreaker. Regardless, Mottershaw devised a trap for Vanucci that would be carried out with the help of Chicago police detectives.

The following week, Oliver went to the meeting on Chicago's West Side, as directed by Vanucci. Chief Mottershaw, a Streator officer named C. C. Goss, and several city policemen watched over him during the transaction. The extortionists were arrested, identified by the Olivers and Persong, and charged with impersonating government agents.

Vanucci came to trial in January 1931, and he and his associates were convicted. Each was sentenced to eight years in Leavenworth and ordered to pay a $3,000 fine. The case was successfully prosecuted, despite the fact that the Olivers and Persong came down with "Chicago amnesia" and claimed they were no longer sure that Vanucci and his men had been the extortionists. Each of the men had received threats by telephone and mail, warning them not to testify. Their "forgetfulness" earned them perjury indictments, thanks to an unsympathetic judge.

After serving out his prison sentence, Vanucci joined the mob's operations in Chicago Heights, under the direction of Frank LaPorte. (LaPorte retained his position with the Outfit until his death from natural causes in 1973—a term of an unbelievable fifty years!) Vanucci worked as muscle for LaPorte for a short time, but his extracurricular activities would eventually lead to his death. In addition to working for LaPorte, he was also stealing slot machines from operations throughout Kane and Kendall counties. This was a hazardous form of employment that fell at cross-purposes to his Outfit employers—and Vanucci had to pay the price.

Early in the morning of May 31, 1938, a farmer named Robert Paul, who was working in his field, came across Vanucci's body in a ditch near Crete. He was lying next to a fence, and his hands and feet had been bound with clothesline. He had been shot in the back more than a dozen times, and investigators surmised that he had been killed with a machine gun.

Vanucci's mother and sister, who had been staying with him in his Chicago apartment, had reported him missing and said that he had last been seen two days before his body was found. They later came to Crete to claim the body, which had been tentatively identified by a silver ring on one of the fingers, bearing the initials "F. V." He had been wearing dark brown trousers and a blue shirt. His jacket and hat were both missing, and one of his shoes was found about sixty feet from the body.

Five miles back, on the same road where Vanucci's body had been found, the police discovered his Dodge coupe abandoned on the side of the road. Registration papers in Vanucci's name were found inside. The headlights of the car were still burning when it was discovered. Police Chief Hans Clausen stated that he believed Vanucci had only been dead five or six hours before his body was found.

Investigators theorized that Vanucci had been run off the road and forcibly taken from his car and placed in another vehicle. A few miles down the road, he was thrown out of the car, and it appeared that he had tried to run, even though his feet were tied together. This is likely when he lost one of his shoes. He was shot to death as he tried to hobble away. Will County Coroner Londos Brannon stated, "The man had been the victim of the old-fashioned gangland ride."

Not surprisingly, the police investigation led nowhere, and no arrests were ever made. To this day, the killers of Fred Vanucci remain unknown and unpunished. Could this explain why some believe his ghost once haunted the roadway where he was killed?

In the early and mid-1940s, stories began to circulate that the stretch of country road between where Vanucci's car was found and where his bullet-mangled body was found was haunted. Witnesses claimed that they heard the sounds of what seemed to be two automobiles racing at high speeds along the road. The loud squeal of brakes signaled an end to the chase, followed by men shouting and loud noises. Whenever the sounds were heard, however, no automobiles or people could be seen on the road. The voices and sounds were literally coming from nowhere!

Others claimed not to hear unexplained things on the road, but to see them. The most commonly reported occurrence involved a weird light that traveled up and down the roadway, almost exactly where Vanucci's body was found. A local farmer connected the "spook light" to the gangster's corpse, and word spread that the site was haunted.

The story of a haunting circulated for a few years, but then apparently faded away. I have been unable to find any recent mentions of Fred Vanucci's ghost. Did he finally find some peace? Or has the strange tale of this little-known mobster simply been forgotten over the years?

The Watseka Wonder

The small town of Watseka, Illinois, is located about fifty miles south of Chicago on the eastern side of the state, just a few miles from the Indiana border. The sensation that would come to be known as the "Watseka Wonder" would first make its appearance here in July of 1877.

It was at this time that a thirteen-year-old girl named Lurancy Vennum fell into a strange, catatonic sleep during which she claimed to speak with spirits. The attacks occurred many times each day and sometimes lasted as long as eight hours. During her trance, Lurancy would speak in different voices, but when she awoke, she would remember nothing. News of the strange girl traveled about the state, and many visitors came to see her.

Doctors eventually diagnosed Lurancy as being mentally ill, and they recommended that she be sent to the State Insane Asylum in Jacksonville. In January 1878, a man named Asa Roff, also from Watseka, came to visit the Vennum family. He claimed that his own daughter, Mary, had been afflicted with the same condition as Lurancy. He was convinced that his daughter had actually spoken to spirits before her own untimely death. In addition, he was convinced that his daughter's spirit still existed.

Mary Roff had died on the afternoon of July 5, 1865, while hospitalized in Jacksonville. She had been committed after a bizarre incident in which she began slashing at her arms with a straight razor. It was the final tragedy in Mary's descent into madness and insanity. In the beginning, it had only been the strange voices that filled her head. Next, she experienced the long periods of being in a trancelike state. Then came her moments of awakening, during which she spoke in other voices and seemed to be possessed by the spirits of other people. Finally, she developed an obsession with blood. Mary was convinced that she needed to remove the blood from her body, using pins, leeches, and at last, a sharpened razor.

After that final incident, her parents took her to the asylum, and Mary endured the "cures" for insanity that existed at the time. She died a short time later.

At the time of Mary Roff's death, Lurancy Vennum was a little more than one year old. In just over a decade, though, their lives would be forever connected in a case that remains today one of the strangest, and most authentic, cases of possession ever recorded.

Lurancy Vennum had been born on April 16, 1864, and she and her family had moved to Watseka when she was seven years old. Since they arrived long after Mary Roff's death, the Vennum family knew nothing of the girl or her family. Then on July 11, 1877, a series of strange events began.

On that morning, Lurancy complained to her mother about feeling sick and then collapsed onto the floor. She stayed in a deep, catatonic sleep for the next five hours, but when she awoke, she seemed fine. The next day, Lurancy once again slipped off into the trancelike sleep, but this time was different, as she began speaking aloud of visions and spirits. In her trance, she told her family that she was in heaven and that she could see and hear spirits, including the spirit of her brother, who had died in 1874.

From that day on, the trances began to occur more frequently and would sometimes last for hours. While she was asleep, Lurancy continued to speak about her visions, which were sometimes terrifying. She claimed that spirits were chasing her through the house and shouting her name. The attacks occurred up to a dozen times each day, and as they continued, Lurancy began to speak in other languages, or at least in nonsense words that no one could understand. When she awoke, she would remember nothing of her trance or of her strange ramblings.

The stories and rumors about Lurancy and her visions began to circulate in Watseka. No one followed the case more closely than Asa Roff. In the early stages of Mary's illness, she too had claimed to communicate with spirits and would fall into long trances without warning. He was sure that Lurancy Vennum was suffering from the same illness as his daughter. But Roff said nothing until the Vennum family had exhausted every known cure for Lurancy. It was not until the local doctor and a minister suggested that the girl be sent to the state mental hospital that Roff got involved.

On January 31, 1878, he contacted the Vennum family. They were naturally skeptical of his story, but he did persuade them to let him bring Dr. E. Winchester Stevens to the house. Stevens, like Asa Roff, was a dedicated Spiritualist, and the two men were convinced that Lurancy was not insane. They believed that Lurancy was actually a vessel through which the dead were communicating. Roff only wished that he had seen the same evidence in his own daughter years before.

The Vennums allowed Dr. Stevens to "mesmerize" the girl and try to contact the spirits through her. Within moments, Lurancy was speaking in another voice, which allegedly came from a spirit named Katrina Hogan. The spirit then changed and claimed to be that of Willie Canning, a young man who had committed suicide. She spoke as Willie for over an hour, and then suddenly, she threw her arms into the air and fell over backward. Dr. Stevens took her hands, and soon, Lurancy calmed and gained control of her body again. She was now in heaven and would allow a gentler spirit to control her.

She said the spirit's name was Mary Roff.

The trance continued on into the next day, and by this time, Lurancy had apparently become Mary Roff. She said that she wanted to leave the Vennum house, which was unfamiliar to her, and go home to the Roff house. When Mrs. Roff heard the news, she hurried to the Vennum house in the company of her married daughter, Minerva Alter. The two women came up the sidewalk and saw Lurancy sitting by the window. "Here comes Ma and

Nervie," she reportedly said, and she ran up to hug the two surprised women. No one had called Minerva by the name "Nervie" since Mary's death in 1865.

It now seemed evident to everyone involved that Mary had taken control of Lurancy. Although she looked the same, she knew everything about the Roff family and treated them as her loved ones. The Vennums, on the other hand, although treated very courteously, were seen with a distant politeness.

On February 11, Lurancy, or rather "Mary," was allowed to go home with the Roffs. Mr. and Mrs. Vennum agreed that it would be for the best, although they desperately hoped that Lurancy would regain her true identity.

Lurancy was taken across town, and as they traveled, they passed by the former Roff home, where they had been living when Mary died. She demanded to know why they were not returning there, and they had to explain that they had moved a few years back.

For the next several months, Lurancy lived as Mary and seemed to have completely forgotten her former life. She did, however, tell her mother that she would only be with them until "some time in May." As days passed, Lurancy continued to show that she knew more about the Roff family, their possessions and habits, than she could have possibly known if she had been faking the whole thing. Many of the incidents and remembrances that she referred to had taken place years before Lurancy had even been born.

In early May, Lurancy told the Roff family that it was time for her to leave. She became very sad and despondent and would spend the day going from one family member to the next, hugging them and touching them at every opportunity.

Finally, on May 21, Lurancy returned home to the Vennums. She displayed none of the strange symptoms of her earlier illness, and her parents were convinced that somehow she had been cured, thanks to intervention by the spirit of Mary Roff. She soon became a happy and healthy young woman, suffering no ill effects from her strange experience.

Lurancy remained in touch with the Roff family for the rest of her life. Although she had no memories of her time as Mary, she still felt a curious closeness to them that she could never really explain.

Eight years later, when Lurancy turned eighteen, she married a local farmer named George Binning, and two years later, they moved to Rawlins County, Kansas. They bought a farm there and had eleven children. Lurancy died in the late 1940s while she was in California visiting one of her daughters.

Asa Roff and his wife received hundreds of letters, from believers and skeptics alike, after the story of the possession was printed on the front page of the Watseka newspaper. After a year of constant hounding and scorn from neighbors, they left Watseka and moved to Emporia, Kansas. Seven years later, they returned to Watseka to live with Minerva and her husband. They died of old age and are buried in Watseka.

Mary Roff was never heard from again.

So what really happened in Watseka? Did Mary Roff's spirit really possess the body of Lurancy Vennum? The families of everyone involved certainly thought so. What other explanation exists for what happened?

To all accounts, Lurancy had the memories and personality of a girl who had been dead for more than twelve years. What really happened? No one knows, but the story of the "Watseka Wonder" causes you to truly wonder if we know as much about the unexplained as we think we do.

The Ghost of Mary Jane Reed

On a dark night in June 1948, a young girl named Mary Jane Reed went out on a date and never returned. Her death, along with the death of her boyfriend, shocked the small town of Oregon, located on the Rock River about one hundred miles west of Chicago. That night was the beginning of a curious, macabre series of events, which included a hushed conspiracy, a purported ghost, and a crime that remains unsolved to this day.

Mary Jane met her date for that fateful night, Stanley Skridla, through the DeKalb/Ogle Telephone Co. Seventeen-year-old Reed worked as a switchboard operator, and Skridla, 28, was a lineman.

Skridla was a Navy veteran who lived in Rockford, but who was working in Oregon at the time. The two were attracted to one another despite their age difference, which was not really a concern for Mary Jane. The pretty young woman had dropped out of high school at fifteen to help take care of her mother, who suffered from severe arthritis.

The Reed family lived on Hastings Road, just east of the Rock River. The area was known as Sandtown because most of the residents worked at the town's silica plant. Sandtown was considered the wrong side of town, but that didn't matter to Mary Jane, a headstrong and independent girl who was determined to never let her circumstances get in the way of what she hoped to accomplish in life. Unfortunately, her dreams would never be fulfilled.

Mary Jane met Stan Skridla on June 24, 1948 for their first—and last—date. Various reports later had them at taverns on the east side and south side of Oregon that night. It's believed that their last stop was the Stenhouse (now known as the Roadhouse), and after that, they drove out to a popular lover's lane on County Farm Road in Skridla's Buick. They were never seen alive again.

The next morning, around 6:00 A.M., a state highway department employee named John Eckerd was driving to work on County Farm Road and noticed a shoe lying alongside the roadway. He stopped to take a look and discovered Stan Skridla's bullet-riddled body lying facedown in a grassy ditch. Police later found five .32-caliber bullet casings at the scene. A pool of blood found on the edge of the road showed where the killer had dragged the young man's body into the grass. Skridla's Buick was found abandoned about an hour later, roughly one mile north of the lover's lane, where Illinois Route 2 and Pine Road intersected. Other than a lipstick-stained cigarette on the floorboard of the car, there was no sign of Mary Jane.

Back in Sandtown, Mary Jane's parents, Clifford and Ruth Reed, were already worried about their daughter by the time they got the news about Skridla's death. Before this, she had always called home if she was going to be late or spend the night at a friend's house. They feared that she had been kidnapped by Skridla's killer. Worried, two of the older children in the family went to see a psychic, who told them that their sister was still alive and being held prisoner in a shack by an older man.

Stan Skridla was buried at Calvary Cemetery in Rockford on June 28. The next day would bring terrible news for the Reeds. On June 29, two policemen came to the door and told them that they had news and it was not good. Mary Jane's brother, Warren Reed, was just five years old at the time, but he still remembers that day. He recalled, "I was holding my mom's hand and I could feel the energy just drain out of her." The officers told Mrs. Reed that Mary Jane's body had been found in a patch of weeds along Silica Road.

She had been shot in the back of the head with what appeared to be the same caliber gun that had been used to kill Skridla. She was wearing brown loafers, a white blouse, and her mother's wedding ring. Her brown slacks were folded neatly on her back. Ironically, the police had checked the area along Silica Road, now known as Devil's Backbone Road, several times after Mary Jane disappeared. Her father had even passed that way several times on his way to work at the silica plant. Her body ended up being found by Harold Sigler, a truck driver who was on his way to the plant. The height of the truck's cab allowed him to see over the weeds and catch a glimpse of the pale body that had been hidden among them. The police recovered a bullet casing at the scene.

The Reed family was devastated. Mary Jane's brother, Donald, was supposed to be married on June 26, and Mary Jane was to be one of the bridesmaids. The wedding was postponed until after the funeral, which was held on June 30. Mary Jane was laid to rest at Daysville Cemetery in Oregon, but she would not rest there in peace.

With two murders on their hands, the Ogle County Sheriff's office enlisted the help of the state and local police. There were very few clues to go on, but Chief Deputy Willard "Jiggs" Burright, the lead investigator, ruled out robbery as a motive. Skridla had still had his wallet, and Mary Jane had still been wearing her mother's ring. Authorities began focusing on Mary Jane's previous relationships, surmising that jealousy may have been a motive for the killings. Detectives interviewed Skridla's family members and other men that Mary Jane had dated. The investigation extended to

Dixon, Rockford, Freeport, and Chicago. Police also looked for a couple that Skridla and Mary Jane had reportedly been seen arguing with before they went to County Farm Road. A witness interviewed at the inquest said that he saw two suspicious men outside one of the taverns the couple had visited. Most of the leads turned out to be dead ends.

As weeks, then months, passed, the slayings vanished from the front pages of local newspapers and eventually left the minds of everyone except for the Reeds. Ruth Reed was never the same after Mary Jane's murder, and family members later sought psychiatric care for her. Warren Reed later reported that his mother would often hide him behind the couch in the living room, convinced that his sister's killer was coming after all of them.

The Skridla–Reed murder case was reopened in the 1950s, but with no success. As years went by, evidence disappeared from the original case files, including the bullet casings, photographs, and investigation reports. Jerry Brooks became the Ogle County sheriff in 1970 and again reopened the case. He re-interviewed witnesses and wrote new reports from scratch because the case file was almost empty. Many of the original interviews could not be re-created, though, because so many of the witnesses had died or too much time had passed for them to remember specific details. His most intriguing lead was the report of the two men outside the tavern, and he theorized that they might have followed the couple to the lover's lane. Brooks worked the case for almost two decades but was no closer to solving it than the detectives were back in 1948. Brooks left office in 1990, but he has never given up on the case; he still believes that a solution is possible.

And he's not the only one. Warren Reed thinks there is much more to the case than meets the eye. In 2005, he pressed for an exhumation order for his sister's body, wondering if clues might be found that were beyond the forensic skills of investigators at the time of the murder. In August of that year, an Ogle County judge approved guidelines for exhuming the body that would allow pathologists to examine Mary Jane's remains. Reed was thrilled with the outcome of the hearing. "I want to wake up the community. People just kind of hushed things up when they shouldn't have. This crime should have been solved. It probably took twenty years off my parents' lives," he told reporters.

The grave was opened on August 23, 2005, and while it did not immediately point out her killer, the exhumation did manage to dispel some of the rumors that had circulated for decades, such as the one that claimed her head was not buried with her body or that a gun had been placed in the casket. Officials were surprised to find that her corpse was mostly intact. She had been buried with all of her organs, and skin still covered her body. Authorities kept the undergarments that she was wearing when she was buried, and oddly, some additional clothing was found inside the vault. A dress and a slip were found wrapped in newspapers dated June 25, 1948, blaring headlines about her murder.

A few months after the exhumation, officials seemed optimistic; opening the grave yielded a few clues and pointed detectives in the direction of two "people of interest," but that optimism soon faded. According to a twenty-four-page report written by Captain Rick Wilkinson (with certain names and details blacked out) in February 2006, the sheriff's department faced too many obstacles when reopening the case. "This investigation, in my opinion, was tainted and mishandled from the start, and nothing that I am aware of can possibly change those facts," Wilkinson said.

Wilkinson followed up on a number of original leads from 1948, as well as leads from the 1950s and the 1980s, when the case was opened again. No new evidence was provided by the exhumation, but as Warren Reed intended, it got people talking, and witnesses came forward with information about two new "people of interest." Unfortunately, both of them were deceased by 2006. "They're not here to defend themselves. They do have families that are still alive, and we can't definitely say they were the people who committed this crime," Ogle County Sheriff Mel Messer said.

After that, the case became cold again, but not everyone is willing to just relegate it to the files of the unsolved. One of those who assisted Warren Reed in getting the exhumation and in his fight for answers was Mike Arians, a former insurance fraud investigator. Arians owned a restaurant in Oregon and was elected the town's mayor in April 1999. He was drawn to the mystery surrounding the murders because he became convinced, after some investigating of his own, that certain aspects of the case were covered up. He spoke at length about his investigation but was more uncomfortable about the other thing that led him to the case: namely, Mary Jane's ghost.

Arians swore that Mary Jane and her mother maintained a "presence" at his restaurant, the Roadhouse, which in its former incarnation was the Stenhouse, possibly Mary Jane's last stop before she and Skridla drove to their doom. As proof of this, he claimed that the same haunting acoustic song, Sergio Mendes and Brasil '66's "After Sunrise," would play spontaneously and repeatedly on the jukebox; that employees had seen apparitions of Mary Jane and her mother; and that, without explanation, drafts of cold air or the overwhelming scent of flowers would permeate the surroundings. He admitted that spirits in the Roadhouse sounded "crazy," but added that he did not believe the ghosts would rest in peace "until this thing is resolved."

Arians' actual involvement in the case did not begin until shortly after he took office in 1999. People soon began coming to him and telling him about the murders, eventually asking him if he would use his investigative skills to look into them. Arians agreed, and soon after, the strange events began. In addition to the ghostly happenings at the Roadhouse, other ominous events began to occur, such as the flower delivery that came to his restaurant for Mary Jane. No one could trace where the arrangement came from, and the Roadhouse was closed that day. He later learned that it had been Mary Jane's birthday.

Will the case ever really be solved? No one can say, but Warren Reed and Mike Arians aren't giving up hope. They have not given up on the idea that, eventually, some incontrovertible evidence will emerge that solves Mary Jane's murder once and for all. Until that time, these two men will continue their investigation, and two lonesome ghosts will continue to walk at the last place that a beautiful young girl was seen alive.

Chicago

Ghosts of the
Fort Dearborn Massacre

It may not have been cold on the April 1803 morning when Captain John Whistler climbed a sand dune around which the sluggish Chicago River tried to reach Lake Michigan—but chances are, it was. A chilling wind would have been a characteristic greeting from the landscape that Whistler had come to change. His orders had been to take six soldiers from the 1st U.S. Infantry, survey a road from Detroit to the mouth of the river, and draw up plans for a fort at this location. After claiming the site, Captain Whistler returned to Detroit to get his garrison and his family. He was forty-five years old, and neither his poor Army pay nor the dangers of the frontier stopped him from living a full and domesticated life. He eventually fathered fifteen children.

Captain Whistler's family was spared the arduous trek over erratic Indian trails to the Chicago River. While the troops marched on foot, the captain and his brood boarded the U.S. schooner *Tracy*, which also carried artillery and camp equipment. It sailed to the mouth of the St. Joseph River, where it met the troops. The Whistler family took one of the *Tracy*'s rowboats to the Chicago River, while the troops marched around the lake.

Sixty-nine officers and men in the contingent had the task of building Fort Dearborn, which was named in honor of Secretary of War Henry Dearborn. The hill where Fort Dearborn was built was eight feet above the river, which curved around it and—stopped from flowing into a lake by a sandbar—flowed south until it found an outlet. To this spot, the soldiers hauled the logs they had made from trees cut on the north bank. The fort was a simple stockade of logs. They were placed in the ground and then sharpened along the upper end. The outer stockade was a solid wall with an entrance in the southern section that was blocked by heavy gates. Another exit, this one underground, was located on the north side. As time went on, they built barracks, officers' quarters, a guardhouse, and a small powder magazine made from brick. West of the fort, they constructed a two-story log building to serve as an Indian agency. Between this structure and the fort, they placed root cellars. South of the fort, the land was enclosed for a garden. Blockhouses were added at two corners of the fort, and three pieces of light artillery were mounted at the walls. The fort offered substantial protection for the soldiers garrisoned there, but they would later learn that it was not protection enough.

Around 1804, a trader named John Kinzie arrived in the region. Kinzie became the first "boss" of Chicago, the self-appointed civilian leader of the settlement. He was known for his sharp dealings with the local Indians over trade goods and furs. He also established close ties with the Potawatomi Indians, and even sold them liquor, which created tension among the other settlers.

Kinzie's business prospered, but it was not without problems. A conflict that he had with Captain Whistler's son, John Whistler Jr., deteriorated so badly that it caused a major rift within the community. Whistler had demanded that Kinzie stop giving liquor to the Indians, but Kinzie refused. The disagreement became so heated that word of it reached officials in Detroit. Whistler, along with all of the other officers at the fort, were recalled and assigned to various posts across the frontier.

In 1810, Captain Nathan Heald replaced Captain Whistler at Fort Dearborn. Heald brought with him Lieutenant Linus T. Helm, an officer, like Heald, who was experienced in the ways of the frontier. Not long after arriving, Helm met and married the stepdaughter of John Kinzie. In addition to her and Captain Heald's wife, there were a number of women at the fort, all wives of the men stationed there. More families arrived, and within two years, there were twelve women and twenty children at Fort Dearborn.

When the War of 1812 unleashed the fury of the Native Americans on the Western frontier, the city of Chicago almost ceased to exist before it got a chance to get started. On August 15, 1812, the garrison at Fort Dearborn evacuated its post and, with women in children in tow, attempted to march to safety. But it was over-whelmed and wiped out, in a wave of bloodshed and fire, after traveling less than a mile. The story of the massacre will be repeated for as long as Chicago continues to stand.

At the start of the War of 1812, tensions in the wilderness began to rise. British troops came to the American frontier, spreading liquor and discontent among the Indian tribes, especially the Potawatomi, the Wyandot, and the Winnebago near Fort Dearborn. In April, an Indian raid occurred on the Lee farm, near the bend in the river (where present-day Racine Avenue meets the river), and two men were killed. After that, the fort became a refuge for many of the settlers and a growing cause of unrest for the local Indians. When war was declared that summer and the British captured the American garrison at Mackinac, it was decided that Fort Dearborn could not be held and that the fort should be evacuated.

General William Hull, the American commander in the North-west, issued orders to Captain Nathan Heald through Indian agent officers. Heald was told that the fort was to be abandoned, the arms and ammunition destroyed, and the goods distributed to friendly Indians. Hull also sent a message to Fort Wayne, which sent Captain William Wells and a contingent of allied Miami Indians toward Fort Dearborn to assist with the evacuation.

There is no dispute about whether or not General Hull gave the order, nor that Captain Heald received it, but some have wondered if perhaps his instruction, or his handwriting, was not clear because Heald waited eight days before acting on it. During that time, Heald argued with his officers, with John Kinzie—who opposed the evacuation—and with local Indians, one of whom discharged a rifle in the commanding officer's quarters.

The delay managed to give the hostile Indians time to gather outside the fort. They assembled there in an almost siegelike state, and Heald realized that he was going to have to bargain with them if the occupants of Fort Dearborn were going to safely reach Fort Wayne. On August 13, all of the blankets, trading items, and calico cloth were given out, and Heald held several councils with Indian leaders that his junior officers refused to attend.

An agreement was eventually reached that had the Indians providing safe conduct for the soldiers and settlers to Fort Wayne in Indiana. Part of the agreement was that Heald would leave the arms and ammunition in the fort for the Indians, but his officers disagreed. Alarmed, they questioned the wisdom of handing out guns and ammunition that could easily be turned against them. Heald reluctantly went along with them, and the extra weapons and ammunition were broken apart and dumped into an abandoned well. Only twenty-five rounds of ammunition were saved for each man. As an added bit of insurance, all the liquor barrels were smashed and the contents were poured into the river during the night.

On August 14, Captain William Wells and his Miami allies arrived at the fort. Wells was a frontier legend among early soldiers and settlers in the Illinois Territory. He was also the uncle of Captain Heald's wife, Rebekah, and after receiving the request for assistance from General Hull, he headed straight to Fort Dearborn to aid in the evacuation. But even the arrival of the frontiersman and his loyal Miami warriors would not save the lives of those trapped inside Fort Dearborn.

Throughout the night of August 14, wagons were loaded for travel and the reserve ammunition was distributed. Early the next morning, the procession of soldiers, civilians, women, and children left the fort. The infantry soldiers led the way, followed by a caravan of wagons and mounted men. A portion of the Miami men who had accompanied Wells guarded the rear of the column. It was reported that musicians played the "dead march," a slow, solemn funeral march that would be a foreboding of the disaster that followed.

The column of soldiers and settlers was escorted by nearly five hundred Potawatomi Indians. As they marched southward and into a low range of sand hills that separated the beaches of Lake Michigan from the prairie, the Potawatomi moved silently to the right, placing an elevation of sand between them and the white men. The act was carried out with such subtlety that no one noticed it as the column trudged along the shoreline.

The column traveled to an area where Sixteenth Street and Indiana Avenue are now located. There was a sudden milling about of the scouts at the front of the line, and suddenly, a shout came back from Captain Wells that the Indians were attacking. A line of Potawatomi appeared over the edge of the ridge and fired down at the column. Completely surprised, the officers nevertheless managed to rally the men into a battle line, but it was of little use. Soldiers fell immediately, and the line collapsed. The Indians overwhelmed them with sheer numbers, flanking the line and snatching the wagons and horses.

What followed was butchery. Officers were slain with tomahawks, and the fort's surgeon was cut down by gunfire and then literally chopped to pieces. Rebekah Heald was wounded by gunfire, but was spared when she was captured by a sympathetic Indian chief. The wife of one soldier fought so bravely and savagely that she was hacked to pieces before she fell. In the end, reduced to less than half their original number, the garrison surrendered under the promise of safe conduct. In all, 148 members of the column were killed; 86 adults and 12 children were slaughtered in the initial assault. The children had been loaded onto a single wagon for safety and were killed in one frenzied attack.

Captain Wells managed to kill eight Indians with his bare hands before he was felled and pinned down by his horse. Warriors pounced on him and killed him, then allegedly cut out his heart and ate it, hoping to ingest some of his ferocious bravery.

In the battle, Captain Heald was wounded twice, while his wife was wounded seven times. They were later released, and a St. Joseph Indian named Chaudonaire took them to Mackinac, where they were turned over to the British commander there. He sent them to Detroit, where they were exchanged with the American authorities.

The surrender that was arranged by Captain Heald did not apply to the wounded, and it is said that the Indians tortured them throughout the night and then left their bodies on the sand next to those who had already fallen. Many of the other survivors suffered terribly. One man was tomahawked when he could not keep pace with the rest of the group being marched away from the massacre site. A baby who cried too much during the march was tied to a tree and left to starve. Mrs. Isabella Cooper was actually scalped before being rescued by an Indian woman. She had a small bald spot on her head for the rest of her life. Another man froze to death that winter, while Mrs. John Simmons and her daughter were forced to run a gauntlet, which both survived. The girl, in fact, turned out to be the last survivor of the massacre, dying in 1900.

John Kinzie and his family were spared in the slaughter. He and his family were supposed to travel by boat to a trading post on the St. Joseph River, but because of the attack, they never departed. Appealing to the Potawatomi chiefs, they were taken away from the massacre site and returned to the Kinzie cabin. There they were joined by Mrs. Helm, the wife of Lieutenant Helm, and Mrs. Kinzie's daughter from her previous marriage. She had been shot, and Kinzie removed the bullet with a penknife. After presenting gifts to the Indians, the Kinzies later escaped to the trading post.

The war ruined Kinzie. He was now deeply in debt and had lost a fortune during the attack on Fort Dearborn. Though in no danger from the Indians, he was captured by the British and accused of high treason since he was a British subject. He was placed in irons and held on a prison ship off Quebec for seven weeks. He was freed in 1814 and rejoined his family. Two years later, he returned to Chicago, but found that much had changed. He failed in restarting his business, thanks to a bad loan, and soon was working for his largest competitor, the American Fur Company. In time, the fur trade ended, and Kinzie worked as a trader and Indian interpreter until his death in 1828.

After the carnage, the victorious Indians burned Fort Dearborn to the ground, and the bodies of the massacre victims were left where they had fallen, scattered to decay on the sand dunes of Lake Michigan. When replacement troops arrived at the site a year later, they were greeted with not only the burned-out shell of the fort, but also the grinning skeletons of their predecessors. The bodies were given proper burial and the fort was rebuilt in 1816, only to be abandoned again in 1836, when the city was able to fend for itself.

The horrific Fort Dearborn Massacre is believed to have spawned its share of ghostly tales. The actual site of the massacre was quiet for many years, long after Chicago grew into a sizable city. Construction in the early 1980s, however, unearthed a number of human bones around Sixteenth Street and Indiana Avenue. First thought to be victims of a cholera epidemic in the 1840s, the remains were later dated more closely to the early 1800s. Thanks to their location, they were believed to be the bones of massacre victims.

The remains were reburied elsewhere, but within a few weeks, people began to report the semitransparent figures of people wearing pioneer clothing and outdated military uniforms scrambling around an empty lot just north of Sixteenth Street. The apparitions reportedly ran about in terror, silently screaming. The most frequent witnesses to these nocturnal wanderings were bus drivers who returned their vehicles to a garage located nearby, prompting rumors and stories to spread throughout the city. In recent times, the area has been largely filled with new homes and condominiums, and the once empty lot where the remains were discovered is no longer vacant. But this does not seem to keep the victims of the massacre in their graves. Current paranormal reports from the immediate area often tell of specters dressed in period clothing, suggesting that the unlucky settlers of early Chicago do not rest in peace.

When the Show Didn't Go On . . .

The city of Chicago has long been a place of horror, tragedy, and death, dating back to the earliest days of the Fort Dearborn Massacre and continuing with the Great Chicago Fire in 1871. Unfortunately, those horrific events were not the only times that Chicago was marked by disaster, and over the decades, the city has seen more than its share. Fires have taken many lives in Chicago and have left a vivid mark on the city. While the Great Chicago Fire was the most famous blaze in the city's history, it was certainly not the only time that the city was scorched with flames.

Perhaps the most heartbreakingly tragic Chicago fire occurred at the famed Iroquois Theater on December 30, 1903, as a blaze broke out in the crowded venue during a performance of a vaudeville show. The fire claimed the lives of hundreds of people, including children, who were packed in for an afternoon show during the holidays. It remains one of the deadliest theater fires in American history.

The Iroquois Theater, the newest and most beautiful show-place in Chicago in 1903, was believed to be "absolutely fire-proof," according to newspaper reports. The new theater was much acclaimed, even before it was unveiled to the public. It was patterned after the Opera-Cominque in Paris and was located downtown on the north side of Randolph Street, between State and Dearborn streets. The interior of the four-story building was magnificent, with stained glass and polished wood throughout. The lobby had an ornate sixty-foot ceiling and featured white marble walls fitted with large mirrors framed in gold leaf and stone. Two grand staircases led away from either side of the lobby to the balcony areas. Outside, the building's façade resembled a Greek temple with a towering stone archway supported by massive columns.

Thanks to the dozens of fires that had occurred over the years in theaters, architect Benjamin H. Marshall wanted to assure the public that the Iroquois was safe. He studied a number of fires that had occurred in the past and made every effort to ensure that no tragedy would occur in the new theater. The Iroquois had twenty-five exits that, it was claimed, could empty the building in less than five minutes. The stage had also been fitted with an asbestos curtain that could be quickly lowered to protect the audience.

While all of this was impressive, it was not enough to battle the real problems that existed with the Iroquois. Seats in the theater were wooden, the cushions stuffed with flammable hemp, and much of the precautionary fire equipment that was to have been installed never actually made it into the building. The theater had no fire alarms, and in a rush to open on time, other safety factors had been forgotten or simply ignored.

The horrific event occurred on the bitterly cold afternoon of December 30. A holiday crowd had packed into the theater on that Wednesday afternoon to see a matinee performance of the hit comedy *Mr. Bluebeard*. Officially, the Iroquois seated 1,602 people, with approximately 700 in the expensive "parquet," the seats down in front that overlooked the orchestra pit; more than 400 in the first balcony; and probably just under 500 in the steep, upper balcony. There were four lower boxes, each seating six people, and two upper boxes designed to hold four people in each, but the owners had managed to crowd eight chairs into those boxes.

Added to those who had purchased tickets to the show in advance were the usual late arrivals. Some came to buy tickets for available standing room; others had guest passes from connections they had with the management, contractors, actors, and theater employees. Others had been given tickets by city inspectors who had done favors for the owners of the theater. Estimates varied, but because the managers wanted to make up for earlier, smaller shows, there may have been considerably more than 200 standees that afternoon. By curtain time, an estimated 1,840 people, most of them women and children, were packed into the house. This was far beyond capacity. The overflow had people filling the seats and standing four-deep in the aisles. Another crowd filled the backstage area with 400 actors, dancers, and stagehands.

By the time the show started, the theater was dangerously over-crowded. Not only was the standing-room-only crowd packed into the designated area behind the last row of seats, they were also sitting in the aisles and standing along both side walls. One usher would later claim there were at least 500 people standing in the auditorium.

Anticipation mounted as the lights dimmed for act one of the show. In accordance with the owner's standard operating procedures, most of the doors leading from the balcony and gallery had been locked or bolted by the ushers to keep out gate crash-ers and prevent those sitting or standing in the upper tiers from sneaking down in the darkness to the more expensive seats. This was done regardless of the fact that it was obvious there were no empty seats anywhere.

The audience was thrilled with the show's first act. During the intermission, those in the expensive sections and boxes retired to the smoking room, or went to freshen up, relax on the plush couches, and mingle on the promenade. Those in the balcony and gallery, behind the locked and bolted gates, flowed through the upper prom-enade and used the restrooms.

By 3:20 P.M., the second act of *Mr. Bluebeard* was well under way. During one of the early scenes, possibly while Foy was riding a baby elephant, Nellie Reed of the aerial ballet was hooked to a thin trolley wire that would send her high above the audience during a musical number. The sequence was made spectacular through the use of hundreds of colored lights. Some of the bulbs were concealed inside two narrow concave metal reflectors that were located on each side of the stage. Called "front lighting," each reflector was mounted on vertical hinges and, when not needed, was supposed to be pivoted by stagehands so that they disappeared into niches in the wall. The lights were not needed for the number that was about to start, but a member of the stage crew, for some reason, had not retracted the right stage reflector. It was left slightly extended, an edge of it in the path of the curtains. In the usual business of moving scenery, adjusting lights, moving backdrops, and the hundreds of other things that needed to be done, no one noticed the error.

In the scene that followed, all of the house lights were extinguished, bathing the stage in a soft blue glow from one of the backstage carbon arc lamps, a powerful spotlight that was created by an electric current arcing between two carbon rods. The spotlight was positioned on a narrow metal bridge about fifteen feet above the stage and within a foot or so of the theater's drop curtains and the fixed curtain that prevented the audience from seeing into the wings. The spotlight was a bulky piece of machinery, with a large metal hood and reflector, and it could generate temperatures as high as 4,000 degrees Fahrenheit.

As the action continued on the stage, bringing beautiful chorus girls and young men in uniform into the softly lit gardens, the carbon arc lamp suddenly began to sputter and spark. A cracking sound was heard, and then a few inches of orange flame appeared and began to spread out, dancing along the edge of the fixed curtain. On the stage below, the cast went into an up-tempo song as stage hands tried to slap at the small flame with their bare hands. Within seconds, though, the tiny blaze had grown, consuming the material above their heads and beyond their reach. It was soon spreading into the heavier curtains, and they shouted to a man on a catwalk above to try and put the fire out. He also began slapping at the fire with his hands.

The audience was engrossed in the romantic musical number onstage while on either side of the garden set, stagehands, grips, and those on the catwalks frantically tried to get to the fire and put it out. But the flames had grown larger and were now out of reach. Black smoke was starting to rise.

William Sallers, the house fireman, was on his usual rounds to make sure that no one was smoking, and as he made his way up the stairs from the dressing rooms in the basement, he spotted the flames. He immediately grabbed some tubes of Kilfyre (a powdery flame retardant), ran up the vertical stairs of the light bridge, and began frantically tossing powder onto the still-growing fire. The platform was only eighteen inches wide, so he had to hold onto a metal rail with one hand as he threw the powder with the other. But it was too late. The flames had spread to the point that the small amount of powder was almost comically ineffectual.

At first, the actors onstage had no idea what was happening, but after a few sparks began to rain down, they knew something was seriously wrong. They continued to sing and dance, waiting for something to happen. Later, some of the actors would recall hearing shouts and bells that signaled for the curtain to come down, but they were muffled by the music.

In the orchestra pit, the musicians spotted the fire, and an order was given for them to play as fast as they could. The tempo picked up, but soon faltered as more of the musicians spotted the flames and began to get rattled. Several of them calmly put down their instruments and exited through the orchestra pit door beneath the stage.

Depending on where they were sitting or standing, some members of the audience saw the fire by simply following the gaze of the actors, who were now looking up. At first, many of them were merely puzzled, but others were becoming alarmed. Most of the children in the front main-floor rows remained in their seats, believing that the glow spreading across the upper reaches of the theater was another of the show's magical effects.

Those in the upper gallery who saw the eerie flickering of the flames had no idea at first about what was happening, until bits of burning fabric began falling down around members of the cast who were still trying to go on with their number. But it was becoming obvious that some of them had fallen out of step with the music and others seemed to have lost their voices. Most were terribly frightened, but survivors of the fire would later say that seeing those girls remaining there, still dancing in an effort to quiet the audience, was one of the bravest acts they had ever witnessed.

Backstage, things became more frightening and chaotic. The stage manager, William Carelton, could not be found (he had gone to the hardware store), and one of the stagehands, Joe Dougherty, was trying to handle the curtains from near the switchboard. But Dougherty was filling in for the regular curtain man, who was in the hospital, and could not remember which drop should be lowered. The asbestos curtain ran on an endless loop of wire-enforced rope, but he was not sure which rope controlled which curtain.

High above him, Charles Sweeney, who had been assigned to the first fly gallery, seized a canvas tarpaulin and, with some of the other men, was slapping at the flames. The fire was out of their reach, however, and it continued to spread. Sweeney dashed down six flights of stairs to a room filled with chorus girls and led them down to a small stage exit. In the rush to escape, most of the girls dropped everything and left the building wearing only flimsy costumes or tights. Other men raced downstairs to rescue girls who were in the dressing rooms under the stage.

High up in the theater's gridiron, The Grigolatis, a group of sixteen young German aerialists (twelve women and four men), had a horrifying view of the scene. Clouds of thick, black smoke were rising toward them, and blazing pieces of canvas the size of bedsheets were falling down on the stage and the footlights. William Sallers, still above the stage, saw the same thing and knew the theater was doomed.

The Grigolatis had only seconds to act. One of them, Floraline, who was perched some distance away from the others, was suddenly engulfed in flames from a burning piece of scenery. Before the others could reach her, she panicked, lost her grip on the trapeze, and plunged to the stage, sixty feet below. By the time her companions were able to unhook themselves from their harnesses and scramble down some metal scaffolding to the stage, Floraline had vanished. They could only hope that she had been carried to safety.

In all of the confusion, no one remembered Nellie Reed, who was still attached to her wire.

In one of the dressing rooms, five young female dancers were sitting and talking when they heard the cries of "fire!" In the rush to get out, one of them, Violet Sidney, twisted her ankle and fell. The other girls ran, but Lola Quinlan stopped to help her. She managed to drag Violet down five flights of stairs and across the back of the burning stage to safety. She was badly burned in the process, but she refused to leave her friend behind.

Voices screamed for the asbestos curtain to come down, but nothing happened. Joe Dougherty and others were still confused about which curtains should be lowered, and more time was lost. A stagehand who had been ordered to sound the fire alarm found that no alarm box had ever been installed. He burst out of the theater and ran as fast as he could through the streets to notify Engine Company 13 of the blaze.

Inside his dressing room, Eddie Foy, in tights, misshapen shoes, short smock, and red pigtailed wig, was preparing for his novelty act as the Old Woman Who Lived in a Shoe. Foy heard the commotion outside and rushed out onto the stage to see what was going on. As soon as he opened the door, he knew something was deadly wrong. He immediately searched for his young son, who had accompanied him to the theater that day, and quickly found him in the darkness. As he stumbled with the boy in his arms, he heard terrified voices raising a cry of "fire!" At that moment, the nearly two thousand people packed into the "absolutely fireproof" Iroquois Theater began to panic.

Some of the audience had risen to their feet; others were running and climbing over the seats to get to the back of the house and the side exits. Many of the standees were blocking the aisles and, since the new theater was unfamiliar to them, were unsure about which way to turn. The initial runners soon turned into a mob trying to get out the same way they had come in. Their screams and cries were muffled by the music and by the show's cast, which was still singing as the burning scenery fell around them. Terrified families were quickly torn apart from one another.

Eddie Foy grabbed his son and rushed to the stage exit, but felt compelled to go back and try and help. He pressed the boy into the arms of a fleeing stagehand and went back to try and help calm the audience and finally lower the curtain. By the time he arrived, the cast had abandoned the stage, and he stood there alone, the blazing backdrop behind him and burning bits of scenery raining down around him. Smoke billowed around him as he stepped to the edge of the footlights, still partially clothed in his ridiculous costume. He urged everyone who could hear him to remain calm, and remarkably, some of the people in the front rows took their seats again. Even some of the people in the gallery sat back down. From the edge of the stage, Foy urged musical director Herbert Gillea to get some of the remaining musicians to play an overture, which had a temporary soothing effect on the crowd.

A few moments later, a flaming set crashed down onto the stage, and Foy asked everyone to get up and calmly leave the theater. He told them to take their time, to not be frightened, and to walk slowly as they exited. Then, he dropped his voice to the stagehand who was on the brink of fleeing from the theater himself. He ordered him, "Lower that iron curtain! Drop the fire curtain! For God's sake, does anyone know how this iron curtain is worked?"

Foy heard timbers cracking above his head, and he made one last entreaty that everyone proceed slowly from the theater, but by now, no one was listening. As he looked out into the auditorium, he later recalled seeing many of the people on the main floor leaving in an orderly fashion, but what he saw in the balcony and the gallery terrified him. In the upper tiers, he said, people were in a "mad, animal-like stampede."

Lester Linvonston, a young survivor who vividly recalled seeing Foy standing at the edge of the stage, pleading for calm, was only distracted from the comedian by a macabre sight that appeared above Foy's head. "Almost alone and in the center of the house," he later said, he watched "a ballet dancer in a gauzy dress suspended by a steel belt from a wire. Her dress had caught fire and it burned like paper." The gruesome vision was Nellie Reed, the British star of the aerial ballet.

Finally, the asbestos curtain began to come down. Most of the stage crew had fled the theater, but someone had figured out a way to lower what was thought would be a fireproof shield between the stage and the audience. It began inching its way down a steel cable between two wooden guide tracks. It descended as if in slow motion, and then, less than twenty feet above the stage, it suddenly stopped. One end was jammed on the light reflector that had not been properly closed, and the other end sagged down to about five feet above the stage. The wooden guide tracks tore apart, and the curtain, which was supposed to have been reinforced and made stiff by steel rods and wires, began to billow out over the orchestra pit and the front rows of seats, pushed by the draft coming from an open stage exit that had been mobbed by the cast and crew.

Some stagehands tried to yank down the curtain, but it was no use. The rest of the crew ran for their lives. The theater's engineer, Robert Murray, ran down to the basement and told his crew to shut off the steam in the boilers heating the building, bank all of the fires to prevent an explosion, then get out as fast as they could. Then he helped a group of chorus girls escape from a basement dressing room by pushing them one at a time through a coal chute that led to an alley. One or two of them were wearing street clothes, but the others were clad in their thin costumes, or worse, in nothing but undergarments.

Murray rushed back up to the stage level and found a young woman whose costume and tights were shredded and burned, and whose skin was charred and blistered. Nellie Reed had somehow unhooked herself from her wire but was seriously injured and in great pain. He managed to get her out into the street, where he handed her to some rescuers.

The entire stage had been turned into a blazing inferno, and if one of the stagehands had not opened one of the big double scenery doors, the entire cast might have perished. Opening the doors undoubtedly saved the lives of the cast and crew, but it sealed the fate of the audience in the upper tiers. The contractors who had built the theater had not only failed to connect the controls for the roof's ventilation systems, but had also nailed shut the vents over the stage and left open the vents above the auditorium, creating a chimney effect. The blast of cold air that rushed in the scenery doors, which caused the curtain to billow out from the stage, instantly mixed with the heated air fueled by the flames, and the result was a huge deadly blowtorch that one fire official later described as a "backdraft."

A churning column of smoke and flames burst out of the opening under the curtain, whirled above the orchestra pit and floor seats, and swept into the balcony and gallery under the open roof vents like a fiery cyclone. The fireball sucked the oxygen from the air, burning and asphyxiating anyone in the upper tiers who remained in their seats or were trapped in the aisles.

Moments later, the last of the ropes holding up the scenery flats onstage gave away, and with a roar that literally shook the building, tons of wood, ropes, sandbags, pipes, pulleys, lights, rigging, and more than 280 pieces of scenery crashed to the stage. The force of the fall instantly knocked out the electrical switchboard, and the auditorium was plunged into complete and utter darkness.

The aisles had become impassable, and as the lights went out, the crowd milled about in blind terror. The auditorium began to fill with heat and smoke, and screams echoed off the walls and ceilings. Many of those who died not only burned but suffocated from the smoke and the crush of bodies. Later, as the police removed the charred remains from the theater, they discovered that a number of victims had been trampled in the panic. One dead woman's face even bore the mark of a shoe heel. Mothers and children were wrenched away from one another and trampled by those behind them. Dresses, jackets, trousers, and other articles of clothing were ripped to shreds as people tried to get through to the exits and escape the flames and smoke. When the crowd reached the doors, they could not open them as they had been designed to swing inward rather than outward. The crush of people prevented those in the front from opening the doors. To make matters worse, some of the side doors to the auditorium were reportedly locked.

In desperation, some of those whose clothing had caught fire jumped from the first balcony to the floor below. Many of them died instantly. Others suffered agonizing deaths from broken backs that were caused by landing on armrests and seat backs.

A brief burst of light illuminated the hellish scene as the safety curtain burst into flames. The curtain, it turned out, was not made completely from asbestos, but from some cheaper material that had been chosen by the theater's co-owner, Will Davis.

At that moment, Eddie Foy made a fateful decision. He needed to get out of the theater as quickly as possible and first considered following the crowd through the Randolph Street doors. But, wanting to find his son, he changed his mind and made his way through the burning backstage and out of the scenery doors. He would only realize how lucky his decision had been after he learned of the hundreds of victims found crushed inside the Randolph Street doors.

Time had been lost because the Iroquois had no alarm system, and the theater had turned into an oven before Engine 13 and other units began arriving. When collecting valuables after the fire, the police found at least a dozen watches that had been stopped at about the same time, 3:50 P.M. This meant that nearly twenty minutes had elapsed from the time that the first alarm had been raised. This certainly accounted for the jamming at the exits and the relatively few people that eyewitnesses saw leaving the theater. Some of the witnesses later stated that nearly seven minutes passed between the time they saw fire coming from the roof of the theater and the front doors on Randolph Street being opened.

Strangely, when Engine 13 arrived at the Randolph Street doors, the scene outside of the theater was completely normal. If not for the smoke billowing from the roof, the firefighters would have assumed that it was a false alarm. This changed when they tried to open the auditorium doors and found they could not—there were too many bodies stacked up against them. They were only able to gain access by actually pulling the bodies out of the way with pike poles, peeling them off one another and then climbing over the stacks of corpses. It took only ten minutes to put out the remaining blaze, as the intense heat inside had already eaten up anything that would still burn.

The gallery and upper balcony sustained the greatest loss of life because the patrons who had been seated there were trapped by locked doors and gates at the top of the stairways. The firefighters found two hundred bodies stacked there, as many as ten deep.

A few who made it to the fire escape door behind the top balcony found that the iron staircase was missing. In its place was a platform that offered a drop of about fifty fee down into Couch Place, a cobblestone alley below. Across the alley, behind the theater, painters were working on a building occupied by Northwestern University's dental school. When they realized what was happening at the theater, they quickly erected a makeshift bridge using a ladder, which they extended across the alley to the fire escape platform. Several people made it to safety, but then as another man was edging his way across, the ladder slipped off the icy ledge of the university building, and the man plummeted to his death.

After the ladder was lost, three wide boards were pushed across to the theater, and the painters anchored them with their knees. The plank bridge worked for a time, but it could not handle the crush of people spilling out of the theater exit. The painters helped as many people as they could, but when what sounded like a bomb went off in the theater (the sound of the rigging and scenery falling to the stage), they watched helplessly as the people trapped inside tried in vain to escape.

Those who swarmed from the fire escape exit were pushed to the edge of the railings with nowhere to go. It was impossible for them to turn back because of the crowd behind them, and they were pushed over the side. Some people tried to crawl across the planks, but in the confusion and smoke, slipped and fell to the alley. Others, whose clothing was on fire, simply gave up and jumped from the railings.

The boards began falling away, and as the fire grew, flames shooting out the doors and windows, many of those hoping for rescue were burned alive in full view of the painters and the students at the dental school. From some of Northwestern University's windows, onlookers could see directly into the theater, which was a solid mass of flames. In the middle of the inferno, they could see men, women, and children running about, and students later said that they did not even look human.

In the aftermath of the fire, Couch Place was dubbed "Death Alley" by reporters who arrived on the scene and counted nearly 150 victims lying on the slush-covered cobblestones. The bodies had been stacked there by firemen, or had fallen to their death from above.

For nearly five hours, police officers, firemen, and even newspaper reporters carried out the dead. Anxious relatives sifted through the ruins, searching for loved ones. As the news spread, public response was immediate and overwhelming. A nearby medical school sent a hundred students to help the doctors who had been dispatched to the Iroquois. A hardware company down the street emptied its stock of two hundred lanterns. Marshall Field's, Mandel Brothers, Carson, Pirie, Scott, and other department stores sent piles of blankets, sheets, rolls of linen, packages of cotton, and large delivery wagons, and converted their ground-floor restrooms and lounges into emergency medical stations. Montgomery Ward sent one of its new, large motorized delivery wagons, but even with its bell ringing, it could not get through the crowds jammed into the streets and had to turn back. Other bodies were taken away by police wagons and ambulances and transported to a temporary morgue at Marshall Field's on State Street. Medical examiners and investigators worked through the night.

Within a short time, small restaurants, saloons, and stores in the vicinity of the Iroquois had been turned into improvised aid stations as medical workers and volunteers began arriving in large numbers. Chicago's central telephone exchange was overwhelmed by emergency calls.

Because the hardware store lanterns were not powerful enough to illuminate the blackened auditorium, the Edison Company rushed over forty arc lamps. When they were turned on, fire and rescue workers were stunned by what they saw. Some of the audience had died sitting up in their seats, facing the stage, staring straight ahead. Others had no burn marks or bruises on them because they had suffocated quickly from the smoke. Many women were found with their heads resting on the back of the seat in front of them. A young boy's head was missing. One woman was bent back over the seat she had been sitting in, her spine severed. Hundreds had been trampled. Clothing, shoes, pocketbooks, and other personal belongings were strewn about. Some of the bodies were burned beyond recognition.

Scores of victims had been wedged into doorways. A husband and wife were locked so tightly in one another's arms that they had to be removed from the theater together. A mother had thrown her arms around her daughter in a hopeless effort to save her, and both had been burned beyond recognition. The number of dead children was heartbreaking. Many were found burned, others trampled. Two dead children were found with the kneeling body of their mother, who had tried to shield them from the flames.

At the edge of the auditorium, a fireman emerged from the ashes with the body of a little girl in his arms. He groped his way forward, stumbling toward Fire Marshall William Henry Musham, who ordered him to give the child to someone else and get back into the auditorium. Another senior officer also ordered him to hand the child off to someone else. As the fireman came closer, the marshal and the other officers could see the streaks of tears on the man's soot-covered face. "I'm sorry, chief," the man said, "but I've got a little one like this at home. I want to carry this one out."

Musham told him to go ahead, and the other officers stepped aside. The weeping fireman carried the little body down the steps of what only an hour before had been the glittering promenade of the grandest theater in Chicago.

With the aid of the Edison arc lights, Deputy Fire Chief John Campion searched the theater's interior while his men continued to douse hot spots that occasionally still burst into flames. Campion called out for survivors, looking around at the burned seats, the blackened walls, and the twisted piles of debris that littered the stage.

The devastated Iroquois Theater was silent.

In possibly less than a quarter of an hour, 572 lives had ended in the Iroquois Theater. More died later, bringing the eventual death toll up to 602, including 212 children. Hundreds more had been injured in what was supposed to be the safest theater in the city. The number of dead was greater than those who had perished in the Great Fire of 1871. A few hours before, the Iroquois had been a luxurious palace but, as newspapers reported that evening, "From the galleries, it looked like a burned-out volcano crater."

The next day, the newspapers devoted full pages to lists of the known dead and injured. News wires carried reports of the tragedy around the country, and it soon became a national disaster. Chicago mayor Carter Harrison Jr. issued an order that banned public celebration on New Year's Eve, closing the nightclubs and forbidding any fireworks or sounding of horns. Every church and factory bell in the city was silenced, and on January 2, 1904, the city observed an official day of mourning.

Someone, the public cried, had to answer for the fire. An investigation of the blaze brought to light a number of troubling facts, including the faulty vents, one of which was nailed shut. Another finding showed that the supposedly "fireproof" asbestos curtain was really made from cotton and other combustible materials. It would have never saved anyone at all. In addition to not having any fire alarms in the building, the owners had decided that sprinklers were too unsightly and too costly and had never had them installed.

To make matters worse, the management also established a policy to keep nonpaying customers from slipping into the theater during a performance—they quietly bolted nine pairs of iron panels over the rear doors and installed padlocked, accordion-style gates at the top of the interior second- and third-floor stairway landings. Just as tragic was the idea they came up with to keep the audience from being distracted during a show—they ordered all the exit lights to be turned off! One exit sign that was left on led only to ladies restroom and another led to a locked door for a private stairway. And as the victims discovered, the doors of the outside exits, which were supposed to make it possible for the theater to empty in five minutes, opened to the inside, not to the outside.

The investigation led to a cover-up by city officials and the fire department, which denied all knowledge of fire code violations. They blamed the inspectors, who had overlooked the problems in exchange for free theater passes. A grand jury indicted a number of individuals, including the theater owners, fire officials, and even the mayor. No one was ever charged with a criminal act, though. Families of the dead filed nearly 275 civil lawsuits against the theater, but no money was ever collected. The Iroquois Theater Company filed for bankruptcy soon after the disaster.

Nevertheless, the building was repaired and reopened briefly in 1904 as Hyde and Behmann's Music Hall and then in 1905 as the Colonial Theater. In 1924, the building was razed to make room for a new theater, the Oriental, but the façade of the Iroquois was used in its construction. The Oriental operated at what is now 24 West Randolph Street until the middle part of 1981, when it fell into disrepair and was closed down. It opened again as the home to a wholesale electronics dealer for a time and then went dark again. The restored theater is now part of the Civic Tower Building and is next door to the restored Delaware Building. It reopened as the Ford Center for the Performing Arts in 1998.

The controversy over the fire may have faded away many years ago, but the lessons learned from it should never be forgotten. The Iroquois Theater Fire ranks as the nation's fourth deadliest blaze and the deadliest single building fire in American history. It remains one of Chicago's worst tragedies and a chilling reminder of how the past continues to reverberate into the present.

The ghosts of the Iroquois Theater tragedy continue to be felt at the site where so many people died. The old theater is long gone, replaced in the 1920s by the Oriental, but ghosts began to be reported in the new theater in its early years—and they remain today.

According to employees, the curtain has a tendency to get stuck at about five feet down, just as the fire curtain did. Others claim that one spotlight—right near the location of the light that started the fire—tends to break off from the now-computerized circuits and behave as though it has a mind of its own. Many employees claim to have seen people in the balcony, particularly during rehearsals, and found no one there—and the doors locked—when they go to make them leave.

Still others have reported backstage encounters with the ghost of a woman wearing a tutu. Traditionally, this has been attributed to Nellie Reed, the aerialist who later died from the burn injuries suffered in the fire. Others believe that it might be Floraline, the other doomed aerialist.

But the woman in the tutu is not the only specter seen around the theater. Recently, several employees have reported the apparition of a man in a red shoulder cape. Several others have reported a ghost in the balcony ventilation system. The identity of the man in the cape would be is anyone's guess—there were more than a thousand costumes used in *Mr. Bluebeard*, and the idea that one might have included a red shoulder cape is certainly possible. The phantoms could also be ghosts of the other employees killed. One other actor, a bit-part player named Burr Scott, was killed in the fire, along with an usher and two female attendants.

It's also possible that some of these ghosts may not be the ghosts of the victims of the Iroquois fire. The theaters that have occupied the spot since 1904 have had their share of horror stories, too. In 1943, a patron attending a movie at the Oriental put a note to his wife, mentioning the song "You'll Never Know How Much I Miss You," a song from the movie of the same name, in his pocket. As the song played in the movie, he shot himself to death. There have also been at least two suicides in the alley behind the theater—Death Alley—in which people have jumped from high buildings to their demise.

Death Alley, in fact, is often said to be more haunted than the theater itself. Cold spots are often encountered here, and many who pass through Couch Place often find themselves very uncomfortable and unsettled there. They say that faint cries are sometimes heard in the shadows, and some have reported being touched by unseen hands and by eerie cold spots that seem to come from nowhere and vanish just as quickly. A number of women claim that they have been touched as they walked though the alleyway, often experiencing something like a small hand holding onto their own as they walk along. Others claim to have heard the sounds of singing, shouting, and perhaps most eerie of all, a group of children laughing and playing.

Is this alleyway actually haunted? And do the spirits of those who met their tragic end inside the burning theater still linger here? Perhaps, or perhaps the strange sensations experienced here are "ghosts of the past" of another kind—a chilling remembrance of a terrifying event that will never be completely forgotten.

Strange Tales of the Eastland Disaster

The afternoon of July 24, 1915, was a special day for thousands of Chicagoans. It was the afternoon that had been reserved for the annual summer picnic for employees of the Western Electric Company. Officials at the utility company had encouraged the workers to bring along as many friends and relatives as possible to the event, which was held across the lake at Michigan City, Indiana. In spite of this open invitation, they were still surprised to find that more than seven thousand people showed up to be ferried across Lake Michigan on the three excursion boats that had been chartered for the day. The steamers were docked on the Chicago River, between Clark and LaSalle streets, and included the *Theodore Roosevelt*, the *Petoskey*, and the *Eastland*.

The *Eastland* was a rusting Lake Michigan steamer owned by the St. Joseph–Chicago Steamship Company. It was supposed to hold a capacity crowd of 2,500 people, but it is believed that on the morning of July 24, more than 3,200 climbed aboard. In addition to being overcrowded, the vessel had a reputation for being unstable. Years before, it was realized that design flaws in the ship made it top-heavy. In July 1903, a case of overcrowding had caused the *Eastland* to list and water to flow up one of its gangplanks. The situation was quickly rectified, but it was only the first of many such incidents. To make matters worse, the new federal Seaman's Act had been passed in 1915 in the wake of the RMS *Titanic* disaster. This required the retrofitting of a complete set of lifeboats on the *Eastland*, as well as on other passenger vessels. The *Eastland* was so top-heavy that it already had special restrictions about how many passengers it could carry. The additional weight of the mandated lifeboats made the ship more unstable than it already was.

The huge crowd, the lifeboats, and the negligence of the crew created a recipe for disaster.

The *Eastland* was moored on the south side of the river, and after the passengers were loaded onboard, the dock lines were loosed and the ship prepared to depart. The massive crowd, dressed in their best summer clothes, jammed onto the decks, calling out and waving handkerchiefs to those who were still onshore. Many of the passengers went below decks, hoping to warm up on this cool, cloudy morning. As the steamer eased away from the dock, it started to list to the port side. Unknown to the passengers, the crew had emptied the ballast compartments of the ship—which were designed to provide stability—so that more passengers could be loaded onboard. They didn't count on a sudden shift in weight that would cause the vessel to lean even farther toward the port side. That sudden shift was caused by a passing fireboat, which fired off its water cannons to the delight of the crowd. The passengers hurried over to the port side for a closer look, and moments later, the *Eastland* simply rolled over. It came to rest on the river bottom, which was only eighteen feet below the surface.

The passengers who had been on the deck were thrown into the river, thrashing about in a moving mass of bodies. Crews on the other steamers, and on passing vessels, threw life preservers into the water, while those on the shore began tossing lines, boxes, and anything that would float to the panicked and drowning passengers. The overturned ship created a current that pulled many of the floundering swimmers to their doom, while many of the women's long dresses were snagged on the ship, tugging them down to the bottom.

The unluckiest passengers were those who had been inside the ship when it turned over. These ill-fated victims were thrown to one side of the vessel when it capsized, and many were crushed by the heavy furniture below decks, which included tables, bookcases, and a piano. As the river water rushed inside, those who were not immediately killed drowned a few moments later. A few of them managed to escape to the upturned side of the ship, but most of them didn't. Their bodies were later found trapped in a tangled heap on the lowest side of the *Eastland*.

Firefighters, rescue workers, and volunteers soon began to arrive and started cutting holes in the ship's hull that was above the water line. The few who had scrambled to safety inside the ship emerged from the holes, but for most of them, it was simply too late. Those onshore eagerly watched for more survivors, but there just weren't any more. The men who had come to rescue the trapped and the injured had to resign themselves to pulling waterlogged corpses from the river instead. The bodies were wrapped in sheets and placed on the *Roosevelt*, or lined up along the docks. The large stores downtown, like Marshall Field's, sent wagons to carry the dead to the hospitals, funeral homes, and makeshift morgues.

Corpses were fished out of the river using large grappling hooks, but those who had been trapped beneath the ship had to be pulled out by police divers and volunteers. According to newspaper accounts, one of these divers, who had been bringing up bodies from the bottom of the river for hours, went into hysterics. He had to be subdued by friends and police officers. City workers dragged the river where the *Eastland* had capsized, using large nets to prevent the bodies from being pulled out into the lake. By the time it was all over, 841 passengers and 4 crewmembers perished in the disaster. Many of them were women and children.

The hundreds of bodies that were recovered on the morning of the disaster were taken to the nearby Reid-Murdoch Building and to local funeral homes and mortuaries. The only public building large enough to be used as a morgue was the Second Regiment National Guard Armory, which was located on Carpenter Street, between Randolph Street and Washington Boulevard. The dead were laid out on the floor of the armory in rows of eighty-five and assigned identifying numbers. Any personal possessions found with the corpses were placed in envelopes bearing the same number as the body.

Chicagoans with loved ones who had perished in the disaster filed through the rows of bodies, searching for familiar faces, but in the cases of twenty-two families, there was no one left to identify them. The families were completely wiped out, including grandparents, parents, children, aunts, uncles, and cousins. The names of these victims were learned through the efforts of neighbors who came searching for their friends. The weeping, crying, and moaning of the bereaved echoed off the walls of the armory for days. The American Red Cross treated thirty women for hysteria and exhaustion in the days following the disaster.

The last body was identified on Friday, July 30. A seven-year-old boy named Willie Novotny of Cicero, number 396, was the last. His parents and older sister had also died on the *Eastland*, and his identification came from extended family members who arrived nearly a week after the disaster took place. After Willie's name was learned, a chapter was closed on one of Chicago's most horrific events.

Officially, the mystery of what happened to the *Eastland* that day was never solved. No clear accounting was ever made to explain the capsizing of the vessel. Several hundred lawsuits were filed, but almost all of them were dismissed by the Circuit Court of Appeals, which held the owners of the steamer blameless in the disaster. After the ship was raised from the river, it was sold at auction. The title was later transferred to the government, and the vessel was pressed into duty as the gunboat USS *Wilmette*. The ship never saw action but was used as a training ship during World War II. After the war, it was decommissioned and put up for sale in 1945. Finding no takers, it was scrapped in 1947.

The *Eastland* was gone, but its story has continued to linger for years—as both a legendary Chicago tragedy and as a series of eerie hauntings.

On the morning of the *Eastland* disaster, many of the bodies of the victims were taken to the Second Regiment National Guard Armory. As the years passed, there was no longer a need for a National Guard armory to be located so close to downtown Chicago. It was closed down by the military, and the building was sold off. It went through several incarnations over the decades, including uses as a stable and a bowling alley, before being purchased by Harpo Studios, the production company owned by Oprah Winfrey. Winfrey is one of Chicago's greatest success stories and is the host of one of the most popular talk shows in television history, as well as a film star, producer, publisher, and well-known personality.

Unfortunately, however, the success of the show filmed in the former armory has done nothing to put to rest the spirits that linger from the *Eastland* disaster. A number of staff members, security guards, and maintenance workers claim that the ghosts of those who perished in 1915 restlessly wander this building. Many employees have had encounters with things that cannot easily be explained away, including the sighting of a woman in a long, gray dress who walks the corridors and then mysteriously vanishes into the wall. There have been many occasions when this woman has been spotted, but each time she is approached, she always disappears. Some have surmised that she is the spirit of a mourner who came here looking for her family and left a bit of herself behind at the spot where she felt her greatest pain.

The woman in gray may not be alone in her spectral travels throughout the old armory. Staff members have also claimed to hear whispers, the sounds of people sobbing, moaning noises, and phantom footsteps. These footsteps, which sound as though they belong to a group of people, are usually heard on a staircase in the lobby. Doors located nearby often open and close under their own power. Those who experience these strange events have come to believe that the tragedy of yesterday is still visiting itself on the former armory as it exists today.

The site of what became the Second Regiment Armory morgue is not the only location in Chicago that still resonates with chilling stories of the *Eastland* disaster ghosts. Reports of the ship being haunted date back to the time just after the disaster and prior to its sale to the Navy. During that period, it was docked near the Halsted Street Bridge and regarded with much superstition by passersby. One lonely caretaker, Captain M. L. Edwards, lived aboard it and said he was awakened by moaning noises nightly, though he attributed them simply to the sound of the ship falling apart. Amused as he was to see people hurry across the bridge, terrified, when they saw a light in his cabin, he was very glad to move off the ship after its sale to the Navy in December 1915.

The site on the river where the disaster occurred has its strange stories, as well. For many years, people who have passed on the Clark Street Bridge have claimed to hear moaning and crying sounds coming from the river, along with bloodcurdling screams and pleas for help. In addition, some witnesses state that the cries are accompanied by the sounds of someone splashing in the river and even the apparitions of people helplessly flailing about in the water. Strange glowing lights are also sometimes seen in the river, but their source remains a mystery.

During several incidents, witnesses have actually called for help from emergency services, believing that someone was actually drowning in the river. At least one man jumped into the water to try and save what he thought was a person unable to swim. When he returned to the surface, he discovered that he was in the river alone. He had no explanation for what he had seen, other than to admit that it might have been a ghost!

In the same way that the former armory seems to have been impressed with a ghostly recording of past events, the Chicago River seems haunted, too. The horror of the *Eastland* disaster may have left behind a memory at this spot, and it continues to replay itself over and over again—ensuring that the luckless victims from the *Eastland* will never truly be forgotten.

The Hand of Death

On the afternoon of Good Friday, April 18, 1924, the members of the Chicago Fire Department's Engine Co. 107 were going about their usual routine. Even though it was a holy day, it would be a day like any other to the firefighters who were on call. They still had to eat, clean, and make sure their equipment and trucks were always ready. And cleaning the large firehouse seemed to be a never-ending task for the men. On this particular day, a firefighter named Francis Xavier Leavy had drawn the duty of cleaning the building's first-floor windows.

Leavy was a good Irish family man who had been with the fire department for thirteen years, after having served an eight-year tour with the Navy, which he had joined at age fourteen. He and his wife, Mary, were the parents of two children, Frank Jr. and a daughter, June. On this day, the usually jovial Leavy was strangely sullen and quiet. He couldn't seem to shake whatever was bothering him, and this put his friends on edge.

Also troubling was the news coming over the telegraph system in front of the firehouse. A four-alarm fire had started in the Union Stockyards, and even though Engine Co. 107 was too far away from it and not expected to respond, the idea that a large fire was burning just a few miles away bothered all of them. Leavy seemed to be lost in his own thoughts, keeping his attention on the window that he was washing. Then, for some reason that remains unknown, he paused in his work with his left hand resting against the pane of glass. He spoke aloud, announcing: "This is my last day on the fire department."

Leavy spoke to no one in particular, but several men heard the strange comment. This, along with his sudden change in personality, puzzled the others, including Edward McKevitt, who had been standing next to Leavy. He started to ask what his friend meant by this, but just then, the station received an alarm call. They were told to go to Fourteenth and Blue Island because the stations that normally covered that area were tied up with the stockyards fire. Just as the other men did, Leavy put on his helmet, coat, and boots and jumped onto the back of the truck as it roared away from the station house.

The burning building they were sent to was Curran Hall, a fifty-year-old brick structure located on South Blue Island, southwest of the Loop. During its heyday, it had been a popular dance hall, but had closed down because of Prohibition. Several small businesses were now operating out of it.

The fire crew stretched a hose up the fire escape and into the building's second story. They crawled through the smoke and fire to aim the water stream at the flames roaring inside. They had no breathing apparatus in those days, so the men had to crawl back and forth to a door or window, following the hose line, to get fresh air. They fought the fire for about a half hour before one of the building's outer walls suddenly buckled, knocking down the entire structure and trapping the firefighters inside. The collapse knocked out the electricity in the area, and the remaining crew had to search for the buried men with flashlights. They dug by hand for hours, ignoring the risk of another collapse, but it was not until cranes were brought in that the bodies of the eight men were discovered.

One of the dead men was Frank Leavy. His eerie prophecy had been fulfilled.

Edward McKevitt had been outside when Curran Hall collapsed, and the following day, he told the other firefighters about Leavy's weird premonition at the window. As he told the story, he looked up at the window that Frank had been cleaning and saw what appeared to be an unusual stain on the glass. It appeared to be in the same spot that Leavy had placed his hand when he made the dire prediction about his own future. McKevitt showed it to the other man and asked whether they thought it could be Leavy's handprint. They tried scrubbing it away and searched for ways to erase the print, but it was no use—the print seemed to be etched into the glass!

The story began making the rounds, and firefighters from all over the city dropped in at the station to see the mysterious handprint. A number of suggestions were made as to how to remove the image, but it refused to come off. Not a single effort, including using ammonia and scraping the glass with a razor blade, ever succeeded. At one point, an expert from the Pittsburgh Plate Glass Company brought in a special solution, guaranteeing that it would remove the print, but it didn't work. It only succeeded in making the handprint more famous.

Hoping to dispel the story, a city official visited the station house after obtaining a copy of Frank Leavy's thumbprint. He planned to compare the print with that on the window and prove once and for all that this was only an anomaly and not the handprint of a dead man. Unfortunately for him, his plan failed. When the fingerprint comparison was concluded, it revealed that the two thumbprints matched perfectly. There was no doubt that the handprint on the window belonged to Frank Leavy.

But what could have caused it? Was it a supernatural occurrence that was left to remind the firemen of their own mortality? Or did the print have a scientific explanation? Some believe that Leavy's fear of a coming tragedy may have caused his body to create a chemical that left behind a permanent stain through his sweat.

No one will ever know for sure, though. The handprint continued to defy all explanation for the next two decades and provided an attraction for visitors to the firehouse. Then, on the morning of April 18, 1944, a careless paperboy tossed the morning edition at the firehouse and shattered the window where Frank's handprint had been. The glass was broken, and the shards were scattered about on the ground, destroying not only the strange window but also any hope that the mystery of the handprint would ever be solved.

Even more eerie than the precise throw of an unknowing paperboy was the date on which the broken window occurred. It was April 18, 1944—exactly twenty years to the day Frank Leavy died!

The St. Valentine's Day Massacre

Perhaps the most famous event to occur in the history of Chicago crime took place on St. Valentine's Day 1929, when mob boss Al Capone attempted to wipe out his competition for the rights to control all the liquor in the city. While this bloody event marked the end of any significant gang opposition to Capone, it was also the act that finally began the decline of Capone's criminal empire.

The bloody events of February 14, 1929, were set in motion nearly five years before with the murder of Dion O'Banion, the leader of Chicago's North Side mob. At that time, control of bootleg liquor in the city raged back and forth between the North Siders, run by O'Banion, and the South Side Outfit, which was controlled by Johnny Torrio and his henchman, Al Capone. In November 1924, Torrio ordered the assassination of O'Banion and started an all-out war in the city. The North Siders retaliated soon afterward and nearly killed Torrio outside of his home. This brush with death led to him leaving the city and turning over operations to Capone, who was almost killed himself in September 1926. The following month, Capone shooters assassinated Hymie Weiss, who had been running the North Side mob after the death of O'Banion. His murder left the operation in the hands of George "Bugs" Moran, a long-time enemy of Capone. For the most part, Moran stood alone against the Capone mob, since most of his allies had succumbed in the fighting. He continued to taunt his powerful enemy and looked for ways to destroy him.

In early 1929, Moran sided with Joe Aiello in another attack against Capone. He and Aiello reportedly gunned down Pasquillano Lolordo, one of Capone's men, and Capone vowed that he would have Moran wiped out on February 14. Capone was living on his estate outside of Miami at the time and put in a call to Chicago. Capone had a very special "valentine" that he wanted delivered to Moran.

Through a contact in Detroit, Capone arranged for someone to call Moran and tell him that a special shipment of hijacked whiskey was going to be delivered to one of Moran's garages on the North Side. Adam Heyer, a friend of Moran, owned the garage, and it was used as a distribution point for North Side liquor. A sign on the front of the building at 2122 North Clark Street read "S-M-C Cartage Co. Shipping—Packing—Long Distance Hauling." Moran received the call at the garage on the morning of February 13, and he arranged to be there to meet the truck the next day.

On the morning of February 14, a group of Moran's men gathered at the Clark Street garage. One of the men was Johnny May, an ex-safecracker who Moran had hired as an auto mechanic. He was working on a truck that morning with his dog, a German shepherd named Highball, tied to the bumper. In addition, six other men waited for the truck of hijacked whiskey to arrive. The men were Frank and Pete Gusenberg, who were supposed to meet Moran and pick up two empty trucks to drive to Detroit and load with smuggled Canadian whiskey; James Clark, Moran's brother-in-law; Adam Heyer; Al Weinshank; and Reinhardt Schwimmer, a young optometrist who had befriended Moran and hung around the liquor warehouse just for the thrill of rubbing shoulders with gangsters.

George Moran was already late for the morning meeting. He was due to arrive at 10:30 but didn't even leave for the rendezvous, in the company of Willie Marks and Ted Newberry, until several minutes after that.

As the seven men waited inside the warehouse, they had no idea that a police car had pulled up outside, or that Moran had spotted the car as he was driving south on Clark Street and, rather than deal with what he believed was a shakedown, stopped at the next corner for a cup of coffee.

Five men got out of the police car, two of them in uniforms and three in civilian clothing. They entered the building, and a few moments later, the clatter of machine-gun fire broke the stillness of the snowy morning. Soon after, five figures emerged and drove away. May's dog, inside the warehouse, began barking and howling.

The landlady in the next building, Mrs. Jeanette Landesman, was bothered by the sound of the dog, so she sent one of her boarders, C. L. McAllister, to the garage to see what was going on. He came outside two minutes later, his face a pale white color. He ran frantically up the stairs to beg Mrs. Landesman to call the police. He cried that the garage was full of dead men!

The police were quickly summoned and, upon entering the garage, were stunned by the carnage. Moran's men had been lined up against the rear wall of the garage and sprayed with machine guns. Pete Gusenberg had died kneeling, slumped over a chair. James Clark had fallen on his face with half of his head blown away, and Heyer, Schwimmer, Weinshank, and May were thrown lifeless onto their backs. Only one of the men survived the slaughter, and he lived for only a few hours. Frank Gusenberg had crawled from the blood-sprayed wall where he had fallen and dragged himself into the middle of the dirty floor. He was rushed to the Alexian Brothers Hospital, barely hanging on. Police sergeant Clarence Sweeney, who had grown up on the same street as Gusenberg, leaned down close to Frank and asked who had shot him.

"No one—nobody shot me," he groaned, and he died later that night.

The death toll of the massacre stood at seven, but the killers had missed Moran. When the police contacted him later and told him what had happened at the garage, he "raved like a madman." To the newspapers, Moran targeted Capone as ordering the hit. The authorities claimed to be baffled, though, since Capone was in Florida at the time of the massacre. When he was asked to comment on the news, Capone stated, "the only man who kills like that is Bugs Moran." At the same time, Moran was proclaiming that "only Capone kills guys like that."

And Moran was undoubtedly right. The murders broke the power of the North Side gang, and while there have been many claims as to who the actual shooters were that day, most likely they included John Scalise, Albert Anselmi, and "Machine Gun" Jack McGurn, all of whom were some of Capone's most trusted men. All three men, along with Joseph Guinta, were arrested, but McGurn had an alibi and Scalise and Guinta were killed before they could be tried.

The St. Valentine's Day Massacre marked the end of any significant gang opposition to Capone, but it was also the act that finally began the decline of Capone's criminal empire. He had just gone too far, and the authorities—and even Capone's adoring public—were ready to put an end to the bootleg wars.

Chicago, in its own way, memorialized the warehouse on Clark Street where the massacre took place. It became a tourist attraction, and the newspapers even printed the photos of the corpses upside down so that readers would not have to turn their papers around to identify the bodies.

In 1949, the front portion of the S-M-C Garage was turned into an antique furniture storage business by a couple who had no idea of the building's bloody past. They soon found that the place was visited much more by tourists, curiosity-seekers, and crime buffs than by customers, and they eventually closed the business.

In 1967, the building was demolished. Strangely, bricks that were sold or removed from the site were rumored to be "cursed" in some way, perhaps affected by the dark and bloody events that occurred in the building.

Whether or not the bricks were somehow "haunted" by what happened, there is little doubt that the site on Clark Street seems to be. Stories say that the site where the St. Valentine's Day Massacre occurred is one of the most haunted spots in the city. People walking along the street at night have reported the sounds of screams and machine guns as they pass the site. The building is long gone now, demolished in a misguided attempt by city officials to erase all vestiges of Chicago's gangster past. A portion of the block was taken over by the Chicago Housing Authority, and a fenced-in lawn that belongs to a senior citizen's development now marks the area where the garage once stood. Five trees are scattered about the site; the one in the center actually marks the point where the rear wall once stood, where Moran's men were lined up and gunned down. The apartment building, where Mrs. Landesman lived and heard the sound of Highball barking in the garage, still stands, but all remnants of the S-M-C Cartage Co. have vanished.

Or have they?

According to reports, residents of the senior housing complex built on one end of the lot have had strange encounters in the building, especially those who live on the side that faces the former massacre site. A television reporter from Canada interviewed a woman who once lived in an apartment that overlooked the small park area, and she often complained that, at night, she would hear strange voices, sounds, and knocking on her door and her window. She complained to the management, who dismissed her claims as imagination but assigned her another apartment. A new tenant moved into the rooms, and she also complained of odd happenings, including knocking sounds that would come at her door at night. When she opened the door to see who was there, she never found anyone nearby. One night, she stated that she saw a dark figure wearing an old-style hat. He remained in place for a few moments and then faded away. Most of the strange phenomena experienced by the new tenant also faded away, and soon, the eerie events either stopped completely or she got so used to them that they no longer bothered her anymore.

Outside, along Clark Street, passersby and the curious have sometimes reported strange sounds, like weeping and moaning, and the indescribable feeling of fear as they walk past the former site of the garage. Skeptics have tried to laugh this off, saying that the sounds are nothing more than the overactive imaginations of those who know what once occurred on the site. Based on the reports of those who had no idea of the history of the place, however, something strange was apparently occurring.

Those who were accompanied by their dogs also reported their share of weirdness, too. The animals seemed to be especially bothered by this piece of lawn, sometimes barking and howling, sometimes whining in fear. Their sense of what happened here many years ago seems to be much greater than our own.

Many believe that what dogs sense here is not the human trauma experienced at the massacre site, but rather the trauma that must have been experienced by Johnny May's German shepherd, Highball. The poor animal must have been terrified by what occurred that morning, from the deafening sounds of the Tommy guns to the bloody slaying of his beloved owner. Tied to the front bumper of the truck, Highball had nowhere to run. It should be noted again that it was not the sound of machine-gun fire that alerted Landesman to the horror inside the garage: it was the howling and barking of the terrified dog.

Could the animals that passed by this empty lot have been sensing the trauma suffered by Highball so many years ago? As any ghost buff can tell you, it's the events of yesterday that create the hauntings of today, and sometimes those who lived in the past can leave a little piece of themselves behind to be experienced in the present over and over again.

Even after all of these years, the violent events of the city's gangster era still reverberate over time. Men like Al Capone, whether city officials want to admit it or not, left an indelible mark on Chicago. It seems that the events of St. Valentine's Day 1929 may have left one, too.

Lonely Ghost of Morton College

While Morton College has only occupied its current campus since 1975, the school has served students from the surrounding communities since 1924. It is the second oldest two-year college in Illinois and a leader in the community college movement. The school got its start in the middle 1920s when eleven teachers began instructing seventy-six young men and women from around the area. For nearly fifty years, classes were held at Morton East High School and in local churches and storefronts. A bond referendum held in December 1966 allowed a much-needed campus to be built on undeveloped land near the Stevenson Expressway. The land was readily available, even though the Jewel Supermarkets chain had been planning to use the property for a new shipping center. An event that took place in 1969, however, stigmatized the land to the point that the proposal was withdrawn.

Ground was broken for the new college campus in December 1973, but it took almost two years for the construction to be completed. The first classes began in September 1975—but even before the school was finished, it was already thought to be haunted.

In the years before Morton College constructed its campus on the land along South Central Avenue, the property was a swampy open lot that local residents considered to be an eyesore. The land went from being a nuisance to a murder site in the fall of 1969.

Emily M. Keseg was an eighteen-year-old business administration student at Morton College and a resident of nearby Berwyn. She was an average girl from a middle class background, somewhat quiet and shy, and she lived with her parents on Maple Avenue. The day of Friday, October 17 began as any normal day for Emily. As her father did each weekday, he dropped her off for her classes, which were then being held at Morton East High School, at 8:30 A.M. She followed her usual schedule, and according to friends, nothing seemed to be bothering her. The only out-of-the-ordinary event to occur that day was an incident between Emily and her estranged sixteen-year-old boyfriend. They got into an argument about a ring he had given her that he now wanted returned.

After her classes ended for the day, at about 6:00 P.M., Emily met a girlfriend who lived in Cicero to make plans for their Friday night. She called her parents at about 8:00 P.M. and told them that she was going out for pizza with friends and would be home around midnight. This is the last time they would ever hear from their daughter.

Emily and three friends met at Pat's Pizzeria on South Roosevelt Road, and according to reports, stayed there until after 1:00 A.M. She and her girlfriend were spotted leaving the pizza parlor with two male friends. As they were leaving, Emily asked the young man who was driving to take her past her boyfriend's house on Central Avenue. She saw him sitting in a parked car in front of his house, so she asked to be dropped off so she could talk to him. Strangely, though, the boyfriend and his parents claimed that they never saw Emily that night.

The last person believed to have spoken with Emily that night, besides her killer, was a twenty-one-year-old motorist who saw a young woman walking west on Thirty-fifth Street near Fifty-sixth Court at about 2:20 A.M. He recognized Emily because he lived near her in Berwyn, and he later told police that he stopped and offered her a ride home, but she declined.

A short time later, she was also spotted by witnesses standing near a pay phone at the northwest corner of Thirty-fifth Street and Fifty-eighth Court (a short distance from the previous sighting). Police investigators later discovered Emily's fingerprints on the receiver, so it's known that she used the telephone, although unknown as to whom she may have called. Some blood spatter was found on the ground near the pay phone, leading to a small pool of blood found around the corner and down an alley. They also found a purse and a shoe that belonged to Emily.

Prior to this discovery, however, a Cicero woman reported the sound of a woman moaning coming from an alley near Thirty-fifth Street and Fifty-ninth Avenue. When her son returned home from his paper route, she sent him to investigate, and he found a wig and a dollar bill with blood on it lying on the ground. A short time later, two telephone repairmen who were working near the alley found several pieces of bloody clothing and Emily's student identification. The police were notified, and a search began around 8:00 A.M.

Investigators combed the area, and shortly before 1:30 P.M., Emily's naked body was found lying in a muddy field on the site of what would someday be Morton College. The cause of death was determined to be strangulation, but Emily's face and head had been badly beaten, and a hole had been punched in at the base of her skull. The medical examiner stated that she had been dead for about ten to twelve hours when found. Her father later identified her bruised and bloody body at MacNeal Memorial Hospital.

The case had an amazing number of contradictions and loose ends. The chronology of the eyewitness accounts really didn't fit the medical examiner's time of death. The police canvassed the neighborhood but could find no other leads and no motive for the girl's murder. She had been carrying little money at the time of her death, which seemed to rule out robbery, but it was speculated that perhaps she had rejected advances by an assailant while walking home. Based on the damage done to her face and head, however, it seemed to be a crime of passion committed by someone who knew her. A number of suspects were proposed, but no one was ever arrested or indicted for the crime.

The final remnant of the case was found three days after Emily's body was discovered. Investigators checked a charity donation bin that stood in a grocery store parking lot on Thirty-fifth Street and found the rest of the girl's belongings inside, including the mate to the shoe that had been found in the alley.

No trace was ever found of Emily's killer, and to this day, the case is unsolved and remains one of the area's most baffling modern mysteries.

The property where Emily's body was found remained vacant for several years after her murder. At the time of her death, Jewel was reportedly making plans to open a shopping center on the site, but thanks to the stigma of the girl's murder, they withdrew their offer to buy the land. Nothing was done with the site until the new campus for Morton College was constructed there.

When work was still being done on the buildings, workmen began reporting strange activity. One day during the construction, a worker saw a girl in a white dress walking along the edge of the roof. He called out to her, but moments later, she jumped from the roof! He ran as quickly as he could, fearing that she was dead after falling from such a height, but when he looked down, there was no one there. Still sure that she must have been killed, he scrambled to the ground level and searched the area at the base of the building—but there was no sign of the young woman.

Since that time, a ghostly form is sometimes seen on the roof, but more common are the stones and pebbles that fly from the top of the building and strike unwitting passersby. Custodians who have witnessed this happening often investigate, only to find that the roof is abandoned and the door leading up to it is closed and locked.

Campus elevators also have a habit of operating on their own, running up and down after classes have ended for the day and there is no one but security guards in the buildings. These same guards have heard the sounds of doors slamming shut in the B, C, and D buildings and have heard the sound of running footsteps on an upper floor, as if someone were dashing back and forth down the hallways. They find the upper floors to be quiet and empty when they investigate the sounds but often hear them again when they return to the first floor.

Building E has also been the scene of water taps that turn on and off by themselves and toilets that flush without assistance. The theater and the library have also been plagued by unexplainable events. Lights often turn out or dim in the theater, and problems with the sound system are always blamed on "Emily." Staff members claim to have seen shadows moving about in the library and have encountered cold chills that should not exist. On one occasion, a dedicated staff member who had recently revamped the entire library abruptly resigned from her position. She had been in the restroom and had been overwhelmed by a flowery smell that she was sure was the ghost. She became too frightened to work there any longer and quit her job.

Based on the long list of strange events that have occurred here, a ghost has apparently taken a liking to Morton College. Most believe that this restless spirit is that of Emily Keseg, whose body was found on the grounds decades ago. Perhaps she stayed behind at the scene of her horrific death—or perhaps she returned to a place she loved when she was still among the living. The current campus was only a dream at the time she was slain, but who can say whether she may have followed the students to the new school after it was built? The answer to the question of the ghost here remains nearly as puzzling as the mystery behind Emily's death.

Haunted Chicago Police Stations

Police stations, jails, and prisons are not uncommon places to find ghosts. In late 1906 and early 1907, a number of police stations came to the Chicago public's attention as being infested with ghosts.

In 1907, officials reported that six Chicago police stations were definitely haunted. Ghosts had been seen at many stations from time to time, but those six stations were regularly haunted. In one of the stations, a patrol driver resigned his position rather than continue in the "ghost-besieged" headquarters where he was assigned to duty. In another station, a ghost attacked one of the patrolmen while he was sleeping in the off-duty quarters upstairs. He was so frightened that he fired his revolver at the phantom and left six bullet holes in the plaster wall. In still another station, a shadowy intruder so affected the mind of a patrolman that he went insane and had to be taken away to an asylum.

The Stockyards, Hyde Park, Grand Crossing, Englewood, Des Plaines, and New City stations were all reportedly haunted. The Stockyards station was said to be the most spirit-infested. The commanding officer and patrolmen vouched for the evidence of the spectral activity. Desk Sergeant William Prindeville, who had been at the station since 1896, had seen so many ghosts in his time, he claimed, that he had become used to them and rather enjoyed their company.

The Stockyards

The first ghost made an appearance at the Stockyards station in the winter of 1902; he was seen on the night following his death in the basement of the building. The "old soldier," as the officers described him, was worn out after tramping through the snow all day and so had come into the station to ask if he could spend the night there. Sergeant Prindeville told the man to go down to the basement, where they often allowed "bojacks," as the homeless were known to the police, to spend the night. The old veteran made his way down to the warm basement and curled up on one of the bunks. Early the next morning, a number of "regulars" found the old man dead on his bunk and reported it to the officers upstairs.

In the early morning hours of the following day, as Sergeant Prindeville was dozing in his chair and waiting for dawn to end the night watch and send him home for breakfast, he heard a slight rapping on the door. He first thought the wind had caused the door to rattle, but listening carefully, he realized that it was a sound made by someone knocking. He went over to the door and opened it. As he turned the knob, a flurry of snow whipped into his face, and in the dim light, he saw the faint outline of the old soldier who had asked him for a place to sleep the previous night. Knowing that the man had died, Prindeville quickly realized that he was facing a ghost. He hurriedly slammed the door and went back behind his desk, unnerved by what would turn out to be the first of many such encounters.

When the shift changed later that morning, Prindeville told the other officers what he had seen. Not surprisingly, they refused to believe him, insisting that the swirling snow must have been playing tricks on his eyes. After that, however, Prindeville began watching for the ghost, and so did some of the other men. Nearly everyone at the station saw the ghost at one time or another, because he returned every winter whenever the snow would fly. Each night following a storm, a knocking would come at the door, and when answered, officers would find the old soldier standing outside. Prindeville stated that he often spoke to the ghost when it appeared, but he never received a reply.

Hyde Park

According to an account from 1907, Detective John Shea, one of the most reliable and trustworthy officers at the Hyde Park police station, nearly shot out the back wall of the station house one night when a ghost invaded his sleeping quarters. Shea had gone to sleep just after midnight in the dormitory on the third floor of the building. Just after 2:00 A.M., he reported, something began tugging on the bed covers, awakening him from a sound sleep. The room was pitch dark, and Shea, who was only half awake, did nothing more at first than reach down and try and retrieve the disappearing blankets.

A few minutes later, the bed covers were again pulled from the bed, and the police officer, now thoroughly awake, thought somebody was trying to play a trick on him. He decided that he would wait until it happened again, and if anyone appeared, he would fire his revolver into the ceiling to frighten them and show that he, too, enjoyed playing pranks. As he lay there with his finger on the trigger, he was horrified to see a phantom shape step out from behind a clothes locker and approach the bed.

Shea later stated that the ghost was shaped like a woman, except that it only had one eye, which shined with a blue sort of light. It slowly approached the bed until it was only about a foot away, and then it reached out a hand toward him. By this time, Shea was as cold as an icicle, and his hand was gripping the butt of his revolver so tightly that his knuckles had turned white. Slowly, the ghost's fingers gathered up the corner of the bed quilts and gradually pulled them onto the floor. The phantom then seemed to draw backward, retreating to the place where Shea had first seen it, as it watched with its one blue eye as he pulled the bed covers back up again.

Shea declared that he stayed there looking at the ghost for nearly an hour. By that time, he said, his courage had returned to him, so he raised the pistol in his hands and fired six times. The sound of the shots created a commotion downstairs, where some of the other night watchmen were playing cards, and across the street at the Holland Hotel, where dozens of guests later reported hearing the sound of shots being fired. Shea's fellow officers crashed up the stairs and burst into the room. The lights were turned on to see what was happening, and all the men saw Shea sitting on the edge of the bed with sweat beaded on his brow and smoke curling from the barrel of his gun. He pointed to the wall on the south end of the room, where there were six large bullet holes.

He only uttered one word: "Ghost!"

Grand Crossing

Patrol wagon driver Thomas Murnane quit his job at the Grand Crossing station rather than put up with the ghost that he, and others, claimed haunted the place. For an entire year before Murnane resigned, the ghost appeared regularly at the station every night and found its chief delight in removing the harness from the patrol wagon horses. As required by the rules of the department, one team of horses had to be kept harnessed all night, and Murnane declared before he left service that the black figure of a man entered the barn every night and calmly removed the harness from his team.

Murnane and two other men who worked on the wagon with him always went to sleep between night runs. One night, Murnane was lying on his cot, not asleep but thinking, when he saw a man walk into the stall occupied by the team and remove the harness from the horses. In the darkness, Murnane thought it was one of the police officers and that he had been wrongly told to keep the horses harnessed all night.

The next morning, he told the other men what he had seen, but they only laughed at him and told him that his night visitor was probably "Johnny Reeves." Murnane had never heard of the man, but not wanting to show his ignorance, he kept quiet and went on about his work. Later that day, though, he asked one of the police officers about Reeves and was told that he had been a tramp who had died one night while sleeping in the barn. Murnane became convinced after this that the figure he saw each night was that of a genuine ghost.

The sightings of Johnny Reeves continued, and the patrol wagon driver, frightened out of his wits by the ghost, tried in vain to sleep as the other men did. Every night, he told them afterward, he lay in a cold sweat, watching the intruder. Finally, after he had worried himself sick, he wrote out his resignation, even though he knew that it meant never fulfilling his dream of being a police officer. Even that lifelong goal was not enough to convince Murnane to stay and brave the nightly visits from Johnny Reeves.

Englewood

One night in the summer of 1906, Denny Lang, one of the detectives at the Englewood station, was reportedly pushed out of bed by a ghost and then chased down Wentworth Avenue for several blocks. Lang had been told that the ghost of a Polish laborer, who had been killed by a switch engine on the Rock Island Railroad tracks just behind the station, had taken up residence in the sleeping quarters on the station's second floor. The ghost was said to carry a bag filled with bricks to attack anyone who came near it.

Lang didn't believe the story and laughed at his fellow officers who were too scared to sleep at the station house. He was determined to prove that he was no coward. One night, about an hour after he had climbed into one of the iron cots used by men on reserve duty, Lang was startled by a heavy thumping on the floor under his bed. He looked around, trying to determine where the disturbance was coming from, and was terrified to see a ghost standing in the far corner of the room. He claimed that it had eyes that glowed like fire and a bag filled with bricks—just as the other men had described it.

Lang's courage immediately vanished, and he ran from the room. He pounded down the stairs and ran out onto Wentworth

Avenue and down the street. He reported that the ghost came after him, hurling pieces of bricks as it pursued him. The ghost eventually vanished, but the experience was not lost on Lang, and he never slept in the station house again.

A remodeling of the station in 1907 caused the ghost to appear less often than it had in the past. Even so, most of the men claimed they still wouldn't sleep there alone.

Des Plaines Street

The ghost that haunted the station on Des Plaines Street was said to be that of a tramp who had been killed there several years before. One night, two tramps were sleeping in cell number three after having been given shelter from the cold weather outside. They got into a fight that led to one of them choking the other to death. After that, men who slept in that cell, prisoners and tramps alike, claimed to be awakened by cold hands squeezing their throats. The cell was soon widely avoided, and old timers, familiar with the story, stated that they would rather sleep on the cold Chicago streets than in cell number three at the Des Plaines station.

New City

According to officers at the New City station, their resident ghost was that of a prisoner who died while trying to escape from his cell one night. After that, officers and prisoners were often aroused at night by an eerie sound like that of a file grating on an iron bar. They came to believe that the prisoner was still trying to escape from confinement, many years after his death.

Hauntings of the Old Cook County Jail

In October 1906, startling reports reached Chicago readers of ghosts and hauntings taking place at the old Cook County Jail, a largely abandoned structure that had been built after the Great Fire in 1871 and had been recently replaced by a new jail. Chicago's executions still continued to occur on the old gallows, and unfortunately, due to overcrowding, some of the cells in the old structure had been put back into use again—much to the dismay of the prisoners and the guards assigned to watch over them.

Many stated that the haunting had already begun when the "car barn bandit," Peter Neidermeir, went to the gallows, but his final words on the scaffold did nothing to ease the minds of those who believed in spirits. Just before his execution, he declared, "You can't kill me, you scoundrels. I will come back, and when I do, you will be sorry for what you have done."

Neidermeir was one of three men sentenced to hang for a series of robberies in Chicago and northern Indiana. Along with Harvey Van Dine and Gustav Marx, Neidermeir had earned his nickname of "car barn bandit" after the murder of two Chicago Street Railway employees at one of the company's barns. He went to the gallows in 1904 and became the forty-fifth man to die at the county jail. Soon after, the haunting of the jail intensified, leading many to believe that Neidermeir had made good on his threat of coming back.

Even before his execution, though, prisoners often reported the sounds of hammers banging away at the gallows. The sounds always occurred at night, when no workmen were present.

Even the most skeptical admitted that the old jail at Dearborn and Illinois avenues, built after the fire and then closed off from view by the courthouse and the new jail, was the perfect setting for a haunting. The place had long since fallen into a state of decay and disrepair and was made up of four grim, brick walls without partitions of any kind. In the center, with corridors all around, were the four tiers of cells that were eventually abandoned. Overcrowding in the new jail put many of the cells back into use again, and thanks to the number of men who died within the walls of the old edifice, it was no wonder that whispers of ghosts began to circulate.

The strange manifestations began before each hanging. Prior to one execution, prisoners and guards came to believe that the resident spirits carried out an execution of their own. The carpenters had put the scaffold in place and made all the preparations for a hanging to be carried out the next night at midnight. The old jail corridor was dark, the workmen had departed, and the lights were turned down low. Then, there suddenly came a loud noise that startled every prisoner in the building and caused the jail guards to come running—the drop of the scaffold had fallen on its own.

No effort was made to investigate the situation that night, but when Jailer Whitman arrived the following morning, he sought to discover the reason for the accident. He found that the executioner's rope, the line that leads back to the small box where a deputy sheriff awaits the signal to use his knife, had been cut just as cleanly as if a deputy himself had severed it.

Whitman was never able to explain the incident, and although he was not a believer in ghosts, he admitted there was something unaccountable about the affair.

In October 1906, an anonymous reporter, hoping to get to the bottom of the rumored haunting, went inside the old jail to speak with the guards and the prisoners. He described the walls of the old structure as being devoid of paint and plaster, just bricks and the cement between them. The old building opened into the new jail, a large structure that faced onto Dearborn and hid the old jail, where the executions took place, from sight. One barred door and a second, steel door separated the two jails, but at the time, only the barred door was being used because the old cells had been put back into service. Because of this, many of the strange sounds reported in the old building were being heard by inmates in the new one.

The reporter wrote, "Yet the prisoners in the new building have no fear, while in the cells of the squatty old structure the occupants are frightened and admit it frankly. They claim they are kept awake at night by poundings at their very heads. One of the prisoners said that almost every night a light was thrown over his eyes until he was awakened and that no sooner did he sleep than the demonstration was repeated. So many things have happened recently in the corridors of the old jail and down in the scaffold room of the basement that the belief has spread that the place is actually haunted. Among the 125 prisoners in the cells of the old structure this belief is supreme, and they assert the punishment by imprisonment is second to their punishment by fear."

According to the guards, prisoners were startled by weird happenings on a nightly basis. Screams were often heard, and men were seen suddenly sitting up on their bunks, their faces a mask of stark terror. When asked what was wrong, most attempted to laugh off their feelings, but invariably admitted to be frightened by the ghosts. Even the guards admitted to often being frightened themselves.

Chairs were moved from place to place in the night and papers often disappeared, only to turn up later in unusual locations. One of the jail guards stated firmly, "I don't believe in ghosts but somehow I am getting creepy in this place. Last night, I sat here and heard someone pounding. I got up and the sound stopped. I went to the place I thought the sound had come from, but there was no one. I asked some of the prisoners and they said they had heard the pounding. So, what are you going to think about that? I wouldn't say the place is haunted, that would make me look foolish, but I want to tell you that I wouldn't stay in this place alone."

The prisoners with whom the reporter spoke freely admitted to being frightened, and most volunteered their encounters with the ghosts. One prisoner stated, "I know there are ghosts here. A few nights ago, I woke up and there was a dim light over my cot. I felt a hand placed on my head, and then the light went out. I jumped up, but the cell door was locked. No living man could have possibly been in my cell. You ask me if this place is haunted—I know it is haunted."

One prisoner, a young man, was so frightened by one night's stay in the old jail that Jailer Whitman, upon hearing his story, had him removed to the new section of the building.

Whitman himself was hard-pressed to believe in ghosts, although sometimes he wondered about the strange incidents in the old jail. He was sometimes inclined to believe in the ghosts, but usually, after an investigation, he was able to explain away most of the mysterious happenings with natural causes.

He told the reporter, "I know of no way to determine whether or not the old jail is haunted. Certainly, it is a likely place for ghosts, if such things exist. Forty-five men have been hanged in those old corridors, and one, at least, vowed to come back and do us injury. I would keep no prisoners in the place if it were not absolutely necessary. The new jail is full, and there are 125 prisoners being kept at present in the old jail. They are frightened at night, every sound disturbs them, and while I know that it is true that they have a creepy feeling the old place is haunted, I am unable to relieve them, except as vacancies are made by discharges from the new jail. When some person more superstitious than others is brought in, I seek to make a place for him that will not cause undue fear.

"And while I personally have no belief in ghosts, I must admit there are some strange happenings in the old jail."

Chicago's Haunted English Pub

While most visitors to Chicago would never believe it, there just happens to be an authentic British pub located on the North Side, just across North Lincoln Avenue from the famed Biograph Theater. For many years, it has had a reputation for being one of the most "spirited" dining and drinking establishments in the city.

The Red Lion Pub opened in 1984 in a two-story building that dated back to 1882. Over the years, it reportedly saw many uses, including a grocery store, apartments, a country and western bar called "Dirty Dan's," and an illegal gambling parlor.

John Cordwell bought the building in the mid 1980s with plans to refurbish it into a pub. Cordwell passed away before the remodeling could be completed, but the project was finished by his son, Colin, and his son-in-law, Joe Heinen. The place soon opened for business and began serving what most consider some of the most authentic pub fare in the city.

The ghost stories of the place are an integral part of the business and date back to long before John Cordwell purchased the property. Former residents of the apartments on the top floor told stories about the proprietor of Dirty Dan's, the bar that once occupied the space, and how he often talked to what he called his "invisible friends" in the building.

During the renovations to turn the place into the Red Lion, workers often found their tools missing or scattered about. There was never any indication of anyone being in the building during their absence, but these strange events continued throughout the renovations and continue to occur in other ways today.

Customers in the pub experienced the strange manifestations as soon as the place opened for business. One of the happenings most often noticed were heavy footsteps that trudged across the upper floor, moving from west to east. Customers and staff members often heard the sound, even though everyone present was aware that no one is upstairs. When anyone went to check on the sounds, they found the second floor abandoned. The phantom footsteps were most active during the cold-weather months, but they occurred at other times of the year, as well. The footsteps were sometimes joined by what sounded like tables and chairs being overturned in the small bar area on the second floor. Alarmed, staff members often ran upstairs to see what was going on only to find the second floor empty and the chairs and tables untouched.

One night, Colin Cordwell and several others on the first floor heard a terrific crash from upstairs. Colin put down what he was doing and dashed up the stairs to see what was going on. The second floor was darkened and silent. As he searched the room, however, he discovered a cricket bat lying on the floor. It had somehow been thrown from where it had been hanging on the wall to a location about twenty feet away. There was no explanation for how this could have happened.

Who the ghosts are in this building is unknown, but there are suspects. There were a couple confirmed deaths in the building, including those of an elderly couple who once lived in one of the second-floor apartments. Years earlier, their daughter had also died in the building. Her name was reportedly Sharon, and according to the remembrances of those who lived in the neighborhood for years, she was mentally disabled. They remembered her often sitting on the front stoop of the building, chatting with passersby. How Sharon died is a mystery, but many believe that she haunts the building today and manifests herself through the strong, sweet smell of lavender perfume. The scent has been encountered all over the pub, although mainly on the second floor.

Another manifestation that might have also been attributed to Sharon was an icy cold spot that appeared in the small bar area upstairs. There were no air ducts nearby, and the cold spot came and went without warning. According to legend, the spot marked the location of Sharon's bedroom before the upper floor was remodeled.

Although it was a rare occasion, ghosts were sometimes seen in the pub. Reports from customers and employees told of a blond-haired man who mysteriously vanished, a bearded man in a black hat, and a man in cowboy clothing, who might have been the specter of "Dirty Dan" himself. Dan Danforth was a reputed troublemaker who cursed the day he was evicted from the building. Before his death, John Cordwell believed that he encountered this nasty spirit. As he was going up the stairs one day, he felt a hard push on his chest, which knocked him back down the steps. Since this was so out of character with the rest of the hauntings in the place, Cordwell was convinced that it was the hard-drinking Danforth who was looking to carry out his threats of revenge. Since that time, no other events that have reportedly occurred at the Red Lion have been particularly threatening or dangerous.

If you get the chance, stop in some time for an order of fish and chips, some Irish stew, or perhaps just a cold glass of beer. The spirits in your glass may not be the only spirits that you find at the Red Lion!

The Ole St. Andrew's Intoxicated Ghost

Although it's known today as the Ole St. Andrew's Inn, this Scottish-themed pub first gained notoriety as the "Edinburgh Castle Pub." The place has operated as a Scottish bar since 1961, but before that, the place was simply a neighborhood bar owned by a colorful character named Frank Giff. Frank had a taste for playing pool, joking and chatting with the customers, and drinking vodka (although not necessarily in that order). He loved to sample the wares of the tavern and dipped into the stock every evening, drinking with the customers until he would become even more loaded than they were. Sadly, one night in 1959, Frank drank himself to death. His wife found the lovable prankster slumped on the floor behind the bar the next morning. Frank Giff had died—but his spirit never left his beloved bar.

Frank's wife, Edna, operated Giff's for a time, but it was never the same without Frank, and she eventually put the bar up for sale. In 1961, Jane McDougall, a native of Glasgow, Scotland, purchased the bar and converted it into a Scottish pub. McDougall brought in tartan carpet, Scottish memorabilia, and a line of ales and whiskeys from the old country, and she dubbed the place the Edinburgh Castle Pub. But even with all of the changes, one thing about the place remained the same—Frank Giff!

As time passed, Jane began to notice large quantities of vodka were disappearing from the stock. As first, she suspected that the bartenders were stealing from her, and thinking that she would catch them in the act, she started covertly marking the level in the bottles with a wax pencil. She was shocked to find that the levels were still dropping and even more shocked when she realized that this was occurring at night, when the bar was empty and no one was in the building! She was not a believer in ghosts, but this weird happening was quickly starting to convince her that the pub was haunted. And she began to believe that it was haunted by a man she knew—Frank Giff—for she recalled his tragic death and his love for vodka.

Other events soon began to lead her to believe that she was right. Glasses started flying across the room and mysteriously breaking. Several times, the glasses were actually taped down to the rack where they hung above the bar. These glasses were hurled with such force that their bases were snapped off and left in place, while the rest of the glass was tossed away. At other times, drinks were disappearing almost in front of startled customers. The drinks, which had been left unattended, would suddenly be drained dry. Ashtrays slid down the bar without assistance. Cash registers and other electronic devices would often stop working, or at least behave erratically, when they were first brought into the bar. Later, they would be left alone—as if Frank had gotten used to them being there.

The pub was remodeled a number of times after 1961, and each time, Frank seemed to make his objections to the changes widely known. Perhaps the most actively haunted spot in the bar was right around the area where Frank died. As things have been changed around quite a bit since Frank's day, the spot can now be found in the dining area of the pub. There is a booth that marks the location, and many people who have eaten there complain of a shifting cold spot that sometimes occurs, as well as a numbness that seems to spread through their legs and feet.

Sometimes, attractive young women who sit in this area (or who just generally visit the bar) encounter the "friendly" spirit of the place. Some of these ladies have reported feeling a cold hand that grabs hold of their shoulder, knee, or even a more sensitive part of the anatomy. They describe it as being like fingers that lightly grasp or brush against their skin or clothing, as if they are being gently caressed. The majority of the women who have reported this sensation have been blonds or redheads. Jane McDougall believed that Frank might be mistaking these women for his wife, Edna, who was a strawberry blond.

The haunting has continued here over the years, despite the changes in ownership and the name of the place. Jane McDougall retired from the bar business and died in 1996, but Frank still remains, greeting customers from the other side. In his time and place, perhaps little has changed here at all, or perhaps the afterlife offers an endless party for Frank and his spectral drinking buddies. So, if you make it down to the Ole St. Andrew's Inn one evening, be sure to lift a glass in honor of Frank Giff.

Chicago's Most Haunted Graveyard

Located near the southwest suburb of Midlothian is the Rubio Woods Forest Preserve, an island of trees and shadows nestled in the urban sprawl of the Chicago area. The rambling refuge creates the illusion that it is secluded from the crowded city threatening its borders, and perhaps it is. On the edge of the forest is a small graveyard that many believe may be the most haunted place in the region. The name of the cemetery is Bachelor's Grove, and this ramshackle burial ground may be infested with more ghosts than most can imagine. Over the years, the place has been cursed with more than one hundred documented reports of paranormal phenomena, from actual apparitions to glowing balls of light.

There have been no new burials here for many years, and as a place of rest for the departed, it is largely forgotten. But if you should ask any ghost hunter just where to go to find a haunting, Bachelor's Grove is usually the first place in Chicago mentioned.

The history of Bachelor's Grove has been somewhat shadowy over the years, but most historians agree that it was started in the early part of the 1800s. Legend has it that the cemetery got its name because only men were buried here, but it actually came from the name of a family who settled in the area. A nearby settlement from the 1820s consisted of mostly German immigrants from New York, Vermont, and Connecticut. One family that moved into the area was called "Batchelder," and their name was given to the timberland where they settled. The settlement continued for some years as Batchelor's Grove, until 1850, when it was changed to "Bremen" by postmaster Samuel Everden in recognition of the new township name where the post office was located. In 1855, it was changed again to "Bachelder's Grove" by postmaster Robert Patrick, but the post office closed down just three years later. Officially, the settlement ceased to exist and was swallowed by the forest around it.

The cemetery itself has a much stranger history—or at least a more mysterious one. The land was apparently first set aside to be used as a burial ground in 1844, when the first recorded burial took place here, that of Eliza (Mrs. Leonard H.) Scott. The land had been donated by Samuel Everden, and it was named "Everden" in his honor. The last burials to take place are believed to be that of Laura M. McGhee in 1965 and Robert E. Shields, who was cremated and his ashes buried in the family plot here in 1989. The last caretaker of the cemetery was a man named Clarence Fulton, whose family were early settlers in the township. According to Fulton, Bachelor's Grove was like a park for many years, and people often came here to fish and swim in the adjacent pond. Families often visited on weekends to care for the graves of the deceased and to picnic under the trees. Things have certainly changed since then!

Problems began in and around the cemetery in the early 1960s. Even before that, the cemetery had become a popular spot along a "lover's lane," and after a nearby road was closed, it became even more isolated. Soon it began to show signs of vandalism and decay, and a short time later, it was rumored to be haunted.

The vandals first discovered Bachelor's Grove in the 1960s and, probably because of its secluded location, began to wreak havoc on the place. Gravestones were knocked over and destroyed, sprayed with paint, broken apart, and even stolen. Graves were opened and caskets removed. Bones were sometimes found strewn about the cemetery.

Was the haunting first caused by these disturbances? Most believe so, but others cite another source for the activity. Near the small pond that borders the cemetery, forest rangers and cemetery visitors have reportedly found the remains of chickens and other small animals that have been slaughtered and mutilated in a ritualistic fashion. Officers who have patrolled the woods at night have reported seeing evidence of black magic and occult rituals in and around the graveyard. In some cases, inscriptions and elaborate writings have been carved in and painted on trees and grave markers and on the cemetery grounds themselves. This has led many to believe that the cemetery has been used for occult activities.

There is no question that vandals have not been kind to Bachelor's Grove, but then neither has time. Roads leading to the place were closed, and people allowed it to fade into memory, just like the poor souls buried there.

Today, the cemetery is overgrown with weeds and is surrounded by a high, chain-link fence, although access is easily gained through the holes that trespassers have cut into it. The cemetery sign is long since gone.

The first thing visitors notice is the destruction. Tombstones seem to be randomly scattered about, no longer marking the resting places of those whose names are inscribed upon them. Many of the stones are missing, lost forever and perhaps carried away by thieves. These macabre crimes gave birth to legends about how the stones of the cemetery move about under their own power. The most disturbing things to visitors, though, are the trenches and pits that have been dug above some of the graves, as vandals have attempted to make off with souvenirs from those whose rest they disturb.

Just beyond the rear barrier of the cemetery is a small, stagnant pond. This pond, while outside of the graveyard, is still not untouched by the horror connected to the place. One night in the late 1970s, two Cook County Forest Preserve officers were on night patrol near here and claimed to see the apparition of a horse emerge from the waters of the pond. The animal appeared to be pulling a plow behind it that was steered by the ghost of an old man. The vision crossed the road in front of the rangers' vehicle, was framed for a moment in the glare of their headlights, and then vanished into the forest. The men simply stared in shock for a moment and then looked at one another to be sure they had both seen the same thing. They later reported the incident, and since that time, others have also reported seeing the old man and the horse.

Little did the rangers know, but this apparition was actually a part of a legend connected to the pond. It seems that in the 1870s, a farmer was plowing a nearby field when something startled his horse. The farmer was caught by surprise and became tangled in the reins. He was dragged behind the horse as it plunged into the pond. Unable to free himself, he was pulled down into the murky water by the weight of the horse and the plow and subsequently drowned.

Even the road near Bachelor's Grove is reputed to be haunted. The Midlothian Turnpike is said to be the scene of vanishing "ghost cars" and phantom automobile accidents. No historical events can provide a clue as to why this might be, but the unexplained vehicles have been reported numerous times in recent years. People who are traveling west on the turnpike see the taillights of a car in front of them. The brake lights go on, as if the car is planning to stop or turn. The car then turns off the road. Once the following auto gets to the point in the road where the first vehicle turned, however, they find no car there at all! Other drivers have reported passing these phantom autos, only to see the car vanish in their rearview mirrors.

It remains a mystery as to where these phantom cars come from and where they vanish to. Why do they haunt this stretch of roadway?

For those searching for Bachelor's Grove, it can be found by leaving the roadway and walking up an overgrown gravel track that is surrounded on both sides by forest. The old road is blocked with chains and concrete dividers, and a dented "No Trespassing" sign hangs ominously near the mouth of the trail. The burial ground lies about a half mile or so beyond it in the woods.

It is along this deserted road where other strange tales of the cemetery take place. One of these odd occurrences is the sighting of the "phantom farmhouse," which has been seen appearing and disappearing along the trail for several decades now. The most credible thing about many of the accounts is that they come from people who originally had no idea that the house shouldn't be there at all.

The house has been reported in all weather conditions, both in the daytime and at night. There is no historical record of such a house existing here, but the descriptions of it rarely vary. Each person claims it to be an old frame farmhouse with two stories, painted white, with wooden posts, a porch swing, and a welcoming light that burns softly in the window. Popular legend states that should you enter this house, you would never come back out again. As witnesses approach the building, it is reported to get smaller and smaller until it finally just fades away, like someone switching off an old television set. No one has ever claimed to have set foot on the front porch of the house.

Also from this stretch of trail come reports of "ghost lights." One such light that has been reported many times is a red, beaconlike orb, which has been seen flying rapidly up and down the trail to the cemetery. The light is so bright and moves so fast that it is impossible to tell what it really looks like. Most witnesses state that they have seen a "red streak" that is left in its wake.

There have also have been many sightings of ghosts and apparitions within Bachelor's Grove Cemetery itself. The most frequently reported spirit is known by a variety of names, from the "Madonna of Bachelor's Grove" to the "White Lady" to the affectionate name of "Mrs. Rogers." Legend has it that she is the ghost of a woman who was buried in the cemetery next to the grave of her young child. She is reported to wander the cemetery on nights of the full moon with an infant wrapped in her arms. She appears to walk aimlessly, with no apparent direction, and is completely unaware of the people who claim to encounter her. There is no real evidence to say who this woman might be, but over the years, she has taken her place as one of the many spirits of this haunted burial ground.

The graveyard continues to be the scene of psychical investigation and ghost research today. In 2006, Chicago psychic detective Ken Melvoin-Berg accompanied a reporter from the *Chicago Tribune* to the old graveyard and encountered the spirit of a young boy. Soon after arriving at the cemetery, Ken heard a child's voice crying to him, telling Ken that he had lost something. A few moments later, Ken understood that it was money. According to the reporter, Ken appeared to "lose it himself" as he staggered out of the cemetery toward the adjacent, algae-filled pond. Wading into the murky water, Ken stopped, bent down, stuck his shaking hands into the muck, and pulled out a 1942 Walking Liberty half-dollar coin—exactly where the ghostly boy told him it could be found.

Is Bachelor's Grove Cemetery as haunted as we have been led to believe? The reader has to decide that for himself, but based on the stories, it seems to be one of the most haunted places in the Midwest.

Haunted or not, Bachelor's Grove is still a burial ground and a place that should be treated with respect as the final resting place of those interred there. It is first and foremost a repository for the dead and should be protected as such by those who hope to enjoy it, and possibly learn from it, in the years to come. It is also a piece of our haunted history that we cannot afford to lose.

Phantoms of Rosehill Cemetery

Rosehill Cemetery began in 1859, taking its name from a nearby tavern keeper named Roe. The area around his saloon was known for some years as "Roe's Hill." In time, the name was slightly altered and became "Rosehill." After the closure of the "dreary" Chicago City Cemetery, Rosehill became the oldest and largest graveyard in Chicago and serves as the final resting place of more than fifteen hundred notable Chicagoans, including a number of Civil War generals, mayors, former millionaires, local celebrities, and early founders of the city.

There are also some infamous burials here as well, such as that of Reinhart Schwimmer, the unlucky eye doctor and gangster hanger-on who was killed during the St. Valentine's Day Massacre. Another, more mysterious grave site is that of young Bobby Franks, the victim of "thrill killers" Nathan Leopold and Richard Loeb. After his death, Bobby Franks was buried at Rosehill with the understanding that his lot number would never be given out to the curious. To this day, it remains a secret, although visitors will sometimes find the site by accident among the tens of thousands of graves in the cemetery.

There are also a number of deceased Chicagoans who are apparently not peacefully at rest here, and they provide the cemetery with its legends of ghosts and strange happenings.

Perhaps the most famous ghostly site on the grounds is the tomb belonging to Charles Hopkinson, a real estate tycoon from the mid 1800s. In his will, Hopkinson left plans for his mausoleum to serve as a shrine to the memory of himself and his family. When he died in 1885, a miniature cathedral was designed to serve as the tomb. Construction was started and then halted when the property owners behind the Hopkinson site took the family to court. They claimed that the cathedral tomb would block the view of their own burial sites. The case made it all the way to the Illinois Supreme Court, which ruled that the other families had no say over what sort of monument the Hopkinson family built and they should have expected that something could eventually block the view of their site. Shortly afterward, construction on the tomb continued and was completed.

Ghost lore is filled with stories of the dead returning from the grave to protest wrongs done to them in their lifetimes, or to continue business and rivalries started while they were among the living. Such events have long been a part of the lore of Rosehill's community mausoleum.

The Rosehill Cemetery Mausoleum was proposed in 1912, and the cemetery appealed to the elite businessmen of the city for the funds to begin construction. These men were impressed with the idea of a large and stately mausoleum, and they enjoyed the thought of entire rooms in the building dedicated to their families alone, which could also be decorated to their style and taste. The building, designed by Sidney Lovell, is a massive, multilevel structure with marble passageways and rows upon rows of the dead. It is filled with a number of Chicago notables from the world of business, including architect Sidney Lovell himself.

One of the funding subscribers for the mausoleum was John G. Shedd, the president of Marshall Field's from 1909 to 1926 and the man who donated the wonderful Shedd Aquarium to Chicago. He guaranteed himself immortality with the development of what he dreamed would be the world's largest aquarium. Even though Shedd died four years before the aquarium would open, his directors remained loyal to his plans and created an aquatic showplace. A little of that extravagance can be found in the Rosehill mausoleum, as Shedd's family room is one of the most beautiful portions of the building. The chapel outside the room features chairs carved with images depicting shells and sea horses, and the window inside bathes the room with a blue haze that makes the chamber appear to be underwater. For this window, Shedd commissioned the artisan Louis Comfort Tiffany and made him sign a contract that said he would never create another window like it.

There have been no ghost stories associated with John Shedd, but there are others entombed in the structure who may not have found the same peace as Shedd has found. Two of the men also laid to rest in the building are Aaron Montgomery Ward and his bitter business rival, Richard Warren Sears. One has to wonder if either of these men could rest in peace with the other man in the same structure, but it is the ghost of Sears who has been seen walking through the mausoleum at night. The business pioneer has been spotted, wearing a top hat and tails, leaving the Sears family room and walking the hallways from his tomb to that of Ward. Perhaps the rivalry that plagued his life continues after death?

Rosehill has been plagued with odd monuments and unusual stories connected to them. One of them is the tombstone of Mary Shedden, who was allegedly poisoned by her husband in 1931.

Those who find the grave may have to use their imaginations a little, but they will likely see two startling visions within the stone of the monument itself. One is the young and happy face of Mary Shedden—and the other is her grinning and cadaverous skull! Skeptics dismiss the tale, saying that the illusion of "faces" is nothing more than the stone's natural markings playing tricks on the eye, but others are not so sure.

One of the most famous mortuary statues in the cemetery, or at least one of the most visited, is the monument to Lulu Fellows, a young woman who died at age sixteen in 1833. Visitors who come here often leave behind coins, toys, and tokens to the girl, whose monument bears the words "Many Hopes Lie Buried Here." A number of visitors claim that they have encountered the scent of fresh flowers around this lifelike monument—even in the winter, when no fresh flowers are present.

Another sad and tragic figure here is that of Philomena Boyington, the granddaughter of architect William W. Boyington, who designed the Gothic gates that lead into the cemetery. According to the stories, people who sometimes pass by the cemetery at night will see the face of Philomena peering out at them from the window to the left and just below the bell tower of the Ravenswood gates. It has been said that the young girl often played near the site when the gates were being constructed back in 1864. She died of pneumonia not long after the structure was completed, and she has haunted the place ever since.

The Italian Bride

Mount Carmel Cemetery can be found in Hillside, just outside of Chicago. In addition to being the final resting place of Al Capone, Dion O'Banion, and other notorious Chicago mobsters, the cemetery is also the burial place of a woman named Julia Buccola Petta. While her name may not spring to mind as a part of Chicago history, for those intrigued by the supernatural, she is better known as the "Italian Bride." Julia's grave is marked today by a life-sized statue of the unfortunate woman in her wedding dress, a stone reproduction of the wedding photo mounted on the front of her monument. While a beautiful monument, there is nothing about it to suggest that anything weird ever occurred in connection to it. Once you know the history behind the site, however, you soon realize that this is one of the strangest tales in Chicago's annals of the unknown.

Julia Buccola grew up on the West Side of Chicago, and when she and her husband married, they moved to a more upscale Italian neighborhood. She eventually became pregnant with her first child, but complications set in and she died giving birth to a stillborn child in 1921. Because of the Italian tradition that dying in childbirth made the woman a type of martyr, Julia was buried in white, the martyrs' color. Her wedding dress also served as her burial gown, and with her dead infant tucked into her arms, the two were laid to rest in a single coffin.

Julia's mother, Filomena, blamed her daughter's husband for the girl's death, so she claimed the body and buried her with the Buccola family at Mount Carmel Cemetery. Shortly after Julia was buried, though, Filomena began to experience strange and terrifying dreams every night. In these nightmares, she envisioned Julia telling her that she was still alive and needed her help. For the next six years, the dreams plagued Filomena, so she began trying to have her daughter's grave opened and her body exhumed. She was unable to explain why she needed to do this; she only knew that she should. Finally, through sheer persistence, her request was granted, and a sympathetic judge passed down an order for Julia's exhumation.

In 1927, six years after Julia's death, the casket was removed from the grave. When it was opened, Julia's body was found not to have decayed at all. In fact, it was said that her flesh was still as soft as it had been when she was alive. A photograph that was taken at the time of the exhumation shows Julia's "incorruptible" body in the casket. Her mother, and other admirers, placed the photo on the front of her grave monument, which was constructed after her reburial. The photograph shows a body that appears to be fresh, with no discoloration of the skin, even after six years. The rotted and decayed appearance of the coffin in the photo, however, bears witness to the fact that it had been underground for some time. Julia appears to be merely sleeping. Her family took the fact that she was found to be so well preserved as a sign from God, and so, after collecting money from other family members and neighbors, they created the impressive monument that stands over her grave today.

What mysterious secret rests at the grave of Julia Petta? How could her body have stayed in perfect condition after lying in the grave for six years? No one knows, and to this day, the case of the "Italian Bride" remains one of Chicago's great unsolved mysteries.

The Miracle Child of Chicago

A grave located in the Chicago suburb of Worth, at Holy Sepulchre Cemetery, is said to have mysterious benevolent properties. In fact, it is said be able to heal the sick and the dying. Many people feel that this is a sacred place and is made so because the grave holds the final remains of a young girl named Mary Alice Quinn. Over the years, hundreds have claimed to experience miraculous healings at her grave site, while others speak of strange occurrences that can only be paranormal in nature. Because of this, Mary's grave has been the site of visits by religious pilgrims and supernatural enthusiasts alike.

Mary was a quiet child who died suddenly in 1935, when she was only fourteen. Born in 1920, she was one of three children of Daniel and Alice Quinn. As a young girl, she was diagnosed with a heart condition and became devoutly religious. Devoted to St. Theresa, Mary claimed to have a mystical experience when she saw a religious image appear on her wall. After that, she became known in her neighborhood for curing the sick. While on her deathbed, Mary told her parents that she wanted to come back and help people after her death. The faithful say that she has done just that. Soon after her passing, she was said to have mysteriously appeared to a number of people in the Chicago area. Throughout the 1930s and 1940s, it was not uncommon to hear of new Mary Alice Quinn sightings.

On one occasion, a sick nun at Mary Alice's former school claimed that she was visited by an apparition of the girl and cured. Others who claimed to see her said that her apparition had a glowing veil over her face. This was attributed to being a "veil of grace," a supernatural manifestation found in cases of people who are saints. Witnesses also began to tell of the spectral scent of roses that surrounded the healings and the apparition sightings. This is note-worthy because of Mary Alice's devotion to St. Theresa, whose motto had been, "I will let fall from heaven a shower of roses." For years after their daughter's death, Daniel and Alice Quinn hoped that the numerous reports of healings and strange phenomena attached to their daughter would attract the attention of the Catholic Church and the girl might someday be considered for sainthood herself. They distributed literature and holy cards and helped to provide documentation for the few articles that were written about Mary Alice in Catholic journals.

While there has been no official interest from the church, Mary Alice's following continues to grow. Today, her healing powers are said to have taken on another manifestation, one that surrounds her grave marker. When she passed away, she was secretly buried in a cemetery plot belonging to the Reilly family. It was thought that this might keep her burial place a secret and prevent the graveyard from being overrun by curiosity-seekers intent on finding her rest-ing place. Word soon spread, however, and a gravestone was even-tually cut with her name on it. Since that time, thousands have come to the site, many of them bringing prayer tokens, rosaries, coins, and photos to leave as offerings and to ask that Mary inter-cede for them in prayer. Many claim to have been healed of their afflictions after visiting the grave, and others have been healed by extension. They claim to have found relief from one of the many spoonfuls of dirt that has been taken from Mary's burial site.

Strangely, the phantom scent of roses has been reported filling the air around the gravestone, even when there are no roses any-where around. The smell is said to be especially strong in the win-ter months, when the scent of fresh roses would be impossible to mistake. Many visitors are alleged to have noticed this smell over the years, and some of them even say that it is overwhelming. The faithful claim that this unexplainable odor is proof that Mary's spirit is still nearby and interceding on their behalf. They say her love and charity continues, even decades after her death.

Father Damen and the Haunting of Holy Family

Located along Roosevelt Road on the South Side of Chicago, the magnificent spires of Holy Family Church point toward the sky—or toward heaven, if you prefer. The Gothic structure stands as the centerpiece of one of Chicago's oldest Catholic parishes and is a wonderful example of local and architectural history, as well as legend and lore.

According to church history, the parish that Holy Family Church serves was founded by Father Arnold Damen, a Jesuit missionary for whom Chicago's Damen Avenue was named. In 1857, the church was built over the running water of Red Creek. The building's main altar is said to be positioned directly over the water. As an aside, tradition has it that the river received the name of "Red Creek" after an Indian battle fought here centuries ago caused the water to run red with blood. The site came to be considered sacred by the Native Americans, making it a perfect candidate for another holy site in years to come.

The church saw what was considered to be its first miracle just a few years after it was constructed. On the east side of the main altar is a large, badly proportioned statue of Our Lady of Perpetual Help that a local man created sometime in the 1860s. One day, a crack that threatened the very structure of the building was discovered, and the statue came to be considered the protective guardian of the church. The crack had made its way down one wall of the church, from the ceiling to the floor. Church officials were warned that if the crack grew larger, a wall, or several walls, could collapse. Father Damen decided to place the church under the protection of Our Lady of Perpetual Help, so he moved the large wooden statue to stand under the crack. Somehow, the church held for many decades and was never repaired until a major renovation in the 1980s. For more than a century, despite years of water damage and decay from rain seeping through the fissure, parishioners were confident in the fact that the building was never in any real danger, thanks to the watchfulness of the church's protector.

Other miracles and strange happenings followed. Perhaps the greatest was the salvation of the church during the Great Chicago Fire of 1871. Although Mrs. O'Leary's cow never really kicked over a lantern, the fire did start near DeKoven and Jefferson streets, just a few blocks away from Holy Family. Father Damen was in New York when the fire broke out, but he received a telegraph from Chicago alerting him to the fact that the city was in flames and the church and parish were in danger. There was little that he could do from so far away, other than to pray and to trust in God and Our Lady of Perpetual Help. Mysteriously, the fire somehow shifted away from the church and burned a path to the north instead, destroying the downtown business district but sparing Holy Family. The parish was saved, and the event was acknowledged as a miracle. When Father Damen returned home to Chicago, he ordered seven candles to be kept burning on a side altar to commemorate the event. After a few years, the candles were replaced by gas jets and then by light bulbs, which have burned brightly ever since.

Without a doubt, though, the most famous story of Holy Family also involves Father Damen and supernatural assistance of another sort. The legend has been referred to in parish histories of the church, and it involves what many believe to be curious additions to the décor of Holy Family. These additions are two wooden statues that depict altar boys dressed in old-fashioned cassocks. The two young boys were said to be brothers who drowned together while on a parish picnic in 1874. No one had any idea at the time that they would return to play a very mysterious part in the history of this spiritual community.

According to the story, Father Damen was awakened one night in the late 1880s, during a terrible snowstorm, by the insistent ringing of the bell at the rectory. When the porter opened the door, he found two young boys on the doorstep, shivering in the cold, anxiously asking for a priest to come and call on a sick woman who was not expected to live through the night.

Father Damen overheard their pleas, and he told the boys that he would come with them immediately. Bundling up in his warmest coat and scarf, he followed the boys out into the night. They trudged for blocks through the nearly blinding snow to a dilapidated cottage on the far edge of the parish. As they reached the door, the boys told the priest that the sick woman had taken to her bed at the top floor of the house. He quickly opened the door, went inside, and began climbing the rickety steps to the upper floor. As Father Damen turned to speak to the two boys, he realized that they were gone.

At the top of the steps, he entered a small room and found an old woman lying on a bed in the corner. She turned to look at him weakly but managed to smile when she saw that her caller was a priest. She thanked him for coming, and he heard her confession and gave her the last rites of the church. The elderly woman was comforted and yet confused by his presence. She asked him how he knew to come to her, admitting that she was very ill and needed a priest, but that she had known no one to send for one.

Father Damen explained that two boys had awakened him and asked him to come. He assumed that they were neighbors, perhaps sent by their parents to fetch him. But the woman insisted that she had spoken with no one. She did not know her neighbors anymore and no one knew she had been ill. There had been simply no one for her to send to summon spiritual help.

"Have you no boys of your own?" Father Damen asked her.

"I had two sons many years ago, altar boys at the church," she replied. "But they have long since died."

Father Damen had the stunning revelation that the two vanished boys had been the woman's sons, returning to help her in her hour of need. He explained his feelings to the woman as she lay dying, and when she passed away near morning, she did so with a smile on her face. She had found peace and believed that she would soon be reunited with her lost children. Father Damen was so moved by what had occurred that he commissioned two wooden statues of altar boys and had them placed high above the main altar of the church. They have been watching over the parish ever since.

Throughout modern times, reported hauntings at Holy Family seem to suggest that Father Damen still makes occasional appearances here, as well, watching over his beloved parish. During the latter part of the 1900s, clergy members and staff reported a figure wearing clerical dress, which passed through the church and patrolled the hallways of St. Ignatius College Preparatory High School next door. These sightings were especially prevalent during the 1990s, when the church and school were being renovated. Just a few years before, the Jesuits had considered destroying the aging landmark and selling off the empty lot, but donations and fund-raising had garnered the necessary funds to restore the place. Many believe that perhaps Father Damen returned because of the all the activity occurring in the building.

Since that time, he has still been occasionally seen, walking the hallways, dressed in his clerical garments. Those who have seen him as he has passed by know who he is—Father Damen, still making his rounds.

The Apparitions at St. Rita's

One of the most bizarre, mysterious, and controversial events ever to ever occur in a Chicago church is said to have taken place at the St. Rita of Cascia Church on All Souls Day, November 2, 1960. To this day, church officials deny that it ever happened, and yet first-hand accounts, neighborhood stories, and family recollections all insist that it did. The event has sparked debate among the faithful in Chicago for nearly fifty years now and has remained an incident of great interest for supernatural enthusiasts for nearly as long. Did an unexplained event really take place, or is the whole thing, as one priest stated, merely "an old wives' tale"?

The Augustinian Fathers of Pennsylvania, who were invited to construct a church in Chicago by Archbishop James E. Quigley, established St. Rita's Church in 1905. They broke ground on the church, and a college later that same year, at Sixty-third and Oakley Avenue. As the parish grew, a new church was constructed north of Sixty-third Street, between Fairfield and Washtenaw avenues. The first mass was celebrated in this church in 1923. In 1948, the cornerstone of the present St. Rita's was laid, building over the old site at Sixty-third and Fairfield. It was in late 1960 that the church's most mysterious event allegedly occurred.

The last days of October and the first days of November are important dates on the calendar of the Catholic Church. Halloween is considered the eve of a holy day, All Saints' Day, when the faithful honor all of the saints of the church. All Souls' Day, the day when remembrance and prayers are offered for those who have died, follows on November 2. It was on this day that a group of fifteen to seventeen parishioners gathered in the sanctuary of St. Rita's to offer prayers and devotions for their deceased loved ones. In the midst of this, a series of inexplicable events began, and though they did not last long, they left an indelible mark on those who were present.

The events began with sounds from the church organ, which was located in a loft over the main doors. The instrument suddenly began to emit shrill tones, even though no fingers had been placed on the keys. The hands of the clock started to spin wildly in opposite directions. The commotion from the organ attracted the attention of those gathered in the church. When they turned in its direction, they were stunned to see six monk-like figures standing on either side of it. Three of the figures wore black robes and three wore white. For some reason that remains unknown to those of us who were not present that day, the parishioners were filled with terror. They scrambled from their seats and began to run toward the doors on the east and west sides of the church. When they reached the doors, however, they were unable to open them. They struggled to get out, but the doors refused to budge, as if some invisible force were holding them closed!

Now paralyzed with fear, the worshippers could only watch as the robed figures began to glide through the air from the organ loft. They settled just above the main floor, passing directly through pews and other solid objects as they traveled toward the front of the building. The organ blared once more, and then a strange voice was heard, croaking in a rough whisper. It cried out: "Pray for me!"

Almost immediately, a strong wind blew through the sanctuary, and the once sealed doors burst open. The trapped congregation ran outside, fleeing in fear from the terrifying scene.

What happened next remains as much a mystery as the event itself. According to some accounts, the church's pastor, Reverend Clement McHale, met privately with those who shared the bizarre experience and insisted that they not speak about it to anyone—for the good of the church. Several of the unnerved parishioners were too frightened to even return to the church, and the story did not remain a secret for long. In fact, it spread through the close-knit community like wildfire. For months after, few could refrain from talking about the terrifying afternoon at St. Rita's.

But what really happened that day? Supporters have long been split over what occurred, torn between a supernatural manifestation and a prank gone awry. There has been talk of devious altar boys, mass hallucinations brought on by fervent prayer, and even the suggestion that the figures were real. Some believe that the day of the event was no coincidence in that some doomed spirit returned to the church to implore the parishioners to pray for his soul. Church officials weren't buying any explanation that reeked of the supernatural, however, and later pastors blamed their predecessors for allowing the story to continue for as long as it has. The late Reverend Francis Fenton grew so tired of the story that he actually denounced it from the pulpit.

But if the event never happened, then how did such a strange story get started in the first place? Was it merely a parable of good and evil (black and white) that became horribly misconstrued, or was it something else? No one knows, although St. Rita's has remained quiet ever since. The puzzling figures have not returned, and each All Souls' Day has passed without incident since 1960—making this Chicago mystery all the more mysterious.

Jane Addams' Hull House

Charles J. Hull constructed Hull House at Halsted and Polk streets in 1856, a time when this was one of the most fashionable sections of the city. After the Chicago Fire of 1871, the "better classes" moved to other parts of the city, and the near West Side began to attract a large immigrant population of Italian, Greek, and Jewish settlers. By the 1880s, Hull House was surrounded by factories and tenement houses, and soon after, it became one of the most famous places in Chicago. Although it was never intended to be known as a "haunted house," Hull House would not emerge from its heyday unscathed by stories of ghosts and the supernatural. Hull himself was interested in Spiritualism, and it's likely that he conducted séances inside of the house around the time of the Civil War.

Hull House would not achieve its fame as a private home but rather as a pioneering effort of social equality started by a woman named Jane Addams and her friend Ellen Starr Gates. They opened the house in 1889 at a time when the overcrowded tenement neighborhoods west of Halsted Street were a jungle of crime, vice, prostitution, and drug addiction. Jane Addams became the "voice of humanity" on the West Side, enriching the lives of many unfortunate people at the house.

Addams, the privileged daughter of a wealthy merchant, was born and raised in the village of Cedarville. Jane was raised under pleasant surroundings, but tragedy came into her life with the death of her father, which occurred the same year that she graduated from the Rockford Female Seminary. She went into a deep depression, and unsure what to do with her life, she spent a portion of her inheritance traveling in Europe. It would be in London, in the terrible slums of Whitechapel, that she would find her calling.

In the company of her college friend and traveling companion, Ellen Starr Gates, Jane would spend time at Toynbee Hall, a settlement house for the poor. Here, young and affluent students lived and worked beside the poorest dregs of London, pushing for social reform and better standards of living. Jane was intrigued by the idea of it, and after her return to Chicago, she began making plans for such a place in the city. She soon discovered the run-down Halsted Street mansion and the terrible neighborhood around it. When she moved in, the house was bracketed by an Irish saloon and an undertaking parlor.

Jane Addams' Hull House appealed to broken-down refugees and immigrants. Jane and Ellen took control of the property in September 1889 and opened the settlement house. Addams was granted a twenty-five-year, rent-free lease by Hull's confidential secretary, Helen Culver, and by the heirs to the Hull fortune, who were enthusiastic about Jane's efforts on behalf of the poor. They soon began turning the place into a comfortable house, aimed mostly at women, but affording food and shelter to the homeless and hungry, as well. The house also provided education and protection for many, and the staff worked to better the lives of the local people for years to come.

At the time Jane Addams took over Hull House, several years had passed since the death of Mrs. Charles Hull, but this apparently didn't prevent her from making her presence known. She had died of natural causes in a second-floor bedroom of the mansion, and within a few months of her passing, her ghost was said to be haunting that particular room. Overnight guests began having their sleep disturbed by footsteps and what were described as "strange and unearthly noises."

Mrs. Hull's bedroom was first occupied by Jane Addams herself, who was awakened one night when she heard loud footsteps in the otherwise empty room. After a few nights of this, she confided her story to Ellen, who also admitted to hearing the same sounds. Jane later moved to another room.

But she would not be alone in noticing the unusual happenings. Helen Campbell, author of the book *Prisoners of Poverty*, reported seeing an apparition standing next to her bed (she took Jane up on the offer of staying in the "haunted room"). When she lit the gas jet, the figure vanished.

According to Jane Addams, earlier tenants of the house also believed the upstairs of the house was haunted. They had always kept a bucket of water on the stairs, believing that the ghost was unable to cross over it. Unfortunately, it was not the only "supernatural" legend connected to Hull House.

Hull House received its greatest notoriety when it was alleged to be the refuge of the Chicago "Devil Baby." This child was supposedly born to a devout Catholic woman and her atheist husband, and it was said to have pointed ears, horns, scale-covered skin, and a tail. According to the story, the young woman had attempted to display a picture of the Virgin Mary in the house, but her husband had torn it down. He stated that he would rather have the Devil himself in the house than the picture. When the woman had become pregnant, the Devil Baby had been their curse. After enduring numerous indignities because of the child, the father allegedly took it to Hull House.

After being taken in by Jane Addams, staff members of the house reportedly took the baby to be baptized. During the ceremony, the baby supposedly escaped from the priest and began dancing and laughing. Not knowing what else to do with the child, Jane kept it locked in the attic of the house, where it later died.

Rumors spread quickly about the baby, and within a few weeks, hundreds of people came to the house to get a glimpse of it. How the story had gotten started, no one knew, but it spread throughout the West Side neighborhood and was reported by famous Chicago reporter Ben Hecht. He claimed that every time he tried to run down the story, he was directed to find the child at Hull House. Many people came to the door and demanded to see the child, while others quietly offered to pay an admission.

Each day, Jane turned people away and tried to convince them that the story was fabricated. She even devoted forty pages of her autobiography to dispelling the stories. Even though most of the poorly educated immigrants left the house still believing the tales of the Devil Baby, the stream of callers eventually died out, and the story became a barely remembered side note in the history of Hull House. Or did it?

As the years have passed, some people still maintain the story of the Devil Baby is true—or at least contains some elements of the truth. Some have speculated that perhaps the child was actually a badly deformed infant that had been brought to Hull House by a young immigrant woman who could not care for it. Perhaps the monstrous appearance of the child had started the rumors in the neighborhood and eventually led to Hull House.

Addams swore to the last that the story had no basis in fact, but regardless, local legend insists that at some point, there was a disfigured boy hidden away on the upper floors of the house. The stories also go on to say that on certain nights, the image of a deformed face could be seen peering out of the attic window and that a ghostly version of the face is still seen by visitors today.

Hull House has not been a settlement house for many years, but people still visit today. They are not just tourists and historians, but ghost hunters, too. The eerie stories told by Jane Addams and the occupants of Hull House are still recalled when weird happenings take place in these modern times. It is common for the motion sensors of the alarm system to be mysteriously triggered. When security officers respond, they find the house is empty and there is no sign of a break-in or any other disturbance. Officers state that no building on the University of Illinois–Chicago campus (which maintains the house) has as many false calls as Hull House. They have also answered reports about people inside the house, or looking out the windows, but the police have never found anyone in the place.

The Irish Castle

In the South Side neighborhood of Beverly stands one of the most unique of the reportedly haunted houses in Chicago. It has been known by several names over the years, from the Givens Mansion to the Irish Castle, although its present incarnation is the Beverly Unitarian Church. After the destruction of Palmer Potter's castle on Lakeshore Drive, this structure became designated as the only actual castle in the Chicago area. It is located on a slight hill at the corner of 103rd and Longwood Drive and has a strangeness about it that contrasts with the elegant homes nearby. If legends and lore about it are any indication, it certainly lives up to its odd appearance!

The Irish Castle was erected by Robert C. Givens, a Chicago real estate dealer of the 1880s. After working for some time with the realty firm of E. A. Cummings & Co., he decided to tour Ireland and Europe for a time and then returned to Chicago to establish his own real estate company. The firm prospered, and soon Givens decided to construct his own home. The story goes that during his tour of Ireland, he became enamored of an ancient, ivy-covered castle on the banks of the River Dee. Possessing some amount of artistic ability, Givens sketched the castle and had plans drawn up for a home to be built on a bluff above Tracy Avenue (now Longwood). The neighborhood at that time was called Washington Heights. The castle was completed in 1886, and legend has it that Givens actually built the place for his wife. She died, however, before she could ever live there.

Heartbroken, he moved into the house anyway and attempted to enjoy the structure that he had labored so long to be able to afford. He moved in a variety of Irish antiques and hung his collection of tapestries on the walls. Givens was never able to realize the quiet, retired life that he had hoped for in the castle, though, and he sold the house to John B. Burdett in 1908.

As time passed, the building went through a variety of owners. It was used by a manufacturer, a doctor, and a girls' school before becoming a church. The house was sold to the Unitarian Church in 1942, and in the late 1950s, new additions were constructed for classrooms. Later, plans were made to tear down the castle altogether for a new building, but these plans were discarded in 1972, and the church remains in the old castle today.

There have been a wide variety of strange happenings in the building. The source of the hauntings is said to be a previous occupant from the time when the castle was the Chicago Female College. According to the story, a young girl became ill with a serious case of influenza and died in the early 1930s. The legends say that her name is "Clara" and that she never left this place.

The ghost was first encountered in the 1960s by a church custodian, who came upon a young girl in a long dress standing in one of the rooms. The two of them chatted for a few minutes, and the young girl remarked that the place had changed much since she had lived there. The custodian left the room and then suddenly recalled that the church had been in the building for more than twenty years. Such a young girl couldn't possibly have lived there before that. She ran back to the room, but the girl had vanished! She then searched the entire building, only to find all the doors and windows locked. She even looked outside and discovered that a fresh layer of snow now blanketed the ground. There were no footprints leading into or out of the church.

Witnesses to the strange events have been numerous and even include a church pastor, who saw two small arms embrace her husband's waist. While the pastor clearly saw this occur, her husband claimed to feel nothing.

Members of the congregation and visitors to the castle have also reported strange phenomena. Several attendees at a wedding reception discovered that a number of utensils mysteriously vanished, only to show up again later. Others have noted half-full wine glasses that have emptied when no one is around. There have also been a number of strange noises. Occupants of the building have described a "jingling" sound, like the tinkling of glasses and silverware at a dinner party. A former pastor, Reverend Roger Brewin, stated that he often tried to track down the source of these mysterious sounds but never could. He said that they seemed to come from everywhere and yet nowhere, all at the same time.

Even the neighbors have seen odd things. They report seeing what appear to be candles drifting past the windows of the castle at night, even when no one is there. One woman also said that she saw a female figure walking across the grounds in the snow. The figure appeared to be solid and yet left no footprints behind. Some believe this spirit might be that of Eleanor Veil, who lived in the castle and maintained it through the Great Depression. It has been suggested that perhaps she loved the place so much she simply decided not to leave.

Who these ghosts are, or why they have remained here, remains a mystery, but it seems certain that they are at peace in this place. No terrifying encounters have taken place within the walls of this sanctuary, and for this reason, officials at the church (who are more open-minded than most) are content to let the ghosts remain. The Irish Castle continues to appeal to not only the spirits of the past, but also to the spiritual side of those who come here. The restless spirits do not seem so restless here, and perhaps have found comfort within these stone walls.

Mysteries of the Schweppe Mansion

The north suburb of Lake Forest has become known over the years for its fabulous mansions and beautiful estates. This is a reputation that the area has gained over time, dating back to the early days of the last century when Chicago's millionaires began to leave the grime and bustle of the city in a search for more bucolic locales.

It was in Lake Forest that newlyweds Charles H. Schweppe and Laura Shedd were presented with a large Tudor Revival mansion as a wedding gift from the bride's father, John Graves Shedd, known in his day as the "dean of Chicago merchants." Shedd was a partner in the Marshall Field Co., and after the death of Field in 1906, he became president of the firm until his retirement in 1922, when he took over as chairman of the board. Before his death, Marshall Field called Shedd "the best merchant in the United States." After the marriage of his daughter Laura to Charles Schweppe, the Shedds moved from their Gothic mansion on Drexel Boulevard to Lake Forest, where Shedd also purchased a home for his daughter and son-in-law.

The Schweppe Mansion, as it came to be called, was the largest private residence in the region, boasting more than twenty acres of surrounding real estate, twenty bedrooms and nineteen bathrooms. It had been constructed on a ninety-foot bluff overlooking Lake Michigan and was designed by prominent architects Frederick Wainwright Perkins and Edmund R. Krause, who had also created the Shedd Mansion in Chicago.

Thanks to the social standing of the family, Charles and Laura held lavish parties for Chicago friends and business contacts, as well as for important political and foreign visitors, including the Duke and Duchess of Windsor, Edward VII, and Wallis Simpson. Sweden's Prince Gustavus Adolphus and Princess Louise stayed here as house guests for a time. They strolled through the luxurious house and gardens, admired the Italian statuary, the shimmering fountains, and the fantastic view of Lake Michigan. But sadly, all good things must someday come to an end.

The Schweppe family fortune began to crumble after the stock market crash of 1929. Charles lost incredible amounts of money during the Depression, and then in 1937, Laura died at the age of only fifty-eight. Charles sunk into deep despair, which only worsened when he learned that his wife had left him little in her will. She had inherited half of her father's vast fortune and even had a personal estate that was valued at nearly $6 million. She left nearly all of her money to her children, though, giving Charles a mere $200,000 with which to try and salvage the wreckage of his own career. He tried and failed, and his financial future and physical health continued to decline. Schweppe began to suffer from chronic insomnia, and he would wander through the vast house each night, stumbling about in his pajamas and robe, pondering the loss of his fortune. When friends insisted that he see a doctor, Charles began to be treated for a nervous condition, but it was too little, too late.

One dark night in 1941, the servants heard the crack of a single gunshot echo though the house. When they reached Charles's bedroom, they found his body thrown back across the blood-spattered bed. A small .32-caliber pistol lay on the covers beside him, his lifeless fingers curled just inches away from its trigger. A red hole could be seen in the center of his forehead, leaving a ghastly wound to the back of his skull that had erupted in blood, bone, and pieces of his brain. Charles had taken his own life, leaving behind a tortured suicide note on the dresser next to the bed. "I have been awake all night. It is terrible," he had scrawled out, never bothering to sign this last missive.

For reasons that remain a mystery, the heirs to the Schweppe estate decided not to live in the house, nor to do anything else with the property. The servants were given their leave, and the house was simply closed up and abandoned. The furniture had been left behind, the table still set for the breakfast that Charles Schweppe would never eat, and the dust of time was left to gather for forty-six years. Although the house and grounds were maintained by a caretaker, it remained 1941 inside the mansion for decades to come.

Not surprisingly, the period of decline spawned many ghost stories about the house. The dark history of the place and the feeling of decadent ruin about the estate were more than enough to attract the interest of ghost enthusiasts and curiosity-seekers. Tales began to be told of phantom servants who still took care of the house, perhaps inspired by the legend of a pregnant maid who was found dead in the elevator years before. The story went on to say that the elevator always behaved erratically after that, coming to life on its own and moving up and down between floors.

Perhaps the most intriguing story, though, involved a mysterious window on the second floor. When the house had been constructed, beautiful leaded-glass windows had been created for it, but only one of them offered a clear view of the walk that led up to the front door of the mansion. Local lore had it that in the last days of Charles Schweppe's life, when his mental health began to decline, he would often peer out of a lower frame of the window, nervously looking out at the front of the house. In the years following his death, curiosity-seekers who visited the estate were chilled to see that this same pane of glass in the old window—and only this pane of glass—managed to always stay clean. The rest of the windows had become weathered and covered with dirt and grime over the years, but somehow, this single pane always looked polished and clean. According to legend, it was kept that way by the ghost of Charles Schweppe, still peering outside as he had done in his final days.

The Schweppe Mansion had become Lake Forest's local "haunted house," that proverbial creature that spawns dark tales and eerie visits on cool October nights. Only this time, the reputation was well deserved.

In 1987, the fate of the Schweppe Mansion took another turn. The house was purchased by a woman who had restored and renovated four other historic properties. She paid a large sum for the property and planned to live here with her family as they tried to undo the damage that time and neglect had done to the mansion. The mansion is now known as Mayflower Place, and the dust and dirt of decades past is gone. The house is once again a North Shore architectural gem and has also been placed on the National Register of Historic Places.

And unlike most cases of renovations, when ghosts seemed to be disturbed by the activity in the house, the renovations of the Schweppe Mansion have had an opposite effect—they have actually laid the ghost to rest. During the work, the old leaded-glass windows were temporarily removed to be restored. When it was no longer in place, the single pane that had looked out over the front walk became dirty just like all the other glass. The ghost had no reason to keep it clean anymore, and Charles Schweppe, if that is who this spirit was, passed on to the other side. There have been no ghostly happenings here since the restoration was completed.

Ghosts of the Congress Hotel

Built in 1893 to accommodate the scores of tourists arriving in Chicago for the World's Columbian Exposition, the Congress Hotel was regarded as the most elegant establishment of its kind in the city. The ballrooms and restaurants inside the hotel were the finest in Chicago and attracted both travelers and city-dwellers to the hotel's doors. History has left quite a mark on this old hotel in the way of both triumph and tragedy—and has left myriad ghosts behind.

A major attraction during the World's Fair, the Congress had been designed by Clinton Warren, a former employee of Burnham and Root, the firm that had constructed the magnificent buildings and pavilions of the White City, as the exposition had been dubbed. After the fair, the hotel began to expand. The south wing was constructed between 1902 and 1907, and part of the new construction included the Gold Room, a massive ballroom that was the first venue of this type in the city to be air-conditioned.

One floor above the Gold Room was the Florentine Room, a slightly smaller room decorated with reproductions of Italian paintings on the ceiling. It was in this room that Theodore Roosevelt made the startling announcement that he was leaving the Republican Party, under which he had served as president from 1901 to 1909. Six weeks later, Roosevelt was back in the Florentine Room, which served as his headquarters during a bid for presidency as the nominee of the Progressive Party. The Florentine Room eventually became a popular spot for women's suffrage meetings, as well as dances, skating parties, and banquets.

Another hall, the Elizabethan Room (later renamed the Joseph Urban Room), became known all over the country when Benny Goodman played a six-month stand with his integrated orchestra in 1935–36; through a series of NBC broadcasts, the shows introduced much of the nation to swing music.

But not everything about the Congress was happiness and light. The hotel had a dark side, as well. Over the years, the place has been plagued by an inordinate number of bizarre occurrences and strange deaths, many of which have led to rumors and whispers of ghosts lingering in the hotel.

In 1900, a U.S. Army officer named Captain Louis Ostheim was found in his room at the Congress, dead from an apparent self-inflicted gunshot to the head. He had suffered from night terrors, and friends speculated that he shot himself in the middle of one of his violent nightmares. Tragically, he was supposed to be married the next morning.

Hotel guests witnessed an elevator operator fall four stories down an elevator shaft to his death in 1904.

In 1908, a murder-suicide occurred over a love triangle, just outside the hotel's front door. A husband and wife, shot by a jealous lover, reconciled as they lay bleeding on the sidewalk.

Also in 1908, a man named Roy Gormely came to drink in the Pompeiian Room and asked the orchestra to play "The Dead March from Saul." The conductor didn't have the music, so instead, Gormley bought drinks for every musician—and paid for another round to be served the following Monday. Having enjoyed a drink with the band, he retired to his room and shot himself. A short while later, a woman called the hotel to ask for him. When she was told that he'd killed himself, she said, "My God? Is that so?" and hung up. She didn't call back.

A girl was poisoned at a party in the Pompeiian Room in 1919 and narrowly survived. The same year, opera singer Charlotte Cail-lies tried to commit suicide by ingesting poison in her hotel room.

In 1930, a showgirl named Jean Farrel died of mysterious causes in the hotel.

A fifteen-year resident of the hotel named Hoyt Smith shot himself in his room in 1932.

In 1938, a Czech refugee named Adele Langer, who had been forced out of her homeland with her family when Hitler invaded, went insane, purportedly because of the persecution she and her family had suffered. Out of her mind with dementia, she threw herself out of a window—taking her sons, Karel, 6, and Jan, 4, with her.

And these weird stories are just a sample of the tragedy that the Congress Hotel has seen. The list of murders in the hotel is long, the list of suicides even longer, and the list of those who died of natural causes in the place longer still. Many of the murders and deaths never even made the newspapers.

Not surprisingly, there are numerous ghosts associated with the hotel. Rumor has it that Franklin D. Roosevelt, Theodore Roosevelt, Thomas Edison, and Frank Lloyd Wright all haunt the place. These rumors appear to have no basis in fact, but the staff has plenty of stories of their own. Several staff members are not shy about admitting that there are certain floors or rooms they prefer to avoid at night.

Guests of the hotel have told of lights and especially televisions turning on and off by themselves. This activity is usually attributed to the ghost of "the Judge," one of the last elderly people to live in the hotel full time. In his declining years, the Judge would entertain himself by wheeling around in his wheelchair with a remote control, confusing people by turning their televisions on and off from the hallway outside.

There have been several reports of a little boy and girl running up and down the hallways. The boy is far more commonly seen than the girl. He has been seen all over, including in the kitchen and in guests' rooms in the middle of the night. He is most active on the twelfth floor of the north wing, which is commonly said to be the spookiest floor of the hotel. There are a couple of theories as to the boy's identity—some say that he may be the ghost of Karel Langer, the six-year-old who fell to his death along with his mother and brother in 1938. Another theory is that the boy and girl are Donald and Zudel Stoddard, two children who were killed in the Iroquois Theater Fire. Their mother spent a frantic day searching for them before retiring, semiconscious, to her room at the hotel, where she soon learned that their bodies had been found. Some say that the ghosts are her children coming to find her.

In 2006, several staff members reported calls from guests on the seventh floor of the south wing saying that a vagrant with an artificial leg was lying in the hallway. Security arrived but found no trace of the man. The ghost—sometimes known as "Peg Leg Johnny"—is thought to be that of a peg-legged hobo who is believed to have died in the hotel in the 1920s. Since then, he's been seen all over the building.

Another story involves a group of U.S. Marines who were scared out of their wits in the middle of the night by a "shadow figure" in their room. The shadow figure, with his connection to the military and to nightmares, is believed to be the ghost of Louis Ostheim, the U.S. Army veteran who shot himself on the eve of his wedding. The shadow figure has been seen all over the hotel, and one security guard claims to have encountered it on the roof one night!

The Gold Room, the largest remaining ballroom, is not without ghosts of its own—a phantom piano has been seen, and a well-dressed ghostly couple is sometimes spotted overseeing the ballroom from the balcony. Shadow figures sometimes show up in photographs taken of the southeastern corner.

As spooky as the Gold Room can be, it is the Florentine Room that the staff seems to regard as the scariest. At least three security guards have reported hearing old-fashioned music coming from the room in the middle of the night. Some attribute this to music played in the room when it was used for roller-skating parties years ago. Others have heard the piano in the room play of its own accord. Still others have reported seeing phantom dancers, and many have reported the feeling of a hand on their shoulder.

Regardless of whom all of these ghosts might be, it's obvious that the Congress Hotel is one of the most haunted places in Chicago—a place where guests check in, and some of them never check out.

"Screaming Lizzie" and Chicago's Other Roadside Ghosts

The tale of the vanishing hitchhiker is truly an American ghost story. There is not a single part of the country that does not boast at least one tale about a pale young girl who gets a ride with a stranger, only to vanish from the car before they reach their destination.

Stories like this have been a part of American lore for many years, and tales of spectral passengers (usually young women) are often attached to bridges, dangerous hills and intersections, and graveyards. Folklorist Jan Harold Brunvand calls the vanishing hitchhiker "the classic automobile legend," but stories of these spirits date back as far as the mid 1800s, when men told stories of ghostly women who appeared on the backs of their horses. These spectral riders always disappeared when they reached their destination and would often prove to be the deceased daughters of local farmers. Not much has changed in the stories that are still told today, outside of the preferred method of transportation.

Today, such tales are usually referred to as "urban legends." They are stories that have been told and retold over the years and, in most every case, have been experienced by the proverbial "friend of a friend" and have no real basis in fact—or do they?

Are all of these stories, as some would like us to believe, nothing more than folklore? Are they simply stories that have been made up and spread across the country over a long period of time? Perhaps this is the case, or perhaps not.

One has to wonder how such stories got started in the first place. Could any of them have a basis in truth? What if an incident—perhaps an encounter with a vanishing hitchhiker—actually happened somewhere, and then was told and retold to the point that it lost many of the elements of truth? As the story spread, it was embraced by people all over the country until it became a part of their local lore. It has long been believed that people provide an explanation for something that they cannot understand. This is usually done by creating mythology that made sense at the time. Who knows if there may be a very small kernel of truth hidden inside the folktales that send shivers down your spine?

Tales of phantom hitchhikers can be found all over the world, but in no city are they as prevalent as in Chicago. There are a number of mysterious phantoms to be found in the region, from the typical vanishing hitchers of legend and lore to what some have dubbed "prophesying passengers"—strange hitchhikers who pass along odd messages, usually involving the end of the world or something almost as dire.

One Chicago story tells of a prophesying nun. A cab driver once recalled a strange and unsettling fare he had picked up in December 1941. He was cruising the downtown streets in his cab one night, and he pulled over to let in a nun who was dressed in the traditional garb of a Catholic order. She gave him the address she wished to be taken to, and they drove off. The radio was on, and the announcer was discussing the events that had taken place at Pearl Harbor a short time before and the preparations that the United States was making for war.

The nun suddenly spoke up from the back seat. "It won't last more than four months," she said, and then didn't speak again for the rest of the ride.

When the cabbie reached the address, he got out to open the door for the sister. He was surprised to discover that she wasn't there! Afraid that the little old lady had forgotten to pay her fare, the driver climbed the steps of the address she had given him and discovered that it was a convent. He knocked on the door and was brought to the Mother Superior. He explained his predicament to her, but she told him that none of the sisters had been downtown that day. She asked the driver what the nun had looked like.

As the driver began to describe her, he happened to look up at a portrait hanging on the wall behind the Mother Superior's desk. He pointed to the picture, and in an excited voice, told her that the woman in the portrait was the nun he had brought to the convent house. He probably thought that he was going to get his fare after all—but he couldn't have been more wrong. The Mother Superior smiled and quietly said, "But she has been dead for ten years."

And the nun, like those passengers who tell of the end of the world, was incorrect in her prediction regarding the short end to World War II. If these beings are truly supernatural, then perhaps they should consider another source from which to get their information about upcoming events!

Another passenger from the Windy City had her own strange prediction to make.

During Chicago's Century of Progress Exposition in 1933, a group of people in an automobile told of a strange encounter. They were traveling along Lake Shore Drive when a woman with a suitcase, standing by the roadside, hailed them. They invited her to ride along with them, and she climbed in. They later said that they never really got a good look at her because it was dark outside.

As they drove along, they got into a conversation about the exposition, and the mysterious woman oddly told them: "The fair is going to slide off into Lake Michigan in September." She then gave them her address in Chicago and invited them to call on her anytime. When they turned around to speak to her again following her doom-filled warning, they discovered that she had disappeared!

Unnerved, they decided to go to the address the woman gave them, and when they did, a man answered the door. They explained to him why they had come to the house, and he merely nodded his head. "Yes, that was my wife. She died four years ago," he said.

"Screaming Lizzie"

On November 18, 1905, a young woman named Lizzie Kaussehull was murdered by a crazed stalker named Edward Robhaut, who had been pursuing her for three months. During that time, Robhaut had tried unsuccessfully to win Lizzie's heart. He constantly bothered her, wrote her letters, sent her flowers, and simply refused to accept her rejection. Neighbors later recalled that he frequently waited around the corner of Lincoln and Carmen avenues, waiting for the streetcar that would bring Lizzie home from her job at Moeller & Stange's grocery store, located farther south on Lincoln. Lizzie did her best to ignore him, but he followed her home every night.

Lizzie became so fearful for her life that her family reported Robhaut's behavior to the police, including the fact that he told Lizzie he would kill her if she would not marry him. Robhaut was arrested, and a restraining order (called a "peace bond" in those days) was filed against him on November 11, but it had no effect on his actions. He continued to follow Lizzie home from the streetcar stop each afternoon, begging her to marry him and threatening to kill her if she did not.

On November 18, Lizzie finished her shift at Moeller & Stange's and, as always, rode the streetcar north on Lincoln. When she reached her stop, she stepped off with several girlfriends, all of them laughing and talking. Then, suddenly, she saw Robhaut leaning against the wall of a nearby storefront. Lizzie's friends froze, and Lizzie shakily put up a hand and stammered in his direction that the peace bond was still in place against him. Robhaut suddenly ran toward her, and Lizzie began to scream.

Robhaut sprang upon her and plunged a knife into Lizzie's chest. She staggered back away from him, but Robhaut attacked again, stabbing her three more times. Finally, her dress soaked with blood, she fell to the sidewalk. Robhaut looked down at the woman whom he claimed to love so much that he had to kill her if he couldn't have her; he then drew a revolver, placed the barrel into his mouth, and pulled the trigger. The back of Robhaut's skull blew out in a red spray of gore, and his body collapsed on top of Lizzie's. They were finally together—in death.

But this was not the end of the story. According to legend, Lizzie's ghost has haunted the intersection at Lincoln and Carmen for more than a century now. The stories claim that, on nights of the full moon, Lizzie returns to the former streetcar stop and can be heard screaming—just as she did when she saw Edward Robhaut lurching toward her on the day he ended her life.

The Flapper Ghost

Another ghostly hitchhiker haunts the roadways between the site of the old Melody Mill Ballroom and Waldheim Cemetery, which is located at 1800 South Harlem Avenue.

The cemetery, once known as Jewish Waldheim, is one of the more peaceful and attractive graveyards in the area and is easily recognizable from the columns mounted at the front gates. They were once part of the old Cook County Building, which was demolished in 1908. This cemetery would most likely go quietly through its existence if not for the tales of the "Flapper Ghost," as the resident spirit has been dubbed.

The story of this beautiful spirit tells of her earthly existence as a young Jewish girl who attended dances at the Melody Mill Ballroom, formerly on Des Plaines Avenue. During its heyday, the ballroom was one of the city's favorite venues for ballroom dancing and played host to dozens of popular big bands from the 1920s to the mid 1980s. The brick building was topped with a miniature windmill, the ballroom's trademark.

This young woman was a very attractive brunette with bobbed hair and a penchant for dressing in the style of the Prohibition era. In later years, witnesses would claim that her ghost dressed like a "flapper," and this is how she earned her nickname. Legend has it that this lovely girl was a regular at the Melody Mill until she died of peritonitis, the result of a burst appendix.

The girl was buried at Jewish Waldheim, and she likely would have been left to rest in peace if strange things had not started to happen a few months later. The events began with staff members at the Melody Mill seeing a young woman who looked just like the deceased girl appearing at dances at the ballroom. A number of men actually claimed to have met the girl there (after her death) and also to have offered her a ride home. During the journey, the young woman always vanished. This fetching phantom was also known to hitch rides outside the ballroom on Des Plaines Avenue, and was also sometimes seen near the cemetery gates. Some travelers who passed the graveyard also claimed to see her entering a mausoleum located off Harlem Avenue.

Although recent sightings have been few, the ghost was most active in 1933, during the Century of Progress Exhibition. She became active again forty years later, during the early 1970s, and stayed active for nearly a decade.

In the early 1930s, she was often reported at the ballroom, where she would dance with young men and ask for a ride home at the end of the evening. Every report was basically the same. A young man agreed to drive the girl home, and she would give him directions to go east on Cermak Road, then north on Harlem Avenue. When they reached the cemetery, the girl always asked the driver to stop the car. The girl would explain to them that she lived in the caretaker's house (since demolished) and then get out of the car. One man stated that he watched the girl go toward the house but then duck around the side of it. Curious, he climbed out of the car to see where she was going and saw her run out into the cemetery and vanish among the tombstones.

Another young man who was also told that the girl lived in the caretaker's house decided to come back during the day to ask about her. He had become infatuated with her and hoped to take her dancing again another evening. His questions to the occupants of the house were met with blank stares and bafflement. No such girl lived, or had ever lived, at the house.

More sightings took place in the early 1970s, and one report even occurred during the daylight hours. A family was visiting the cemetery one day and was startled to see a young woman dressed like a flapper walking toward a crypt, where she suddenly disappeared. The family hurried over to the spot, only to find that the girl was not there, and there was nowhere to which she could have vanished so quickly.

Since that time, sightings of the Flapper have been few, possibly because the old Melody Mill is no more. The days of jazz and big bands were gone by the 1980s, and attendance on weekend evenings continued to slip until the place was closed down in 1985. It was later demolished, and a new building was put up in its place two years later. Has the Flapper Ghost simply moved on to the other side since her favorite dance spot disappeared? Perhaps—and perhaps she is still kicking up her heels on a dance floor in another time and place, where it's 1933 every day.

The Little Hitchhiker of Evergreen Park

Another phantom hitcher haunts the roadways near Evergreen Cemetery in Evergreen Park, a Chicago suburb. For more than two decades, an attractive teenaged girl has been roaming out beyond the confines of the cemetery in search of a ride. A number of drivers claimed to have spotted her, and in the 1980s, a flurry of encounters occurred when motorists in the southern and western suburbs reported picking up this young girl. She always asked them for a ride to a location in Evergreen Park and then mysteriously vanished from the vehicle at the cemetery.

According to the legends, she is the spirit of a child buried within the cemetery, but there is no real folklore to explain why she leaves her grave in search of travelers to bring her back home again. She is what some would call the typical "vanishing hitchhiker," but there is one aspect to this ghost that sets her apart from the others. In addition to seeking rides in cars, she is resourceful enough to find other transportation when it suits her.

In recent years, encounters with this phantom have also taken place at a bus stop located directly across the street from the cemetery. Many have claimed to see a dark-haired young girl here who mysteriously vanishes. On occasion, she has also climbed aboard a few Chicago Transit Authority buses.

One evening, a young girl climbed aboard a bus and breezed right past the driver without paying the fare. She walked to the back of the vehicle and sat down, seemingly without a care in the world. Irritated, the driver called out to her, but she didn't answer. He finally stood up and walked back toward where she was seated. She would either pay, he thought, or get off the bus. Before he could reach her, however, she vanished before his eyes!

According to reports, other shaken drivers have had the same eerie experience at this bus stop. The other drivers have also seen this young girl, and every single one of them has seen her disappear as if she had never been there in the first place.

The Naked Hitchhiker

One of the most intriguing of Chicago's phantom hitchers was the spirit dubbed the "Kennedy Road Phantom." This mysterious female ghost was first seen around Byron during the frigid months of December 1980 and attracted so many curiosity-seekers that traffic was often bumper-to-bumper along Kennedy Road. Our guess is that many of these would-be ghost hunters were male—for this slender young woman was allegedly dressed, despite the cold weather, in very little clothing!

The sightings continued for several weeks, and a number of reliable witnesses came forward to police officers and newspaper reporters, all claiming to have seen the phantom. One witness, Dave Trenholm, stated that he was driving along Kennedy Road with Guy Harriett of Oregon at about 9:00 P.M. on the night of January 2, 1981. He told the *Chicago Tribune* that he saw the girl step out from behind some bushes at the side of the road and he had to look twice because he was so shocked by her appearance. He couldn't believe his eyes! He described her as being "tall, slender, nice-looking, about twenty. All she was wearing were some black panties and some kind of scarf around her neck." The woman seemed to be unaffected by the cold weather (it was about 10 degrees that night), and after she spotted the car, she turned and ran toward a nearby farmhouse—and then vanished.

There were a number of theories as to who the woman might be, ghostly or otherwise. Some thought that she was a mentally handicapped girl who had been reported missing by her parents around Christmas. This turned out not to be the case, and after all of the standard theories of pranksters were dismissed (for what woman would go to the length of standing on the side of the road nearly naked in December for a joke?), many ideas turned to the supernatural.

Initial thoughts were that she was a car accident victim who had been killed along Kennedy Road and had now come back to haunt the highway. Others speculated that she was the ghost of a woman who had been buried in a nearby abandoned cemetery, which had been destroyed.

Regardless of who she was, additional sightings continued through January and began to include varying reports of the phantom's description and clothing. Different witnesses stated that she was wearing a pair of light-colored shorts and a sweatshirt; shorts and a light jacket; and even a skimpy halter top. Again, because it was the dead of winter on a remote rural roadway, the ghost didn't seem to be a joke or a hoax, so what was going on?

In late January 1981, the *Rockford Register-Star* published a report that an Ogle County Sheriff's car had run over a mysterious woman around 8:00 P.M. The woman had suddenly appeared in the middle of the road, and the squad car had slammed into her. According to the officers, the woman was pulled beneath the car, and they heard her bones crunch and felt the impact of the tires rolling over the body. Needless to say, they quickly came to a stop and jumped out of the car to investigate and assist her if possible.

But when they ran back up the road, they found no woman lying there. A police lieutenant called the story "crazy and untrue," but the stories and the strange sightings continued.

By the end of January, the stories started to die out, and finally, despite many people still looking for her, the ghostly woman faded out of existence. Does she still haunt this lonesome stretch of road? No one knows for sure, but even though she has not been seen in quite a while, we have a feeling that many male ghost hunters are still keeping an eye out for her!

Resurrection Mary

Chicago is a city filled with ghosts, from haunted houses to ghostly gravcyards. But of all the tales, there is one that rises above all of the others. Her name is "Resurrection Mary," and she is Chicago's most famous ghost.

According to legend, the story of Resurrection Mary began with the death of a young woman who was killed while hitchhiking on Archer Avenue in the mid 1930s. This is the popular version of the story and has all the elements of Chicago's greatest haunting—a beautiful blonde, a lonely highway, a popular big-band ballroom, and of course, a hitchhiking ghost.

Many would dismiss this story as nothing more than an urban legend gone awry, a bedtime story that has taken on a life of its own over the years. Others would argue this and recount the most widely told version of the tale, never wavering from the idea that they believe the story to be true. Unfortunately though, the story of Resurrection Mary is filled with mystery—and myth—and nothing about it is simple. It's a complicated tale of two young women and a single legend that became, without question, American's greatest ghost story.

The legend of Resurrection Mary began at the Oh Henry Ballroom (now known as the Willowbrook Ballroom), a popular place for swing and big-band dancing during the mid 1930s. The ballroom is still located today on the south stretch of Archer Avenue in

Willow Springs. Many years ago, this was a somewhat secluded place, nestled among the trees in a small town with a "wide open" reputation for booze, gambling, and prostitution. Young people from all over the South Side came to the Oh Henry Ballroom for music and dancing, and owner John Verderbar was known for booking the hottest bands in the Chicago area and the biggest acts that traveled around the country.

The story goes that Mary came to the Oh Henry one night with a boyfriend, and they spent the evening dancing and drinking. At some point, they got into an argument, and Mary stormed out of the place. Even though it was a cold winter's night, she decided that she would rather face a cold walk home than another minute with her obnoxious boyfriend. She left the ballroom and started walking up Archer Avenue. She had not gotten very far when she was struck and killed by a passing automobile. The driver fled the scene, and Mary was left there to die.

Her grieving parents buried her in Resurrection Cemetery, wearing her favorite party dress and her dancing shoes. Since that time, her spirit has been seen along Archer Avenue, perhaps trying to return to her grave after one last night among the living. Motorists started picking up a young woman on Archer Avenue, who offered them vague directions to her home, but would then vanish from the automobile at the gates to Resurrection Cemetery.

But is there any truth to this legend? Did a young woman actually die after leaving the Oh Henry Ballroom and then begin haunting Archer Avenue? Many say that none of this ever happened. They speculate that "Mary" never existed at all. They dismiss the idea of bothering to search for her identity and believe she is nothing more than an urban legend and a piece of fascinating folklore. She is, they say, nothing more than Chicago's own version of the "vanishing hitchhiker."

While the story of Resurrection Mary does bear some resemblance to the classic bit of American highway lore that we call the vanishing hitchhiker, the folklorists have forgotten an important thing about Mary's story that other versions don't have—credible eyewitness accounts, places, times, and dates. Many of these reports are not just stories that have been passed from person to person and rely on a "friend of a friend" for authenticity. In fact, some of the encounters with Mary have been chillingly up close and personal and remain unexplained to this day.

In addition, the story of Mary includes something that the urban legends leave out—physical evidence of her presence. And Mary, unlike our highway legends, springs from real-life counterparts for whom evidence remains about their lives—and deaths. We confess that, in the pages ahead, you will not find evidence that any of the "Marys" in question died after leaving the Willowbrook Ballroom, but you will find some pretty compelling evidence that Mary still haunts Archer Avenue to this day.

The first accounts of Resurrection Mary on Archer Avenue came about in the spring of 1934. At that time, a number of drivers who passed Resurrection Cemetery at night began to report strange occurrences with a girl who tried to flag down rides from them and, sometimes, tried to climb onto the running boards of their cars.

Aside from the harried motorists who encountered Mary along Archer Avenue were those who came face-to-face with her under other conditions. One of these people was a young man named Jerry Palus. His experience with Mary took place in 1939 but would leave such an impression that he would never forget it until his death in 1992. Palus remained an unshakable witness and appeared on a number of television shows (including *Unsolved Mysteries*) to discuss his night with Resurrection Mary. He never doubted the fact that he spent an evening with a ghost!

Palus met the young girl, who he described as a very attractive blond, at the Liberty Grove & Hall, a music and dancing venue near Forty-seventh Street and Mozart in the Brighton Park neighborhood. As it happens, this dance hall, which was a "jumping spot" on the South Side for many years, was located not far from the homes of both the women who are usually believed to have been the girl who became Resurrection Mary.

That night at the Liberty Grove & Hall, Jerry asked the girl to dance. He had been watching her for some time that evening, although he admitted in later interviews that he never saw her come into the place. She spent a couple of hours sitting by herself, since she didn't seem to know anyone, and Jerry finally gathered the courage to take her out onto the dance floor. The girl accepted his invitation, and they spent several hours together. Strangely, she seemed a little distant, and Palus also noticed that her skin was very cold, almost icy to the touch. When he later kissed her, he found her lips were also cold and clammy.

At the end of the evening, the young woman asked Jerry for a ride home. He readily agreed to give her a lift. When they got to his automobile, she explained that she lived on South Damen Avenue but that she wanted to take a ride down Archer Avenue first. Jerry shrugged and told her that he would be happy to take her wherever she wanted. By this time, he was infatuated with the girl and likely wanted to extend the night for as long as he could. He knew that it would be quite some distance out of the way to drive down Archer Avenue, but he didn't mind, so he put his car into gear and drove off.

To reach Archer Avenue from the Liberty Grove & Hall, Jerry only had to travel west on Forty-seventh Street. Once he made it to the old roadway, they traveled southwest to Summit and then on to Justice. It was a dark, dimly lit road in those days, but Jerry was somewhat familiar with the area, so he just followed the course of the road, heading eventually, he thought, toward Willow Springs.

But as they approached the gates to Resurrection Cemetery, the girl asked him to pull over. She had to get out here, she told him. Jerry was confused, unable to understand why she would want to get out at such a spot, but he pulled the car to the side of the road anyway. He agreed that he would let her out, but only if she allowed him to walk her to wherever she was going. There was a row of houses to Jerry's right, about a block off Archer Avenue, and he assumed that she was going to one of them. He wanted to be sure that she made it there safely.

The beautiful young girl refused to allow this, however. She turned in her seat and faced Palus. She spoke softly, saying, "This is where I have to get out, but where I'm going, you can't follow."

Jerry was bewildered by this statement, but before he could respond, the girl got out of the car and ran—not in the direction of the houses but across Archer Avenue and toward the gates of Resurrection Cemetery. She vanished before she reached them—right before Jerry's eyes! That was the moment when he knew that he had danced with a specter.

The following day, determined to find out what was going on, Palus visited the address the girl had given him. The woman who answered the door told him that he couldn't have possibly been with her daughter the night before because she had been dead for years. However, Palus was able to correctly identify the girl from a family portrait in the other room.

Needless to say, Jerry was stunned by this revelation, but apparently the address and identity of the woman were forgotten over the years. Sometime later, when Palus was contacted again about his story (when the passage of time had renewed interest in the elusive ghost), he was unable to remember where he had gone on the day after his encounter. Despite this memory lapse, Palus's story remains one of the most credible of all the Resurrection Mary encounters.

This was only the beginning for Mary, and starting in the late 1930s, she began making regular appearances on Archer Avenue. Stories like the one told by Jerry Palus became almost commonplace over the years as other young men began to tell of picking up a young woman, or meeting her at a local ballroom, only to have her disappear from their car.

The majority of the reports seemed to come from the cold winter months, such as the account passed on by a cab driver who picked up a girl walking along Archer Avenue one night in 1941. It was very cold outside, but she was not wearing a coat. She jumped into the cab and told him that she needed to get home very quickly. She directed him to go north along Archer, but a few minutes later, he looked back and she was gone. He realized that he was passing in front of the cemetery when she disappeared.

The stories continued, but starting in the early 1970s, the number of "Mary sightings" began to increase. People from many different walks of life, from cab drivers to ministers, claimed they picked her up and gave her rides. They encountered her in local nightspots and saw her vanish from the passenger seats of their automobiles.

It was during this period that Resurrection Cemetery was undergoing some major renovations, and perhaps this was what caused her restlessness. There are others who believe that Mary's grave was disturbed many years before that. It is thought that she was buried in the single grave section of the cemetery, and just after World War II, the graveyard needed more space. Some of the graves were moved to other locations, while others, according to the relatives of some who had loved ones buried in the cemetery, were reportedly bulldozed under the earth. Whatever the cause of the increased activity, there is no denying that things on the Southwest Side started getting very interesting!

In 1973, Mary was said to have shown up at least twice at a nightclub called Harlow's, which was located at 8058 South Cicero Avenue, almost directly east of Resurrection Cemetery. Bob Main was the night manager at Harlow's at the time, and he is perhaps the only person to ever encounter Resurrection Mary on two different occasions. He saw her on a Friday night that spring and then saw her again about two weeks later on a Saturday.

He described her: "She was about twenty-four to thirty years old, five-foot-eight or nine, slender with yellow-blond hair to the shoulders that she wore in these big spooly curls coming down from a high forehead. She was really pale, like she powdered her face and her body. She had on this old dress that was yellowed, like a wedding dress left in the sun. She sat right next to the dance floor, and she wouldn't talk to anyone. She danced all by herself, this pirouette-type dance. People were saying, 'Who is this bizarre chick?'"

When Main and some of the other staff members tried to talk to the young woman and make sure that she was okay, the woman only shook her head. Main described her expression as though she "seemed to look right through you."

Bob had no idea who the girl might have been, and while he doesn't dismiss the idea that it could have been some sort of prank, or even a mentally disturbed woman, he did add something rather disconcerting to the story: "The strangest thing was, even though we carded everyone who came in there—I worked the door and there were waitresses and bartenders and people there—nobody, either night, ever saw her come in and they never saw her leave."

He added that he never would have assumed the woman was Resurrection Mary until he read a newspaper article about her a few years later. After that, it was the only thing that really made sense.

Other types of accounts began to surface around this same time, and Mary was reported running out into the middle of Archer Avenue and being struck by passing cars. These reports, although unknown to most of those who submitted them, hearkened back to the early 1930s and they had an eerie similarity to the very first Mary stories from that time.

In these new accounts, drivers began to report a young woman with light brown hair and wearing a white dress, who ran out in the front of their automobiles. Sometimes, the girl would vanish just before colliding with the car, and at other times, they would feel the impact and see her crumple and fall to the road as if seriously injured. When the motorist stopped and went to help the girl, she would either disappear or no sign of her body would be found.

On August 12, 1976, Cook County Sheriff's Department officers investigated an emergency call about an apparent hit-and-run victim near the intersection of Seventy-sixth Street and Roberts Road. The officers found a young female motorist in tears at the scene, and they asked her where the body was that she had allegedly discovered beside the road. She pointed to a wet grassy area, and the policemen could plainly see a depression in the grass that matched the shape of a human body. The girl said that just as the police car approached the scene, the body on the side of the road vanished!

In May 1978, a young couple was driving north on Archer Avenue when a girl suddenly darted out in the road in front of their car. The driver swerved to avoid her but knew when he hit the brakes that it was too late. As they braced for impact, the car passed right through the girl! She then turned and ran into Resurrection Cemetery, melting right past the bars in the gate. Another man was on his way to work in the early morning hours when he spotted the body of a young girl lying directly in front of the cemetery gates. He stopped his truck and got out, quickly discovering that the woman was apparently badly injured, but still alive. He jumped into his truck and sped to the nearby police station, where he summoned an ambulance and then hurried back to the cemetery. When he came back, he found that the body was gone! The outline of her body, however, was still visible on the dew-covered pavement.

In October 1989, two women were driving past Resurrection Cemetery when a girl in a white dress ran out in front of their car. The driver slammed on the brakes, sure that she was going to hit the woman, but there was no impact. Neither of the women could explain where the apparition had gone. They had seen the young girl clearly, though, and described her as having light brown, curly hair.

The most bizarre account of Resurrection Mary occurred on the night of August 10, 1976. On this occasion, Mary did not just appear as a passing spirit. It was on this night that she left actual evidence behind!

A driver was passing by the cemetery around 10:30 P.M. when he happened to see a girl standing on the other side of the gates. He said that when he saw her, she was wearing a white dress and grasping the iron bars of the gate. The driver was considerate enough to stop down the street at the Justice police station and alert them to the fact that someone had been accidentally locked in the cemetery at closing time. A patrolman named Pat Homa responded to the call, but when he arrived at the cemetery gates, he couldn't find anyone there. He called out with his loudspeaker and looked around with his spotlight, but there was no one to be seen. He finally got out of his patrol car and walked up to the gates for one last look. As far as he could tell, the cemetery was dark and deserted, and there was no sign of any girl.

But his inspection of the gates, where the girl had been seen standing, revealed something that chilled him to the bone. He found that two of the bronze bars in the gate had been blackened, burned, and—well, pulverized. It looked as though someone had taken two of the green-colored bars in his or her hands and had somehow just squashed and twisted them. Within the marks was what looked to be skin texture and handprints that had been seared into the metal with incredible heat. The temperature, which must have been intense, blackened and burned the bars at just about the spot where a small woman's hands would have been.

The marks of the hands made big news, and curiosity-seekers came from all over the area to see them. In an effort to discourage the crowds, cemetery officials attempted to remove the marks with a blowtorch, making them look even worse. They finally cut the bars out of the gate and installed a wire fence until the two bars could be straightened or replaced.

The cemetery emphatically denied the supernatural version of what happened to the bars. In 1992, they claimed that a truck backed into the gates while doing sewer work at the cemetery and that groundsworkers tried to fix the bars by heating them with a blowtorch and bending them. The imprint in the metal, they said, was from a workman trying to push them together again.

While this explanation was quite convenient, it did not explain why the marks of small fingers were clearly visible in the metal or why the bronze never reverted back to its green, oxidized state.

As mentioned, the bars were removed to discourage onlookers, but taking them out actually had the opposite effect. People soon began asking what the cemetery had to hide. The events allegedly embarrassed local officials, so they demanded that the bars be put back into place. Once they were returned to the gate, they were straightened and left alone so that the blackened area would oxidize to match the other bars. Unfortunately though, the scorched areas continued to defy nature, and the twisted spots where the handprints had been impressed remained obvious until 2002, when the bars were finally removed for good. At great expense, Resurrection Cemetery replaced the entire front gate, and the notorious bars vanished for good.

Just a few minutes after midnight, in the early morning hours of Friday morning, January 12, 1979, a taxicab driver had an unsettling experience with Resurrection Mary. It was a cold winter's night, and at the time the driver picked up his unusual passenger, a major blizzard was just hours away from hitting the Southwest Side of Chicago. As he traveled along Archer Avenue, rain and sleet pelted the windshield. The driver reached over to crank up the heater one more notch. *It is the kind of night that makes your bones ache,* he thought.

He was returning to the city after dropping off a fare in Palos Hills. His route took him past the Old Willow Shopping Center, located at the intersection of Archer Avenue and Willow Springs Road, just a short distance away from the Willowbrook Ballroom. As he passed the collection of stores at the shopping center, a pale figure, blurry through the wet and icy glass of the window, appeared along the road. The driver craned his neck and saw a woman standing there alone. He later recalled: "She was a looker. A blond. I didn't have any ideas or like that. She was young enough to be my daughter."

The young woman was strangely dressed for such a cold and wet night. She was wearing only a thin white cocktail dress. The girl never stuck out her thumb or anything. She just stood there looking at the cab, but the driver pulled over and stopped the car anyway. The girl stumbled as she walked toward him, and he rolled down the window to speak to her. She was beautiful, the driver saw, despite her disheveled appearance. Her blond hair was damp from the weather and plastered to her forehead.

He invited her into the cab, and she opened the passenger door and slid into the seat. The cabbie looked over at her and asked her what was wrong. Had she had car trouble or something? The girl didn't answer, so he asked her where she wanted to go and offered her a free ride. It was the least that he could do in that weather, he told her.

The girl simply replied that he should keep driving north on Archer Avenue, so the cabbie put the car into gear and pulled back onto the road. He noticed that the young woman was shivering, so he turned up the heater again. He commented on the weather, making conversation, but she didn't answer him at first. She stared out the window in such a vacant way that he wondered if she might be drunk. Finally, she answered him, although her voice wavered and sounded almost fearful. The driver was unsure if her whispered words were directed to him or if she was speaking to herself. "The snow came early this year," she murmured. After that, she was silent again.

The cabbie agreed with her and attempted to make some more small talk, but he soon realized the lovely young girl was not interested in conversation. "Her mind was a million miles away," he said.

The girl finally spoke, but when she did, she shouted at him. She ordered him to pull over to the side of the road. She needed to get out!

The startled driver jerked the steering wheel to the right and stopped in an open area in front of two large, metal gates. He looked across the road, searching for a house or a business where this girl might need to go. He knew there was nothing on the right. She couldn't get out there—it was a cemetery.

He looked back at the girl and realized what had just occurred. "And that's when it happened. I looked to my left—like this—at this little shack. And when I turned back she was gone. Vanished! And that car door never opened. May the good Lord strike me dead, it never opened," he insisted.

The beautiful young girl had simply disappeared.

At the time of this encounter, the driver (a fifty-two-year-old working man, father, veteran, churchgoer, and Little League coach) had no idea that he had just had a brush with the region's most enigmatic and sought-after ghost. He wouldn't find out until a friend put him in touch with a newspaper columnist, who began looking into the story for himself.

After looking into the story of Resurrection Mary, the reporter's trail led him to the Willowbrook Ballroom, which was once known as the Oh Henry. He discovered that the cab driver had picked up the young girl just about ten minutes after midnight, a few blocks from the Willowbrook on Archer Avenue. Was this merely a coincidence? The reporter didn't think so, especially based on the strange occurrences connected to Mary that had taken place at the Willowbrook Ballroom over the years.

The site of the ballroom in Willow Springs, right on Archer Avenue, started as a beer hall operated by the Verderbar family in 1920. In 1929, the original structure burned down and was replaced by an elaborate ballroom. They called it the Oh Henry, but the name was later changed to the Willowbrook. Starting in the 1930s, the ballroom gained a reputation as one of the best dance clubs in Illinois and attracted customers from all over the area. The Oh Henry, and later the Willowbrook, developed a strong following, and today it is one of the last of the old-time ballrooms in Chicago. Times and musical tastes may have changed, but a visit to the Willowbrook is like taking a trip back in time. The old dance floor, the tables, the cocktail bar, and even the restrooms are just as they were back in the days when Mary reveled here. It's a place where the big-band sound can still be heard and is a time capsule of another era.

In 1998, the Verderbar family decided to sell the ballroom to Birute and Gedas Jodwalis, who decided to keep the Willowbrook just the way it was. Longtime customers most likely breathed a little easier when they found out the big bands would still be coming to the ballroom—as did the ghost buffs and Resurrection Mary enthusiasts. If the big bands kept coming, then Mary would too!

Since the 1930s, Mary has been encountered numerous times on the dance floor by customers and employees alike. Reports commonly tell of an attractive young woman in a white party dress who is seen from the opposite side of the ballroom. Occasionally, she is dancing, but at other times, she is just standing at the edge of the floor, watching people with a slight smile on her face. At times, she vanishes without warning, and on other occasions, she has disappeared whenever someone tries to approach her.

Aside from the white dress, the descriptions of the girl vary just a little. She is always beautiful, but some have stated that she was a blond and others say that she was a brunette with curly hair. Each time, she disappeared—leaving little doubt that she was a ghost—but also leaving behind the question as to which Mary the witness actually saw!

There is one thing that each of these sightings have in common, no matter what the girl looked like. That one thing is that Mary has never been reported by anyone who actually went to the Willow-brook with the intention of seeing her. Every sighting seems to come from someone who had a chance encounter with the phantom.

Don't let that discourage you from spending an evening at the Willowbrook Ballroom, though. Even if you don't get to meet Mary face-to-face, you will still get a chance to experience a place that is a unique part of Archer Avenue history and an integral part of the roadway's most famous haunt.

Sightings of Mary continued into the 1980s and the 1990s, and even though Mary sightings and first-hand encounters have slacked off in recent years, they still continue to occur today. While many of the stories are harder to believe these days, as the tales of Mary have infiltrated our culture to such a degree that almost anyone with an interest in ghosts has heard of her, some of the stories still appear to be chillingly real.

One of the most commonly asked questions of those who have researched Resurrection Mary is this: Who was Mary when she was alive?

Over the years, many have searched for the earthly counterpart of Resurrection Mary, and a number of candidates have emerged. Some are more likely than others. One of the options is Mary Duranski, who was killed in an auto accident in 1934. Another is a twelve-year-old girl named Anna Norkus, who died in another tragic auto accident in 1936. That same year marked the date of another accident that some believe spawned Resurrection Mary. In this case, a farm truck collided with an automobile, and three of the four passengers in the sedan were killed. One of the victims, a young woman, may have become Resurrection Mary. Others believe Mary can be traced to another accident near Resurrection Cemetery that occurred in the 1940s. In this case, a young Polish girl had taken her father's car to meet her boyfriend in the early morning hours. She died in an accident and was buried in the nearby cemetery. Most believe this to be little more than a neighborhood "cautionary tale" told by protective parents, but it certainly adds another element to the legend.

It's possible that any one of these young women could still haunt Archer Avenue and may have contributed to the Resurrection Mary legend. However, I believe there that the majority of the sightings can be connected to two young women who, ironically, lived only a few blocks away from one another in life.

The first reports of Resurrection Mary began to appear in the late spring of 1934. It was at this time that motorists on Archer Avenue, passing in front of Resurrection Cemetery, began telling of a young woman who would appear on the roadway, as if trying to hitch a ride. On some occasions, she became frantic as cars passed her by, and many times, she seemed actually desperate. Motorists told of the woman running toward them across the road, trying to climb onto the running boards of their automobiles, and sometimes even trying to climb into the open back windows! They all described her in the same way, wearing a light-colored dress and having curly, light brown hair that reached to her shoulders.

What made matters worse is that many of the people in these automobiles, who were residents of the Southwest Side, actually recognized this young woman. Her name was Mary Bregovy, and some of these motorists were her friends. They laughed with her, drank with her, and often danced with her at their favorite spot, the Oh Henry Ballroom. Of course, all that had happened in the past—when they began seeing Mary trying to flag them down on Archer Avenue, she had been dead for several weeks!

Mary Bregovy was twenty-one in March 1934. She had been born on April 7, 1912, and attended St. Michael's Grammar School a short distance from her home. She lived in a small home at 4611 South Damen Avenue, which was in the stockyards neighborhood of Bridgeport. She was of Polish descent and was employed at a local factory, where she worked hard to help support her mother, father, and two younger brothers, Steve and Joseph, during the early days of the Great Depression.

Friends would later remember her as an extremely fun-loving girl who enjoyed going to parties and loved to go out dancing, especially to the Oh Henry Ballroom, which was her favorite place. Her friend LaVern Rutkowski, who grew up with Mary on the Southwest Side and lived just two houses away from her, recalled in a 1984 interview, "She was personality plus. She always had a smile and you never saw her unhappy."

Mrs. Rutkowski, or "Vern" as she was commonly known, spent Mary's final day with her on March 10, 1934. The two of them spent a lot of time together, and years later, Vern would vividly recall going out with Mary to dance halls all over the Southwest Side. Ironically, Mary's parents had forbidden her to go out on the night of March 10, and Mary might have listened to them if she and Vern had not met a couple of young men earlier that day. These two men, who are believed to have been John Reiker and John Thoel, were in the car the night that Mary was killed.

Mary and Vern spent that Saturday afternoon shopping at Forty-seventh Street and Ashland Avenue, and it was in one of the stores there that they met the two men. After getting into their car to go for a ride, Vern took an instant dislike to them. "They looked like wild boys and for some reason I just didn't like them," she said. Vern added that they drove recklessly, turning corners on two wheels and speeding down narrow streets. Vern finally demanded to be let out of the car a few blocks from home. She asked Mary if she planned to go out with the young men that night, and Mary said that she did. Vern urged her to reconsider, not only because she didn't like the boys but also because Mary's parents had already told her that she couldn't go. Mary shrugged off her friend's warnings and simply replied, "You never like anyone I introduce you to."

Vern stood watching on the street corner as Mary and the young men roared away in the car. It was the last time she would ever see her friend alive.

No one knows how Mary Bregovy spent the rest of the day, but a few clues have emerged from family members over the years. The wife of Mary's younger brother, Steve, reported in 1985 that she had received a letter from a friend of Mary's years before stating that Mary had planned to attend a novena at church before she went out dancing that night. The Bregovys were devout Catholics, and this would not have been out of the ordinary for Mary to do. She also said that she believed Mary had been going to the Oh Henry Ballroom that night.

But did she ever arrive there? No one knows for sure, but tradition holds that Mary and her new friends, who now included a young woman named Virginia Rozanski, did go dancing at the Oh Henry Ballroom that night. After the ballroom closed, it is believed that they drove into the city, where most of the clubs stayed open much later. They were leaving downtown in the early morning hours, traveling along Wacker Drive, likely headed for Archer Avenue, which would take Mary home to Bridgeport, when the deadly accident occurred. One has to wonder if alcohol, combined with the reckless driving described by Vern Rutkowski, combined to cause the crash.

The accident occurred along Wacker Drive, just as it curves to the south and away from the Chicago River. At the point where Wacker crosses Lake Street, there is a large, metal support for the elevated tracks overhead. If a driver was coming along Wacker too quickly, it would be easy to not make a complete turn and collide with the support column, which is almost in a straight line around the curve. This is apparently what happened to John Thoel that night.

When the automobile collided with the metal column, Mary was thrown through the windshield and instantly killed. She was also badly cut up by the glass. Before her funeral, the undertaker had to sew up a gash that extended all of the way across the front of her throat and up to her right ear. Tragically, Mary was not even supposed to be sitting in the front seat when the accident occurred. Her parents would later learn that she had switched places with Virginia Rozanski because Virginia didn't like John Thoel, next to whom she had been sitting in the passenger's seat. She had asked Mary to sit in front with Thoel, and Mary had agreed. Unfortunately, her good-natured personality would turn out to be fatal for her.

Vern Rutkowski accompanied Mary's mother and her brother, Joseph, to the morgue to identify the body. Mary was taken to the Satala Funeral Home, located just a couple of blocks from the Bregovy home, to be prepared for burial. The owner at the time, John Satala, easily remembered Mary. In 1985, he recalled, "She was a hell of a nice girl. Very pretty. She was buried in an orchid dress. I remember having to sew up the side of her face."

Mary was buried in Resurrection Cemetery, and this is where some of the confusion about her story comes along. According to records, Mary was buried in Section MM, Site 9819. There was a Mary Bregovy buried here, but it was not the young woman who was killed in March 1934. A search for this grave site revealed that the Mary Bregovy laid to rest here was a thirty-four-year-old mother who was born in 1888 and died in 1922—a different Mary Bregovy altogether.

Family members of Mary Bregovy said that Mary was actually buried in a term grave and never moved. After World War II, when space was needed for more burial sites at Resurrection Cemetery, some of the term graves were moved, but others, like Mary's, were simply covered over. For this reason, according to Mrs. Steve Bregovy, the location of Mary's grave is unknown. Could this be one of the reasons that her spirit is so restless?

The stories of Mary Bregovy's ghost began a very short time after her death. In April 1934, a caretaker at Resurrection Cemetery telephoned funeral home director John Satala and told him that he had seen the barefooted ghost of a young girl walking around the cemetery. She was a lovely girl with light brown hair, and she was wearing a pale, orchid-colored dress. The caretaker was positive that the ghost was the woman that Satala had recently buried. Satala later said that he recognized the description of the girl as Mary Bregovy.

Soon after, other reports began to surface, such as the earlier-mentioned accounts of a woman matching Mary's description who was trying to hitch rides in front of the cemetery. These Archer Avenue sightings also included reports from people who actually recognized the ghost as Mary Bregovy.

We're convinced that these reports were the beginning of the Resurrection Mary legend. These were the first stories of a young woman hitching rides on Archer Avenue, and thanks to the destination of many of these motorists, combined with the fact that the Oh Henry Ballroom was Mary's favorite dance spot, the story began to grow. We believe that many of the reports of a ghostly woman being seen around Resurrection Cemetery can be traced to Mary Bregovy—the "original Resurrection Mary."

But Mary Bregovy does not haunt this stretch of Archer Avenue alone . . .

She may have started the legend of Resurrection Mary, but she was not the only phantom haunting Archer Avenue and the area around it. The stories of a "beautiful blond" don't physically match Miss Bregovy, who was certainly beautiful, but definitely not a blond. She had naturally curly, light brown hair, which means that she is not the same spirit so frequently being picked up by motorists and spotted on the side of the road.

However, thanks to a letter I received in 2005 (and the interviews that followed it), I believe that I may have the identity of the second woman who has contributed to the legend of Resurrection Mary—who may also be the same woman that Jerry Palus met at the Liberty Grove & Hall in 1939.

The name of Mary Miskowski is a familiar one to Resurrection Mary buffs. There have been numerous brief mentions of her in ghostly literature, listing her as a possible candidate for the identity of the legendary ghost. Little has been known about her except for the fact that she was killed in October 1930 by a hit-and-run driver. She was allegedly crossing the street while on her way to a Halloween costume party.

In July 2005, I received a vague letter from a woman who promised information about Resurrection Mary, claiming that the real-life counterpart of Mary had once been her mother's babysitter when she was a child. If I was interested, I could call her and get more information. Her mother was still alive and would be happy to speak with me about it. Out of curiosity, I decided to give the woman a call. She gave me a few details of the story and then gave me the telephone number of her mother, who was eighty-five years old, and urged me to contact her. The next afternoon, I called the number and was soon speaking with Mrs. Martha Litak, who grew up on South Damen Avenue on Chicago's Southwest Side. I told her why I was calling and asked her what she could tell me about the story of Resurrection Mary.

Her answer surprised me. She laughed and said: "Resurrection Mary was my babysitter!"

According to Mrs. Litak, Mary Miskowski had lived just down the street from her family when Mrs. Litak was a child. Mary's house was located at 4924 South Damen Avenue (interestingly, just three blocks away from Mary Bregovy, so it seems possible these two women could have known one another), and she often watched neighborhood children to earn extra money. Mrs. Litak was not sure if Mary had a regular job or not. She lived with her parents but she was old enough to be out of school.

Martha remembered Mary very well. "She was a very pretty girl. She had light blond hair with just a little bit of curl to it. It was cut short, just a little below her ears. All of the boys in the neighborhood were in love with her. I do remember that she liked to go on dates but I don't recall that she had any one boyfriend in particular," she said.

Martha said she had spoken with her younger brother, Frank, after her daughter told her that I might get in touch. She had asked him if he could remember anything about their old babysitter,

Mary Miskowski. Frank was only seven at the time Mary died, but he recalled what she looked like and remembered some of his older cousins talking about Mary after she had been killed. The cousins said that Mary loved to go out dancing, including to the Oh Henry Ballroom, which had opened in 1921. Her favorite place, though, was the Liberty Grove & Hall, which was located only about twelve blocks from her home.

I couldn't help but wonder if Mary Miskowski might have been the ghost that Jerry Palus encountered at the dance hall that night. She certainly matched the description that Palus (and many others over the years) later gave of the young woman he met who then vanished from his car in front of Resurrection Cemetery.

There is also no question that Mary Miskowski had long since passed away by that time. Martha Litak confirmed that Mary had been killed by a hit-and-run driver in October 1930. A car had struck her as she was crossing Forty-seventh Street and had sped away. Whoever the driver was, he was never caught. Martha surmised that perhaps this incident was how the story got started about Resurrection Mary being run over by a car and left for dead on Archer Avenue. With the Oh Henry Ballroom, and later the Willowbrook, being so closely tied to the legend, she was not surprised that the accident had been moved to a location closer to the dance hall. Mrs. Litak also confirmed that Mary had been on her way to a costume party that night. She had been dressed as a bride, wearing her mother's old wedding dress. Martha didn't know what Mary had been buried in, but she did believe that perhaps the white dress that so many people reported Resurrection Mary wearing could have been this dress from the early 1900s.

Mrs. Litak further connected Mary Miskowski to the legend by adding that she had been buried in Resurrection Cemetery. I have been unable to confirm this, but Martha and Frank were both sure this was the case. They told me that she had been buried in a term grave (just like Mary Bregovy), but she did not know the ultimate location of the site.

If any of this is accurate, it may explain the Resurrection Mary encounters that don't match the description and behavior of Mary Bregovy. Could the presence of Mary Miskowski explain the sightings of a pretty, blond phantom that hangs out in dance halls and vanishes from cars? And could she be the ghost who is seen running across the road in front of the cemetery where she is buried, perhaps reenacting her final moments over and over again as she is struck by a passing automobile?

It's possible, perhaps even likely. It's a fascinating and compelling story—compelling enough that it prompted our theory that Resurrection Mary is not one ghost but two, or maybe even more.

So, who was Mary? And does she really exist?

I believe that she does, and I also believe that I know the identities of at least two of the girls who have created her enduring legend. But many other theories also exist. Mary Bregovy and Mary Miskowski may be just two of the girls, and there may be many more.

Many still remain doubtful about her, but I've have found that their skepticism doesn't really seem to matter. Whether these people believe in her or not, people are still seeing Mary walking along Archer Avenue at night. Motorists are still stopping to pick up a forlorn figure that seems inadequately dressed on cold winter nights, when encounters seem to be the most prevalent. Curiosity-seekers still come to see the gates where the twisted and burned bars were once located, and some even roam the graveyard, hoping to stumble across the place where Mary's body was laid to rest.

We still don't know for sure who she really is, but that has not stopped the stories, tales, and songs from being circulated about her. She remains an enigma, and her legend lives on, not content to vanish as Mary does when she reaches the gates of Resurrection Cemetery. You see, our individual belief, or disbelief, does not really matter. Mary lives on anyway—a mysterious, elusive, and romantic spirit of the Windy City.

Bibliography

Adams, Joseph. "A Lost Village." *Historic Illinois*, August 1999.

Allen, John. *It Happened in Southern Illinois*. Carbondale, IL: Southern Illinois University Press, 1968.

———. *Legends and Lore of Southern Illinois*. Carbondale, IL: Southern Illinois University Press, 1963.

Asbury, Herbert. *Gem of the Prairie*. New York: Alfred A. Knopf, 1940.

Banton, O. T. *History of Macon County, Illinois*. Decatur, IL: Macon County Historical Society, 1976.

Bettenhausen, Brad. "Batchelor Grove Cemetery." *Where the Trails Cross* newsletter, 1995.

Bielski, Ursula. *Chicago Haunts*. Chicago: Lake Claremont Press, 1998.

Churney, Dan. *Capone's Cornfields*. Charleston, SC: Booksurge, 2003.

Cowdery, Ray. *Capone's Chicago*. Lakeville, MN: Northstar Commemoratives, 1987.

Crowe, Richard. *Chicago's Street Guide to the Supernatural*. Chicago: Carolando Press, 2000.

Davis, James E. *Frontier Illinois*. Bloomington, IN: Indiana University Press, 1998.

Drury, John. *Old Illinois Houses*. Springfield, IL: Illinois State Historical Society, 1948.

Everett, Marshall. *The Great Chicago Theater Disaster*. Publishers Union of America, 1904.

Fliege, Stu. *Tales and Trails of Illinois*. Urbana, IL: University of Illinois Press, 2002.

Howard, Robert. *Illinois—A History of the Prairie State*. Grand Rapids, MI: William B. Erdmans Publishing, 1972.

Kaczmarek, Dale. *Windy City Ghosts*. Alton, IL: Whitechapel Press, 2000.

———. *Windy City Ghosts II*. Alton, IL: Whitechapel Press, 2001.

Lewis, Lloyd. *Myths After Lincoln*. New York: Harcourt, Brace & Co., 1929.

Neely, Charles. *Tales and Songs of Southern Illinois*. Manasha, WI: George Banta Publishing Company, 1938.

Norman, Michael, and Beth Scott. *Haunted America*. New York: Tor, 1994.

———. *Historic Haunted America*. New York: Tor, 1995.

Parrish, Randall. *Historic Illinois*. Chicago: A. C. McClurg & Co., 1905.

Quaife, Milo. *Chicago Highways Old and New*. Chicago: D. F. Keller & Co., 1923.

Russell, Dorotha. *Squire of Voorhies*. Monticello, IL: Illinois Pioneer Heritage Center, 1967.

Scott, Beth, and Michael Norman. *Haunted Heartland*. New York: Dorset Press, 1985.

Taylor, Troy. *Bloody Illinois*. Decatur, IL: Whitechapel Press, 2008.

———. *Haunted Alton*. Alton, IL: Whitechapel Press, 2000 and 2003.

———. *Haunted Chicago*. Alton, IL: Whitechapel Press, 2002.

———. *Haunted Decatur*. Decatur, IL: Whitechapel Press, 2006.

———. *Haunted Illinois*. Alton, IL: Whitechapel Press, 2004

———. *Haunted President*. Decatur, IL: Whitechapel Press, 2005.

———. *Mysterious Illinois*. Decatur, IL: Whitechapel Press, 2006.

———. *Resurrection Mary*. Decatur, IL: Whitechapel Press, 2007.

———. *The Possessed*. Decatur, IL: Whitechapel Press, 2007.

Winer, Richard, and Nancy Osborn Ishmael. *More Haunted Houses*. New York: Bantam, 1981.

About the Author

*T*roy Taylor is the author of nearly sixty books about history, hauntings, crime, and the supernatural in America. He is the founder and president of the American Ghost Society and the owner of the Illinois and American Hauntings tour companies. Along with writing about the unusual and hosting tours, Taylor is also a public speaker on the subject of ghosts and hauntings and has appeared in newspaper and magazine articles about ghosts. He has been interviewed hundreds of times for radio and television broadcasts about the supernatural. He has also appeared in a number of documentary films, several television series, and in one feature film about the paranormal. He currently resides in central Illinois.